From Depression to War

From Depression to War

American Society in Transition—1939

August C. Bolino

PRAEGER

Westport, Connecticut
London

Library of Congress Cataloging-in-Publication Data

Bolino, August C. (August Constantino), 1922–
    From depression to war : American society in transition—1939 /
August C. Bolino.
      p. cm.
    Includes bibliographical references and index.
    ISBN 0–275–96064–1 (alk. paper)
    1. United States—Civilization—1918–1945. 2. Nineteen thirty-
nine, A.D. I. Title.
E169.1.B683   1998
973.91—dc21   97–38542

British Library Cataloguing in Publication Data is available.

Library of Congress Catalog Card Number: 97–38542
ISBN: 0–275–96064–1

First published in 1998

Praeger Publishers, 88 Post Road West, Westport, CT 06881
An imprint of Greenwood Publishing Group, Inc.

Printed in the United States of America

The paper used in this book complies with the
Permanent Paper Standard issued by the National
Information Standards Organization (Z39.48–1984).

10 9 8 7 6 5 4 3 2 1

To TJ

Contents

Preface

The obvious question is, why write about 1939? A simple answer is that it was a great time to be alive. For most Americans, it was a time of calm and more optimism, although conditions "over there" were worsening. We escaped by listening to and dancing to big bands; by tuning in to soap operas, comedies, and dramas on radio; and by going to ball games that cost pennies to attend.

When I attended the fiftieth reunion of my graduation from Mechanic Arts High School in Boston (now Boston Technical), several speakers stressed the special nature of the graduates and highlighted the unusual events of that year. It was surely a golden year for radio and for Hollywood, a golden time for sports and a golden period for science (much of it on parade at the New York World's Fair). But whereas these happenings were serene, war came to Europe. It was a war that was an extension of events that led up to it: the Japanese invasion of China, the Spanish Civil War, Russia's invasion of Finland, and Italy's grab of Albania.

Readers will learn that I have defined 1939 broadly, because no subject exists in isolation, and I have chosen to fill in biographical information where it is relevant. A note on my search for sources: Once again, I bow to the librarians at The Catholic University of America, who willingly led me to materials about 1939, and to those faceless persons on the Maryland Telephone Reference Service, who came up with answers to my most esoteric questions.

I must thank my wife T. J. for doing the bibliography, for editing the entire manuscript, for doing some of the word processing, and for being my best supporter in this effort. I must also thank my son Gregory for formatting all the chapter files and for preparing the final manuscript for the publisher.

Introduction

The year 1939 was a defining year. John Brooks wrote: "I see 1939 as the watershed year between the older America and the newer one, partly because various technological developments that were to be of great importance happened. . . . I see it as such because it marked the end of one era, that of the Depression, and the beginning of the war that was to be the basis of our transformation."[1] The signs of economic improvement could not mask the lingering gloom. Escapism took many forms: some joined the dancing craze doing the jitterbug, the Lindy Hop or marathon dancing; others fled to movie theaters. The most desperate took to the road (blacks heading northward and Okies westward).

The month of January foreshadowed coming events: General Franco captured Barcelona; Field Marshall Goering convened a meeting on the emigration of Jews; Czech and Hungarian troops clashed near the Ruthenian border and Hitler declared that Germany "wants peace." The year ended with Moscow refusing to negotiate with Finland; with the German battleship *Graf Spee* limping into Montevideo, Uruguay with thirty-six dead, and with Pope Pius XII calling for adoption of a five-point peace plan.

LIVING IN 1939

If you were alive in 1939, you were born before television, before penicillin, before polio shots, before frozen foods, and before Xerox. You were born before radar, before atomic energy, before laser beams, before ballpoint pens, before pantyhose, before electric blankets, and before air conditioners. You were born before FM radio, before tape decks, before electric typewriters, before word processors, before McDonald's, and before instant coffee.

In 1939, "Made in Japan" was an American joke, meaning junk. When you went shopping, you went to a 5 & 10 cent store, where you actually bought things for five cents and ten cents. You could buy an ice cream cone for a nickel, and for a nickel you could make a phone call, buy a Pepsi, or buy stamps to mail a letter and two postcards. You could buy a Chevy or a Ford for $600 (but who could afford one?). You could buy gasoline at eight gallons for a dollar, but most people took the street car or public transportation for a dime. It was also the time for fads. One of the wildest was reported in the March 4 issue of the *Boston Daily Record*, which told us that Harvard University freshmen were eating live goldfish.

The income tax burden in 1939 did not affect many families. Only 3 percent of families paid any income tax, despite the fact that 4 million families (out of 130 million) had incomes of over $2,000. On the richer side, over 42,000 families reported incomes of over $25,000, and two-thirds of the families paid 90 percent of all money collected by the Bureau of Internal Revenue.[2]

Prices and wages made the salaries of the rich appear colossal. Louis B. Mayer, of Metro-Goldwyn-Mayer, was paid over $1 million. Business executives and show-business stars commanded an equal largess. And while many starved, the rich had their "coming out" parties. The most lavish and expensive was Brenda Frazier's. The affair was held in the Main Ballroom of the Ritz-Carlton Hotel—it lasted until 7 A.M. the next morning, although poor little Brenda left at 4 A.M., after hours of champagne and dancing. The rest of the fifteen hundred guests enjoyed the $50,000 worth of entertainment provided by her mother and the executor of her estate (which totaled more than $4 million).

Americans didn't live like Brenda, but they had a security that we lack now. Anne Lindbergh caught the feeling after visiting the World's Fair and seeing a young couple walking up Madison Avenue. They were young, nice looking, and obviously in love. She thought they had the happiness of security; they were the only persons on the street, but they were not hurrying as "they sauntered on into the darkness."[3]

Americans of 1939 heard expressions such as "don't be a sap." They depended much on slang, and, considering that they made up two-thirds of the English-speaking persons in the world, the influence of their slang was spreading, much to the chagrin of purists, who felt that slang was corrupting the language of Shakespeare and Milton. The visit of the King and Queen of England to the United States in 1939 brought up the issues of our common tongues. It has been said that the two great English-speaking nations can agree on most things, except how to speak English, or as one person put it, "We are divided by a common tongue."

There was the fear that American English would become the English of the world. The truth is that colloquialisms that are slang survive because they describe conditions better than other words. This was true for Shakespeare and for O. Henry. It was the immigrants from southern and eastern Europe who gave the American language its vitality. The juxtaposition of words in Yiddish gave us "Yes we have no bananas."

Many words, that were thought to corrupt the English language, such as "guy," "greenhorn," "bubble," "bully," "hot dog," "iron horse" and "talk turkey," have become part of the "dignified English speech." And think of how much time and paper we save by using "pro" instead of professional. And what expression could replace that beautiful metaphor of "highbrow"? The influence of American slang may be exaggerated, because in two hundred years, we have added about a thousand words to the language. And remember that American English is the language of Abraham Lincoln and Walt Whitman.

Although we are a classless society, what we wore in 1939 depended on what we did and where. The 1930s saw a very different style of dress than did the 1920s. The prosperity decade featured the flapper look in women (high-hemline skirts) and the collegiate look in men (sweaters, two-toned shoes and even straw hats). In the 1930s, the hemlines came down and more men went for conservative styles.

In 1939, society was polite. Women still wore hats and gloves to social events, and men always covered their heads outdoors (and removed their hats indoors). There were taboos: Women did not wear shorts, and many men still wore tops to their bathing suits. Gelernter tells us that the average World's Fair goer "was a fiftyish man in a gray hat and suit, brown shoes, blue socks with garters, white shirt, blue bow tie and a small American flag in his lapel."[4]

Though adults had some choices about what to wear, children usually did not (it was the time of "children should be seen but not heard"). Clothes were for the occasion. One did not wear the same outfit for church as for a sports event or for school. The rigid dress codes were meant to retain recognitions of honor. A child showed deference for a parent or a minister or a teacher. As a teenage high school student, I was required to wear slacks, dress shirt, and tie in a public school. Dress requirements were part of a larger scheme that fostered respect for authority, age, and status. Children stood when adults entered the room, and men—including boys—stood when a lady entered.

It is a theory of marketing that in booming times, all dress (male and female) becomes skimpier, while in depressed times the amount of fabric increases, which is a good segue to the zoot suit. Hipsters (those who were hip) wore zoot suits, usually called zoots. These suits, often of sharkskin grey, had a big, long coat, heavily padded shoulders, and pants that ballooned out at the knees and tapered down to the cuffs as ankle chokers. One had to remove shoes to get these pants on and off. The appropriate hat was very wide brim, usually of straw with a multicolored feather. Of course, this outfit required bold new shoes—the kind with pointed toes and a light tan or orange-brown color. These were described as a "drape shape, neat pleat and stuffed cuff." There were women zooters, who wore their "juke jackets." The zooters became a symbol of unpatriotic and rebellious behavior.

The Depression and worries of war seemed to accentuate the dancing craze. Marathon dancing remained popular, but the "Big Band Sound" created the first "danceteria" in the heart of Times Square in 1939. It was three floors of dancing and eating. Each year, saw new steps. In 1939, it was the Samba, the Lambeth Walk, (imported from England), and the Glide.

Arthur Murray commented that more people than ever were taking dancing lessons to learn the new steps. The *New York Times* (April 2, 1939) told us that more men than women took dancing lessons. It was an era never equaled for popular music and for dancing. It was the time of the "Jitterbug," the "Shag," the "Big Apple," the "Susie Q," and the "Lindy Hop." This dancing craze required a new language to describe the new beat. The music was "in the groove," or "solid," or a "killer-diller." When the dancers "got with it," they often screamed, "send me," or "feed it to me," or "beat me daddy with a boogie beat." In the unlikely event that the music didn't send one, they called it, "schmaltzy" or "square."[5]

The words to "The House of Blue Light," a boogie-woogie song of the time, illustrate how jazz buffs influenced our speech:

Man:	What you say. You look ready as our Freddy.
Woman:	What's that homey. If you think I'm going dancing on a dime, your clock is ticking on the wrong time.
Man:	What's your pleasure, treasure. You call the plays, I'll make the ways.
Woman:	I'm in there and I mean way back.
Man:	You snap the whip; I'll make the trip.

This was the language of jive; it was free, wild, and unencumbered by logic. It was also confusing to the uninitiated, who might have thought they had walked into a foreign country. Let us extricate the confused by a few definitions: Musicians are cats—some "cool" cats. If you cut the rug, you were dancing to swing music. If you were very knowledgeable about swing, you were a hepcat. If you were not, you were "ickie" or "square." If you were in the groove, you were carried away with the music. If you were watching a jam session, you were not dancing but were enjoying the improvisations of the group, usually small, making the sounds. To be knocked out by the music meant that you were really sent (you were totally unfazed by your environment).

The Lindy Hop, named in honor of Charles Lindbergh, grew into the jitterbug, which originated in Harlem. It featured acrobatic gyrations, unusual movements, and an amazing amount of stamina. The male led the woman into twirls and spins. Band leaders shifted the beat from the 1/3 count of the fox trot to the 2/4 count of the swing rhythm.[6]

Having a zoot suit was an invitation to the dance. Almost everyone did the Lindy Hop. In this dance of twirls, the girls were flipped around so rapidly that their skirts snapped outward. They were flung over hips, under legs, overhead, and even in over-the-back postures without missing a single beat. In doing their variations of the "kangaroo" and the "split," the men, with their zoots, looked like balloons when they swung out.

Malcolm X, in one of his lighter moments, describes well the process of Lindy-hopping: "If you've ever lindy-hopped, you know what I'm talking about. With most girls, you kind of work opposite them, circling, side stepping, leading. Whichever arm you lead with is half-bent out there, your hands are giving that little pull, that little push, touching her waist, her shoulders, her arms. She's in, out, turning, whirling, wherever you guide her."[7]

Blacks who danced in places where the races mixed often straightened their hair. They were called "conk-heads" or just "conks." They spoke of "stud cats," "chicks," and "cool hips." If they danced with white women, these were known as their "fay chicks."

Mark Judge called swing the "Dance of Democracy." The syncopated swing beat was the medium for bringing together persons of different classes. It did not matter who you were or where you worked (if you had a job), as long as the two persons could touch as they flung each other in diverse ways that proclaimed their repertoire.[8]

At the depth of the Great Depression, many Americans ate beans; it was all they could afford in the grinding poverty. But by 1939, the American diet was markedly different. Rising incomes, new farm methods, and better storage facilities broadened available food supplies. Changing dietary patterns are best seen from the proportion of calories derived from the major food groups. Family food consumption at all incomes showed a decreasing emphasis on grain products and meats and a greater reliance on fruits, vegetables, milk, fats and sugars. This continued a trend of fifty years, during which the proportion of calories from milk, cheese, fruits, and vegetables doubled.[9]

Nutritionists called for Americans to consume at least one-half of their calories from the "protective foods"—milk and milk products, fruits, vegetables, and eggs. At the time, they were taking only one-third from those sources. This shortage led to deficiencies in vitamins A, B, and C.

The restaurants of 1939 were a relatively unimportant part of life. The menu, which was called "the bill of fare," was more agrarian oriented. Meat of all kinds was featured regularly, and no part of an animal was wasted. As one person said, "Americans ate every part of the pig except the oink." This was true even at the higher scale restaurants. Note, for example, that Marshall Fields offered sweetbread salad for sixty-five cents, chicken giblets for thirty-five cents and minced tongue for twenty-five cents.

NOTES

1. Brooks, *The Great Leap*, p. 11.
2. Brooks, *The Great Leap*, p. 132.
3. Lindbergh, *War Within and Without*, p. 12.
4. Gelernter, *1939: The Lost World of the Fair*, p. 215.
5. Allen, *Since Yesterday*, p. 213.
6. Villacorta, *Ballroom Dancing*, p. 47.

7. Malcolm X, *Autobiography*, p. 64.

8. *Washington Post*, October 1, 1995.

9. U. S. Department of Agriculture, *Yearbook*, 1939, p. 127.

Part I

DOCUMENTING AMERICA

1

This Transitional Year

The year 1939 stood between the Great Depression and World War II. What were conditions like in this transitional year? The birth rate was falling, and demographers were predicting gloomily that the United States would suffer a long-term population decline. Americans living outside central cities seemed to be in the poorest straits. Almost 40 percent lived without a bathtub or shower, and 35 percent of homes had no flush toilets. The average American had completed only eight years of schooling and was 29 years old; one in six was foreign born. The average wage for all workers in manufacturing was sixty-three cents per hour, which was just about the cost of an average lunch. Only 3 percent paid any income tax. The federal budget was $9 billion, most of which went for social welfare expenditures.

The average educational attainment of Americans was just over eight years. Religious leaders lamented the rise of godlessness, and they called for a return to traditional values and beliefs. They decried the increasing popularity of the bikini and "nakedness" on our beaches, and they seemed to be linking these to the lack of purpose of the nation's youth.

More Americans were purchasing homes in 1939. The last urban building boom collapsed after the mid-1920s, and recovery did not come until a decade later. Urban construction was beginning to revive, as new buildings appeared, many of which were low-cost housing projects. These were plain rectilinear boxes, but they provided very necessary housing for the poor and low-income families—a major plank in the New Deal program. Fifteen percent of homes had their own telephones. In the suburbs, Tudor and Colonial houses, some with fieldstone, were very popular. They were priced in the $10,000 to $20,000 category. In the small towns, homes surrounded the old hotel, with its Cape Cod or mansard roof and its wraparound screened porch. The hotel always stood near the railroad station. On the outskirts of town, drivers could stop in one of the small "tourist cabins," which were heated with a single kerosene stove.

By 1939, the Depression was finally waning, but vestiges remained. Unemployment, which had declined each year from its peak of 24.9 percent in 1933 (13 million persons), was still at 17 percent—nine and one-half million persons. And the WPA rolls were still over 2 million persons for most of the year. In the North, the violent strikes that characterized most of the decade continued in 1939, and in the South and West, as Steinbeck wrote in his *Grapes of Wrath*, the poverty of sharecroppers was crushing.

Anne Lindbergh gave another perspective, of one who had lived outside of the United States. On returning in 1939, she said she was shocked by "the material shell of America . . . the speed, the brightness, the flash and advertisement. Nothing solid or real or quiet." (But she was living on Long Island, New York!) She longed for France and "the maturity of life there, the sense of tasting and touching and relishing life as it goes by. Here you can't. It goes by too fast." But she did say that she did not want to be a "Henry James American."[1]

FAIRS EAST AND WEST

In the summer of 1939, there were two world fairs. They each glorified their past—the one in California recalled its Spanish and Asian history, and the New York fair was a celebration of the sesquicentennial of the inauguration of President George Washington.

"Shine-for-39"

The Golden Gate International Exposition, which was known affectionately as "Clean-Up-and-Shine-for-39," was held on Treasure Island. It opened on February 18 to the words of dignitaries and President Roosevelt and the music of Count Basie and Benny Goodman. The Governor recalled the last fair, the Panama-Pacific Exposition of 1915, which brought the states and nations of the Pacific region together. He hoped the 1939 fair would do likewise. The Mayor of San Francisco reminded his audience that it was the Spanish padres who first carved out the western hills, and that the city was named for Saint Francis, the gentle saint who loved people and animals and all of God's creatures.

From the front gates, one saw the beautiful vista of San Francisco Bay and the impressive skyline of the city, with its precipitous hills. To the right were the peak of Tamalpais, Sausalito, and the rocks of Alcatraz. From the hills of San Francisco, two miles across the blue waters of the Bay, one could see the coral walls of the exposition city on Treasure Island—the four hundred acres made it the largest man-made island in the world.

It was a massive construction jobs. Trucks bringing equipment and supplies had to use the Bay Bridge to Treasure Island, where they unloaded their tons of material for exhibitions. The cleanup lived up to its name, as hundreds of office buildings, apartments, and private dwellings got a thorough "jazzing up" for the fair. It produced three million man-hours of work—a necessary condition for the continuing depressed times. The task involved planting one million new trees, using two million gallons of paint and adding ten million hours of candlepower for illumination.

Recalling their past, San Franciscans were happy to name the road from the ferry to the fair the "Path of Gold." It seemed appropriate, because everything about the exposition glittered. Gold paint trimmed with blue was added to most buildings along the pathway to the fair—all dazzling from the lamps that were installed for the purpose.

The city was ready for the one-half million visitors who came to tour famous places while lounging in the blue and gold touring buses. The forty-nine mile scenic drive took fairgoers to Chinatown, Telegraph Hill, Fisherman's Wharf, the Presidio, Golden Gate Park, and over the Bay Bridge. Those who wanted to venture further could motor out to the north country to see the redwoods or the Carmel coast.

Visitors saw the blending of Asian, Mayan, Incan, and American cultures, industries, and arts. As they entered, they confronted Antonio Sotemeyer's terracotta map, designed as a fountain, that was a key to the location of exhibits. The choice was one of abundance. There were the Chinese city and gardens that duplicated life in ancient Cathay, the Japanese Samurai feudal castle, the marvelous wonders of the Hawaiian volcanoes and the crude habitat of the Maoris from New Zealand. For those who preferred local exhibits, the choices were relics of the gold rush days, the specimens of giant sequoias, a science laboratory of "Hollywood Boulevard."

They saw the Palace of Fine Arts for those inclined toward local, American, and European art; the Cavalcade of the Golden West, with its huge stage against a mountainous background; the Pageant of America, the history of the United States, as told by the federal government; the Treasure Island Rodeo, with the usual steer roping and bull dogging; the Toy Symphony, featuring instruments from the 16th to the 18th centuries. The ethnics had their days also: there was Czecho-Slovakia Day, Belgian Day, Peru Day, Hawaii Day, and the Welch Music Festival. In all, twenty-six nations participated, and the fair lost $4 million.

New York, New York

Compared with San Francisco, the New York World's Fair was a colossus. Its emblem, the "World of Tomorrow," was the Trylon and Perisphere (a tall spire rising out of the globe).[2] The fair featured a plenitude of new technology. Attendees saw fluorescent lighting and a ten-million-volt lightning bolt that was discharged at sporadic intervals. The grounds were replete with innovations in housing, transportation, and recreation (the entertainment of the future). Agriculture was not slighted. There was an "Electrified Farm," which exhibited the marvels of hydroponics (the cultivation of plants in water). And there was even a national poetry contest conducted by the Academy of American Poets—to select the official poem of the Fair. The rules stated, "No contestant may submit more than three poems."

It was the largest fair ever. Three hundred buildings were constructed to house the fifteen hundred exhibits. There were twenty-two foreign pavilions astride the Court of Peace. It was there that the political condition was prominent. Germany had no pavilion; Italy featured a large waterfall; Japan showed a Shinto shrine within a replica of the Liberty Bell, which was made of eleven thousand cultured pearls and four hundred diamonds; and the Soviet Union showed off a towering figure of a worker holding the Red Star aloft.

Whereas Germany did not participate, Czecho-slovakia, which had lost its independence to Germany after the Munich pact, chose to carry on—a fruitless effort of imitative freedom. When the fair opened, the Czecho-slovakian pavilion was incomplete—a stark reminder that the Czech nation had been absorbed by Hitler. The Japanese exhibit at the fair displayed only quiet, serene traditional housing, gardens, and culture. It did not indicate that Japan had built a war machine that it was already using against China. Yet, despite these hypocrisies and ironies, the triumph of technology was manifest in the twenty-nine million paid admissions.

Idea and Execution

The idea for the New York World's Fair came from Joseph Shadgen by way of his daughter Jacqueline. She learned in school about the Declaration of Independence and about George Washington's inauguration in New York City in 1789. In discussing this with his daughter, Shadgen realized that 1939 was the 150th anniversary of the inaugural. He spoke to his business partner, who spoke to merchants, who spoke to bankers, who spoke to Mayor La Guardia, who must have spoken to President Roosevelt. Everyone recognized a good commercial idea, and in October 1935 the New York World's Fair Corporation was formed, with George McAneny, a banker, as chairman of the board and Grover Whalen, of the Wanamaker department store, as president.[3]

The fair could not have been possible without the help of Robert Moses, who was head of the Long Island State Commission, the New York City Park Department, and the Triborough Bridge Authority. He had dreamed for a decade of creating a large park in Queens. The idea of a fair gave him his chance. He proposed that the swampland known as the "Corona Dump" be used as a fairground. It would be part of his plan to extend the Grand Central Parkway to Queens. The Parkway, which curved along the western edge of the park, went through a mountain of garbage. Moses used $59 million of federal funds to buy the Flushing site.

He selected Flushing Meadow in Queens for the big event. Because it was a marsh and a dump, it had to be drained and filled in (for $7.5 million). The city built a special subway spur to the site and an amphitheater (where Billy Rose could hold his Aquacade). The total cost was $150 million, with the corporation paying $42 million—$29 million for construction and $13 million for "organization, promotion, and other expenses."[4]

Starting in July 1936, laborers worked twenty-four hours per day for nine months to fill in the swamp with six million cubic yards of ash and garbage. They carved out two lakes, using the sludge for top soil (after treating it with chemicals). They rid Flushing Bay of pollution, controlled drainage, and installed underground utilities and landscaping, The "Official Guide Book" of the fair called the project "the largest single reclamation project ever undertaken in the eastern United States."

By the spring of 1939, twelve thousand workers had converted the twelve-hundred-acre site at Flushing Meadows into "The World of Tomorrow." They built more than two hundred buildings and paved sixty-five miles of streets and walks for the fifteen hundred exhibits. These included large industrial firms, fifty-eight foreign countries, thirty three states, and Puerto Rico. E. B. White captured the essence of the transformation when he wrote:

The Road to Tomorrow leads through the chimney pots of Queens. It is a long, familiar journey, through Mulsified Shampoo and Mobilgas, through Bliss Street, Kix, Astring-O-Sol, and the Majestic Auto Seat Covers. It winds through Textene, Blue Jay Corn Plasters; through Musterole and the delicate pink blossoms on the fruit trees in the ever-hopeful back yards of a populous borough, past Zemo, Alka-Seltzer, Baby Ruth, past Iodent and the Fidelity National Bank, by trusses, belts, and the clothes that fly bravely on the line under the trees with the new little green leaves in Queen's incomparable springtime. Suddenly you see the first intimations of the future, of man's dream—the white ball and spire.[5]

White continued, "The refurbished ash heap, rising from its own smolder, is by far the biggest show that has ever been assembled on God's earth."

When President Roosevelt opened the fair on April 30, 1939, he spoke before sixty thousand persons of "a star of peace." During a day of sunshine and pelting rain, of parades, and fireworks, 206,000 persons paid the seventy-five cent admission charge. The *New York Times* of May 1 told us, "They came in hordes down the railroad and subway ramps, forty or fifty abreast to gaze upon the wonders." The official attendance figures were kept by a counting machine that revolved on top of the National Cash Register building.

Albert Einstein, the refugee from Germany, was asked to throw the switch that lit up countless fountains and floodlights. Overhead, two blimps cast their shadows over the President as he spoke, and in the harbor and on the Hudson River, a large contingent of the twelve thousand officers and men of the "Atlantic Squadron" sailed by. Thirty-eight ships were ordered to the fair, including the battleships *New York* and *Texas*, the heavy-cruiser *Wichita*, the light-cruiser *Honolulu,* and the aircraft carrier *Ranger.*

The Trylon, the three-sided pointed needle that thrust seven hundred feet into the air, symbolized the "Fair's lofty purpose." Connected to it by a bridge about sixty feet above the ground was the Perisphere, a smooth globe two hundred feet in diameter. Architects Wallace K. Harrison and J. Andre Fouilhoux stated that the Trylon represented limited flight and the Perisphere controlled stasis.[6]

Futurama: The Magic Carpet

A Gallup poll substantiated what every fairgoer knew: that the General Motors' Futurama was the hit of the show. Norman Bel Geddes' Futurama, according to one observer, "Combines the thrills of Coney Island with the glories of Le Corbusier." It was a stunning presentation, in miniature, of a visionary plan for the cities and countryside of the United States in the year 1960.

Bel Geddes, a native of Adrian, Michigan, who did short stints at the Cleveland School of Art and at the Chicago Institute of Art, turned his attention to the stage, leading to his appointment as stage designer for the Metropolitan Opera Company. His innovations of design drew the gasps of the audience from his more than two hundred productions. During the 1930s he expanded his horizons by becoming an industrial designer and by linking up with George Howe, a well-known architect. One assignment was to loom much larger: Bel Geddes designed the medal commemorating the twenty-fifth anniversary of General Motors. He was surprised when General Motors called again to ask him to design its exhibit at the New York World's Fair.

In Bel Geddes' Futurama, the traffic system he created was an example of his fertile mind; autos moved in controlled lanes and were segregated by speed, which was controlled automatically. This $7.5 million project was a gigantic model of nearly one-half million structures, which were viewed while sitting for fifteen minutes in a comfortable blue-velour wing chair that moved by conveyor belt past the dioramas.

As the rubber-tire train of twelve cars left the station, a voice invited passengers to enjoy an airplane ride sixteen hundred feet over the United States of 1960. The moving system by which spectators were carried through the exhibits was called the greatest contribution of technology at the fair. Bel Geddes decided that if the millions who were to see his Futurama had to walk through the exhibit, they would see it all through fatigued eyes. It would all be a test of stamina rather than the wonders of technology.

The chair-train was designed by James Dunlop, an engineer from Westinghouse Electric. It was a daunting task. It required an endless track, 1,586 feet long (almost a third of a mile long), that would wind in and out of a building that contained forty-four thousand square feet. At one point, the track was 23 feet high, and the loading and unloading platform stood 13 feet above the floor. In addition to this engineering problem, the conveyor was to be smooth and silent.

The conveyer system was both a train and an escalator. It consisted of 322 cars with a driving motor on every fourteenth one. The Futurama was a succession of three-dimensional pictures that portrayed our technological evolution. The millions who went through the Futurama (including this writer) were awe-struck at the one-half million miniature houses, its one million trees and its fifty thousand miniature automobiles, as they progressed smoothly over a complex network of superhighways and bridges. Each seat had its own speaker that narrated the scene around you. The trip began in blinding sunshine past orchards and fruit trees; it wound along farmhouses on magnificent highways as the speaker told you that these were the roads of 1960. Next you flew over a dairy, by a small town and on the superhighway at one hundred miles per hour.

Other Exhibits

White chose the American Telephone & Telegraph Exhibit as his personal best, because as he stated, "There are millions of people who have never either made or received a long distance call." AT&T allowed anyone who had drawn a lucky number to make a phone call to anywhere in the United States. White relates how "Eddie Pancha, a waiter in a restaurant in El Paso, Texas, hears the magic words, 'New York is calling. Go ahead, please,' he is transfixed in holy dread and excitement."[7]

The "Democracity" of the Fair would presage the modern suburb. It would replace tenement slums, those "quaint" buildings without central heat or bathtubs, with apartments on the fringes of cities. Fairgoers were introduced to this wonderful world of tomorrow by a film called *The City*. It was purely an American enterprise: produced by the American City Planning Institute; narrated by that dean of American technocrats, Lewis Mumford and embellished by the serene strains of music by Aaron Copland.

The movie contrasted the noise, the fumes, the sirens, the railroad yards, the traffic jams with the playgrounds, and the green fields that suburbanites would see as they drove around the factories and tenements that they would desert. In the suburbs, where adults walk along their manicured walkways, children ride their bicycles or play ball on diamonds that are clearly demarcated.

The fair also included a Children's World; a City of Tomorrow; a miniature rocket voyage to the moon; and a transparent man. And there was the less serious aspect of the fair. Thousands of persons visited the "Amusement Loop," especially the girlie shows and the Aquacade. Ketchum believed that "science does not seem to compete with an undressed woman."[8]

One particularly obnoxious show, "Twenty Thousand Leagues Under the Sea," featured a scantily dressed woman who always was in the clutches of an octopus, that made what appeared to be obscene gestures as she wrestled to get free. It is easy to see why he was called "Oscar the Obscene Octopus." By contrast, Aquacade, produced by Billy Rose, was quite refined; it starred Olympic champion Eleanor Holm and her "Aquafemmes," who did precision swimming to semiclassical music. These shapely "femmes" were a big crowd pleaser.

Equally popular was the parachute jump from the 250-foot Life Saver tower. Those who dared were strapped in their seats and hoisted into the air slowly to get a spectacular view of the fair below. They sat above the Lagoon of Nations, the rides, restaurants, and fountains, astride the Japanese and Russian exhibits. As they gazed at the marvelous panorama below, they reached the top of the ride, and swiftly stomachs heaved as the parachute opened. The thrill was over quickly as the chute took in air and floated to the ground.

On at least one occasion, the chute failed to descend. A couple from Baltimore was stuck on the top of the Life Saver tower. A reporter arrived before the engineer who was to remedy the malfunction. The crowd grew quickly as drivers, hearing the news on the radio, turned off Grand Central Parkway into the World's Fair Boulevard Gate. As the reporter gave a running commentary, he was asked not to reveal the names of the stranded couple. When he inquired why not, he got his answer, "He's from Baltimore, and that's not his wife."

THEIR MAJESTIES COME TO VISIT

On June 7, 1939, a blue and silver train crossed the suspension bridge at Niagara Falls and entered the brick railroad station, having arrived from a point just twelve miles south of Quebec, via Canadian Pacific Railroad. The American delegation, headed by Secretary of State Cordell Hull, met the great-great-great grandson of George III, George VI, the first British King to visit the United States. On disembarking, their majesties, King George VI and Queen Elizabeth of England, stepped onto the small length of red carpet and the King extended his hand to the Secretary.

His Most Excellent Majesty George VI, by the Grace of God, of Great Britain, Ireland, and of the British Dominions Beyond the Seas, King, Defender of the Faith, Emperor of India, whose subjects accused him of having "no wit, no learning," had been on the throne for only two years when he came to North America.[9]

Prince Albert, who became George VI, was no Edward VIII, who was good looking and warm, and who had abdicated his crown for "the woman I love." By contrast, George VI was stiff and not at ease in social settings (but he did improve with some champagne). Worse for him, he stammered when he spoke, which troubled him greatly. But George VI plodded and did well, and he won the respect, admiration, and love of the English people. He often remarked about his good fortune in marrying Elizabeth Angela Marguerite Bowes-Lyon, a very sociable, attractive brunette, who made up for his shortcomings at lawn parties. She had charismatic qualities, but they did not stop English reporters from commenting on her dull-looking, frumpy clothes that did not flatter her more-than-adequate figure. It was unfair characterization, because the Queen was not dowdy; she looked regal.

The English were relieved to be rid of Edward VIII, who in rebellion against the strict disciplinary approach of his father George V, modernized the monarchy in all matters of politics and love. Prime Minister Stanley Baldwin, in particular, disapproved both of Edward's shocking sexual escapades that he flaunted to the horror of the royal family and its public and his meddling in state affairs. Baldwin was flabbergasted when King Edward visited Germany and gave the Nazi salute. George VI, dominated by the Periclean Winston Churchill, preferred to stay in the background.[10]

Before their majesties came to Washington, D.C., the Secret Service stationed fifty thousand servicemen along the way. When the train arrived at Union Station in Washington on June 8, it was greeted by the President and Mrs. Roosevelt and a group of congressional notables. The temperature was a very uncomfortable 94 degrees Fahrenheit, and the King was perspiring heavily in full-dress, epauletted uniform, but no more than our President, who was attired in cutaway coat, striped trousers, and top hat.

The following day, the royal visitors were given a twenty-one-gun salute and a triumphant motorcade through the streets of Washington, where (*Time* of June 19 tells us) six hundred thousand persons, many standing on peach baskets, cramped their necks to get a glimpse of royalty. Overhead, ten Flying Fortresses roared their way to the White House. There was agreement: that her majesty was the heroine of the day. "She was the perfect Queen: eyes a snapping blue, chin tilted confidently, two fingers raised in a greeting as girlish as she was regal. Her long-handled parasol seemed out of a storybook."

Then it was Congress's turn. Many were very fearful of entangling alliances; others were grumbling about the unpaid debt of World War I (over $5 billion). When the guest list for the State dinner was announced, these same legislators tried all their tricks to get the scarce tickets. Senator Ellison "Cotton Ed" Smith declared that he would not kowtow to royalty, but he dug out his old morning suit for the dinner, and when the King called him Cotton Ed, all icicles melted. Smith jokingly offered to cancel the war debt if we could keep Queen Elizabeth.

Despite this attempt at humor, there was bitterness among the British delegation over the ill-breeding of Americans. Vice President John Nance Garner screamed, "Here comes the British," and gave the King a Texas slap on the back. Congressman Nat Patton, also a Texan, called King George "Cousin George" and Queen Elizabeth "Cousin Elizabeth."

The entertainment included Lawrence Tibbett, Marion Anderson and Kate Smith. Later, Mrs. Roosevelt wrote of her visit to Kate Smith, who was particularly pleased that His Highness had requested that she sing "When the Moon Comes over the Mountain."

That evening, the President and fourteen hundred guests joined the King and Queen for a cruise down the Potomac River to Mount Vernon on the presidential yacht. During the formal dinner at the British embassy, which followed the cruise, the slender Queen again stole the show. She looked exquisite in her embroidered white gown, matching hat, and parasol. The whole affair was like a fairy tale, and the Americans loved every chapter.

On June 10 the visitors took a train to Red Bank, New Jersey, where they met Governor Herbert Lehman and Mayor Fiorello La Guardia of New York. They drove to Sandy Hook, in lower New York Bay. An estimated two hundred thousand persons lined the route. They were greeted by a choir singing "God Save the King" and ten U.S. Army Air Corps bombers. At the battery in lower Manhattan, they received a second twenty-one-gun salute. The *New York Times* estimated that 3.5 million persons watched the motorcade, which it said was the second largest crowd ever (only Lindbergh's was bigger in 1927).

The final stop for the day was the New York World's Fair. This time the expressions of friendliness were more boisterous. Grover Whalen was joined by brass bands and thousands of fair attendees. The royal visitors were given an exhausting tour on a trackless motor train. As Richard Ketchum reminds us, no one thought that a king ever went to the bathroom. It was quite embarrassing for him to inform his driver that he had to relieve himself. Following a brief visit at the British Pavilion, which was the official purpose for the visit, they were on their way along the Hudson River for the eighty-mile journey to the Roosevelts' home at Hyde Park, where all the formalities ended.

The President had martinis ready, and the King accepted one gladly with hands that were swollen from handshaking. The President and the young King were joined by Canadian Prime Minister Mackenzie King, and they talked for hours. Roosevelt spoke to the King "as a father to a son," giving advice concerning the ominous conditions in Europe. The President spoke as an admirer, and promised help if war came.

For the following day (Sunday), the Roosevelts scheduled an American-style picnic of hot dogs, Ruppert beer (made in New York), ham, smoked and plain turkey, salads, donuts, cookies and strawberry shortcake. The King could have done without the hot dogs, but as Allen said, "He knew well that a hot dog eaten smilingly in America might be worth a dozen battleships." Folk singer Alan Lomax and a Choctaw-Chickasaw half-breed Indian telling stories provided the entertainment.

Dinner that evening was intimate and informal, and while they were still dressed in their dinner clothes, the royal couple entrained for their return trip to Quebec. The crowd sang "Auld Lang Syne" and "For He's a Jolly Good Fellow." The President added, "Good luck to you. All the luck in the world," as the train pulled away.[11]

THE DOMINANT RELIGION

The Trylon of the New York World's Fair pointed skyward; it promised a future. Inescapably, it was linked with religion, which helps you to "see" the promise of perfect political and social systems. In 1939, Americans were optimistic; they believed in technology and the wonders of their age. The future was accepted on faith.

The United States was firmly White Anglo-Saxon Protestant (WASP) in 1939, especially in the small towns of the Midwest and the Southwest. These churchgoers praised toleration, but they were intolerant of atheism, Judaism, socialism, communism and Catholicism. The tensions between Catholics and non-Catholics were long-standing, their roots being the nativist elements in the population who believed that the large Catholic immigration was a Roman plot to overthrow the democratic institutions of America.

Because Protestants were not a homogeneous group, their attitudes on Catholicism were wide ranging. Some offered expressions of good will; others were rabidly venomous in their hatred for "the Church of Rome." Dislike, however, was a two-way street. Some Roman Catholics harbored unpleasant feelings towards Protestants. It was all fueled by the assertion that "outside of the Catholic Church, there is no salvation."[12]

But the most serious charge made by Catholics was leveled against the public schools. Universal free education was considered to be the strongest pillar of a democratic American society, but Catholics challenged the Protestantism of those schools and concluded that the only solution was a school system of their own.

Indubitably, the Catholics who immigrated to the United States came to a "Gospel of Wealth," and strong notions of economic self-interest were foreign to them. They had trouble adjusting to the unparalleled prosperity of American society. As Lally wrote, Roman Catholics were not "socially progressive" until the New Deal years.[13]

Negro churches were another problem for the WASPs.[14] The migration of blacks into the major industrial cities that commenced during World War I continued throughout the 1930s. Their churches became less emotional and more formal. There were fewer "spirituals" in tents, but there were more small, storefront places of worship that had names such as "Church of the Living God," "The Kingdom of God," "Church of our Savior," "The Christian Zion Church," and "The Sanctified Holy Church." These black churches were one more manifestation of the growing schism within Christianity—a division caused by a clash between what Hudson calls "the older agrarian and the newer urban society."[15]

Blacks also had their fringe churchmen. One evangelical in particular "Father Divine" promised to deliver God in his own person. His real name was George Baker. He ministered in a New York ghetto where all races were equally welcome. In his church, he preached love and peace, and his supporters claimed, "Father Divine is the supplier and satisfier of every good desire."

Most white denominations also were beset by troubles throughout the 1930s—the diminishing influence of conservative fundamentalism and the growth of secularized liberal theology. This decade saw a new evangelism in the churches. There were traveling teams, city missions, and the media that worked among the derelicts and the Park Avenue dwellers. The ministers sought confessions and conversions, and they preached against pagans and sinners. In 1939, this movement was given a new name—Moral Re-Armament—and, according to Hudson, it drew thirty thousand people into the Hollywood Bowl for an assembly and an additional ten thousand persons were turned away.

When World War II began, American theology was in an incipient revival phase, sparked by a number of European writings that were heavily influenced by existentialists Kierkegaard, Tillich, and Bonhoeffer. They seemed to favor moving to the right in theology and to the left in politics. This religious revival was aborted (temporarily) when World War II began.

In the 1930s the local Protestant churches considered themselves to be the watchdogs of the moral elements of American society. Although their values were under attack from Darwinians and Freudians, the Protestant clergy continued to believe that they spoke directly to God. And so their stewardship over the churches, the schools, and the community was largely unchallenged. They thought that we were still and should remain a Protestant nation.

Events posed a challenge and bid to change the Protestant reality. One was the God-is-dead movement, a product of the Great Depression. Polls indicated that the more educated were less prone to remain with organized religions, yet even at the highest intellectual levels, belief in a creator flourished. In the debate about God, theologian Reinhold Niebuhr declared that one could not and need not prove the existence of God by reason. In time of economic depression, which leads to frustration and despair, humanity must look to God for strength and perseverance.[16]

The second challenge was immigration, because 55 percent of immigrants who passed through Ellis Island were Catholics and Jews. How should the Protestant establishment confront this alien element in our society? There was a religious earthquake shaking the establishment door; the question was, who should be let in?

During the 1930s the local churches could not avoid the problems of poverty and economic justice. In the pulpits they had to confront the issue of poverty and the social gospel. How should the churches react to the spreading poverty of the Great Depression? Where were the leaders who could speak forcefully on world issues from a Christian perspective? One answer was to use the print and radio media to gain control over the forces of Godless Communism, socialism, and secularism.

George E. Haynes, a leader in the Protestant church on race relations, was very suspicious of all attempts to link the black social movement to the class struggle. He insisted on taking a nonconfrontational approach, even in the face of the violence that Negroes tolerated. He worked diligently to divorce the National Negro Congress from the communist movement and to adhere to his strategy of promoting more contacts between whites and blacks in the churches.

In the mid-1930s Haynes agreed to work on the Joint Committee on National Recovery, which desired to unite blacks to fight for the abolition of Jim Crow laws, a reduction and eventual abolition of lynching, more relief programs, and greater economic opportunity, including the acceptance of black labor unions in the national federations. It was here that he tangled with A. Philip Randolph, President of the Brotherhood of Sleeping Car Porters, who at that time was a socialist. Haynes resisted supporting communists and socialists because they represented the antithesis of Christianity. By the end of 1939 Randolph recognized the defeat of his approach, when he said, "Negro people cannot afford to add to the handicap of being black the handicap of being red."[17]

In 1938, a group of representatives met in Utrecht, Netherlands, to draft a constitution for a World Council of Churches. Although World War II intervened, this group continued to press for church unity. But the Council's work was hampered because the leading churches refused to send representatives, including the Roman Catholics, the Russian Orthodox, the Missouri Synod Lutherans, and the Southern Baptists. The Roman Catholic position was most easy to state. It believed it was the one true church, and therefore it could not adjust to others, for this would negate its already existing perfect union with God. The refusal of the Lutherans and the Baptists was, according to Sweet, "most baffling."

Will Herberg, in his "Protestant-Catholic-Jew," wrote of the serious tensions and distrust that faced these religions in their interreligious relations. Catholics and Jews were the victims of bigotry; they were accused of being separatists, because each in its way believed it was worshiping the "one true God." They were constantly required to prove their patriotism. Catholics had to prove that they were not "Papists," and Jews that they were not clannish. Catholics were called undemocratic because they insisted on shunning public (American) schools and establishing their own parochial schools. Protestants chose not to notice that the public schools used the King James Bible for their morning prayers. Not many, then, paid much attention to "the separation of church and state."

The burdens upon Jews were particularly onerous, because, as the largest non-Christian group, they not only wanted acceptance on social and cultural levels, but they were advocating foreign policies that were anathema to many Americans. For this, they were labeled politically subversive. In 1939, it was difficult for Jews to be model Americans and to retain their Jewishness. Jews wanted to be insiders, but their concerns (Palestine, immigration) militated against creating the kind of coalition they were anxious to create.

The American Catholic Church, the largest Christian group in the United States, faced an equally antagonistic Protestant establishment. Catholics had to defend their legitimacy and demand their equality in an environment that Kraut called "ambivalent." He denounced the "deep-seated anti-Catholicism" as morally offensive, intellectually unjustified, and religiously mis-guided."[18]

Envoy to the Vatican

The appointment of Myron C. Taylor, the retired Chairman of the United States Steel Corporation, as Roosevelt's personal envoy to the Vatican during Christmas week of 1939 shocked many Americans. Taylor, a native of Lyons, New York, was educated as a lawyer but made his mark as a businessman. He began by practicing law but turned to running textile mills. He catapulted to the top of the financial world by completing a $2 billion merger.

This success led him to the United States Steel Corporation, where he replaced J. P. Morgan as Chairman. His negotiating skills became obvious in 1936, when he convinced John L. Lewis, head of the CIO, to make peace with U.S. Steel, which had long been a nonunion company, thereby avoiding a serious labor stoppage.

Taylor resigned in 1939 to meditate on the problems of modern civilization. He did not meditate long, however, because President Roosevelt appointed him to lead the U.S. delegation to the Evian Refugee Conference. This resulted in his appointment as the American associate of the Intergovernmental Committee for Refugees.

Taylor's appointment to the Vatican was an historical event, because it came in wartime, and it was the first such appointment in American history. As envoy, Taylor, an Episcopalian who was raised a Quaker, was named an ambassador, but without portfolio. He was the first American to visit the Vatican in an official capacity since Rufus King in 1868. The new "ambassador of peace," a large man with a fierce look, was just the opposite in manner; he was gentle and totally in control of his emotions. He relished his appointment to Italy, because he always had a great interest in all art. As a businessman, he was a regular visitor to the American Academy in Rome and the Metropolitan Museum of Art in New York.

The restoration of diplomatic relations with the Holy See inflamed sectarian rivalries. The Protestant churches, which had been working for church unity in the 1930s, were particularly chagrined. But Roosevelt saw the appointment as an attempt to meld democracy and religion. It was his answer to the call to love and respect your neighbor. Whether he was motivated by this sense of civility or whether he was thinking of the growing number of Catholics in the electorate, this appointment created a storm for him, and the choice of Christmas eve for the announcement must not have pleased those who opposed the move.

The Radio Priest

Father Charles Edward Coughlin, an Irish Canadian, was the leader of one of the most influential "America First" movements. He called Christianity the answer to the nation's economic problems. Coughlin, true to the encyclicals he studied in the seminary, considered economics a branch of the moral law. His sermons became harangues that dealt with money matters, as he denounced "the filthy gold standard," which he called Jewish currency. Parroting some of the ideas of William Jennings Bryan, he stated that a gold standard would lead to war and destroy mankind. To replace that filthy gold, Coughlin urged that all silver be monetized, because silver is gentile currency. He began where William Jennings Bryan left off: that humankind was crucified on a cross of gold. The answer, then, was "free silver" and an inflated money supply.[19]

Coughlin claimed that he was a simple priest, but his Sunday broadcasts had made him the most powerful figure in radio. His beautiful baritone voice had a marvelous range. He began his talks in a slow, low, rich pitch, gradually increasing the tempo, finishing with passion as his spirits soared with his words. So vehement was his delivery that the veins in his neck reddened and protruded. Although his diction was flawless, he could not conceal his Irish brogue, which made the words flow musically.

Coughlin built an empire through his brilliant radio orations and his manipulation of the media "exploiting aspects of the national character which were then but little understood: American innocence, the nation's yearning for simple solutions, its joiner complex, and the carnival instinct for collecting shiny junk."[20]

Coughlin was not a large man. His round face and extra flesh made him appear plump. But he was handsome, with his brown hair well trimmed, his blue eyes visible beneath his heavy steel glasses, and his tailored suits. His manner, not his physique, was what overwhelmed his visitors. He played out his princely role, but he also entertained with stories, some having sexual connotations, and by playing the piano and accompanying himself. It was a perfect blend of the spiritual and the material (he was rendering to Caesar what was Caesar's).

Americans were bewildered as to how this Canadian could have reached such prominence in American politics. Coughlin took his priestly vows in 1916, and for the next seven years, he taught at Assumption School near Detroit. He was a Basilian priest, but he came to prefer the parish life to the cloistered one. Accordingly, he accepted posts in several Michigan parishes, until he was asked to establish a new church in Royal Oak, Michigan, only twelve miles from Detroit. He built a much bigger church than his parish could support, but a tragedy started him on his way as the "radio priest." When the KKK burned down his new church, the director of radio station WJR asked him to go on the air to give a series of sermons that would help finance a new church. These came to be called the "Golden Hour of the Little Flower," broadcast on CBS. He was a sensation. His mellow, florid voice, which exuded intimacy, was described by Wallace Stegner as "without doubt one of the great speaking voices of the twentieth century."[21] Coughlin was a man of ability and ambition, a man who was to use the priesthood to satisfy his "obsessive desire for acclaim."[22]

The seeds of Coughlin's National Union for Social Justice are found in the words of Leo XIII. The Pope wrote of the "pressing question" of the hour, of the "Misery and wretchedness . . . of the working class," of society being "divided into two widely different castes," of the "greed of unchecked competition," of the yoke put upon "the teeming masses," and then he gave his prescription: "A workman's wages should be sufficient to enable him comfortably to support himself, his wife and his children."

When the 1930s began, Coughlin had a radio audience of over forty million. At first, he stuck to Biblical stories, but when the economic situation worsened, he remembered Catholic social thought. He was compelled to address the plight of the working man. In Detroit, the effects of the Depression were everywhere, and Coughlin's "sermons" became totally political in content. He received more mail than anyone else in America—more than any movie star or sports hero, more than the President. In a typical, self-deprecating manner, Coughlin declared, "I am neither Republican, Democrat nor Socialist. I glory in the fact that I am a simple Catholic priest endeavoring to inject Christianity into the fabric of an economic system woven upon the loom of greed by the cunning fingers of those who manipulate the shuttles of human lives for their own selfish purposes."

When money poured in from the sale of chromium-plated crucifixes, "The Little Flower" rebuilt his church (with, it was claimed, nonunion labor). On the marble and granite seven-story tower, he placed a bas-relief of Christ, which, when lit up, could be seen all over the city. Beneath the figure was the single word, "Charity." Farmers nearby thought the tower looked like a silo, so they began to call Coughlin "Silo Charlie."

By 1939 Coughlin owned a forty-seven-station network; headed a political organization, the National Union for Social Justice; headed the Social Justice Poor Society, and published a newspaper—*Social Justice*. He was the only stockholder of the Radio League of the Little Flower (its Board of Directors was his two secretaries. He was also the sole stockholder of Social Justice, a profit-making organization that was the spearhead of Father Coughlin's anti-communist and anti-Semitic campaigns.

Coughlin encouraged the Christian Front—an anti-Semitic, pro-fascist organization—in a speech in July 1939 in which he counseled them to follow the "peaceful way." But his printed policies had no planks that mentioned democratic government or free speech. John McCarten wrote that much of the anti-Semitic material used by Coughlin came from a Nazi propaganda publishing organ—"World Service." Coughlin declared that Jews were natural conspirators, he blamed them for introducing an international banking system run by communists," and he named Bernard Baruch and Eddie Cantor as America's most dangerous Jews.[23]

Coughlin presented a major dilemma for the Catholic Church. Although he was attacked by some eminent cardinals, the Church was unable to exercise control over him, because he had the full support of his own Bishop, Michael J. Gallagher of Detroit. And so Coughlin's sermons became more inflammatory and demagogic. As proof of the Jewish conspiracy, he published the "Protocols of the Elders of Zion," a patently false, bigoted document that had circulated for years. It was "an ancient plot whereby the Jews would impose financial slavery upon the world."[24]

Irish Americans had a certain affinity with his preaching. Boston, with its heavy Irish Catholic population, was a stronghold of the Coughlinites. Mayor James Michael Curley once said that Boston was the "strongest Coughlin city in America." Coughlin's popularity there was achieved despite the denunciation of William Cardinal O'Connell, the Archbishop of Boston. O'Connell called Coughlin an hysterical cleric, saying that Christians could not accuse bankers and financiers publicly, because the Church is for everyone. The growing hordes of Coughlin's followers caused friction in the downtown areas of Boston and New York. The Jews were buying real estate and starting businesses in areas previously held by Irish Americans, which led to attacks of Jews by Irish-American gangs.

When war began in Europe in 1939, Coughlin made a peculiar switch. He had been advocating the establishment of "sports clubs" to train young men to accept discipline and to engage in military drills, but when fighting commenced, he became a strong advocate of American neutrality. Coughlin organized a "Christian Front," under which groups of bullies went into large cities imitating the terroristic tactics of Hitler's Storm Troopers. Coughlin's approach disturbed Catholics and confused the many existing fascist groups, who abhorred Catholics, Jews, communists, and liberals. When Protestant minister Gerald L. K. Smith organized his "Committee of One Million," he offered to support Coughlin, but most of his followers were vehemently anti-Catholic.[25]

THE DAR AND JIM CROW

Irish Catholics were not the only bigots in 1939. On a cold Easter Sunday in 1939, a quiet Negro woman did more to reduce discrimination than the activities of most intellectuals and labor unions. Marian Anderson, a native Philadelphian, began singing in church choirs at the age of six. Her father was an ice dealer, and her mother scrubbed floors so their girl could study voice. Because she wanted to break into the white world of classical song, she confronted discrimination everywhere. In her teenage years, she was refused admittance to a good school in Philadelphia, but she stuck to her formal voice training. As she matured, she kept hearing, "No Negroes need apply." Discouraged, she headed for Europe, where Sol Hurok heard her sing. He signed her to a contract in 1935, and she debuted in New York. The reviews were sensational.

In April 1939 Anderson, a shy, dignified, and deeply religious woman, wanted only to use her extraordinary voice at Constitution Hall in Washington, D.C., which happened to be owned by the Daughters of the American Revolution. Instead, she broke the color line and exposed the racism of the DAR with her beautiful voice. Anderson's struggle against the DAR was a milestone in the fight for racial justice, but she was not comfortable in her role as a crusader. She quietly went about being the best Negro vocalist of her time.

The DAR began discriminating against blacks in 1935 by inserting a clause in all of its contracts that said, "Concerts by White artists only." When Howard University sponsors applied to lease Constitution Hall in 1939 for a concert by Marian Anderson, the DAR management refused them, saying there were no open dates. But Anderson's manager, impresario Sol Hurok, was unbelieving. When he had a friend call for dates that were supposedly taken, they were quickly granted. It was clear to Hurok that Anderson could not sing there because it was reserved for whites only. When the DAR manager realized that he had been trapped, he was furious and he said, "No Negro will ever appear in this hall while I am the manager."

When Eleanor Roosevelt learned of this episode, she resigned from the DAR in protest, but the Daughters stuck to their Jim Crow rules. Next, Anderson tried to sing in the auditorium of Central High School (now Cardozo High), but school officials told her that Central High School was a "whites only" school. Mrs. Roosevelt, seeing the total frustration of the situation, asked Secretary of the Interior Harold Ickes to reserve the steps of the Lincoln Memorial for Anderson's concert.

When she sang on that windy April day, her concert was attended by cabinet members, Supreme Court Justices, members of Congress and thousands of Washingtonians. Her crystalline voice floated down the mall over the large crowd. The high point of the evening came in the beginning when she opened the concert with a moving rendition of "America," which brought tears to many eyes. There followed several spirituals, including "Gospel Train" and "Nobody Knows the Trouble I've Seen."

Edward T. Folliard, covered the event for the *Washington Post.* He wrote: "It was another kind of communication. It was not a communication of mind, the heart or the flesh. It was a communication of the soul of man, which never dies and never will die. . . . The sight of Abraham Lincoln with this black woman standing in a beautiful fur coat in front of a big Steinway piano singing, 'My Country Tis of Thee,' is a thing you don't see or hear or feel every day."[26]

Conductor Arturo Toscanini, speaking a few years later when Anderson was auditioning for the Metropolitan Opera, said that she had the kind of voice heard "once in a hundred years."

APPROACHES TO CRIME: HOOVER AND DEWEY

Bootleggers and Gamblers

The year 1939 was a struggle of good and evil. Religious leaders strove to reconcile their differences; those who ran organized crime (Luciano, Genovese, Buchalter, and Valachi) were pursued relentlessly by the nation's two leading crime fighters—Hoover and Dewey.

John Edgar Hoover, always known as J. Edgar, had a coterie of fervent admirers, including Shirley Temple and Walter Winchell (and those thousands of boys who ran around the streets emulating G-men). He was born and grew up in a modest section of Washington, D.C., where he was called "Speed," despite his being the smallest person in his class at only 110 pounds.

He stuttered badly as a boy but overcame it by speaking rapidly. His speech problem did not prevent him from graduating as valedictorian. John Edgar seemed destined "to go places." As a young man of ambition, by day he worked as messenger in the Library of Congress and evenings he studied law at George Washington University. He was appointed Special Assistant to the Attorney General. In that post he served as director of the newly created General Intelligence Division, which was responsible for investigating "antiradical" behavior. In 1921 Hoover was made assistant director of the FBI, and three years later, he was appointed director, despite not spending a single day in the field chasing criminals.

John Dillinger provided Hoover's "coming out party." Dillinger had said, "I don't drink, I don't gamble. I guess my only bad habit is robbing banks." But what rankled Hoover was Dillinger's habit of embarrassing the FBI. He thumbed his nose at the law, and he gave money away to the poor, which made him a kind of folk hero. The flustered Hoover went on the radio and declared, "John Dillinger is Public Enemy Number One"—the first so designated and vowed that the FBI would get him. In short time, his G-men gunned down Public Enemy Number One in an alley behind the Biograph Theatre on Lincoln Avenue, Chicago. He was betrayed by a friend of his girl friend, Anna Sage— "The Woman in red."

Hollywood inflated the Hoover legend by producing a series of anticrime movies in which the G-men always won. The steady procession included *The Public Enemy, Little Caesar, Scarface,* and *G Men.* In all these cases, the government was pursuing public enemies.

Only much later would we learn that the myth was greater than the man. In the 1930s, Hoover created a network of internal security files of people who had committed no crimes. There were files of labor organizations, subversives, racketeers, pacifists, cabinet members, and congressmen. He even had a file on Mrs. Roosevelt. By 1939 Hoover ruled over a large bureaucratic agency and was a law unto himself.

The FBI never stopped collecting and filing information about alleged radicals. In the years from 1924 to 1939, this information was sent to special agents. Hoover kept files on the ACLU, on Felix Frankfurter (a dangerous man), on Helen Keller (who wrote on "radical subjects"), and on Jane Addams, a Nobel Prize winner, who J. Edgar said was a supporter of revolutionary movements.

Tough-guy Hoover "assailed the parole system, with its 'sob-sister judges,' 'criminal coddlers,' 'shyster lawyers and other legal vermin.' He blamed them for 'human rats' like John Dillinger." Hoover told the world, "I'm going to tell the truth about these rats. I'm going to tell the truth about their dirty, filthy, diseased women. I'm going to tell the truth about the miserable politicians who protect them and the slimy, silly or sob-sister convict lovers who let them out on sentimental or ill-advised paroles. If the people don't like it, they can get me fired, But I'm going to say it."[27]

As his popularity rose, Hoover sought a distinctive name for his bureau. He preferred one that would have catchy initials, such as the Criminal Investigation Division of Scotland Yard, which yielded the initials CID. One of his top assistants, Edward Tamm, came up with the winning choice. He recommended the Federal Bureau of Investigation, which Hoover wasn't keen about until Tamm told him that the initials FBI stood for Fidelity, Bravery, and Integrity, the words that fit his special agents. Hoover, the man with the gigantic ego, ordered new stationery, which put Attorney General Cummings in a rage, because the words "FEDERAL BUREAU OF INVESTIGATION" were larger than "The United States Department of Justice."

Until recently, Clyde Tolson's rapid (one could say spectacular) rise in the FBI was seen as a puzzle. It was a unique case in the history of the Bureau. He was named a special agent in April 1928, an inspector in 1930, and an assistant director in 1931. Tolson and Hoover were inseparable. They were both bachelors. They worked together, they ate together, they recreated together, and while in New York City, they shared a complimentary suite at the Waldorf Astoria. They usually spent the Christmas season together in Florida, and they always went to California for the start of the racing season at Del Mar.

As Hoover obtained and wielded more power, he became the target of a wider group of enemies, who wanted to bring him down because of his abuse of authority. But it was Hoover himself who almost wrecked his agency. It happened during his appearance before the House Appropriations Subcommittee on November 30, 1939. The FBI director told the committee that he had hired 150 new special agents for his General Intelligence Division, which compiled extensive data on subversive organizations, alphabetically and geographically. This is the same organization that Attorney General Stone had ordered abolished in 1924, and what is more incredible, Hoover had not even changed its name!

J. Edgar Hoover's problems were much more serious. According to Anthony Summers, Hoover was also involved with personal corruption, fraud and dishonesty. Summers writes that Hoover ignored the real threat of the 1930s— the Mafia—because he was a fanatical gambler and he had a homosexual lover, Clyde Tolson, an FBI agent. Summers' most impressionistic charge against Hoover is that he was a transvestite, who attended orgies with "young blond boys." These charges are not included in Richard Powers' earlier biography. But for Summers, it was not a case of his homosexuality but rather of Hoover's dereliction of duties. William Turner, a former FBI man, wrote that Hoover neglected field cases; he preferred to focus on notorious persons. As a consequence, the FBI handled only 1 percent of crimes in the United States, and it ignored completely the growth of organized crime.[28]

Each summer, Hoover and Clyde Tolson went to Del Mar Race Track in California as guests of Clint Murchison, the Texas oil man. Murchison took care of everything—free room, free bets, and even free investments in oil. The Mafia said that it was immune from investigation by the FBI because Lansky had photos of Hoover and Tolson *flagrante delicto*, having oral sex. It was alleged that these photos kept the FBI off the Mafia and compelled Hoover to deny that there was a crime syndicate.

Hoover said consistently that FBI agents were incorruptible—that his men were an elite group. He said that FBI stood for Fidelity, Bravery, and Integrity. But he was homophobic, being especially obsessed with problems of homosexuality among his agents. He feared they could be blackmailed. Sadly, Hoover was his own worst enemy, because he did not deal with "the enemy within." The rumors of Hoover's homosexuality did not tarnish his image, because he had a first-class public relations department. Psycho-historians might make something of Hoover's claim that "the closest thing to a love affair" he ever had was his deep affection for child star Shirley Temple, with whom he was often seen.[29]

Messick's assessment of Hoover is not kind: "For a half century John Edgar Hoover, unique among Americans, had the power to destroy the infamous syndicates of organized crime. He failed to use it. Instead, as crime grew into the nation's biggest business, Hoover used his power to enhance his reputation."

Scarface Al

Al "Scarface" Capone was released from Alcatraz prison in California in November 1939 to enter Union Memorial Hospital in Baltimore, Maryland for treatment of paresis, a brain ailment. He arrived under very heavy police surveillance with his mother, his wife, and his brother. Al Capone, the squat man with the beady eyes, came to personify evil. He seemed not to value life on any terms. His career was a very long series of murders and accommodations to them. It was a case of loyalty and betrayal. He came to public prominence during the Chicago gang wars in the Prohibition era. In his time, and to an extent today, his life was deplored and celebrated.

For better or for worse, he was an American icon. He was the most brutal gangster of his time—Public Enemy Number One. He was born Alphonse Caponi in New York City in 1899. His parents, Gabriel and Teresa, could neither speak, write, nor read English. With their first child, Vincenzo, age six, and with Teresa eight months pregnant, they emigrated from the slums of Naples to the slums of Brooklyn. It was there that they Americanized their name.[30]

Gabriel struggled as a grocer and barber and watched his family grow to a total of nine children, seven sons and two daughters. The poor, uneducated Southern Italians challenged the concept of the melting pot. The *contadini* (the peasants), a majority of the immigrants, were clannish and suspicious of outsiders. In Italy, they did not trust the police and local politicians, who often protected the rich and powerful. In their adopted country, they thought their only recourse was to be loyal to family and the *paisani*.

With their lack of education, and their inability to speak the English language, they were confined to the lowest-paid and most back-breaking jobs as ditchdiggers and bricklayers, or they sold fruit and vegetables from stands and stores as did Gabriel Capone. Italian immigrants were law-abiding, but they suffered from a myth that was hard to dispel: that they had a natural impulse toward criminal activities. All the research indicated otherwise.

Alphonse, the fourth child, saw everything differently. He abhorred his family's poverty and rejected his father's way of life, which was based on Italian traditions. Capone took no pride in his Italian roots. When the press reported that he was born in Italy, he protested, "I'm no Italian . . . I was born in Brooklyn."[31]

Alphonse became part of that small minority who believed that in America only crime led to the good life. Al, as he was now known, was involved early with gangsters and violence. He had the raw vitality and the brains to become the CEO of crime. Violence was his currency. But he yearned for respectability. He loved opera and expensive clothes. He looked shorter than he was in his 5' 10 ½ inch frame, and he was flamboyant, preferring the colors yellow and green. Although he frequented houses of prostitution, where he was a constant, lusty client, he fathered a child and married Mary Coughlin, a lovely Irish girl.

Believing that the payoff was higher in Chicago, which was a totally corrupt city, he moved there in 1920. Capone had rivals, and at first, he allied himself with them in a "combine," but by the early 1920s, gangs were common on the streets of Chicago. The killings were facilitated by the newly developed Thompson submachine gun, which gave us the name "Tommy Gun."

During the Depression, public relief funds in Chicago became scarce. When bills were introduced to raise taxes for the needy, the rich protested, but Capone, playing up his sense of community, fed three thousand unemployed per day. In six weeks, he donated twenty thousand meals at a cost of $12,000. But true to his gangster life style, Capone spent more than $100,000 a year on himself.

Capone stood supreme as head of the mob; he was *capo dei capi* (chief of chiefs), but there was a growing spirit of rebellion within the Mafia (also known variously as the Syndicate, the Firm, the Mob, and *la Cosa Nostra*—our thing). The conflict was between Neapolitan and Sicilian families and between old-line Italian traditions and American versions of organized crime.

Schoenberg focuses on Capone as a "businessman of crime," who believed that "the proper business of crime was business."[32] Capone once said, "I make my money by supplying services," and "I am part of the capitalist system." But Capone's life shows him to be devoid of those aspects of character that would have enabled him to lead a legitimate business. Bergreen agrees that Capone's work bore a strong resemblance to the activities of legitimate American businessmen. There was just as much paper shuffling, delegation of authority, and occasional visits to his sublieutenants for peptalks and inspirational meetings.[33] In one real sense, Capone was a businessman, because he employed thousands and his income was estimated at over $100 million per year.

Although Capone controlled local police, he could not buy federal law-enforcement officers. In 1931, unable to obtain enough evidence to convict on murder charges, the government sued him for income tax evasion. He was indicted on twenty-two counts for the years 1925 to 1929, and he faced a maximum prison sentence of thirty-four years. It took five years for Internal Revenue to untangle his financial empire. Capone, in his arrogance, tried to control the legal process, but the judge wasn't playing the game. He set aside a plea bargain that would have given Capone only a two-and-one-half-year sentence, and he ordered the trial to proceed on all the indictments.

The primary question of the case was whether the statute of limitations would be six years or only three. A U.S. District Court of Appeals had ruled in favor of the three-year rule. If this interpretation prevailed, it would preclude prosecution of Capone. Ignoring these legal technicalities, the government proceeded with its case. The verdict showed that the jury was also confused. In the three indictments, it voted guilty of tax evasion for some years and not guilty of failure to file a return for others. Capone was sentenced on Saturday, October 24, to eleven years' imprisonment, a $50,000 fine, and $30,000 court costs. It was the stiffest sentence ever given for tax evasion.

Capone was taken to the Atlanta prison, where he was given number 40,822. The penitentiary was overcrowded, so it could not honor his request for a single cell. He was given a Wassermann test, which proved negative. Capone had contracted syphilis three years earlier. Capone bragged that he would be out of prison soon, but when J. Edgar Hoover visited the prison, the buzzing was about Alcatraz. A month later, Capone crossed the desert in mid-afternoon, was loaded onto a barge, and alighted at the Alcatraz dock. He was at the "Island of Pelicans"—the Big House.

It was meant to be hell; there was no talk of rehabilitation. The guards stripped the fifty-eight prisoners who had come on the train, examined all apertures for narcotics and items that could be fashioned into weapons. Life at Alcatraz was extremely regimented. The day began at 6:30 A.M. with clanging bells and flashing lights. At 6:50, another bell signaled the morning count. A third bell indicated that all prisoners were accounted for. The fourth bell was for breakfast. The prisoners, who all sat facing in the same direction, ate ten to a table in silence. Negroes were segregated.

Capone, who was assigned to the laundry room, stuck to his task. He refused to join in on a prisoner's strike, for which he was called a scab. But his goal was to get out of prison alive. He succeeded, but not as he envisioned. In February 1938, he began to act irrationally, and he was prone to vomiting. He did not hear commands and seemed to want to vomit. The examining psychiatrist suggested that Capone was in the last stages of syphilis (it was rumored that he was a cocaine addict also). A spinal fluid was taken, something that he refused to have done early in his imprisonment. The results confirmed major damage to the central nervous system. His ten-year sentence was reduced to six years and five months for good behavior and working credits.[34]

When he was released from Alcatraz on January 6, 1939, he was a pitiable creature who was incapable of understanding. He still had a one-year sentence in Illinois for failing to file an income tax return, but because his disease left him with fever and mental confusion, it was decided not to return him to the Cook County jail in Illinois and to allow him to finish his imprisonment at the Federal Correctional Institution at Terminal Island near Los Angeles.

Bergreen writes of an interesting irony in Capone's family. His brother Vincenzo disliked intensely his brother's lifestyle, so he ran away from home, changed his name to Vincent Hart (after Hollywood film star William Hart) and became a law enforcer! When they had family reunions, the brothers sat next to each other—the killer and the policeman.

Mr. Lucky

Capone was the chief of the Neapolitans; Lucky Luciano was the Young Turk of the Sicilians. In one of the many wars between Mafia families, Luciano leaped to the top of the gangster world by deceit. He tricked his boss in a double-cross to have lunch in a Coney Island restaurant on the promise that his enemy could be taken there. Instead, Luciano arranged his killing—he took six bullets to the head and back.

This effectively ended the gang war, allowing Luciano to reorganize the Mafia. Luciano reserved prostitution and drugs for himself and assigned Meyer Lansky and Bugsy Siegel the gambling concessions in the West. In the new scheme of things, Capone headed the list, followed by Joe Costello and Luciano.

At ten o'clock in the evening on August 24, 1939, a four-door sedan driven by Albert Anastasia, the head of Murder, Inc., pulled up to the curb at 101 Third Street in Brooklyn to pick up a passenger and drove over the Brooklyn Bridge into Manhattan. He stopped behind a large, black limousine at Fifth Avenue and Twenty-eighth Street. The passenger in Anastasia's car got out and walked to the limousine. Its driver, Walter Winchell, opened the front door, looked at the figure standing outside, leaned over towards the man in the back seat, and said, "Mr. Hoover, this, is Lepke."[35]

He was referring to Louis "Lepke" Buchalter, who had disappeared in 1937. Buchalter got his nickname from his mother who lovingly called him Lepkela, meaning little Louis. As Maas described him, he was slender, reticent, and sad-eyed, he looked more like a shoe clerk than the mastermind of a huge narcotics ring, as well as the absolute ruler of labor and management extortion in trucking, in restaurants, in movie theaters, and in the baking, garment, and fur industries.[36]

By 1937 Lepke was wanted for murder and indicted on charges of narcotics peddling and extortion. Because he was "hot," he decided to hide while he ordered the death of anyone who could testify against him. In the process, one of his killers gunned down a person who resembled a potential witness, causing a public uproar. They wanted Lepke dead or alive.

Hoover had called him "the most dangerous criminal in the United States." The FBI had spent two years and thousands of dollars searching for Lepke. To find Lepke, they needed to visit Lucky Luciano at Dannemora prison, New York. In his "Last Testament" Luciano tells how he destroyed the Godfathers and took over the Mafia. He broke a cardinal rule of the Mafia by linking with several Jewish mobsters, including Meyer Lansky and Benny Siegel. Together they used force to bring discipline to the rackets, especially after Prohibition.

Hoover nodded, Lepke entered the car and took the seat next to the FBI director. When Hoover spoke, it was clear that there was no deal. Hoover informed Lepke that he would be tried on the narcotics charges in federal courts. Lepke was stunned. He had been promised a fix, but now he faced a prison term of more than a hundred years.

Even in prison, Lucky Luciano carried much weight with the FBI. They went to see him to obtain information about their "Most Wanted List." Who was this "Boss of Bosses?" He was born Salvatore Lucania, son of Antonio and Rosalie, in the poverty of Sicily. At age nine, in 1906, Luciano was brought to the United States with his family. They settled in that maze of immigrants on New York's Lower East Side, where he could watch neighborhood crooks with their flashy clothes and big cars. It was then that Salvatore decided that he wanted to be rich.

His first job was legitimate, as a runner for the Goodman Hat Company, but his six dollars per week were not enough for his desired lifestyle, so he turned to heroin peddling. He served one year for unlawful possession, but from that time (1916) until 1936, he stayed out of prisons. He recruited partners who were to help him dominate the rackets. One was Frank Costello; for the others, he chose Jews over the "Mustache Petes."

He met Meyer Lansky and Benny Siegel on Manhattan's East Side. Like him, they were tough, ambitious kids. Lansky was born Maier Suchowljansky in Grodno, Russia. Benjamin Siegel was American-born. Meyer was smart (they said he was a math genius), and Benny was fearless. They became fast friends, which troubled all the Lucanias and the Sicilians. In dealing with his Jewish friends, Salvatore changed his name—he became Charles Luciano, later Lucky. He once was so beat up—his head was nearly decapitated. He said, "I guess I'm just lucky to be alive," which gave him his nickname. At the same time, Benjamin became Bugsy Siegel and Francesco Castiglia became Frank Costello. They called themselves the Four Horsemen. According to Luciano, in bribing New York politicians later, it did not hurt to have an Italian with an Irish name.

When the Volstead Act was repealed, the mob moved into industrial racketeering. They controlled the garment industry, trash collection, window cleaning and building materials. The Chicago Crime Commission estimated that Murder, Inc. controlled thirty-two industries.[37]

Enter Dewey

In this era of high crime, Thomas Edmund Dewey became an American hero, because he was free of scandal. He was the envy of all parents—as a boy he was a scout, he sang in a choir, and he was never absent or late for school. Although he was stiff in demeanor, he won debating contests; but no one would have predicted his spectacular rise in law and politics.

A native of Oswego, New York, he graduated from the University of Michigan and Columbia Law School. Throughout his educational career, he continued to sing with his excellent baritone voice, but he gave this up in 1931 when he was appointed Assistant to the United States Attorney for the Southern District of New York. It led to his nomination and election as New York City's District Attorney. He was the first Republican to hold this position in nearly two generations.

Dewey launched his assault on crime by hitting the prostitution industry, in which Lucky Luciano was called the "King of Vice." He quickly targeted Dutch Schultz and Lucky Luciano (who was "Public Enemy Number One in New York."). Dewey called Lucky "The Grand Pimp," because he was shaking down pimps, and he put up their bail money.

When the grand jury refused to act on the mounting evidence, Governor Lehman named Dewey to clean up the city. The case of the *State of New York v. Charles Lucania, et al.* took place on May 8, 1936. There were ten defendants. Dewey won his case when a prostitute, Cokey Flo, testified that Luciano ordered the beating, drugging, and torturing of girls to force them to work. Luciano took the stand and lied at every statement. He was found guilty and sentenced to thirty to fifty years in the state prison.

From the time that Lepke went into hiding in 1937 until 1939, the "big heat" was on. Hoover, Dewey, and Police Commissioner Lewis J. Valentine agreed to pool all information. Dewey announced a $25,000 reward for the capture of Lepke. The crime syndicate was nervous, because the hunt was interfering with their rackets, especially smuggling narcotics. A plot was conceived by Meyer Lansky to get rid of Lepke. When the FBI came to Luciano asking about Lepke, he told them he would produce Lepke in twenty-four hours if his sentence was commuted. No promises were made, but Lucky knew he had to do something to pacify Dewey and Hoover and the mob.[38]

Within a month, Lepke was tried on federal charges for being part of a narcotics conspiracy, for which he was sentenced to fourteen years. Just as quickly, he was in the state court where Thomas Dewey won a conviction on charges of extortion, and the mobster was given thirty years to life.

The thirty-one-year-old Dewey compiled an outstanding record of crime fighting. In what Allen calls "one of the most extraordinary performances" in the history of prosecution, Dewey assembled a brilliant group of young lawyers who fanned out all over New York City gathering evidence against the rackets. Dewey's crew closed down restaurants and crooked businesses, and they indicted seventy-three racketeers. For this effort, Dewey was elected District Attorney in 1937, and he was on his way to the Republican nomination for President.[39]

Dewey's attack on crime made him a sensation. He went after the big names and the small. He was particularly incensed when he learned of violations that resulted in harm to many who could not fend for themselves (for example, building code laws). Luciano's conviction, and Dewey's investigations of curruption in the trucking and restaurant businesses made him known to all New Yorkers.

It was no surprise, therefore, when in the fall of 1939 his name kept coming up for a candidacy for national office. When the Gallup polls showed that over 60 percent of Americans favored Dewey for President, he announced on December 1, 1939, that he would accept the Republican nomination for President if it were offered, but his trip to the White House was blocked by Roosevelt, and later by Truman.

NOTES

1. Lindbergh, *War Within and Without*, p. 4.
2. The spire and globe rendition may not have been entirely original, since the Shrine of the Immaculate Conception in Washington, D.C., features a Gothic spire and an adjoining Romanesque nave, which symbolizes the catholicity of the church. The church was planned in 1920 and construction began in 1931.
3. *New York Times*, March 5, 1939.
4. Ketchum, *The Borrowed Years*, p. 159.
5. White, *One Man's Meat*, p. 71.
6. Meikle, *Twentieth Century Limited*, p. 192.
7. White, *One Man's Meat*, p. 77.
8. Ketchum, *The Borrowed Years*, p. 163.
9. Ketchum, *The Borrowed Years*, p. 154.
10. Some of this story is based on the excellent PBS television account of "The Windsors," which was shown in November 1994.
11. *Time*, June 26, 1939.
12. This was the title of a book by Michael Muller, a Redemptorist Father, published in 1886.
13. Lally, *The Catholic Church in a Changing America*, p. 48.
14. In discussing this problem, we need to deal first with the issue of terminology. Should we call persons of color Negroes, Colored, Blacks or African Americans? In the 1930s, the term "African Americans" was seldom if ever used to denote blacks. Malcolm X's mother said this about the question, "We shouldn't call ourselves Negroes or Niggers. We should be called Blacks." We would like to take her advice, but many books and writings of the period called colored persons Negroes. We believe that at times it is more accurate and necessary to retain that term. No disrespect is intended.
15. Hudson, *Religion in America*, p. 371.
16. Sweet, *The Story of Religion in America*.
17. David W. Wills, "Black Americans and the Establishment," in Hutchison, *Between the Times*, p. 179.

18. Benny Kraut, "A Wary Collaboration: Jews, Catholics and the Protestant Goodwill Movement," in Hutchison, *Between the Times*, p. 194.

19. Although Father Coughlin was sometimes called the Little Flower of Detroit, no one can ever confuse him with Fiorello La Guardia, the Little Flower of New York.

20. Manchester, *The Glory and the Dream*, p. 108.

21. Quoted in Manchester, *The Glory and the Dream*, p. 92.

22. Brinkley, *Voices of Protest*, p. 84.

23. *American Mercury*, June 1939, pp. 129-141.

24. Brinkley, *Voices of Protest*, p. 266.

25. Malone and Rauch, *War and Troubled Peace*, p. 271.

26. *Washington Post*, April 9, 1993. Anderson was the winner of the Spingarn Medal in 1939 for being "an outstanding Negro in the United States." She was considered America's greatest contralto. But it was not until 1943 that she got to give her concert at Constitution Hall.

27. Gentry, *J. Edgar Hoover*, p. 179. The following information draws heavily on this excellent and exhaustive biography.

28. Compare Summers, *Official and Confidential* and Turner, *Hoover's FBI*.

29. Messick, *John Edgar Hoover*, p. 143.

30. This section draws heavily from Kobler, *Capone.*

31. Kobler, *Capone*, p. 22.

32. See Schoenberg's 1992 biography *Mr. Capone.*

33. Bergreen, *Capone.*

34. Kobler, *Capone*, p. 380.

35. This account was dictated by Lucky Luciano to Martin A. Gosch and Richard Hammer as the "last testament" of one of America's worst gangsters. See their *The Last Testament of Lucky Luciano.*

36. Maas, *The Valachi Papers*, p. 157.

37. This figure was offered on the Fox TV program, "Loyalty and Betrayal," July 25, 1994.

38. Messick, *John Edgar Hoover*, p. 80.

39. Allen, *Since Yesterday*, p. 148.

2

Conditions of the Working Classes

THE NUMBER ONE ECONOMIC PROBLEM

In 1939, unemployment was still America's number one economic problem. An average of 10.5 million persons were unemployed—2 million more than the low reached in 1937 and 17 percent of the labor force. In the decade of the 1930s, the highest unemployment rates were found in the building trades, railroads, mining, and wholesale and retail trades, whereas employment gains were made in government, education and the service industries.

Statistics show that the South lagged other areas in 1939. A high school graduate in the South earned an average annual income of $965, compared to $1,300 in the non-South; and for college graduates, the figures were $1,370 in the South and $1,680 in the non-South. The discrepancies were larger by race. Nonwhite males in the South earned $625, compared with $855 in the non-South, and the figures for college graduates were $777 and $925.[1]

The southern leadership in Congress was the major obstacle to the elimination of poverty in the American South. In the spring of 1938, the National Emergency Council, a group of young, liberal, southern social scientists provided Roosevelt with the grim picture of southern poverty. This report stressed the paradox of the southern condition: the region was blessed by nature with great wealth, but its people were the poorest. Roosevelt was appalled, and in his inaugural address he stated, "It is my conviction that the South presents right now the Nation's No. 1 problem—the Nation's problem, not merely the South's." He was more determined to offer an agenda to redress these wretched economic conditions.

The Great Depression was a shattering experience for most families. Husbands and wives argued constantly. A California woman told of her husband going North for three months to find work. At first, he wrote often, but then there was no word from him. She lamented: "Don't know where he is or what he is up to," but it was clear that her man had simply deserted his family.[2] When someone found work, there was enormous tension. Foremen and supervisors looked over shoulders for mistakes, knowing that there was a ready supply of replacements. A very experienced, efficient secretary who found work after being unemployed a year, was so nervous on the job that she was not able to take simple dictation from her boss. She could only cry.

The Depression also took its toll on some cherished democratic institutions. Police were unusually rough on vagrants, and some judges lacked sensitivity. Local officials were even harsher: they recommended that all persons on relief be fingerprinted, and others questioned their right to vote.

UNIVERSAL PENSION PLANS

From Townsend to Ham and Eggs

Dr. Francis E. Townsend, the sixty-six-year-old physician from Long Beach, California, was very moved by the number of old persons who had lost their jobs and life savings in the Depression. Townsend, who was born in a log cabin on a farm, saw the problem of pensions as one of organizing the people to demand what the Congress, the military, the police and government workers already had. He asked for volunteers and quickly got thousands of signatures on petitions. Townsend raised almost a million dollars from "donations, card parties, dances, quilting bees, raffles and box suppers, as well as by subscriptions to the 'Townsend Weekly,' where homey inspiration was interlarded with advertisements for trusses and artificial teeth."[3] When his movement gained strength faster than he could handle it, he sought help from Robert E. Clements, his landlord. Clements, a Texan, was only thirty-nine years old, but he was a shrewd real estate promoter, who knew how to assess the chances of making a dollar from Dr. Townsend's plan.

Townsend appeared before the House Ways and Means Committee to explain his plan. When he spoke, he made clear that his bill was about much more than pensions. It had two other objectives: it would help solve the unemployment problem and it would restore purchasing power to the people, thereby returning the economy to full employment. Under the plan every citizen who attained the age of sixty qualified to receive $200 a month from the federal government if they retired, had no criminal record, no other income, and if they agreed to spend all of the $200 every month. Because this plan was applied to individuals, a husband and wife over sixty would get $400 a month.

At that time, there were about ten million older Americans, but Townsend believed that only about eight million would qualify for pensions. To raise the $1.6 billion per month, a 2 percent tax would be levied on every commercial transaction, including a tax on every waiter, every beautician, every book sold, every barber, every telephone call, every theater ticket, every sports event, every lecture, and every Wall Street transaction.

E. B. White attended a New York meeting of Townsendites, where Townsend explained that the business world was stymied and he scoffed at the New Deal with all of its alphabet-soup agencies. White described the meeting as "an impressive performance." "It was no time for cynicism," and, he added, "Most of what Dr. Townsend had said, God knows, was true enough. If anybody could devise a system for distributing wealth more evenly, more power to him."[4]

Congressman Robert Doughton, Chairman of Ways and Means, told Townsend that the total cost of providing eight million pensions, including administrative costs, would be about $20 billion. Townsend seemed uninterested in discussing the cost of the plan. Critics claimed that Townsend's estimate of eight billion was too low; for others, the concern was that those over sixty, who made up one-seventh of the population, would receive almost one-half of the national income. It would surely ruin many businesses, and, worse, it would make criminals of those who did not spend their $200. Townsend's lackadaisical testimony before the Committee did not endear him to the members, who refused to order the bill out for a vote. But the good doctor said he would press on, and then he lambasted the "brain trusters" and added, "God deliver us from further guidance by professional economists!"[5]

By this time, rumors were everywhere that he planned to run for President of the United States by splitting the two major political parties. When Townsend supported the idea of replacing the two-party system, there was the question of what to do with Father Coughlin's followers, whose numbers were substantial. Townsend had publicly denied that he wanted to join forces with Coughlin. Undoubtedly, Roosevelt's opposition to Townsend kept his support to a minimum.

From the ashes of the Townsend plan arose the phoenix of "Ham and Eggs," which was promoted by a group of technocrats, led by Rho Owens, who was accused of garnering a fair share of the proceeds. In November 1939, California voters went to the polls to vote on the "Ham and Eggs" plan, otherwise known as "Thirty Every Thursday." It would provide $30 in cash each Thursday to all the unemployed aged fifty and over. The money would be raised by a state tax on incomes above $3,000 a year and on securities sales. A two-cent stamp would be placed on the dollar warrants each week, which would be redeemed by the clearinghouse of the Peoples Bank of California.

"Ham-and-Eggers" enrolled four hundred thousand dues-paying members; they trained twelve thousand volunteer workers. In all of their hundreds of rallies and demonstrations, there was the endless, impassioned chant of "Ham and Eggs, Ham and Eggs." When they marched, they sang "Onward, Pension Soldiers, Marching as to War."[6] The "Ham and Eggs" plan was defeated at the polls in 1938, but its prospects seemed bright in 1939.

EPIC

Another famous deviationist was Upton Sinclair, the socialist author who joined the Democratic Party in California to run for governor under the EPIC slogan (End Poverty in California). Sinclair had borrowed $5 to get to the Golden State, which had 25 percent unemployment and no safety net for the elderly or disabled.

He advocated that the federal government take over idle factories and make them available to the unemployed, that as many persons as possible be "returned to the land." He plugged the Marxian notion of "production for use, not for profit," and he too believed that capitalism would eventually wither away. Sinclair's book, *I Governor of California*, was a huge success, and his campaign for governor took off. There were over one thousand EPIC clubs in the state.

Sinclair's candidacy caused confusion among the Democratic ranks. How would they deal with a socialist? Roosevelt favored his program for social security, but thought he was too radical. Everything got more confused when Harry Hopkins endorsed Sinclair, who also received the support of Father Coughlin. Blacks were not attracted to EPIC; they wanted to get inside the existing capitalist system, not to abolish it. Republicans, who called Sinclair a communist while stealing his program, agreed to a deal with Roosevelt. The Democrats would support the Republican candidate, Merriam, while the Republicans would back the New Deal programs.

THE GREAT STENTORIAN

At its June 12, 1939 meeting, the executive board of the CIO proposed that all needy persons over sixty receive a maximum monthly pension of $60. Under the plan, all state assistance programs would be replaced by a federal plan.

Until 1935, the American Federation of Labor stood supreme and alone in the labor movement. By organizing craftsmen with skills, the leaders were able to pursue Samuel Gompers' notion that all the unions wanted was "more." Passage of the Wagner Act set the basic governmental attitude toward labor, it upheld the right to organize. Employers were forbidden to "interfere with, restrain, or coerce employees in the exercise of the rights" to bargain. When the AFL refused to grant charters to the new unions, these members bolted the Federation and formed a separate union—the Congress of Industrial Organizations (CIO).

This precipitated a rapid rise in the "vertical" unions—those organized along industrial rather than skill lines. Union organizing, which had been thwarted by business's antiunion practices, such as the yellow-dog contracts, could now proceed under legal protection. The new CIO grew in spectacular fashion. It organized one-third of the maritime and textile industries, 60 percent of the steel industry, and 75 percent of the automobile industry.

The war was on for new members. By 1939, both the AFL and the CIO were thriving with active government support. The AFL had about four and one-half million members; the CIO had roughly four million. Nearly a million workers belonged to independent unions. The CIO gains came in the vertical unions (rubber, steel, autos, mining).[7]

Although there were many leaders in the organizing group of the CIO, John Llewellyn Lewis towered over the new union. Manchester describes him as a "preposterous figure. A barrel-chested, beetle-browed, six-foot three-inch goliath of a man, who read the Bible, Shakespeare and Greek tragedies."[8] This curious stentorian was a Republican who championed the cause of the working man. He was hated or loved but never ignored, because his viperous tongue cut quickly and deeply. He accused William Green, president of the AFL, of uttering "fluttering procrastinations."

The crowning bit of irreverence for Lewis came in early August 1939 as he sat in the witness chair during the hearings of the House Committee on Labor. He spoke softly at first, but gradually the mumble escalated to a crescendo as he shouted his rage pounding on the table. He screamed that labor was only asking for twenty five cents per hour and that the source of the opposition was the Democratic party, and especially from the "labor-baiting, poker-playing, whiskey-drinking, evil old man whose name is Garner." When he referred to Vice President John Garner in those words, everyone gasped. Lewis pounded the table again. "Yes, I make a personal attack on Mr. Garner for what he is doing, because Garner's knife is searching for the quivering, pulsating heart of labor. And I am against him. I am against him officially, individually and personally, concretely and in the abstract, when his knife searches for the heart of my people. I am against him in 1939 and I will be against him in 1940 when he seeks the Presidency of the United States."[9] Columnists speculated that Garner had just won the drinking and card-playing vote.

Lewis wasn't finished with Garner. He said, "There are millions unemployed. And this Congress has made no contribution to the well-being of the average American." Then he aimed this zinger, "I have no objection to Mr. Garner if he wants to do it and his neighbors let him get away it, to debasing sheep men and cattle men in Texas by charging them extortionate interest for loans through the banks that he controls."

The AFL had always pledged to stay out of politics and to reward "friends of labor" of either party. The industrial unions, which had a heavy communist contingent, chose instead to align themselves with a very leftist legislative program. This CIO political effort in 1939 became a major force in the United States. Whereas the AFL gave lukewarm support to the New Deal, CIO members rang doorbells, handed out circulars, and made speeches on the radio and on the stump.[10]

The CIO adopted a much more egalitarian approach. These younger, idealistic union members understood and accepted the need for racial integration. They embraced nondiscriminatory policies, including supporting the

NAACP, the Negro churches, and the National Urban League. While this was a strong moral position, it was also a practical approach, because many of the members of the industrial unions were black.

The AFL responded by launching organizing drives in new fields, thereby creating a war within labor's ranks. It was this competition for members that caused the AFL to alter its racial restrictions. Both unions gave more attention to racial matters. Presidents Philip Murray (AFL) and Walter Reuther (CIO) served as members of the NAACP Board of Directors. Both unions also supported civil rights legislation. Thurgood Marshall, the NAACP's chief legal adviser, favored the CIO program, calling it "a Bill of Rights for Negro labor in America." Although the CIO was viewed with great favor in the Negro community, it was limited by social and economic factors in following its own egalitarian policies. In the South, for example, some CIO locals barred Negroes from membership.

Lewis also had his problems with President Roosevelt. At one point, when a strike was threatened over jurisdictional issues, FDR declared "a plague on both your houses." Lewis was quick to answer: "It ill behooves one who has supped at labor's table and who has been sheltered in labor's house to curse with equal fervor and fine impartiality both labor and its adversaries when they become locked in deadly embrace."

Sit Down and Fight[11]

On February 27, 1939, the United States Supreme Court decided the sit-down strike case brought against the Fansteel Metallurgical Corporation. It sustained the right of the employer to discharge the strikers, thus ending a very remarkable episode in the organizing drive of the automobile workers. In the 5-to-2 decision, Chief Justice Charles E. Hughes called the sit-down strike "a high-handed proceeding without shadow of legal right." He added, "The ousting of the owner from lawful possession is not essentially different from an assault upon the officers of an employing company."

While it persisted, it was a very powerful weapon during which workers simply sat down in the factories, refusing to leave. The sit-down strike prevented the auto industry from replacing striking workers with scabs. The Depression had shown that there were thousands of unemployed who would willingly cross picket lines.

It began in 1936, when the CIO met in South Bend, Indiana. It was there that the United Automobile Workers Union was born, with Walter Reuther as its chief organizer. His task was to organize the Big Three automobile companies, and he chose the sit-down strike as his weapon. Reuther (who was called "Big Red," for the color of his hair) was the big victor. He was born in West Virginia into a militant family of socialists. His father was so inclined, but he always said he was not a Marxist. When Walter Reuther was fired from his job as a foreman in an automobile plant, he traveled all over Europe and Asia studying union movements.

The CIO members, who sat down inside the factory, often sang a ballad to describe their efforts:

When they tie the can to a union man,
Sit down! Sit down!
When they give him the sack they'll take him back,
Sit down! Sit down!
When the speed-up comes, just twiddle your thumbs,
Sit down! Sit down!
When the boss won't talk, don't take a walk,
Sit down! Sit down!

Next came General Motors at the Fisher Body plant in Flint, Michigan. The workers sat down in December 1936, and two weeks later, General Motors obtained an injunction from a judge who held a sizeable block of company stock. When the workers refused to leave the plant, the police attacked in full riot gear, including gas masks. When the workers were gassed, women went around the factory breaking all the windows to allow air to enter. On February 11, 1937, the UAW and General Motors signed a contract agreement. It was the first of the Big Three to accept the union.

What began at Flint, Michigan, became a whirlwind of sit-down activities, spreading to fourteen states and involving 135,000 persons. Governor Frank Murphy of Michigan, fearing for his political life, refused to call out the National Guard, choosing instead to serve as a negotiator, which ended the strike with a huge victory for the unions. A Gallup poll reported that 56 percent of respondents favored the General Motors position against the CIO tactic.

The great climax came at the bridge near the River Rouge Ford plant. Harry Bennett, who was given the title of Head of the Service Department at the Ford Motor Company, had a ready supply of three thousand goons to enforce Henry Ford's no-union policy. Bennett's army of former policemen, prize fighters, and even jailbirds believed in using all tactics to discourage union membership.

They destroyed union flyers, tore membership badges off the clothing of members, and were prepared to fight. They gathered a gang of former convicts for what Bennett called "rehabilitation meetings," and when they were ready, they attacked the unionists on the bridge. Several were thrown into the water, and the River Rouge lived up to its name. Walter Reuther was beaten on the head with clubs. Ford was not to accept the union for four more years.

Lewis Calls a Halt

The battle between the AFL and the CIO was a jurisdictional one. By the beginning of 1939, there appeared to be no end to the three-year labor war. If there was to be a marriage, it would be a union of unlike partners. The AFL was established. William Green, the president, ran a big business. He answered countless telephone calls, took care of paperwork. He was a veteran of older labor battles, and his grey hair showed the effects. In a real sense, he was satisfied with his union's progress and did not welcome a battle with a younger adversary, John L. Lewis, head of the CIO.

On February 25, President Roosevelt addressed letters to John L. Lewis of the CIO and William Green of the AFL asking for "a constructive negotiated peace" and "a unification of the labor movement." The President wrote identical letters to each of the union heads, but, in each, he added a personal touch. For Lewis, he wrote, "My dear John, I have a great satisfaction in knowing that I am dealing with a man whom I respect, a man of honor, intelligence and good will." For Green, the last paragraph read, "It is with confidence that I write you, dear Bill, as a man of good-will, of experience and high principles."[12] The President wrote:

"The American people sincerely hope that a constructive negotiated peace with honor may come about between the American Federation of Labor and the Congress of Industrial Organizations within the early months of the new year. . . I wish to reiterate the sincerity of my belief in labor's capacity to end this breach and my faith in the intuition of the wage earners of Anorexia to play their part along with all other groups in our community in overcoming our mutual problems and bringing about the good American democratic life."

And seven months later in a letter to the AFL Convention, September 30, 1939: "And so I ask you, as I shall ask the Congress of Industrial Organizations in its convention a little later, to continue whole-heartedly and generously the search for an accord. The men and women working daily in the mills, factories, and stores, and in transports, want this accord. The American people want it and will hold in honor those whose insight, courage and unselfishness can effect it."

Optimism was very high in Washington that the rift could be healed, but the AFL was blurring lines between craft and industrial unions, and it was attempting to broaden its jurisdiction over industrial units. In one case, the AFL claimed that its engineer's unit in a radio station should be included with all other employees in that department, thereby cutting out the CIO attempt to organize that department. The AFL was appropriating the main CIO argument that the bargaining unit was all employees.

The AFL counteroffensive included strikes and boycotts against the CIO and supporters of political candidates who favored the CIO. The AFL used dirty tricks by telling employers that they should prefer the AFL's "conservative organization" over the CIO's "radical organization dominated by Communists."[13]

NEW DEAL SOLUTIONS

The unemployed fended for themselves in a variety of ways. Some relied on family, some went on relief, and some obtained federal employment. The largest segment (over 27 million) depended on unemployment insurance. The adults signed up for WPA work, and the youth enrolled in one of the CCC camps or joined the National Youth Administration. In 1939 the CCC was at its full authorized strength of 300,000, and the NYA took care of the "work needs of some 611,588 young people."[14]

The Civilian Conservation Corps

The Civilian Conservation Corps was proposed in 1932 by President Franklin D. Roosevelt, as part of the Emergency Conservation Act to help end the nation's economic crisis. This program gave hope to youth; it kept idle youngsters from riding the rails, "living off soup kitchens and sleeping in hobo jungles."[15] The idea of the work camps came from Secretary of Labor Frances Perkins, with an assist from New York Senator Robert F. Wagner, although critics of the CCC said it was a page from the Nazi Youth Corps.

The U.S. Labor Department selected the junior enrollees; the Veterans Administration and the Bureau of Indian Affairs chose the special enrollees. The Departments of Agriculture and Interior planned and executed the work projects at all camps, and the National Park Service oversaw work on the national parks. Some called the CCC Roosevelt's "tree army," because so many youth were involved with natural resource and conservation efforts. But, most of the young men came to the camps for the $30-per-month wage, and they sent an average of $25 back home as a family allotment.[16] There were generally more applicants than openings in the CCC until 1939, when the advent of war in Europe and the defense buildup in the United States began to deplete enrollments.

Although she approved of the idea in concept, Eleanor Roosevelt was not satisfied with the operation of the CCC camps. She insisted that they should be under civilian control, especially after she read of abuses that were perpetuated at the camps by the military and the lack of experience of many of the teachers. She told Franklin that with all the unemployed teachers, this condition could be remedied easily. She also noted that because war was imminent and the Army was calling up many reserve officers, there would be a shortage of military teachers. On June 15, 1939, Director Robert Fechner announced that he was discontinuing the policy of assigning reserve officers as company commanders. All former military men would be retained in their jobs as physicians, dentists, bakers, and chaplains, but they would serve as civilians at rates of pay that were comparable to those established by the Classification Act of 1923.[17]

Enrollees at Work

The typical CCC camp had between 150 and 200 trainees who worked outdoors, trained in the workshops, played in the recreation room and read or wrote letters home in the library. Enrollees got up at 6 A.M., had breakfast at 6:30, policed and cleaned their barracks and campgrounds, and started work at about 8. Some had to board trucks to get to the work site. The workday was completed at 4 P.M. After dinner, they played sports, attended vocational classes, hiked in the woods, listened to the radio or read until 10 P.M. when the lights went out. The vigorous nature of their work, the wholesome food, and the regular hours built up many a run-down body.

The boys got free transportation to camp, free medical services, and plenty of clothes (woolen pants, workpants, flannel shirts, socks, underwear, blankets, shoes, raincoats, workhats, belts, and ties). These were kept in a barracks bag. For eating, they were issued a mess kit. From this description, the military atmosphere of the camp is obvious. Some campers lived in tents, but most were housed in wooden barracks, which were usually constructed by the CCCers out of trees that grew nearby. City boys and farmers stood shoulder to shoulder at work and at play.

Ellis wrote of a New York boy who was sent to Utah. He was enthralled by the ride up the mountains, and he was confused when the old truck stopped in the middle of some thick woods. "Where's the camp?" he asked. The sergeant in charge pointed to the trees all around them and said, "This is it. Break out the axes and chop." Not wanting to sleep on the cold ground, the boys chopped wood and built cabins and a mess hall. But in most camps, union labor constructed the buildings.

Because of the heavy demand, administrators limited the stay to six to nine months. Because the program was voluntary, an enrollee could leave anytime, and many just walked out complaining about the "chickenshit regulations." A fair percentage left to take employment or to go back to school.

For most, the CCC experience was exhilarating. City boys got to climb mountains, and they saw places they knew only from motion pictures and news films. Bostonians went to Vermont, Wyoming, and Oregon; New Yorkers were sent to Utah and Washington; and Philadelphians were shipped out to Alabama and Kentucky. Little did they know that some were in the presence of future celebrities. A young army officer named George C. Marshall, who became Army Chief of Staff in 1939, was commander of twenty seven CCC camps in the Northwest, where a young Walter Matthau was in training. Not far away another young boy was digging ditches, and we know him as the late actor Robert Mitchum.

The official CCC handbook stated, "No discrimination shall be made on account of race, color, or creed," but there were charges of prejudice, particularly because the Army was segregated at the time. About 10 percent of CCC enrollees were black, but most of them were in segregated camps in the South, where black leaders insisted that racial quotas be met.[18] Although black enrollees made up about 10 percent of the total, which was about equal to their ratio of the total population, they constituted a much larger percentage of the unemployed and were clearly more disadvantaged. Fechner, although living in Boston, was a southerner who showed little interest in this problem.

The CCC was voluntary, but one program was compulsory—literacy training. The elimination of illiteracy was a primary goal of Howard W. Oxley, the educational director of the CCC program. Approximately 15 percent of all persons in CCC camps had no formal education, and we must presume that they were illiterate. They were given instruction in literacy by WPA personnel or in nearby high schools, usually in the evenings. The elimination of illiteracy was but one goal; others included job training and assistance in finding employment. From 1935 to 1939, between 57 and 64 percent of trainees were enrolled in vocational programs.

The boys gained in health and self-respect, roads and trails were built, and forests were cleared. Anderson relates how anxious one official was to have his work understood: "You are a writer. Can't you tell them? Can't you make them understand that we are builders? These CCC camps. We are taking these city boys and making builders of them."[19] Anderson, who pursued ideas sought by Rousseau, extolled the natural element of the CCC. Everything about the camps was temporary, but Anderson thought, "Suppose they shouldn't be temporary. Suppose what is going on here is but a beginning. . . they have been jerked out of that environment [East Side of New York], hauled in fast trains across two-thirds of the United States. . . They had to build camps, keep themselves clean, learn to swing an axe. . . . It's the beginning of some kind of revolution in life— for them at least."

But Blakey records the impression of a Kentucky enrollee in 1939:

I've raked most of Ft. Knox.
I've cut down some stumps
I'm safe from typhoid,
And even the mumps.

I'm safe from the women,
But that aint no fun.[20]

The CCC enjoyed more popularity than most New Deal programs. Americans were pleased with these efforts to keep idle youth busy. There were four thousand camps established in the forty eight states. The boys in these camps built recreation buildings, picnic sites, roads, and bridges. Much of their work is still evident today. They cleared streams, built truck roads, sprayed for pests, saved wildlife, and helped eradicate Dutch elm disease. They constructed dams, eliminated gypsy moths in the East, and attacked spruce flies and crickets in the West. They restored Revolutionary and Civil War battlefields. They stocked our streams with almost a billion fish, they built more than thirty thousand wildlife shelters, thinned 4 million acres of trees, and they helped plant 190 million trees. It was truly an incredible accomplishment.[21]

Even two-thirds of all Republicans were in favor. In 1939, nearly 80 percent of the American people and President Roosevelt favored making the Corps a permanent agency. Employers also looked favorably on graduates of the CCC. They believed that the boys had learned the value of doing a full day's work and took pride in the final results.

I conclude with a personal note. I served at CCC camp number P-62 at Brunswick, Vermont in 1939 when I was 16 years old. Technically, I was too young, but because I was 16 3/4 years old, I was admitted. The work project was gypsy moth control, timber survey, and fire hazard reduction. This work was under First Lieutenant John C. Vaughan, the Company Commander, and Arthur F. Heitman, the Superintendent. My group was assigned to build a forest ranger station on Mount Monadnock, about twenty miles away. Each day we would be taken by truck to the mountain, we climbed to the top (just over three thousand feet) and dug a trench about a foot wide and a foot deep for the telephone lines that would serve as communication for forest rangers who were spotting for forest fires.

My lasting recollection of the camp was lunch. Each day we were given three sandwiches—nearly all of liverwurst, which I hated. To this day, fifty-nine years later, I have never eaten liverwurst.

The Works Projects Administration[22]

The WPA received popular support because it came at a time when the United States had no unemployment compensation and few relief projects. It became the major thrust in a giant New Deal rescue operation. It was assigned the task of providing "socially useful" employment and "enhancing prior occupational skills and aptitudes." WPA projects were sponsored by other government agencies, and the states were expected to contribute at least 25 percent in cash or in kind of the total cost of the program. Ninety-five percent of the projects were planned by city councils, county commissioners, and boards of education

These WPA employees constituted 20 to 27 percent of total unemployment between 1935 and 1941. Who were these people? They were the families who President Roosevelt kept calling the "ill-fed, ill-housed and ill-clad third of the nation." A *New York Times* headline of July 16, 1939, stated that the "WPA is Full of Average Americans." The average age was thirty-nine, and 97 percent of them had held a job in the private sector. They were high school and college graduates, and they held every type of professional and skilled and unskilled job titles. The WPA employed more persons than the automobile, coal and steel industries combined, and WPA officials claimed that their programs touched fifty million persons directly.[23]

WPA employees were not on relief; they considered themselves on a government payroll. Wecter quotes a North Carolina farmer, who was living with his family in a one-room filling station: "I'm proud of our United States, and every time I hear the Star-Spangled Banner I feel a lump in my throat. There aint no other nation in the world that would have sense enough to think of WPA and all the other A's."[24]

By 1939, most of the direct relief payments were made by the states alone. In January, when there were nearly thirteen million persons unemployed, the total

WPA employees numbered 2,985,620. They received between $50 and $60 per month in wages, and this may be compared to the $25 they were receiving under direct relief. In March, President Roosevelt told Congress that under Harry Hopkins, 86 percent of the WPA funds were allocated to wages.[25]

The WPA was often described as a model of inefficiency, and it added the word, "boondoggle," to the nation's vocabulary—a Scottish import meaning "an unearned reward," which Americans took to mean "a wasteful project." Roosevelt responded, with a smile, that in so vast a program, there was bound to be some inefficiency. The President knew that the people were behind him. He remembered the day when he was in Marietta, Ohio, when an old woman knelt down kissed his footprint in the dirt.

These Are Our Lives (stories from the Federal Writers Project) presented interviews of persons in various Federal programs in North Carolina, Tennessee and Georgia. Typical are these:

Mr. Pugh owns the shoe plant. . . he sure is a Christian man. . . I'm on piecework now. . . I make just a whole lot now. Highest I ever made in one week was eleven dollars. . . I usually hit in between and make eight or nine dollars.

Well there was nothin' to do but apply for relief. I did, and finally got a job on the WPA. Worked on a labor project; dug ditches, rolled wheelbarrows, and things like that. I did all sorts of temporary jobs. . . And I kept up my union activities. I became secretary of an Unemployed Workers' Union. Yeah, it was a WPA union.

Millard Ketchum had just come in from his day's work in the field. He was still in his blue CCC work uniform. This is better clothes than I ever had at home. . . before I got to the CCC. . . couldn't have much clothes to wear and in summer time we just didn't wear no shoes and no shirts much, nor nothing else much.

I ain't never been much to school. Just went to the second grade, that's all, excepting what I learned here in the CCC. I got one brother that went to the second grade, too, and my sister she went to the first. Then she quit. I quit that old second grade when I was fourteen. I left home and went to work.

The attack on illiteracy was one of the most spectacular phases of the WPA program. Teachers were sent into rural counties, remote mountain valleys, city slums, public schools, farm houses, mountain shacks, and churches to teach people to read and write.

The WPA administrator, Colonel F. C. Harrington, attempted always to confine projects to work that could not be accomplished by free enterprise. These included the New York City North Beach Airport (later La Guardia Field), which cost $40 million and nearly six hundred other airfields. The WPA was primarily a financing agency for construction. Forty-seven percent of the workers were employed on highway and street projects, 9 percent on public building, 7 percent on parks, 8 percent on sewers, 11 percent on educational and recreational programs and 8 percent on sewing production. In its six years, it employed more than eight million men and women—about 20 percent of the labor force, built twenty thousand schools, libraries and gymnasiums. They put roads where none existed before. It was a bureaucratic nightmare, but it was the largest and most successful work relief program in American history.

ANATOMY OF DEPRESSED AREAS

Dust Bowl Refugees

Father Coughlin stated that the droughts and dust storms of the 1930s were God's punishment to the American people for the sin of electing Franklin Roosevelt as President. Americans must have wondered whether the Almighty was offended by the New Deal practices of killing little pigs and plowing under cotton. Christians compared it to the first Good Friday when the sun was blotted out at noon.

This dark moment in American history resulted from overexploitation of the land. No one was concerned about the possibility of overplanting. Lacking nutrition, the top soil blew away. Crops shriveled in the 120-degree sun. Cattle wandered until they dropped dead of dehydration. The dust was so thick that street lights burned at noon. Rivers, wells, and everything else dried up. Even the prickly-pear cactus were dying. Railroads stopped running because they had no water to make steam. Forest fires could not be doused. Farmers kept planting, hoping for rain, but eventually despair set in, causing one farmer to pass out cards that read, "If at first you don't succeed, the hell with it."[26]

The small towns had to haul in water to survive, and the sheriff was told to arrest water rustlers on the spot. The nights were pitch black, because the stars could not penetrate the layers of dust. Roads, homes, automobiles, and even some telegraph poles were buried in dust.

The area of the "Dust Bowl" cannot be defined exactly, because it encompassed land that stretched from the Canadian border to Southwestern Texas. But the southern part of the plains states, including the panhandles of Texas and Oklahoma, Eastern Colorado, Western Kansas and New Mexico—an area of nearly one hundred million acres, received the most damage. The height of the storm was in 1936, when about sixteen million acres of top soil literally blew away.

By 1939, 350,000 thousand farmers crossed the Arizona border heading westward. This rising tide alarmed Californians, who began to warn others not to come to California seeking employment. One Californian described the invasion as "Worse than a plague of locusts."[27] In the worst year, a million persons escaped the dust of Oklahoma, Texas and Missouri. A federal program offered money in an attempt to dissuade others from making the trip, but the caravan never ceased until 1939.

It was the Okies who were the most famous—the subject of Steinbeck's *Grapes of Wrath* (1939). They were the last of the homesteaders, the ones who stampeded toward the Cimmaron River on April 22, 1889, to file their claims.

Now, after struggling for over fifty years, they abandoned their homes and acres and went west on Highway 66. The popular song said that "You get your kicks on Route 66," but the farmers, lawyers, school teachers, bankers, ministers, college students, and groups of vagrants were called scum and filthy Okies.

Those who went to California to farm found no heaven there. In the first half of 1939, twenty thousand crossed the Arizona border seeking employment, bringing the total for the four years to three hundred thousand migrants (one-fifth from Oklahoma). If they found work, it was probably with the Associated Farmers of California at pitifully low wages.[28] The Okies replaced the Mexicans, who previously had filled the vacated slots of stoop labor.

The state of California exhausted every means in trying to restrict the number who crossed from Arizona. New entrants were required to produce $10, a practice that produced a great public outcry. The police set up border patrols, which turned back many, but there were too many highways to block, so the numbers of migrants just kept growing. The state offered to pay the return fare to anyone who wanted to return, and a few did accept. Still, California couldn't deal with the numbers, and it was left to the federal government to provide a temporary respite for the travelers, in what were called Federal Migratory Labor Camps.

The Arvin Camp, twenty miles from Bakersfield, was famous because Steinbeck wrote part of his *Grapes of Wrath* in the library there. Flanking the main street was the administration building, hospital, nursery, laundry and toolshed. The residential section was several rows of tents, which had rusting, decrepit hulks of wagons sitting besides the wooden platforms.

Those fortunate enough to find employment could rent one of the "labor homes," the permanent cottages nearby. Each family was allotted three-fourths of an acre for plowing and planting in the good soil of Kern County. Because only twelve camps were constructed that could handle only twenty-five hundred families, near riots ensued at the gates for any vacant beds.

Each camp had a capacity of two hundred families, and they were restricted to a one-year stay. Culture shock confronted the newcomers. Many found indoor plumbing for the first time, and women had to wrestle with the intricacies of electric washing machines. For recreation, administrators scheduled boxing matches, smokers and dances in the evenings. One teenager spoke as follows: "I realize that conditions are terrible, and there was an excuse for their not having food or money. But there wasn't any excuse for their not having some kind of covering for the children. Even an animal will fight for his little ones. Maybe he couldn't buy blankets, but even burlap bags or rags are better than nothing."[29]

Both Texas and California built a small number of migratory labor camps, patterned after the federal model, but it was the growing prosperity of the farm sector that eventually ceased the tide of human migration. By the end of 1939, the wheat crop was the best in six years. The demonstration farms of the Soil

Conservation Service showed that contour cultivation, terrace farming and preservation of rain water would yield a more abundant crop.

The Missouri Roadside Protest

The Great Depression forced hordes of owners of small farms into the dependent status of tenancy. Several forms of sharecropping developed. Cash renting was the highest form, under which the tenant paid a rent, supplied the working capital, and kept all the profits. This was common in the North, but rare in the southern regions. Another form of sharing allowed the tenant to supply labor, tools, and some farm animals. In the cotton belt, a system prevailed under which the tenant contributed nothing, but his and his family's labor qualified him to receive one-half of the cotton and one-third of the grain that was produced. Although Iowa, Kansas, Nebraska, and South Dakota had more tenant farmers than Virginia, Kentucky, and Florida, there was "no pandemic misery" in the Middle West, because many farmers there chose to conserve scarce capital to purchase equipment.[30]

In January 1939 one thousand tenant farmers established an outdoor camp in Southeast Missouri during a brutally cold winter to dramatize the extreme nature of their poverty. Their roadside demonstration was a peaceful attempt to affect public policy. The demonstration occurred in the region of Missouri popularly known as the "Bootheel," a name resulting from its peculiar geographical shape—in the southeastern corner of the state, where the Missouri line gives the appearance of a boot.

The history of Bootheel agriculture commenced with the stripping of the land by lumber companies, after which levees were built and drainage districts were created. The reclaimed soil, inside of miles of levees and dikes, was a major contributing factor in the economic misery that followed.[31]

By 1939, the plight of the sharecroppers worsened. Living conditions were pitiable. They lived either in wooden unpainted crude shacks or box houses made of weatherboard. Spaces between boards were covered with old newspapers or pieces of cardboard. Worse, in spite of a high infant death rate in the Bootheel, the population kept rising, because of the high birth rate.

Landlords chose tenants with large families for work in the peak seasons, making children a valuable economic asset. This system of using child labor guaranteed that there was no hope of their achieving upward mobility. The children dropped out of school early or never began. For those who attended, the schools were disgraceful, few being approved by the State Board of Education.

Realizing these conditions, the farmers made a bold move: they sought to organize both blacks and whites in a single union to attack the inequities of the AAA program. They saw the fallacy of the 1938 Act, whereby all payments were made to the landlords, who were supposed to make payments to the tenants. The Southern Tenants Farmers Union (STFU) got to Southeast Missouri largely because of Thad Snow, a University of Michigan graduate who had studied the writings of Thorstein Veblen. Snow was a plantation owner, but one who showed enormous concern for his tenants, and for this, he was known as the "cotton field Confucius" and the "Sage of Swampeast Missouri." The education he acquired at Michigan must have tilted his support towards "the poor devils who bend their backs to do our work."[32]

Although Owen H. Whitfield did not organize the STFU local in Missouri, he became its leader and he was the person who conceived of the highway demonstration. Whitfield, a Negro Mississippi sharecropper and a preacher, attended Okolona College for two years. He worked in and out of college as a railroad fireman, a farmer, a tap dancer, and as a minister. He settled, finally, as a sharecropper on the farm of Al Drinkwater, near Charleston, Missouri. He worked hard, and as his family grew, he worked harder. One day, he had a conversation with God. It was an angry discussion, but it gave way to reconciliation. God had always provided; it was up to him to do something. And so he joined the STFU to get a fairer share of what God was providing.

But Whitfield's efforts for reform commenced when sharecropping was dying in Missouri. As the number of farms decreased, many plantations were converted to large-scale mechanized farms, and the sharecropper was made unnecessary. When a sharecropper was evicted, it was the practice to serve him with two notices: one on November 1, and the second sixty days later, on January 1 of the new year. The first notice gave the cropper time to look for another arrangement.

Whitfield learned late in 1938 that evictions of Southeast Missouri sharecroppers were to take place in January 1939. He could not determine the exact number, because few croppers received written notices, but he estimated that there were about nine hundred.

The idea of a roadside demonstration had nebulous roots. According to Thad Snow it all began as a joke. A sharecropper when asked where he would go if he was evicted said, "Out on the road, I guess." Whitfield picked up the idea. If we have to starve, we will do it together. The idea of a roadside strike had been tried in Mississippi. But what gave his plan more promise was that Missouri was not the deep South. The planners did not expect a bloody confrontation, because it was Missouri and because it would take place in the winter months.

The planned strike hit the newspapers on January 8, 1939, as Reverend Whitfield compared it to the exodus of Moses leading the children of Israel out of bondage. The strikers had nothing to lose; they preferred to starve on the highway rather than in their meager shacks. When the strikers placed their household belongings along the road, motorists were shocked to see the conglomeration of beds, autos, and kitchen supplies along U. S. Highway 60.

The day before the roadside demonstration, the participants pleaded for local financial support. But even the STFU's largest contributor refused to help. They tried next to obtain a $1,000 loan from the CIO, but that failed. In desperation they turned to the socialists, and they were able to get funds from Norman

Thomas. They raised enough funds from private committees to alleviate the immediate financial crisis, and in time, they tapped into the funds for Strikers Relief.

A *Washington Post* reporter counted forty infants along Highways 60 and 61, most of whom had no milk. But lack of milk was not the chief problem; rather, it was the elements. Only those in their dilapidated automobiles were relatively safe. Strikers reserved those places for women and children.

On January 11, 1939 the temperature along the route fell into the thirties and the next day a cold rain added to the general misery. The situation worsened when the rain turned to snow. Some composed tents using sticks and sheets or mattresses. As the strikers shivered in the Missouri cold, the demonstration became a national issue. Representatives came from the newspapers, the Social Security Administration, the CIO, the Red Cross, and the Communist Party. The police, fearing violence, charged Butler, the STFU president, with "inciting to riot." He was escorted to the Arkansas line and ordered out of the state of Missouri. He ignored the order, as he made several trips into the Bootheel with supplies.

To remove this black eye from Missouri, state officials removed the sharecroppers from the highway and sent them to what was generally referred to as a "concentration camp." Whitfield was told that the strikers were removed for health reasons. Police guards were provided to prevent people from entering or leaving.

Some relief grants were made to tenant farmers in Southeast Missouri, but the amounts were very small. The FSA announced that an investigation would be made and that emergency grants would continue for families based on need. In fact, checks were stopped and the situation was as desperate as ever since the church fund of the Sharecroppers' Committee was depleted.

The roadside demonstration focused national attention on the Bootheel and projected Owen Whitfield into the limelight. But the residents of Southeast Missouri refused to believe that Whitfield, a poor Negro, could have masterminded this event. Thad Snow decided to oblige them. He had remained outside the main events, but now he would produce the devil that the natives sought. He concocted a confession. Not just a confession, but a very absurd one.

Just before the January demonstration, he had visited Mexico, and so he placed his confession within that setting. He wrote of meeting Leon Trotsky and Diego Rivera about the Bootheel problem. They arranged for discussions with co-conspirators President Cardenas of Mexico, Secretary of State Cordell Hull, President Roosevelt, Upton Sinclair, Al Smith, and even Norman Thomas.[33]

The confession first appeared in a Sikeston newspaper on February 2, 1939, and it got the desired effect. Many residents believed the absurdity, but in time it was recognized as the joke that it was. Snow's confession had one more unexpected effect: Secretary of Agriculture Henry Wallace, on learning of the events, suggested that Attorney General Frank Murphy ask the FBI to make its own investigation. The STFU joined in demanding that the FBI examine the violations of civil liberties. The FBI report denied the planter's contention that the entire scheme was the work of outside agitators. It condemned their lack of sympathy for the sharecroppers, who could not survive with the existing wages, and it decried their excessive interest in the system of "absentee landlordism."

By the end of 1939, evictions of tenant farmers continued. Snow threatened to lead another demonstration in January 1940 if the state did not deal with the homeless problem. This time everyone listened, attitudes were different, but the results were the same. The demonstration had failed to alter the essential economic condition of farm tenancy. There was plenty of fault all around. Secretary Wallace certainly caved in to southern congressmen, and President Roosevelt seemed not to notice the injustice of the system, even though he stated early in his first administration that the conditions in the South were "the number one domestic problem."

Bloody Harlan

Far from Washington and Hyde Park is the Cumberland plateau, which Harry Caudill called that "serrated upland." It is the region of Kentucky in the eastern and southeastern part of the state. Its hills total ten thousand square miles and cover nineteen counties and parts of a dozen more.[34]

In 1939, the nearly one-half million inhabitants of Kentucky were some of the most colorful in the United States and were among the most poor. These mountaineers, the product of European cultures and the American environment, were in these hills long before the United States was dreamed of. Their rugged life was unstable and unique. Their lamentations on the banjos, fiddles, and dulcimers permeated the cold evenings of their crude cabins. Some of the ballads were imports from their English or Scottish heritage, but most were created as they played. Their music, as well as their family tales, were never written down. Often the Saturday night "hoe-downs" produced violent ends. The square dances were lively, but the mixture of corn liquor, women and the ever-present rifles often produced shootings or stabbings. These uneducated people confined their creative urges to utilitarian objects.

Because these mountain people had few recreational opportunities, the radio had a major impact in their lives. In the 1930s, it was a treasured object for the poorest families. Daily programs began with sermons from fundamentalist preachers, then the ladies soaked up the soap operas, and in the evenings, the family got a mixture of hillbilly music and exhortations on how to solve the crucial problems of the time. The solution was often linked to a Biblical passage.

The loss of the region's young men to the popular CCC broke down old ways. The mountainmen flocked to the Corps, often encouraged by parents who could not provide for them and who looked forward to receiving their monthly allotment checks. The region was further destabilized when thousands of the

CCC enrollees were sent to the far western states. Many did not return. For many, this experience was an overture to "signing up" in World War II.

How the Cumberland region acquired this extreme poverty is the story of corrupt management of the land, wanton spoilage of natural resources, and the terrible toll of mining coal. Harry Caudill's words are sad and plaintive: "Coal has always cursed the land in which it lies. When men begin to wrest it from the earth it leaves a legacy of foul streams, hideous slag heaps and polluted air. It peoples this transformed land with blind and crippled men and with widows and orphans. It is an extractive industry which takes all away and restores nothing. It mars but never beautifies. It corrupts but never purifies."[35]

It fell to the WPA to save the miners and farmers from starvation. The hurry-up projects that were designed to absorb the thousands of unemployed had to be make-work efforts. The directors of the federal programs had to contend with destitute men who outnumbered the tools required for completion of the work. Someone conceived of the brilliant notion of allowing the men to bring their own picks and shovels and hammers. If a federal project was delayed, the director had to keep the men busy, in which case, they were often employed in making blasting holes for highway construction. Hundreds of men dotted long stretches of highways drilling holes and filling them with wooden pegs (to keep them from refilling with dirt) until the road was blasted later.

Relief changed the political landscape after the 1938 campaign, when young Albert B. Chandler, the Governor of Kentucky, always known as "Happy," decided to challenge Senator Alben Barkley, the senior senator and majority leader. It was a bold and brash move, because Barkley was a favorite of President Roosevelt, a strong supporter of the New Deal and a powerful speaker on behalf of social programs. His defeat would be a stunning blow to the President. Chandler, the always-smiling one, was a great vote-getter in Kentucky, but he was a conservative and not warm about economic reform.

Although federal relief was "nonpolitical," the bureaucrats, sensing a threat to their livelihoods, quietly converted the relief program into a political machine. Programs became political patronage. Chandler saw it happening, but he could only denounce it with little effect. Barkley appointed loyal campaign managers in each county and asked them to visit him in his office in Louisville. There, behind closed doors, he explained the mission—to defeat Chandler. Mission accomplished. Before the largess, the plateau had been overwhelmingly Republican since the Civil War.[36]

By 1939, 22 percent of Kentuckians were union members, one of the highest percentages in the South. Fifteen thousand miners belonged to the UMW from Harlan County, which became a battleground. Kentucky Governor Chandler equivocated. He tried to be both pro-labor and pro-business at one time. He praised the Wagner Act but spoke out against strikes in the mines.

Sheriff J. H. Blair and his deputies attempted to free Kentucky of unions. Nearly all of the mine owners declared that their mines were nonunion. The coal operators did not respond to pressure from the federal government to break the string of violent acts of both sides to the dispute. A major point of contention was the appointment of persons with criminal records as sheriff's deputies. At Governor Chandler's request, the Kentucky General Assembly banned these appointments and gave the state treasurer control over the deputies' salaries. But for the miners, the bigger issue was the conduct of the deputies in labor disputes.

The federal answer was to try several mine operators for depriving miners of their civil rights under the Wagner Act. They had evaded Blue Eagle codes, which guaranteed the right to organize; they ignored rulings of the National Labor Relations Board. The case was deadlocked, and the judge declared a mistrial. The mine owners submitted and signed contracts with the UMW. Blakey contends that they "spent nearly a million dollars to insure a hung jury."[37]

It seemed to be a time for calm, but John L. Lewis shattered the fragile labor peace by calling a nationwide strike in April 1939 when Governor Chandler and the coal operators opposed the UMW proposal to ban the employment of nonunion workers, who would have to cross the picket lines to get to work. Violence was expected, and it came.

The governor then gave the parties until May 14 to reach an agreement or he would call out the National Guard to protect property and lives. He was under great pressure, because in this tail end of the Depression, many nonunion miners wanted desperately to return to work. As Blakey related, several miners requested "protection so that we might resume our work and support our families," but UMW members warned that the use of troops and scab labor to dig coal would "cause blood to run trickling down these little streams."

When Chandler's deadline came, most operators had accepted the UMW, affecting 86 percent of the miners in the Appalachian region, but not in Harlan County. Chandler stuck to his promise: he ordered five hundred national guardsmen to keep order in the mines and in the region. The violent acts escalated. It was Blakey who wrote of "unprecedented carnage and bitterness." Chandler, who brought more troops, said he was not antiunion; he was only protecting the right of Kentuckians to choose where to work. As the strike dragged on and the mine families went hungry, the federal government supplied food under the WPA, which caused more resentment from the owners and the nonunion miners.

In "Bloody Harlan" County, each side buried its dead, as the fighting escalated. One man was shot in the head the first night the troops were in Harlan, and a second was shot in the leg the next day. Trucks filled with troops continued to roll into town, as the Harlan Coal Operator's Association said it would send the soldiers into the mines in the evening.

John L. Lewis asked President Roosevelt to intervene in Kentucky to ascertain what civil rights were being violated in the mining camps. Speaking at a CIO convention, Lewis showed his usual oratorical skills when he shouted, "I know Happy Chandler. . . . He was in favor of collective bargaining and was against the hiring of gunmen, the exploitation of mine workers and the suppression of civil liberties. . . . We believed Happy Chandler because we did not know he talked with his tongue in his cheek."[38] Lewis reminded Chandler of the CIO aid in getting the governor elected, but Chandler must have remembered that the union sided with Alben Barkley in the last senate campaign.

By this time, the nation faced a real coal emergency. There was a month's supply aboveground, but most of it was in the West. For the industrial Northeast, the supply situation was critical. President Roosevelt ordered both sides to submit a plan for the resumption of coal mining by May 10. He reminded the disputants that they were first American citizens and that failure to agree would bring on a "stern alternative."

When the deadline approached, John R. Steelman, chief of the United States Conciliation Service, announced, "The deadlock is over." The settlement contained an approval of the union shop, which Lewis had been seeking for a long time. To accommodate FDR's demand for an easing of the coal shortage, Lewis agreed to have his miners return to work in all areas except in the Appalachian region.

In July 1939 an armistice was arranged. The dead and wounded were cared for, the National Guard left Harlan County, and the mines reopened. Chandler boasted that "Kentucky won a victory for itself." But the struggle for unionizing the mines, which had gone on for two decades, was not finally resolved until World War II, and even then, Lewis challenged the United States by calling for other strikes in wartime.

NOTES

1. Colberg, *Human Capital in Southern Development*, p. 4.
2. Ellis, *A Nation in Torment*, p. 235.
3. Wecter, *The Age of the Great Depression*, p. 204.
4. White, *One Man's Meat*, p. 97.
5. Ellis, *A Nation in Torment*, p. 437.
6. Perrett, *Days of Sadness*, p. 22.
7. At this time, the CIO unions chose also to rename themselves the Congress of Industrial Organizations.
8. Manchester, *The Glory and the Dream*, p. 130.
9. "Evil Old Man," *Timecapsule / 1939*, p. 34.
10. Wecter, *The Age of the Great Depression*, p. 112.
11. This is the title of the September 6, 1993 PBS television program on sit-down strikes, which was part of "The American Experience" series.
12. "Roosevelt Letters to Labor Chiefs," *New York Times*, February 26, 1939, p. 2.
13. "C.I.O.-A.F.L. Row Enters New Phase," *New York Times*, August 13, 1939, p. 10E.
14. "Unemployment Remains Major Economic Worry", *New York Times*, July 30, 1939, p. 6E.
15. Wecter, *The Age of the Great Depression*, p. 185.

16. Hill, *The School in the Camps*, p. 7.

17. "CCC Camps Will Be Put on Civilian Basis," *New York Times*, June 16, 1939, p. 27.

18. Blakey, *Hard Times and New Deal in Kentucky*, p. 81.

19. Anderson, *Puzzled America*, p. 61.

20. Blakey, *Hard Times and New Deal in Kentucky*, p. 82.

21. Ellis, *A Nation in Torment*, p. 305.

22. The WPA began as the Works Progress Administration, but under the Reorganization Act of 1939, the name was changed to the Works Projects Administration and put under the new Federal Works Agency.

23. Bolino, *A Century of Human Capital*, p. 193.

24. Wecter, *The Age of the Great Depression*, p. 96.

25. "WPA Knit Into Nation's Life," *New York Times*, March 19, 1939, p. 6E.

26. Ellis, *A Nation in Torment*, p. 455.

27. Todd, "Okies Search for a Lost Frontier," *New York Times*, August 27, 1939, p. 11.

28. Wecter, *The Age of the Great Depression*, p. 175.

29. Todd, "Okies Search for a Lost Frontier," p. 16.

30. Wecter, *The Age of the Great Depression*, p. 136.

31. Conrad, *The Forgotten Farmers* (1965).

32. Snow's memoirs *From Missouri* is the best popular account of the 1939 strike.

33. Cantor, *A Prologue to the Protest Movement*, p. 124.

34. Caudill, *Night Comes to the Cumberlands* (1963).

35. Caudill, *Night Comes to the Cumberlands*, p. i.

36. The Great Depression and the new programs of the Democrats converted the territory into a Democratic stronghold for years to come. Barkley, for all of his efforts, was later nominated to be Vice President under Harry Truman.

37. Blakey, *Hard Times in Kentucky*, p. 164.

38. "Mine Chiefs Move For Harlan Peace," *New York Times*, May 16, 1939, p. 1.

3

FDR's New Dealers

FDR

Franklin Delano Roosevelt, that patrician in the White House, was a remarkable man. Like Shakespeare's Julius Caesar, FDR "bestrode his narrow world like a colossus." A distant cousin of Theodore Roosevelt, Franklin championed the causes of the oppressed, of the poor, and of the handicapped (of which he was one). His political rise could have been predicted. He took a politically unpopular position by supporting Catholic Al Smith for President in 1928. It did not hurt him when he ran for and won the governorship of New York in 1929.

FDR was born and grew up with great riches and with a renowned family name in a matriarchy. He was a mama's boy. His mother, Sarah Delano Roosevelt, dominated him. As a boy, she did not allow him to play games or swing a baseball bat. His life was totally regulated and lonely. He was an extroverted, loquacious boy who was penned up at Hyde Park—that tight little island of snobbish people.

When Franklin went to Groton, where sports was everything, he was an outcast. Not until he got to Harvard College did he find himself and his first love—Eleanor Roosevelt, a distant cousin. She thought Franklin was sympathetic, sociable, charming, warm and good looking. He was many things she wasn't.

When Roosevelt became president in 1933, his preparation for the job was complete. He had traveled widely as a boy and young man, he read constantly, especially history, and political science and his education was rounded off at Harvard University. He learned early to depend on experts, and no president since has had such an illustrious "Brain Trust." President Roosevelt was resolute, charming, politically savvy, and he got the trust of the American people.

Examples of his charm are legendary. Countless persons came to his office to resign; very few did. He simply turned on the charm. He told one person they were married for better or for worse. When Jerome Frank, head of the SEC, told FDR that he could not afford to stay in Washington at his current salary, the President told him, "Why Jerry, after this crisis is over, do you think that either of us will ever have trouble earning money?" Frank stayed. On another occasion, all six New England governors marched into his office sternly. The President looked at them with that FDR smile and said, "You're not going to secede are you?"

Roosevelt was a gentleman, in the old sense. He was educated, civilized, kind, and he was never crude. He never excoriated anyone in public. Some said he was too nice, but he would have smiled at such a possibility. He delighted at sending personal notes, each of which had a witty little saying. For example, he wrote Congressman Rayburn on his birthday that it must be awful (in capital letters) to be so old, then he added that he wouldn't be that age "for 23 days."

Because Roosevelt was a decent person himself, he believed in the decency of humanity. He trusted the people in their democracy. He knew that the people would select the right persons and the right programs for human progress. In discussing human advancement, he once said, "But I would rather be a builder than a wrecker, hoping always that the structure of life is growing, not dying."[1]

Roosevelt had no fear of the unknown. He knew that things would be alright, even in those darkest moments. He was infinitely confident of his own ability. Doris Goodwin has the right words to describe him, "Whether sorting his stamp collection with Missy LeHand, inspecting the troops in the company of his wife, probing the latest Hollywood gossip with Harry Hopkins, enjoying the company of a stylish woman, co-opting a potential rival, delivering a fireside chat, charming a disgruntled Cabinet officer, exchanging repartee with reporters or confidences with Churchill, Roosevelt's ebullience permeated every aspect of his leadership."[2]

When he spoke on the radio, his audience thought he was speaking directly to them. Such was the power and popularity of his fireside chats. He had an uncanny ability to choose the right words, and they were always words that Americans could understand. He used homey examples (he compared lend-lease to loaning your neighbor something he needed at the moment). His speech writers said that he tried to picture the people in their kitchens and their living rooms as he delivered his words, and to him they were family.

A SUCCESSFUL WIFE

Anna Eleanor Roosevelt was born into a famous family in New York City. Her uncle Theodore was the President of the United States. She was shy, awkward, clumsy, gangling, and had a high, squeaky voice, but she was not ugly. She tired early of the debutante scene, as she saw injustice in the world. She was appalled by the sights of child labor, of the sweat shops and of unsafe working conditions. It helped to make her a lifelong friend of labor. This extraordinary woman was courageous, unselfish, and devoted to making humankind a little more secure and comfortable. She summed up her life's philosophy in one sentence, "I always looked at everything from the point of view of what I ought to do."

Her cousin Franklin must have seen the fine qualities she was to exhibit as a mature woman. They courted and were married on March 17, 1905. Their first child was Anna Eleanor, but then they had five sons. From the beginning, her marriage was one of combining social work and family responsibilities. She was a member of countless youth, women, and consumer organizations, and she was the first First Lady to hold a press conference, which she did shortly after Franklin was sworn in as President.

Franklin's first federal job was as Secretary of the Navy in World War I, but he was to stay out of the public arena for a long time, recovering from infantile paralysis. When he contracted polio, he was despondent and he wanted to give up, but Eleanor insisted that he try to get up and walk. She used her discipline, energy, and will to serve as his voice, his servant, and his constant companion (but she was not his lover; by agreement, they had consented to sleep in separate beds after she found love letters describing his affair with Lucy Mercer).

Franklin said his political career was over, but Eleanor nursed him mentally and physically through months of hospital stays, convalescence, and rehabilitation. Through her efforts, he became the only handicapped President in American history. She simply became his legs, his eyes, and his ears to the people of the United States. FDR gave more weight to her opinions, because he knew she was always on the high ground.

She worked tirelessly to promote her husband's political career. On several occasions, she attempted to pursuade writers to either alter or not print stories that were less than favorable towards her Franklin. She was friendly and warm, but she was iron willed, and she had a much greater commitment towards social welfare programs than did her husband. She was a straight arrow and was the most daring and effective first lady in American history.

When Franklin was pursuing his goals of becoming governor of New York and president of the United States, Eleanor Roosevelt made her own career in social services, teaching, lecturing, and writing. The title of one of her books epitomized her belief—*This Troubled World* (1938) was a plea to "love thy neighbor." Overcoming her shyness, she championed the plight of the blacks, the unions, and the unemployed.

Mrs. Roosevelt often worked most effectively through the women her husband appointed. She watched those appointments carefully, hoping to find allies for her many causes. She also attempted to pressure Franklin to make sure that these women were selected on the basis of merit for all jobs. When women in the administration were attacked, Eleanor immediately came to their defense.

Mrs. Roosevelt's primary concern was the nation's youth—she called them our "messengers of the future." She feared that if we did not act to save them, we would lose a whole generation. It was the germ for FDR's National Youth Administration, which he created by executive order. Under it, students in high school and college could work after school at prescribed wages. The program had three objectives: to provide for financial assistance for families, to reduce the unemployment rate, and to keep the youth in school.

Eleanor Roosevelt's achievements were astounding: in the seven years between 1932 and 1939, she traveled 280,000 miles, wrote over a million words, made hundreds of speeches, and attempted to answer the 150,000 letters she received in 1939 (mostly in support of her efforts to help those in need).[3]

John Gunther described her as "one of the most magnificent women of modern times," and historian James McGregor Burns called her a "heroine of social change." The Gallup poll of January 1939 showed that she was more popular than her husband. She even received a majority of favorable votes from upper-income groups (which her husband did not).

This remarkable approval rating was unequaled anywhere in the world; she had an enormous influence on public opinion, which was amazing because, when she became First Lady, she was derided, she was caricatured, and she was joked about. But as she pursued her multiplicity of interests for the public good, the people slowly came to admire her. She wasn't just the president's wife and White House hostess. A woman of great wealth, she preferred a simple picnic of hot dogs and hamburgers (which she usually cooked herself) to an elaborate state dinner.

In 1939 Americans paid attention to the ubiquitous Mrs Roosevelt. She tackled subjects that others could not. She became everywoman—a champion.[4] This gawky, tall, plain-looking woman accomplished as much as any other woman in the twentieth century, yet she faced derision and mockery everywhere she went. She was accused of attempting to do too many things, but she answered by being a successful wife, mother and hostess.

Being so much in the public eye made her treasure her private moments more. Whereas Franklin thrived in the spotlight of the capital, she preferred to spend her time at Val-Kill, the fieldstone cottage that he had built for her on the grounds of the Hyde Park estate. It was there that she spent many private hours with Joe Lash. She met him in November 1939, when as a student leader he was called to testify before the House Un-American Activities Committee. She was drawn immediately to this radical who favored so many of the social programs that Eleanor sought. They became lifelong friends (Goodwin called it an "intimate friendship"). Morison added his praises:

She visited and talked to all sorts and conditions of people, giving them a feeling that the government really cared about them. She took a particular interest in the disoriented and confused young people then graduating from schools and colleges, and was instrumental in preventing thousands of them from going Red. Among the colored people she became a legendary benefactress; and, in so doing alienated the white South. She maintained the atmosphere of a gentleman's country home in the White House, amid all the hurlyburly of the New Deal.[5]

She never escaped the vicious press. The campaign literature published by the Almina (Kansas) Plaindealer is just a sample:

Gallivanting Gal

Strike up the Band!
Here's our Globe Trotter!

Call off the bombing for today
Wheel out the Army ship
Hold up the war so Eleanor
Can take another trip.

For 20,000 miles she goes
To have her weekly fling,
And rub her nose against the nose
Of some wild Zulu king!

'Twas by design and not by luck
She chose this distant shore ;
The only place she hasn't stuck
Her nosey nose before.

Now, having rubbed the royal nose
She crossed another sea,
To scare the natives I suppose
And watch them plant a tree.

The happy thought occurred to me
As homeward bound she sped ;
Why couldn't they have shipped the tree
And planted her instead?[6]

Her life was spent on matters of substance, but too much of it was devoted to the superficial aspects of being First Lady. According to Goodwin, "In 1939, her secretary recorded that Eleanor received 9,211 tea guests, 4,729 dinner guests and 323 house guests." These routines kept her up after midnight on many days.[7] Despite her many accomplishment and world fame, she still clung to those elements of insecurity that never left her.

FDR'S NEW DEALERS

A Right Thorough Thinker

Cordell Hull, the quiet, drawling Tennessean, was sworn in as Secretary of State five hours after Roosevelt became President. Hull's appointment was considered unusual, because his views were not totally consistent with those of the President, and he did not seem to possess the brilliant analytical powers of the younger members of the Brain Trust. Some thought Hull was a payoff to the fundamentalists of the South for their backing of a party that was controlled by Ivy Leaguers. They called Hull "Mr. Milquetoast."

But Roosevelt respected his Secretary of State. FDR always opened his cabinet meetings by calling on Hull to give his latest assessment of conditions overseas. By 1939 Hull was a senior citizen and a senior diplomat. He slumped in his chair and he spoke slowly, but his words were cogent, and the cabinet paid attention.

Cordell was his father's favorite son (there were five of them). Billy Hull described him as follows: "Cord wasn't set enough to be a school-teacher, wasn't rough enough to be a lumberman, wasn't sociable enough to be a doctor and couldn't holler loud enough to be a preacher. But Cord was a right thorough thinker."[8]

He was not spectacular, he was not popular, but he forged a reciprocal trade agreement that was revolutionary in content. It was an unusual internationalist position for a man who was born in a log cabin and was raised in a backwoods community that had one telephone. Hull's manner was undoubtedly influenced greatly by his part-Indian mother, nee Elizabeth Riley, who helped him to grow into that studious and quiet man who was an effective speaker and debater.

Cord went to a one-room school and to Montvale College, where he studied anatomy, Greek, geometry, and surveying under Professor Joe McMillan (it was said he was half of the faculty). It was as a student that Hull got into Tennessee politics, and he became a lifelong Democrat. He finished law school, practiced briefly, but left it all to form the Fourth Tennessee Regiment in the Spanish American War. From there it was a judgeship and election to Congress. As a congressman, he favored low tariffs (he was a Jeffersonian free trader) and income redistribution. He wrote the first income tax bill in 1913, and as his seniority grew, his advocacy turned national.

His stint as Secretary of State was off to a poor start. In June 1933 he headed the American delegation to the London Economic Conference, which was a major failure, but Hull, who did not look like or have the manners of a diplomat, quietly impressed a lot of people who had mistaken his low-key approach for incompetence. When he went to the Pan-American Conference at Montevideo, his southern, folksy approach won over the Latin Americans who believed they had a friend in the State Department. The result was the "Good Neighbor Policy," which established an important, new approach. The agreement stated that no country in this hemisphere had a right to interfere in the affairs of another country.

Hull's monument was the reciprocal trade agreement, under which there was created a "most favored nation status" for twenty-two nations, which accounted for over 60 percent of our overseas trade. The trade agreement act gave President Roosevelt the authority to raise or lower any tariff up to 50 percent for those countries willing to make reciprocal concessions.

By 1939 Hull had achieved a spectacular international and domestic record. He avoided commitments on controversial issues, choosing instead to respond with a calculated vagueness. He always promised to "look into" any situation that was questioned at a press conference. By then, his views were indistinguishable from Roosevelt's, and Hull's esteem had risen to the point where he was considered a leading candidate to replace the President if he did not run in 1940.

Hopkins and Ickes

Harry L. Hopkins, who worked in social welfare programs in New York City and was appointed administrator of Federal Emergency Relief, was born on August 17, 1890, in Sioux City, Iowa. Robert Sherwood relates how Hopkins always kept coming back to his humble beginnings. After his first encounter with Stalin, Hopkins told a companion, "I couldn't believe it. There I was, walking up the staircase of the Kremlin, going to talk to the man who ruled 180 million people. And I kept asking myself—what are you doing here, Hopkins, you—the son of a harness maker from Sioux City—?" His friend broke in: "Now, for God's sake, Harry—don't give me that old line again. You told me when you first set foot in the White House that there you were, the son of a harness maker. . . . Can't you ever stop boasting about your humble origin?"[9]

He enrolled at Grinnell College with the class of 1912, where he showed his ability to get votes. One teacher, in particular, had a profound effect on his future career: Professor Edward A. Steiner, who taught social science. Steiner, a Czecho-slovakian Jew who became a Congregational minister, taught Hopkins much about the Christian ethics and the communist world. Steiner, the author of *On the Trail of the Immigrant* and *The Immigrant Tide*, influenced young Harry to appreciate the multicultural aspects of American life in the pre World War I days.[10]

Hopkins was a frail man, who had several long periods of serious illness, but he was a man of intellect, who could plumb the bottom of social issues. Churchill called Hopkins "Lord Root of the Matter." It was said that Hopkins and Roosevelt were twins—one person with two heads. Harry Hopkins came into Roosevelt's life through Eleanor. She was always seeking good persons to run one of her husband's new programs. He was perfect for FDR. Together, they talked for hours; they bantered; they cajoled; they poked fun at each other. The President liked to be buttered up, but he wanted it done with flair and irreverence, and Hopkins was his man. Hopkins became a trusted adviser who brought many competent persons into the Roosevelt Administration. FDR seldom argued against any of his choices.

In 1939, during the hearings for his appointment as Secretary of Commerce, Hopkins was called a radical and a revolutionary. He was confirmed, but he had to mend his political fences. He devoted more time seeing corporate America, and he catered more to the demands of the U.S. Chamber of Commerce. That summer, Hopkins revisited Grinnell where in speaking to the student body, he disclosed that as a student he did not have the "vaguest knowledge about government" and "The less government interfered with me around this town, the better I liked it."—that's quite a statement from a person who was to manage the WPA and the Commerce Department.

When Congress passed the reorganization bill in 1939, which brought together all relief operations under the Federal Works Agency, Roosevelt had a problem: who should run the new agency. Should it be Harold Ickes, the old curmudgeon of the PWA or Harry Hopkins of the WPA? The two men were not enemies, but they were not friends. Roosevelt bucked the problem by establishing a unique troika to run the agency: he placed an old friend Frank Wallace on the same level with Ickes and Hopkins to control the giant system of grants. Wallace was to act as bookkeeper, and Ickes and Hopkins spent the money.

Many persons confused the WPA and PWA; they could not comprehend why there should be two agencies with the same three initials. The differences in the two organizations were really linked to the two men who ran them. Hopkins had the job of putting those on relief into jobs quickly. It was a shift from dole to work.

Ickes had a more difficult assignment: he had to prime the pump in such a way as to achieve the greatest employment results on a long-run basis. This Keynesian approach was meant to offset a deficiency of private investment with public works.

Harold Loy Ickes, the WPA administrator from 1933 to 1939, was an independent Republican who was a reformer. Although he was born in Pennsylvania, his experience was all Chicago: University of Chicago undergraduate, a reporter on the *Chicago Record*, and campaign manager for candidates for the office of mayor of Chicago. He was always on the liberal side of issues: he was a supporter of Theodore Roosevelt and Hiram Johnson, the progressive governor of California. Ickes was a civil rights lawyer who defended blacks and Jews when it was not popular to do so, and he was president of the local NAACP Chapter. When he took over the CCC, he did not approve of the antiblack policies of Robert Fechner, the southerner who administered it.

President Roosevelt, who was trying to bring progressives into his administration, appointed Ickes Secretary of the Interior, which put him in charge of the public lands and the Public Works Administration. The value of PWA cannot be questioned; it built the Boulder Dam, the TVA, Bonneville Dam, the Tri-Borough Bridge in New York City, public airports, sewer systems, water works, and public buildings. It promulgated a new, revolutionary policy towards Indian Americans that protected their lands and their cultural heritage. T. H. Watkins, who wrote admiringly of Ickes, said that he was first a conservationist and he was more interested in the National Park Service than other more-urban programs.[11]

"Tommy the Cork" (et al.)

Thomas Gardner Corcoran, who was called "Tommy the Cork" by FDR and who drafted much of the New Deal legislation, met President Roosevelt when singing Irish ballads to him during a White House party. Corcoran, with his partner Ben Cohen (together they were called the "Gold Dust Twins"), became an indispensable part of Roosevelt's plans. A Rhode Island native, Corcoran was a brilliant student at Brown University, where he won prizes for debating and English composition. At Harvard Law School, he was greatly influenced by Professor Felix Frankfurter, who labeled him "little hot dog." Corcoran was first in his class, which led to his appointment as secretary to Supreme Court Justice Oliver Wendell Holmes. Corcoran read the classics in the Latin and Greek texts to Holmes, and they became good friends.

Tom was very Irish in his approach. He was pleasant, easy to approach, and he learned to handle politicians by singing to them in off-hours. He knew Gilbert and Sullivan, he was a fair concert pianist, and he could cook. Tom had an encyclopedic knowledge of literature, which he used generously when he was called on to ghostwrite one of the President's speeches. But Corcoran's real job was in drafting legislation.

Corcoran and Cohen lived together, they were inseparable, and they were gluttons for work, often putting in consecutive twenty-hour days. They were premier architects of New Deal legislation—their bills were "models of legal brilliance."[12]

Roosevelt had a long list of "helpers"—ghostwriters. They were big names and unknown names. Robert Sherwood was prolific. He wrote several speeches to Congress, many with felicitous phrases. On one occasion Mrs. Sherwood sent Roosevelt a congratulatory telegram after a particularly good speech that her Bob had written, to which the President observed, "Bob and I are awfully glad you liked it."[13] In addition to Sherwood, the team of writers included Archibald MacLeish (too literary), Sumner Welles and Raymond Moley.

Joe Joe Kennedy Kennedy

Joseph P. Kennedy's life was full enough for several men. His breadth of achievements was astonishing. Born in an immigrant area near the waterfront in East Boston, he rose to great wealth and great power. He succeeded in everything he tried, except becoming president of the United States. His early successes were tied to athletics, but later they were all tied to money. Because his father Patrick was in the coal and saloon businesses, the Kennedys were relatively well off. This enabled Joe to go to parochial school, Boston Latin High School, and Harvard University. He was a star athlete. At Boston Latin, he played basketball and football and was a leading batter on the baseball team. At Harvard, where he majored in economics, he was on the basketball team, but he was a loner, because his classmates did not encourage him to run for any of the prestigious clubs there.

Joe showed his entrepreneurial ability at a very early age: he sold tickets on an excursion steamer when in high school, and while at Harvard, he saved $5,000 by running a sight-seeing bus to Lexington in the summers. He was bright and eager to conquer the world around him, especially the WASP world of Boston. He decided then that he would be a millionaire at age 35. Not long after graduating, he was running a bank at the corner of Meridian Street in Maverick Square, East Boston. He began as a bank examiner for the Columbia Trust Company, where his father was a director, and in just months, Joe borrowed enough money to buy a large part of the stock of the bank.[14]

By making these fortunes, he met the Bostonians on their terms. He bought in Hyannisport, he gave his children all the trappings of class, but he still was not accepted by those who mattered in Massachusetts because of his Roman Catholicism. So he set his sight higher. He courted and won the daughter of the Mayor, John "Honey Fitz" Fitzgerald. Rose Fitzgerald was a steadying influence for him as he reached for his political stars. She bore him five children in the first six years of marriage and four more after. As a dutiful wife, she stayed in Boston as he traveled to Hollywood and New York.

His pace in the business world was frenetic: he went into shipbuilding, then investment banking. He was on Wall Street in the prosperity decade of 1920s. He bought a chain of movie houses, then he went to Hollywood to try to buy it. He was determined to show the proper Bostonians his worth, and so he made several fortunes. He made a fortune in Hollywood after moving there in 1926. It was a gold mine to his liking. His low-budget films made plenty of money, and he made millions on his RKO theaters. Because of his success, he was appointed to manage the funds of Gloria Swanson, one of the most beautiful and richest women in Hollywood. Soon they were lovers. It is alleged that he made another fortune in running whiskey from Canada to the United States during Prohibition. His third fortune was acquired on Wall Street. He joined in the frenzy of the late 1920s, but he knew when to get out. As he said, "Only a fool goes for the top dollar."[15]

After selling all his stock in 1929 before the crash, Kennedy made a wise decision: he jumped on the FDR bandwagon. Kennedy was sure that the government would play a much larger role in the 1930s, and he wanted some of that action. In 1930, when he was only forty-two years old, he was a powerhouse in the Democratic party. He gave thousands for Roosevelt's first run at the White House, for which he was allowed to ride on the campaign train with the nominee. His payoff came later when he was appointed Chairman of the new Securities and Exchange Commission.

It startled everyone that Roosevelt should put a speculator in charge of a commission that was responsible for controlling speculators and protecting the public interest. Everyone said that Roosevelt had put the fox in the chicken coop, because Kennedy had been accused of manipulating stock. But Kennedy knew all the angles and could more effectively control them. He was an able chairman of the SEC, and when Kennedy left that office in a year and a half, he was praised by both the liberal and conservative presses. After leaving the SEC, he worked for a time as a floating consultant, helping to reorganize RCA, Paramount Pictures, and some of the W. Randolph Hearst properties. Still aiming for a cabinet post, he published a book, *I'm For Roosevelt*, in 1936, just in time for the campaign for Roosevelt's second term. But again, there was no cabinet job for him.

His managerial wizardry got him another federal assignment. In 1937 Roosevelt asked him to chair the newly created Maritime Commission, which was set up to administer the United States Merchant Marine Act. In his two months at the commission, he reorganized the agency, settled a major labor dispute, and strengthened the United States merchant fleet. As Chairman, Joe used all of his public relations skills to keep his name in the newspapers. He called for a large study of the merchant marine, and when the report came out, it was a reasoned economic analysis. His star was rising. In 1938 a poll showed him to be the fifth most popular person for the presidency in the coming (1940) election.

But Roosevelt wanted him out of the country; the ambassadorship to Great Britain was the solution. Kennedy, who was called the richest Irish-American on earth, was appointed ambassador in December 1937 when he was forty-nine years of age (he was the first Irish-Catholic to hold that post). According to Kennedy biographers, his appointment as ambassador followed one comical episode. As they tell it, Kennedy was ushered into the Oval Office where Roosevelt told him, "Joe, would you mind taking your pants down." The bewildered Kennedy "slowly unhooked his suspenders, let his pants fall to the floor, and stood in his shorts looking silly and embarrassed." The President said, "Joe, just look at your legs. You are just about the most bow-legged man I have ever seen. Don't you know that the Ambassador of the Court of Saint James'. . . has to wear knee breeches and silk stockings? We'll be the laughing stock. You're just not right for the job Joe." Kennedy stared at the President and said he would get permission to wear a cutaway coat and striped pants. The President, knowing that the British would stand on tradition, agreed to give Kennedy two weeks before appointing a new ambassador. Before the allotted time, Kennedy returned with the King's permission.[16]

When FDR appointed him to be Ambassador to the Court of St. James, a position that put him among the most elite in the English-speaking world, everyone took notice, especially the Brahmins of Boston, who had shunned him since his days at Harvard. After being rebuffed in his effort to become a cabinet officer, Kennedy had plucked the top American diplomatic post. He would be the most important American in Europe. How he must have reveled in this appointment, because it meant that he could jibe at all the proper Bostonians in Yankee land. The Brahmins ranks, wrote Rose Kennedy, "closed around 1820, and that nobody has been taken in since." She also wrote that her father, John F.

Fitzgerald, the Mayor of Boston, had been mentioned for the same appointment in Wilson's time, but the President knew that Fitzgerald could not be approved for the post.[17]

When the Kennedys stormed London, the British press was fascinated by this large Irish-Catholic family from Boston. Rose Kennedy thought that the British people had adopted the family. But their mission was diplomatic, not social, so Rose Kennedy set about making the embassy livable for her large family. After settling in at the embassy, the Kennedys began their official and social events. They prepared Kathleen (Kick) for her coming out party and prepared to be received by the Queen, a custom for all ambassadors and their wives. Ambassador and Mrs. Kennedy arrived at Buckingham Palace at the designated time of 7 P.M. and were met by the master of the household. As Joe Kennedy sized up the situation with all its splendor, he commented, "Rose, this is a helluva long way from East Boston."[18]

The English welcomed the new ambassador as "Jolly Joe Kennedy." They were astounded by his casual demeanor. He greeted the British press with his feet propped up on his desk, and he joked that, "You don't expect me to develop into a statesman overnight." His informality was probably strained to the limits when he refused to wear knee breeches when presenting his credentials to King George; it meant that he was the only person in the room wearing long pants.

In London, there was a very warm greeting for the Kennedy children— Britishers called Kennedy the "U.S.A's Nine-child envoy." The children were accepted graciously in the best British circles. Rose Kennedy had done her job well; she turned her brood into a collection of persons of breeding and culture. They were ready to meet Dukes and Marquesses. Ambassador Kennedy had reached his goal of full acceptability. The British seemed to forget that he was a Roman Catholic.

As American ambassador, Kennedy had nearly constant contact with Prime Minister Neville Chamberlain. They respected each other because they both came from the working class—both being descended from tradesmen. Neville was the son of Joseph Chamberlain, who at one time suggested that Queen Victoria relinquish her crown in favor of a republic. The press refused to cease its relentless criticism of the Prime Minister, who they said was a better Chairman of the Birmingham Town-Planning Committee than a Prime Minister. Chamberlain squelched the criticism when he said that "he had never met anybody in Birmingham who in the least resembled Adolf Hitler."

While all the talk in London was of Kick and Eunice, John Kennedy was soaking up history as a student at Harvard when his father was appointed ambassador. Young John divided his time for two years between Cambridge and London. He was an observer of the events of the summer and fall of 1938. Because Joe Kennedy believed that war was inevitable, he suggested that Jack postpone his second semester and return to England to observe the momentous events as they unfolded.

As soon as Jack arrived back in London in February 1939, his father put him and brother Joseph to work writing reports on impressions of English society concerning the possibility of war. It was at that time that Jack Kennedy's notions about the coming war began to deviate from his father's. Rose wrote that, "Joe despised everything about Hitler and naziism," but this stretched the truth a bit. Jack offered his reflections on these times in his senior thesis and later in a book, *Why England Slept*, whose publication was financed by his father.[19]

Jack experienced a memorable result of the first year of war. The ambassador sent him to Glasgow to interview American survivors of the sinking of the *Athenia*. Young Jack faced a raucous crowd, who believed that they were in jeopardy because President Roosevelt had announced that the United States could not provide escort convoys for the returning refugees. Kennedy calmly informed them that the United States was a neutral nation and that they would be safer on one of our ships than on a British transport.

By 1939 Joe Kennedy had become disenchanted with the New Deal, but he refused to resign. He was too enamored of his diplomatic importance. For Roosevelt, who never liked him, Kennedy was a pain. The President thought he was too British and was too taken in by royalty and plumage. If 1938 was a Kennedy high, 1939 was a disaster. When Hitler invaded Austria, Kennedy was impressed with German might. He was unimpressed with "British Steel." When war came in September 1939, he sent his children home, because he said the British would lose the war. In a press conference, Kennedy stated that democracy was finished in Great Britain and perhaps in the United States. It is ironic that Joe Kennedy, the consummate politician and expert at public relations, should have made such a PR gaffe.

He was lampooned at Harvard, where Professor Milton Katz, of the Law School penned a poem:

Joe Joe Kennedy Kennedy

Went to the Court of Saint James
Where he was frequently seen
With the King and the Queen
At cricket and other games.

Said Joe Joe Kennedy Kennedy
Before England went to war,
These stories will do for the tories
That's what God made me for.

But when the bombs began to fall
All over London town,
Said Joe Joe I must go,
England has let me down

The red-haired Boston Irishman sent a priority cable on Sunday, September 3, to Secretary of State Hull stating that the British had given a new deadline to Adolf Hitler. If he did not act by 11 A.M., there would be war. *Time* called the Ambassador a "legman in a tail-coat." He interviewed people to get news and reported to the State Department or the President. Kennedy was able to do this well in England, because he had the confidence of the British people, who seemed to love the smiling, profane Irishman. The English viewed Ambassador Joe Kennedy as an exemplar of the U.S. businessman—a good family man, who was a shrewd trader in the marketplace and who could communicate his views forcefully.

Kennedy did not sleep much on September 3. He caught a nap on a folding cot, and at 3 A.M. he received a phone call telling him that the British ship *Athenia* was sinking, having been torpedoed by a German submarine, with 1,418 passengers, about three hundred of them Americans. Kennedy, who worked with his coat tossed over a chair, his sleeves rolled up, and suspenders showing, got quick results. He contacted consulates to obtain the names of American passengers. Everyone agreed that he had performed well.

Joe Kennedy was a newsboy, a bus driver, a Harvard athlete. He was a bank examiner, a bank president (the youngest in the United States, at age twenty-five). He built ships for Bethlehem Steel, when Franklin Roosevelt was Assistant Secretary of the Navy. If one reads his Vita, one could get the impression that he was a fly-by-night, undependable, flitting kind of person. Of course, the opposite was more true. He had brief stints with RCA, with the Film Booking offices of America, with Keith-Albee-Orpheum, and with Paramount Pictures, but in actuality, he was a Wall Street player who knew when to get out and how to make the most of his wealth.

The Little Flower of New York

Fiorello Henry La Guardia, the short, swarthy-faced mayor of New York City, had one the toughest political jobs in the United States. Yet he was recognized as one of the best mayors in New York history, attested by his election as president of the U.S. Conference of Mayors. He was a human dynamo, working an incredible schedule and flying almost daily to Washington to argue for more funds for New York City.

He was born in New York City. His father, Achilles La Guardia, was a cornetist and a conductor, who came to the United States with his wife, the former Irene Coen Luzatti, a Sephardic Jewess from Venice who was a piano accompanist. In the United States, Achilles became an army bandmaster, traveling to remote posts at Fort Sully, South Dakota, and to Whipple Barracks near Prescott, Arizona. Young Fiorello attended high school in Arizona; he learned to play the cornet and to share his mother's love of operas. He also learned to make an excellent pasta sauce in his mother's kitchen.

Achilles La Guardia died in Arizona after eating some tainted army rations, and Fiorello was taken by his mother to Budapest and Trieste, where he acquired some of the language skills he would use at Ellis Island and as mayor. He was only nine years old when he got a job in Trieste as an interpreter. In 1906, La Guardia returned to New York City, where he became the most famous interpreter who worked on Ellis Island. He was hired because he spoke Croatian, Italian, Yiddish, and Hungarian. He worked seven days per week for two years, at a time when immigration was at an all-time peak (1906-1907). His strenuous schedule called for more stamina than most people possessed; the grind was constant from the moment he put on his uniform until he took the boat back to the mainland to go to evening classes at the New York University Law School.

For a time in 1907, Ellis Island was processing ten thousand persons per day. It was at Ellis Island that La Guardia began his reform movement that eventually would propel him into the mayor's office. His duties were many: he worked with the sane and the insane, with the sick and the well; he often accompanied couples who were about to be married to New York City Hall. La Guardia would accompany bride and groom, witness the ceremony, and then give the bride clearance to enter the country. He soon learned that the alderman who was performing the weddings was overcharging the couples and taking bribes. As mayor, he fought "this contemptible petty thievery."[20]

During World War I, the obstinate Little Flower refused to accept his rejection for military service because of his height (he was only five-feet-two), so he took flying lessons and served in the American squadron in France. Following the war, he was elected a Republican member of Congress, where he was frustrated by the lack of progress in fighting political "pork." His opponents called him "Blackguardia," but he was a success in combatting "Yellow Dog" contracts and in fighting for the repeal of Prohibition. He was so popular that he received the votes of Socialists, Liberals, and Progressives. He also won the Italian and Jewish votes by making campaign speeches in those languages.

He lost his seat in Congress in 1932 with the Roosevelt sweep, but when the people rebeled against the philandering, fraudulent leaders of Tammany Hall, he was chosen as a reform candidate on the nonpolitical Fusion ticket for mayor. At one of the rallies La Guardia thanked his sponsors but told them, "Don't expect any patronage if I'm elected." He was true to his word. He got a new city charter; balanced the budget; cut his own salary; obtained funds for hospitals, highways, and low-cost housing developments; and even built a new airport at North Beach (which they later named for him).

La Guardia carried on a workload that was reminiscent of his days on Ellis Island. His grueling schedule was featured in the *New York Times* of August 17,

1939, which called him a "human dynamo." He abhorred dictators. One time, when he was called to provide an escort for a German delegation visiting the city, he assigned an all-Jewish group for the task.

Gunther calls him "the most spectacular mayor the greatest city in the world ever had," and then he tells why: "the volatile realism, the rubber-supple grin, the flamboyant energy, the zest for honesty in public life, the occasional vulgarisms, the common sense."[21] In an interview with Gunther, La Guardia gave some telling responses:

Gunther:	"Whom do you hate most?"
La Guardia:	(Grunting). "Hitler."
Gunther:	"What do you like most?"
La Guardia:	"Music."
Gunther:	"What do you believe in most?"
La Gurdia:	(Smiling). "Children."

The Little Flower could be intense, religious, puzzling, or holy. He often quoted Scripture, and he pounded his desk when riled, especially when he believed that he saw injustice anywhere in his administration. On more than one occasion, he screamed in that high, squeaky voice of his, "So long as I'm the mayor, regardless of race or religion, everybody in this city gets treated on merit and alike."

La Guardia, the half-Italian, half-Jew, the five-foot man with the squeaky voice and the corn-cob pipe, had an enormous impact on New Deal spending. He inherited several troublesome projects. One was the Triborough Bridge—"the bridge to nowhere." It was supposed to connect Manhattan, Queens, and the Bronx. Fiorello decided that his best bet in getting funds to complete the project was personal contacts with President Roosevelt. The mayor made almost daily flights to Washington. One in five jobs created by the Roosevelt Administration went to New York City. La Guardia opened up jobs for Jews and Italians, who had been shut out by Jimmy Walker and the Tammany Hall Irish.

But Robert Moses was the instrument of the Mayor's successes. In 1939, in addition to being the chief executive of the New York World's Fair Commission, he was the City Parks Commissioner, the State Parks Commissioner and Chairman of the Triborough Bridge Authority. In reshaping New York City in the 1930s, Moses often broke the mayor's rules and city laws, over which they fought constantly. They were a sight: the stocky, ebullient Mayor and the grand, hauty Commissioner who was a foot taller. Their love-hate relationship produced an urban miracle. Moses built three new bridges, miles of new highways and 255 new playgrounds—more than double the existing number. Although Caro denounced Moses as ruthless and power-hungry, he recognized Moses' genius for being a quintessential visionary.[22]

As Fiorello went about building roads, clearing slums and cleaning up the city, he faced two problems, only one he knew about. What he didn't know was that Robert Moses had feuded with President Roosevelt. Moses had ridiculed the

President as a "cripple" and had mocked Eleanor's high voice. Roosevelt ordered Fiorello to fire Moses. When the mayor refused, Secretary Ickes cut off all of New York's funds.

This served to emphasize the other problem that Fiorello faced. Unemployment reached over 50 percent in Harlem. Congressman Adam Clayton Powell, Jr., led the picketers and protesters against City Hall and against Jewish merchants who refused to hire blacks. When the Long Island to Harlem bridge was completed to 125th street (the very heart of black New York City), no blacks were hired in the construction, because unions controlled hiring practices. La Guardia, who knew discrimination from experience, was sympathetic, and by 1939, blacks had much more influence in the La Guardia Administration.

FDR AND THE "JEW DEAL"

Franklin Roosevelt had it both ways. On the one hand, he was accused of being an anti-Semite, because he refused to allow the Jewish refugees from the *Saint Louis* to land at an American port, and on the other hand, he was vilified by some of the American press for having so many Jews in his Administration. He was accordingly called "Rosenfeld" and his Administration was labeled the "Jew Deal." The Frankfurter-Brandeis connection at Harvard provided many of these "Happy Hot Dogs"—as they were known. Roosevelt, who was a strong liberal, thought that he should appoint talented people, regardless of their religion, but he had to contend with the anti-Semitism that pervaded American society in 1939. A typical description was, "You can't find an official in the whole government who hasn't got a damned Jew lawyer sitting by him at his desk."[23]

Many of these attorneys were compelled to accept government jobs, because the WASP tycoons of Wall Street would not hire them. The Harvard Law School for years followed an unwritten quota system for the admission of Jews. President Abbott L. Lowell excused this discrimination by explaining that it was in the best interest of the university to limit the number of Jews, especially those less desirable Jews from Eastern Europe. Admissions officers spoke of "good" and "bad" Jews—the bad ones being persons who lived up to the stereotypes. Other professional schools also had their quotas, and scientists were not exempt. Einstein, being German, was a "good" Jew.

But even FDR was ambivalent on this subject. As a member of the Harvard Board of Overseers, he had voted earlier in favor of quotas that were designed to reduce the percentage of Jews in the freshman class from 30-15 percent. Roosevelt preferred Jews who were more "American" and less "Jewish." Yet, he was very pleased with his many Jewish lawyers; he thought they were some of "the best minds."

At one point, FDR spoke of a preference for "tenement lawyers," but few of his appointments came from a tenement home—most of his Jewish lawyers came from the middle and upper classes. These included, in addition to Brandeis and Frankfurter, Bernard Baruch, Samuel Rosenman, Joseph Lash, Henry Morgenthau, Jr., Jerome Frank, Benjamin Cohen, David E. Lilienthal, David Niles, and Abe Fortas. Oddly, the Jews comprised approximately 15 percent of his top appointments—the exact ratio that the Harvard Board had agreed on earlier.

POLITICS, NOT AS USUAL

The Second New Deal

The New Deal produced an unusual condition: the President and the Vice President disagreed over policy. Roosevelt and John Garner agreed on regulations regarding abuses of power in the capitalist system, but they began to disagree when Roosevelt suggested abandoning the balanced budget idea to promote his welfare state. Garner was willing to accept the concept as a temporary measure, but he believed that the President was using welfare to build up his political power.

When Garner opposed some labor policies that he considered abuses of power, John L. Lewis called him a "Tobacco-chewing, whiskey-drinking, poker-playing evil old man." The Vice President was piqued. He drank whiskey and chewed tobacco only moderately, but there was nothing evil about this man. As Majority Leader and Speaker of the House, he was loyal to New Deal programs. Garner accepted those that were far to the left of his liking, but when Roosevelt tried to pack the Supreme Court, the Vice President got off the bandwagon. This rift made Garner unacceptable as a running mate.

Roosevelt remained a liberal to his death. He explained what that meant to a Young Democrats Club, on August 8, 1939:

Liberals are those who, unlike the radicals who want to tear up everything by the roots and plant new and untried seeds, desire to use the existing plants of civilization, to select the best of them, to water them and make them grow—not only for the present use of mankind, but also for the use of generations to come. That is why I call myself a liberal, and that is why, even if we go to the modern contraption of polls of public opinion, an overwhelming majority of younger men and women throughout the United States are on the liberal side of things.[24]

On another occasion, he differentiated liberals and conservatives.

I am reminded of four definitions:
A Radical is a man with both feet firmly planted in the air.
A Conservative is a man with two perfectly good legs who, however, has never learned to walk forward.
A Reactionary is a somnambulist walking backwards.
A Liberal is a man who uses his legs and his hands at the behest—at the command—of his head.[25]

Roosevelt was a master at consensus building; he was good, but he also wanted to be liked by everyone. He told visitors what they wanted to hear. The compromises he made in his second term diminished the accomplishments of his first term. The growing number of opponents saw him surrendering to big business and giving in on the Jewish question and the matter of fiscal conservatism. In all these cases, his advisers disagreed.

Kenneth Davis adds another disappointment of Roosevelt's second term: his foreign policy, which failed to challenge a small, vocal band of isolationists. He opines that a stronger show of power could have defeated the neutrality lobby, which contributed to Europe's inability to confront Hitler. Davis claimed that the President was speaking out of both sides of his mouth, thereby missing several chances to diminish the chances of war.[26] Roosevelt was a complicated person. It would be difficult to find a better description of the complex being that was FDR than the statement of Robert Sherwood, who wrote many of Roosevelt's lines. He found the President impossible to understand.

His character was not only multiplex; it was contradictory to a bewildering degree. He was hard and he was soft. At times he displayed a capacity for vindictiveness which could be described as petty, and at other times he demonstrated the Christian spirit of forgiveness and charity in its purist form. He could be a ruthless politician, but he was the champion of friends and associates who for him were political liabilities, conspicuously Harry Hopkins, and of causes which apparently competent advisers assured him would constitute political suicide. He could appear to be utterly cynical, worldly, illusionless, and yet his religion was the strongest and most mysterious force that was in him.[27]

The Third Term

The chief political question of 1939 was whether President Roosevelt would run for a third term. Since George Washington's definitive statement against the practice, no president had given it serious thought. But 1939 was different. Europe was at war, and if the United States were to enter, it would mean changing Commanders in Chief in the middle of fighting.

Roosevelt, the consummate politician, knew that he did not need to disclose his hand early. He wavered, because he longed to be home with his children, his stamp collection, and his boats, but he feared the international crisis. Eleanor was just as confused. She knew that there was so much undone, especially for the blacks and the poor. As she ruminated: the first term restored hope, reformed government, and added welfare; in the second term, FDR was more helpless, and he could not prevent war in Europe. What could he accomplish in a third term?

If he did not run for a third term, how, FDR wondered, could he keep his foreign and domestic policies alive? He was concerned because in 1938 Congress had defeated his plan to enlarge the Supreme Court, and conservatives of both parties were blocking his reform legislation. Roosevelt worried that this growing trend would place a conservative in the White House, and he feared most for the unemployed.

The President jibed at reporters about a third term and said he would be available to students in the summer of 1941. Not only would he not run again, but he would not recommend a choice for his successor. His dilemma was that Cordell Hull, his Secretary of State, was the most knowledgeable about foreign policy, but he was fairly conservative on most domestic issues. There was much talk of a combination ticket of Vice President John Garner and a young liberal such as Justice William O. Douglas.

Even facing retirement, the President seemed to put politics into all his moves. When FDR appointed Myron Taylor to be his special envoy to the Pope, he said it was because of the importance of the Vatican as a listening post, but the President also hoped that the designation might induce American Catholics to look more favorably towards his foreign policy.

War complicated Roosevelt's decision on a third term. Roosevelt needed to build a new American consensus on foreign policy—one that would permit him to oppose dictators and at the same time, to find new ways of dealing effectively with the Congress, while preserving his status in public opinion polls. FDR knew that an isolationist policy would be disastrous; he fully expected us to be in the war, as Churchill kept telling him. His safest political course was to work within the hemisphere. His first result came out of a Conference of the Latin American States in Panama. He proposed a Declaration of Panama, under which there would be a neutral zone created, which would extend three hundred miles out to sea.

FILLING THE HIGH COURT

The Jewish Seat

On January 5, 1939 Felix Frankfurter was nominated to be Associate Justice of the Supreme Court of the United States. It was not a popular choice. Father Coughlin called him the "Iago of the Administration," and others called him a Bolshevik and a Marxist. He was neither.

Frankfurter may be the most distinguished alumnus of Ellis Island. Born on November 15, 1882, in Vienna, Austria, to Leopold and Emma Frankfurter, he came to the United States in 1894 aboard the *Marsala*, a "typical immigration tub," having come steerage. Frankfurter was a stocky 5' 5" man with a balding head, beady eyes, and a keen mind, but because his father was a merchant of modest means, young Felix attended Public School No. 25 on New York's East Side. He next enrolled at the College of the City of New York (now CUNY) in 1902 and the Harvard Law School in 1906. Upon graduating, with the highest honors, he became an assistant to Henry L. Stimson, the U.S. Attorney for the Southern District of New York State.

During World War I, Frankfurter served on the War Labor Policies Board, and when the United States entered the conflict, he served as Assistant to Secretary of War Newton Baker. He resigned his government work to accept the Byrne Chair of Administrative Law at Harvard. He took leave from this post to serve as visiting professor at Oxford, returning to Harvard, where he remained until 1939, when President Roosevelt appointed him Associate Justice to succeed Benjamin N. Cardozo, to what was considered to be the "Jewish Seat" of the Court. Frankfurter established a reputation for his attempt to interpret the law while taking social and economic conditions into consideration. He was aware that the Court must have a role in "the dynamic process of American society."

Frankfurter was a Brandeis disciple. They each came from the economic side of law. Both were involved with monopoly, labor law, and public utility regulation—subjects which Frankfurter taught at Harvard. One student expressed his view of Frankfurter's teaching:

> You learn no law in Public U
> That is its fascination
> But Felix gives a point of view
> And pleasant conversation.[28]

Frankfurter believed that monopolies engaged in predatory practices, and he distrusted corporate lawyers who defended them. Having rejected the corporate view, he encouraged his students to take up union causes. But his sympathy for labor did not cause him to embrace the common man. He only cavorted with "first-rate" people. In Felix Frankfurter, the President found a justice who had a grasp of economic matters and a passion for justice. His technical knowledge of the law was unsurpassed, and he combined it with a zeal for the problems of humanity.

The Other Seat

William Orville Douglas was nominated to the Supreme Court on March 20, 1939. At forty years of age, he was the sixth youngest nominee ever. He followed Hugo Black, Stanley Reed, and Felix Frankfurter as Roosevelt appointees. In appointing Douglas, FDR showed that he was less interested in where a justice resided than whether he believed fervently in the principles of the New Deal.

Douglas, the son of an itinerant Scottish minister, was born in Maine, Minnesota, near Sauk Center of Sinclair Lewis fame. When his father died, the family moved to Yakima, Washington. In the family struggle to survive, young Bill sold newspapers and collected junk.

He came to the nation's capital from Columbia University, but he grew up and kept a summer home at Goose Prairie, Washington. He contracted polio as a child, which gave him his life-long interest in outdoor activities. He hiked for miles to restore strength to his weak legs.

He left Columbia for Washington in 1936 when President Roosevelt appointed him to the new Securities and Exchange Commission, where he served first as member and then as chairman until he was called to a vacant chair on the Supreme Court. He went to the Court well versed in corporation finance and business organization, topics that were the subjects of his legal teachings at Yale. As the Sterling Professor of law, he was voted the nation's outstanding law professor.

He was passionately attached to the concept of due process, which made him one of the most liberal justices ever to serve on the Supreme Court. He was a constant defender of First Amendment rights. He also believed that the law should be a growing, progressive instrument—one that should serve "the over-complicated social and economic problems of today."[29]

A Klansman on the Court

Supreme Court Justice Hugo La Fayette Black rose above the bigotry of his youth to become a dominant figure in the reinterpretation of American law. Black, a native Alabaman, graduated from the Alabama Law School and started practicing in Birmingham. He had to fight within himself to define his political position. Would he join the conservative Democrats or the Populists (there were few Republicans in Alabama at that time)?

Black knew that in the 1920s the Ku Klux Klan controlled the politics of most of the South and much of the Midwest. To win in Alabama, he needed the support of the Klan, therefore Black became an active member, and he agreed to serve as an officer of the local chapter. The support of the KKK helped him to win a seat in the United States Senate in 1926. His political posture there reflected his roots: he ranted against miscegenation, against allowing blacks to vote, and against the threat of increased immigration. To all appearances, he was another southern racist.

But slowly, he realized that the law was just only if it protected the rights of individuals, including blacks. His metamorphosis was nearly complete during his second term in the Senate, when all his bigoted speeches ceased, and he commenced making liberal speeches about the rights of individuals. These utterances convinced Roosevelt that Black would be a liberal and effective justice; his nomination to the Court came in 1937. Somehow, the President did not know that Black had been a member of the KKK—he found out when the news was emblazoned across all of the country's newspapers. How could the liberal Roosevelt appoint a bigot to the high court, they asked. By then, Black had long resigned from the Klan and acknowledged his membership publicly.[30]

Black was captivated by the words of the First and Fourteenth Amendments. These principles were upheld in a 1939 case, for which Black wrote the opinion of the Court. In *Chambers v. Florida*, the conviction of four black men was overturned because they had been arrested and held without bail or counsel. Black wrote: "No higher duty, no more solemn responsibility, rests upon this Court than that of translating into living law and maintaining this constitutional shield deliberately planned and inscribed for the benefit of every human being subject to our Constitution—of whatever race, creed or persuasion."

HUAC

Martin Dies

The congressional power to investigate was used often to arouse public opinion against New Deal policies. At the start of the 1939 session of Congress, the Republicans announced their intentions of investigating the improper use of funds in the WPA. The task was to assuage Martin Dies, the square-jawed Chairman of the House Un-American Activities Committee (HUAC), who feasted on jibes at cabinet members. Roosevelt had to move cautiously because Dies had managed to obtain a huge increase in appropriations for his committee. It could continue its fishing expedition looking for communists in the executive branch.

Dies had the support of America Firsters. They were a powerful lot, including Senators Hiram Warren Johnson of California, William Borah of Idaho, Burton K. Wheeler of Montana, Robert A. Taft of Ohio, Gerald P. Nye of North Dakota, Robert M. LaFollette of Wisconsin and aviator Charles A. Lindbergh. Their speeches included excerpts from the Washington Farewell Address, and especially from the Monroe Doctrine. They were honest, superpatriots who railed against any form of tyranny, even if some of their methods were tyrannical.

The Joseph McCarthy of his day, Martin Dies, of Orange, Texas, gained a certain legitimacy when his committee found a few Communists in the Department of Labor, in the Federal Theatre and in the unions. Young Martin grew up in Washington, D.C., not Texas; his father was a congressman from 1913 to 1919. When Martin ran for Congress himself, his only plank was against the Ku Klux Klan, which had little power in his district. Reelection came easy. Dies, the boyish-looking six footer, spent a lot of time telling Texas tales. His long cigars made him appear older, and he was quick to take up any issue that involved God or country. He swore, however, that he had no political ambitions; he was only interested in protecting the United States for his wife and three boys.

When Dies was elected to Congress, he was a staunch New Dealer; he believed in inflating the depressed economy, and he was a critic of the conservative Supreme Court. Although his academic achievements were somewhat tainted (he had a law degree from the National University of Washington, D.C.), he achieved a seat on the powerful House Rules Committee, because it was said that he was a protege of Vice President Garner.

Beginning in 1936, Dies's stripes began to change. He was ceaseless in his efforts to convince House leaders that there were situations that should be investigated. He said that all aliens should be deported, and he took a strong position against the sit-down strikes. Dies saw immigration as the cause of city slums and the "isms" that crowding engendered. Each year, he put in bills that would have acted on these issues, but they went nowhere.

As Dies kept whispering John Garner's name everywhere, he gained prestige and became one of the leading anti-Roosevelt Democrats. Dies was determined to stake out an area in which he could make his name. He found it in 1938 when he learned from Representative Dickstein of New York that Fritz Kuhn and the German-American Bund were acting like Nazis. They convinced the leadership of the house to establish the Committee to Investigate Un-American Activities, with Dies as Chairman and with an appropriation of $25,000.

By some devious scheming, Dies was selected chairman of the new HUAC, which set the stage for him to turn the committee against the Jews in the name of anticommunism. Dies was a nativist who was opposed to anything involving immigration. He particularly disliked aliens, he called them all "enemy aliens," and he wanted to deport them. In fact, in his first day in the Congress, he introduced legislation to cease all immigration for five years.

Representative Dies seemed like a jovial, cigar-smoking clown, but his pursuit of communists in the government and out was not funny. He knew the ways of Washington; he knew that those who headed congressional committees got the limelight. It mattered not what you investigated.

At a news conference, President Roosevelt accused the Dies Committee of making no effort to get to the truth and allowing personal opinion to pass as facts.[31] But Dies persisted. He was able, in January 1939, to have the Committee's appropriation increased substantially, allowing him to increase the staff with former FBI agents.

Dies and his committee were just beginning. The tentacles of their investigative octopus reached out further. No group was safe. The American Youth Congress was listed with the Consumers' Union and the League of Women Shoppers as "transmission belts" for the communist movement in the United States. Dies was fortunate, because he found a suitable target when the American Federation of Labor accused the CIO of being communist dominated. In this, he had found his niche; he received mountains of mail from people who were willing to expose communists in the labor movement.

During his first committee hearings he promised to be impartial and fair and courteous. He even promised not to use smear tactics. But soon he began to malign innocent people. Witnesses singled out Frank Murphy, the Michigan nominee for governor and the Hollywood Reds (someone mentioned Shirley Temple in this category).

It is one of those major ironies of history that the House Committee on Un-American Activities (HUAC) was created to investigate Nazi propaganda in the United States. The idea for a committee on un-Americanism originated with

Representative Hamilton Fish, the congressman from President Roosevelt's Hyde Park district.

The Jews of Hollywood

The Jews of Hollywood generally backed liberal causes—they called them "good causes." They were strong New Dealers, and they supported the Republican side in the Spanish Civil War. The cause that motivated them most was the Anti-Nazi League. By 1939 it was the primary vehicle of activism in the Hollywood Jewish Community.

The League's mandate was very broad: it condemned Hitler, but it also offered strong support for the Federal Theatre Project, which was in danger of abolition. It published its own weekly newspaper, which encouraged those who were attempting to pass legislation dealing with child labor, youth unemployment, and women at work. For this, it was called a communist front. The charges, though false, had a certain validity for the time, because the Communist Party of the United States (CPUSA) had a group in Hollywood addressing many of the same causes. The League and the CPUSA tended to work together, so it was simple for the right wing to link them.

The Communist party in Hollywood was a writer's party, and it was heavily populated with Jews. Budd Schulberg may be prototypical of the young Hollywood writers of the 1930s. The son of B. P. Schulberg, the head of production at Paramount Pictures, he joined some liberal causes, then became a member of the Communist party in 1937. In that year, he wrote a short story, "What Makes Sammy Run," which was published in *Liberty Magazine*, and which was turned into a novel in 1939. It was the story of Sammy Glick, who rose to the top of Hollywood by using indecent and immoral strategies.

It became a sensation as "the" Hollywood novel. It was seen, rightly, as a work on the psychology of the Hollywood mogul, but it raised all the old stereotypes anew. Did all Jews have money? Were they all pushy? Or was Sammy simply rebelling against his father's pushiness? Mayer and the other Hollywood Jews were not seeking answers to these questions: they wanted B. P. Schulberg to tell his son not to publish the novel, which touched so many nerves.

Dies was convinced that the Anti-Nazi League was communist dominated. He challenged the very essence of what it meant to be a Jew in the United States. He suggested that Jewish movie producers create some anticommunist films to prove their Americanism.[32] Although the Jews spoke of taking the offensive against HUAC, it was just talk, and the committee was free to leave the impression that there was a link between Judaism and communism and that Jews were somehow "an alien element" in the United States.

Some of Dies's friends were openly anti-Semitic, and he constantly spoke of his Christian heritage. It got worse for Jews. His first witness was a member of the Nazi Bund; the second was a publisher of a fascist magazine. Then came some big names, such as Gerald L. K. Smith, the reverend who was an anti-Semite, and James Colescott, the Imperial Wizard of the Ku Klux Klan. Dies was after communists, not fascists. It was Christ against Marx. And when Dies saw communists, he saw Jews.

Dies found plenty to scrutinize, especially Roosevelt's programs and policies. By September 1939, when HUAC had been in existence for almost a year, Dies arranged to start publishing names of communists and "fellow travelers" who were government employees. The first included 563 names taken from the membership rolls of the League for Peace and Democracy—a group Dies suspected of being communist dominated.[33]

The House Un-American Activities Committee was very popular with Americans—three-fourths of whom wanted the work of the committee to continue. But Dies did not have the stage to himself, because he was treading on the turf of J. Edgar Hoover. The FBI head was far more skillful in massing public opinion in his favor, so Dies was constrained in his efforts to hog the conspicuous position in the public eye. Hoover, not Dies, was the personification of the decent, honest and democratic way of life.

Communists in the CIO

On September 11, 1939, the House Un-American Activities Committee heard testimony from Ben Gitlow, a former Communist party leader, that the party was "instrumental to a very large degree" in the establishment of the CIO. His statement contradicted the contents of a letter received earlier from John Brophy, Executive Director of the union, which denied that the CIO had ever received money from the communists. According to Gitlow, the Communist International had sent funds regularly since Brophy ran for the presidency of the United Mine Workers of America in 1926.

Gitlow alleged that a dozen or more leaders of the CIO were recent or former members of the party and were beneficiaries of the party's financial support. He claimed they were all "followers of the party line." Gitlow brought with him minutes of the 1927 meeting of the Trade Union Committee of the Communist party, which recommended that Brophy claim that John L. Lewis had stolen the election, and it urged Brophy to issue a statement so indicating, to which Martin Dies, chairman of HUAC said, "I don't see how you could have more convincing evidence than that."[34]

Among those named by Gitlow as communists or former communists were: Lee Pressman, CIO general counsel—who was called "one of Stalin's main men;" Donald Henderson, head of the Cannery Workers Union—his Communist party membership was "a matter of public record; "Marcel Scherer, head of the Federation of Architects, Engineers, Chemists, and Technicians, who Gitlow claimed, was a member "since the party's inception"; Ben Gold, head of the Furrier Union; Harry Bridges, head of the West Coast Maritime Union; Powers Hapgood, head of Shoe Workers' Union; and Heywood Broun, head of the

American Newspaper Guild. Gitlow said, also, that "Sidney Hillman, head of the Amalgamated Clothing Workers Union, supported the communists until 1922."

Harry R. Bridges, whom Gitlow had named as a Communist party member, was at that very time fighting deportation on that charge. John Gunther wrote that Bridges was "Lean, boyish, alert, with hawklike humor and a touch of the dapper," which reminded him of Jimmy Walker, the Mayor of New York City.[35] The Labor Department served a warrant for Bridge's arrest on March 5, 1938, but on April 6, 1939, the United States Circuit Court of Appeals ruled in the Strecker case that membership in the communist party was not grounds for deportation.

Bridges had a long history of making Marxist-type statements, some of which he learned from his uncles in his native Melbourne, Australia. These ideas undermined his idea of becoming a priest, and they led him to the sea and San Francisco. He married there, became a member of a longshoremen's union and applied for American citizenship.

During the 1934 maritime strike, which was a general strike in San Francisco, Bridges rose to the top of the union. His cries of unity thrust him into the lead of the Joint Strike Committee, and when Lee Holman, president of the longshoremen's union, was removed from office, Bridges was ready. Partly to allay fears of communist domination, Bridges broke up the Maritime Workers Industrial Union in favor of his International Longshoremen's and Warehousemen's Union.

Bridges antagonized San Franciscans by siding with the farm workers in their efforts to unionize. His union allowed fruit to rot on the docks of Los Angeles, Seattle, San Diego, as well as San Francisco. This caused more intense resentment and hatred towards Bridges, who rankled labor leaders as well. He refused to adopt the views of Harry Lundeberg on union tactics. Lundeberg preferred the IWW (Wobbly) approach of avoiding political ties in favor of economic pressure. Their friendship soured considerably when John L. Lewis chose Bridges to head the West Coast branch of the CIO.

Bridges hated Dave Beck, the vice president of the Teamsters Union, and Beck hated him back. Beck loathed socialism. He was an ardent admirer of capitalism, because he believed that he could achieve wage increases if business was prosperous. Curiously, he was a staunch advocate of the New Deal, though being a conservative at the state level. These views put him at odds with Harry Bridges.

The U.S. Commissioner of Immigration Edward Cahill was urged to start deportation proceedings. He investigated and reported that he could find no worthy evidence that would be admissible in court that Bridges was a communist or that he had advocated the overthrow of the United States government. When faced with the same pressure, Secretary of Labor Frances Perkins stated that she would act when the Supreme Court decided the Strecker case. Bridges' trial was conducted on Angel Island, California by James M.

Landis, Dean of the Harvard Law School. The flimsy evidence was chiefly the statements of two rival labor leaders, who hated Bridges. Dean Landis quickly dismissed the case.[36]

HUAC and the German-American Bund

As Hitler gained power in Germany, German-Americans began to use propaganda and fifth-column activities in the United States. In 1932, they formed the "Friends of the New Germany" in Chicago, which was closely connected with the Nazi party in Germany. Most members were German immigrants who became American citizens. They were prepared to help Hitler "at the critical moment." Meanwhile, they held German Day celebrations that had little support among non-Germans.

When the Bund had been known as the Friends of the New Germany, it was controlled by Heinz Spanknoebel and Fritz Gissibl, two veterans of Hitler's 1923 attempt to take over Germany. Arriving in the United States, they tried unsuccessfully to take over the German-American organizations, some of which dated to the nineteenth century. When Hitler did take command of Germany in 1933, Spanknoebel and Gissibl began a bitter struggle for control of the Friends. The Hitler government considered the fight so damaging that it forbade membership in the Friends for all German nationals in the United States.

At this point, seizing the opportunity, Fritz Julius Kuhn became national leader of the Friends. He was a German immigrant who was also one of Hitler's original followers in Munich in 1923. He came to the United States and got a job at the Ford River Rouge plant at Dearborn, Michigan. Soon he became a leader of the Detroit Bund. There is no record that Henry Ford ever knew of Kuhn's subversive activities, although Ford had a penchant for hiring persons of questionable character.

Kuhn announced that there would be a new direction. He would lead the Bund into an era of "German principles," and it would be called Americanism. Kuhn's first step was to change the name of the organization from the Friends to the German-American Bund; then, he changed its uniforms—dropping the black breeches and riding boots—and adopting one that looked like that of the American Legion. He declared, further, that the German flag would not be flown at meetings, except on German national holidays. The American flag and the Bund flag, with its swastika, would wave side by side, as a sign of "Aryan supremacy."[37]

On February 20, 1939, the German-American Bund held a rally at Madison Square Garden. The gathering was a celebration of Washington's birthday. Mayor La Guardia acknowledged that he had received both protest and bomb threats against the Bund, but he said, "If they bomb it, we'll catch the bombers." Nevertheless, fearing violence, the police had blocked all side streets from 47th to 51st streets, to guarantee that only Bund members could enter the Garden.[38]

By 8:00 P.M., when the rally began, there were 15,000 persons in their seats, the number reaching 18,900 shortly after. Nazi banners proclaimed the views of the attendees: "Smash Jewish Communism." Outside there were different signs: "Smash Anti-Semitism," and "Drive the Nazis out of New York."

The meeting commenced with the singing of "The Star Spangled Banner." The national secretary began his speech with the phrase, "My fellow Christian Americans." There were cheers, but a thunderous roar filled the Garden when a speaker denounced President Roosevelt (pronounced Rosenfeld). Kuhn was the featured speaker, and he did not disappoint the Jew haters. He swore that he would protect his children and his home from those who would turn the United States into a "Bolshevik paradise."

Roosevelt, who was roasted by Bund members, was also a target of the German press. They accused him of contriving tensions among European nations, especially over the forthcoming trade talks between England and Germany. The Germans called them a positive step following the Munich accord, but Churchill and Roosevelt were not impressed with this gesture as a peace move. The *Deutsche Allgemeine Zeitung* blamed any tensions on "the presumptuous speeches and utterances of the American President."

Fearing that FDR would have a major impact on the policies of the Western nations, the German press leveled new attacks. The Germans denigrated Roosevelt's talks of a European crisis as an effort to divert attention from his domestic difficulties. The *Nauchtausgabe* accused him of "seeing ghosts." At the same time, Captain Fritz Wiedemann, on Hitler's orders, was sent to San Francisco as German Consul General to promote good will between Germany and the United States.

Although most Jews were outraged at the Bund rally, the American Jewish Committee supported the Nazis right to meet. It stated that the management of the Garden was correct in allowing the meeting. But the committee sent a letter on February 18 to go on record that the Bund was an "anti-American and anti-democratic organization."

In May, following the February meeting of the Bund, Representative Dies found his cause when he learned from Representative Samuel Dickstein of New York that Fritz Kuhn and his German-American Bund had marched on the streets of New York City wearing Nazi regalia and carrying Nazi flags. Dies called hearings to investigate charges made by Bund members. Major General George Moseley testified to the existence of a Jewish-led communist organization that would soon overtake the country in a revolution. Moseley defended the meeting of the German-American Bund as "an antitoxin for the disease of Communism."

Fritz Kuhn was in and out of court. He got a summons for speeding on March 21, 1939; he was held for drunkenness and swearing at a policeman on July 17; and he pleaded guilty to speeding on September 10. But more serious was the charge that he had embezzled $14,548 of the society's funds.

The Charges Against the Federal Theatre

The Federal Theatre was the largest of the Works Progress Administration's projects. At its zenith, it employed thirteen thousand persons in thirty one states. It was one of the most controversial New Deal programs.[39] Over thirty million people attended WPA theatre project productions. These productions introduced Americans to names that would later be featured on theater marquees: William Bendix, William Baird, Joseph Cotton, Ed Gardner, Arthur Kennedy, Burt Lancaster, Arlene Francis, Rex Ingram, Canada Lee, Orson Welles, John Houseman, Arthur Miller, John Huston, and E. G. Marshall.

The HUAC approach against the Theatre was typical. The committee first reported on activities of communists who produced dramatic plays. John Lawson's drama of the class conflict between coal miners and the mine owners portrayed the striking miners as victims of the warmongering capitalists. It featured vigilantism and the KKK-staples of communist rhetoric of the time. Many plays produced by the Federal Theatre were seen by Congressman Dies as "un-American." The producers saw them as exposing injustices in American society—the same injustices that President Roosevelt cited in his second inaugural address, when he spoke of one-third of a nation being "ill housed, ill clad, and ill nourished."

Dies, not impressed with this argument, responded that a large number of employees on the Federal Theatre Project in New York City were members of the Communist party or were communist sympathizers. When questioned, Dies admitted that his committee had never attempted to quantify the "large number." In truth, when research was done, the numbers involved were a small minority of all the theatrical employees. These actors were seeking an organization that would offer hope against the unemployment lines, the hunger marches, the Hoover villages, and the growing ranks of the poor. They also feared that the capitalists would create a war fever against the Third Reich.

Hallie Flanagan, the Vassar professor who ran the Theatre, had confidence in the democratic process. She was quite willing to allow producers and actors to emphasize the injustices of the system without it overly influencing the ideologies of the audiences. Not so for Martin Dies, who had sworn to ferret out these malcontent laborers, whites and Negroes, farmers and intellectuals who were inciting "class consciousness"—a step away from communism.

Responding to the charge that communists were behind the Federal Theatre, that they were "peddling the party line" using drama as a prop for winning audiences, Flanagan issued orders that no communist plays were to be presented. At least one member of the Congress was not mollified. Everett M. Dirksen of Illinois, who was later to serve as the Republican minority leader of the Senate, had no kind words for the WPA productions. He mocked the titles of plays he had not seen, especially "Be Sure Your Sex Will Find You Out," "Cheating Husbands," and "A New Kind of Love" (he wondered aloud what that could be). It was good Republican fun, but it failed to note all of the excellent plays and musicals by leading Americans that were put on the stage.

The Federal Theatre began in 1934 with an expenditure of $28,000, and it ended with a budget of $27 million. From the beginning, it was the subject of intense Congressional investigations. HUAC called a long list of witnesses to prove that the Theatre was run by a bunch of communists. He worked closely in his search for communists with J. Parnell Thomas, a Republican member of his committee. Dies wanted Hallie Flanagan before his committee. She was ordered not to respond to these charges, but although many saw comedy in the hearings, she said, "It never seemed funny to me."[40]

When she did testify, reporters and stenographers jammed the high-walled chamber with the large chandeliers, which was filled with materials from the Federal Theatre. Because witnesses before the House Committee had questioned Flanagan's loyalty, on December 5, 1939, she responded to the charges: "I am not and never have been a Communist; that I am a registered Democrat; that I have never engaged in any communistic activities, or belonged to any communistic organizations. . . . I had planned and directed Federal Theatre from the first as an American enterprise."

The committee's questions exasperated her, and she called their methods "un-American." And she asked whether the committee members had ever read the plays they were criticizing, which inflamed Congressman Starnes, who forced her to apologize, and then he lectured her. "You are not here to ask the Committee questions. You are here to answer questions."

In only one case was Dies's claim of communist control on a more firm basis, because the Workers' Alliance (the theater union) was dominated by party regulars. Howard Lawson was a party member in 1939 who had written "Processional," a play about exploited coal miners. It was an expressionistic piece about social relevance that dealt with "cheating capitalists" and the noble proletariat. Many of the dance productions also had social themes. It seemed to follow Arthur Koestler's notion that the goal of the Communist party in the United States was to infiltrate the labor unions and the theatre groups.[41]

A second House Committee got involved in the investigation—the Sub-Committee on the House Committee on Appropriations (Clifton A. Woodrum, Chairman). Before this committee, the situation worsened for the Federal Theatre, because the committee used H. R. Burton, a paid investigator, to lead the probe. His job was to study the plays, their budgets and "any other matters relating thereto."

Again, the question of subversives came up. Dinsmore Walton, the manager of a New York project, claimed that he had been demoted for testifying against the Federal Theatre before the Dies Committee, and he intimated there were subversives in the WPA. The Committee ignored a long list of excellent productions that emanated from the Theatre, including *Abe Lincoln in Illinois*, *Pinocchio*, *Androcles and the Lion,* and *Playboy of the Western World.* For Congress, as Flanagan said, "Art seems like boondoggling to a congressman who is looking for a club with which to belabor the administration and there is always something in the Federal Theatre that can be blown up into a scandal. But . . . the Federal Theatre, which has brought art and ideas within the range of millions of people all over the country and proved that the potential theatre audience is inexhaustible."[42]

At one point in her testimony, Flanagan described the actors as exhibiting "Marlowesque madness," to which Democratic Congressman Joseph Starnes of Alabama asked, "Is he a Communist?" Again, Flanagan kept her cool, answering matter-of-factly that he was one of the greatest dramatists of Shakespeare's time. And, she added, the audiences at these WPA shows included teachers, industrialists, union leaders, ministers and priests, and thousands of young persons who had never seen a play before.

Roosevelt could not help, because the popularity of the New Deal was waning and the Congress had recently dealt him a number of political defeats, including the Supreme Court bill, the wages-and-hours bill, and the reorganization bill.[43] The WPA program was under total attack. There were charges of mismanaged funds in several places. The Federal Theatre had to go.

HYDE PARK

Toward the end of his second term, Roosevelt spoke more about retirement and about establishing a presidential library. Roosevelt intended to retire to Hyde Park, New York, where his books, papers, and mementos would be located. He hoped that Harry Hopkins would join him there. FDR promised him a cottage and a professorship at Vassar. Hopkins was very ill in 1939, so these options were attractive to him, particularly because he had become very close to Eleanor Roosevelt in his daily administration of the WPA programs. The two Roosevelts were very fond of the "down-to-earth, unsentimental reformer who understood the political game."[44]

When FDR chose Hyde Park for his library, many did not approve. They said it was too remote, to which the President responded that the place was just two and one-half hours from New York City and just over four miles from Poughkeepsie, where there were ample hotels. Some objected to the fragmentation of presidential papers, and for them what was good enough for Washington and Jefferson (the National Archives) was good enough for Roosevelt.

The President was adamant. He asked the archivists to survey the magnitude of the collection to be housed there, and he requested that the Democratic party commence a fund drive to pay for the entire cost of construction. As expected, the most caustic comments came from Republicans. One in Chicago wrote: "The decent citizens of this country are only anxious to forget the stench of your egotistical, incompetent, unscrupulous and unspeakably costly administration." Another called FDR an "egocentric megalomaniac."[45]

After some legislative finagling by Majority Leader Sam Rayburn, the bill to authorize the federal government to accept Roosevelt's papers passed the House on July 3, 1939 (the Senate had approved it earlier). On November 19, 1939, when the cornerstone was laid, Roosevelt was the principal speaker at the ceremony. He remembered the tranquility of his youth, then he said, "This is a peaceful country-side and it seems appropriate that in this time of strife we should dedicate the library to the spirit of peace." At the ceremony, poet Archibald MacLeish said these are the records of "the man who refused, in the name of his generation, to continue to accept what was no longer acceptable— the man who demanded, for his generation, what his generation had the courage to expect. . . . They belong by themselves, here in this river country, on the land from which they came."[46]

THE LEGACY OF THE NEW DEAL

How did Americans of 1939 view the record of the New Deal? A Gallup poll in June indicated that they rated relief as the major issue of their time, and they gave the federal programs a high place in their assessment—28 percent listed it as the "greatest achievement." The second-place finisher is surprising—21 percent voted for banking reform. Other favorable programs were as expected: The Civilian Conservation Corps, Social Security legislation, and farm programs followed next. On the negative side, the poll showed that "spending policy," "crop control," and foreign policy "meddling" were concerns.[47]

The people either loved FDR or hated him. He received five to eight hundred letters per day, in which he was a savior or a scoundrel. But fully 85 percent of American newspapers were anti-FDR, led by the venomous *Chicago Tribune*. The letters ran a wide gamut:

Mr. President:

   If you could get around the country as I have and seen the distress forced upon the American people, you would throw your damn NRA and AAA, and every other God-damned A into the sea, before you and your crooked crowd are taken out as they are in Germany and that is just what you and the rest deserve.

Dear Honored Mr. Roosevelt:

   I never saw a President I would write to until you've got in your place, but I have always felt like you and your wife and your children were as common as we are.

My Dear Sir:

   It is expensive and a headache to have a playboy as a President. Wipe that grin off your face.[48]

Economic historians have tried for years to answer the question, "Did the New Deal fail?" Those who agree state that it was World War II that restored

American prosperity, not the New Deal. They say flatly that Roosevelt failed to solve the unemployment problem; when war began in Europe in September 1939, there were still eight to nine million unemployed Americans.

But economic arguments cannot provide a full answer to the question. The Great Depression ripped the fabric of our society. It was sundered worse than at any time since Lincoln faced the problems of a nation trying to dissect itself. For a short time, it appeared that the economic engine would stop. Revolution was in the air as angry bonus marchers tried to raid the Capitol Building in Washington, and communists tried to foment a nationwide revolution.

Roosevelt, acting deftly, thwarted communists and fascists by moving slightly leftward and by offering a revolutionary, peaceful response to the crisis. He was successful in shifting power, through a social revolution, from Wall Street to Main Street. It was a peaceful and bloodless shift (President Hoover had used the army to drive the bonus army from Washington).

The immediate effect of the New Deal was the shift of political power to Washington. The Democratic party was strengthened immensely, and the Republican party was greatly liberalized. New Deal spending had a lasting impact. It was more than an attack on the Great Depression; it was a fundamental reform of a system of capitalism that had broken down in a massive way. When it passed into history, it was noted for its relief, rehabilitation and reform.

Franklin Roosevelt started slowly and badly. He spoke of balancing the budget! But he learned quickly by listening to his excellent advisers. He restored the nation's self-respect; he gave the people hope ("There is nothing to fear but fear itself"); he put millions to work. Roosevelt's reputation rests on these accomplishments: he is usually linked with Abraham Lincoln and Thomas Jefferson as America's greatest presidents.

NOTES

1. Gunther, *Roosevelt in Retrospect*, p. 118.
2. Goodwin, *No Ordinary Time*, p. 606.
3. *Current Biography*, 1940, p. 492.
4. "Temporary Extinguishment," *Timecapsule/1939*, p. 49.
5. Morison, *Oxford History of the American People*, p. 952.
6. Gunther, *Inside U.S.A.*, p. 845.
7. Goodwin, *No Ordinary Time*, p. 109.
8. Quoted in *Current Biography*, 1940, p. 412.
9. Sherwood, *Roosevelt and Hopkins*, p. 14.
10. Steiner, who knew and talked to Tolstoy, helped to prepare Hopkins for dealing with the Soviet Union, which may explain why Hopkins was appointed Envoy to Russia by Roosevelt and Special Assistant to Truman on the Soviet-Polish border dispute.
11. Watkins, *Righteous Pilgrim*.
12. *Current Biography*, 1940, p. 193.
13. Gunther, *Roosevelt*, p. 122.

14. As a young boy, I remember banker Joe Kennedy standing in front of the Columbia Trust Company in East Boston with his legs apart, hands on hips, and sleeves rolled up to his elbow greeting us as we walked home from school. Each day he waited for us and gave us that large grin and a handshake.

15. This brief narrative is based in part on the PBS television production "The Kennedys."

16. Collier and Horowitz, *The Kennedys*, p. 86.

17. Cutler, *Honey Fitz*, p. 278.

18. Rose Kennedy, *Times to Remember*, p. 204.

19. *Time*, September 18, 1939.

20. La Guardia, *The Making of an Insurgent*, p. 14.

21. Gunther, *Inside U.S.A.*, p. 578.

22. Caro, *The Power Broker*.

23. Schwarz, *The New Dealers*, p. 129.

24. Hardman, *Rendezvous With Destiny*, p. 143.

25. The *Herald-Tribune* Forum, October 26, 1939.

26. See the fourth volume of Davis's biography of Roosevelt, *FDR: Into the Storm*, 1937-1940.

27. Sherwood, *The White House Papers of Harry Hopkins*, I, p. 10.

28. Quoted in Schwarz, *The New Deal*, p. 132.

29. "Mr. Douglas to the Court," *New York Times*, March 26, 1939, p. 4E.

30. Newman, *Hugo Black*. Newman details a fascinating picture of this complex man who believed that the Supreme Court was the primary voice guaranteeing the right of Americans to speak freely concerning their opinions and their hopes and dreams, without government interference.

31. *Atlantic*, February 1940, pp. 232-37.

32. Gabler, *An Empire of their Own*, p. 353.

33. Perrett, *Days of Sadness: Years of Triumph*, p. 88.

34. "Gitlow Links Reds to Forming of C.I.O.," *New York Times*, September 12, 1939, p. 23.

35. Gunther, *Inside U.S.A.*, p. 24.

36. The attempt of the government to deport Harry Bridges went on for six years. Finally, the case against him was dropped and he was allowed to become an American citizen.

37. "Kuhn Loses Fight to Get Jury Data," *New York Times*, June 3, 1939, p. 5.

38. "22,000 Nazis Hold Rally in Garden," *New York Times*, February 21, 1939, p.1.

39. Lally, *History of the Federal Dance Theatre*, p. viii.

40. Flanagan, *Arena*, p. 335.

41. Koestler, *Arrow in the Blue*, p. 249.

42. Flanagan, *Arena*, p. 355.

43. Rosenman, *Working With Roosevelt*, I, p. 181.

44. Lash, *Roosevelt and Churchill*. p. 114.

45. Quoted in *Smithsonian*, December 1989, p. 61.

46. *Smithsonian*, December 1989, p. 68. Construction was not fully completed until July 1941, when the library was dedicated to "the spirit of peace. " Hyde Park is a monument to our only President to serve four terms. It houses the papers of nearly one thousand press conferences, thousands of letters by persons who were helped by his New Deal, and the record of his attempt to move Americans off the isolationist road.

47. "Relief Top Issue, Survey Indicates," *New York Times*, June 4, 1939, p. 27.

48. *The Fabulous Century*, p. 137.

Part II

SOME GOLDEN AGES

4

The Golden Age of Film and Radio

THE GOLD IN HOLLYWOOD

The Wall Street crash shattered the euphoria in Hollywood, but thanks to the "star system" and new investments, it survived the crisis. These alone might not have succeeded without the major studios, each of which had its own coterie of stars, directors, and technicians. It was said that MGM had more stars than there were in heaven. Its huge financial resources allowed it to produce films like *The Wizard of Oz*. Warner Brothers, by contrast, was the frugal studio of the working class. It featured Edward G. Robinson and James Cagney as gangsters, and in so doing it criticized the penal system.

The smaller studios made great movies on much lower budgets. Columbia depended on the genius of Frank Capra, and RKO relied on Fred Astaire and Ginger Rogers, Katharine Hepburn, and Cary Grant to keep it afloat. 20th Century-Fox used Shirley Temple as its money machine.

In the Great Depression, movies offered an escape from the cold economic times. Americans patronized the neighborhood theater zealously to beat the heat or cold, to take off on a Hollywood fantasy, or to complete a set of dinnerware (one piece per week, usually on a Friday or Saturday night). While politicians and economists focused on the travails of the time, Hollywood hummed. As Wecter wrote, "By 1939 box-office receipts at the country's fifteen thousand motion-picture theaters had risen to nearly seven hundred million dollars, a yearly average of twenty five dollars per family."[1]

For prices ranging from twenty-five cents to a dollar, viewers could watch a standard newsreel (for example, Pathe or Fox), a comedy or two (Popeye or Mickey Mouse), a short subject (travelogue), a serial (Rin Tin Tin was my favorite), and two feature movies. The largest theaters also sponsored the Big Bands and vocalists. Benny Goodman and Sinatra were big draws in 1939.

"With an investment of two billion dollars and 282,000 persons regularly employed at the start of the year," reported Brooks, "the industry in 1939 turned out 530 feature films and more than seven hundred short subjects."[2]

Despite the prodigious output, there was argument about the precise role of films in the Depression. Did "escapism" account for the phenomenon of *Gone With the Wind?* Fleischhauer and Brannan did not find this notion "particularly instructive." They ask, Why did the people choose this "particular vehicle"? Why should a novel about the American Civil War relieve the anxieties of the worst economic crisis in American history?[3] For them, films were a pursuit for redemption, "a theme that penetrated much of Depression culture." This affirmation of individual and societal regeneration permeated the mores of the Great Depression, and it manifested itself in Hollywood films.

We see the same cycle of despair and hope in Steinbeck's *Grapes of Wrath*, published in 1939, when the Joad family loses its forty-acre farm, sells all its possessions to buy an ancient car and heads to California. After being exploited and hounded by the system, Ma Joad cries out, "We ain't gonna die out. People is goin' on—changin' a little maybe, but goin' right on." This linking of the Civil War and the Okies may seem like a strained dichotomy, but each tackles the chief problem of the time: devastation, ruin, and hope for revival. The totally different cultures receive our sympathies because they confront the universal plight of the Dust Bowl refugees and the fading romanticism of a decaying South. Hollywood expressed the tragedy of American life, but it portrayed the people as having the ability not only to endure but to triumph. They were hungry and miserable, but the Depression could not kill their strength.

Motion pictures were the most common form of art for the masses. Though the radio provided some succor from the grimness of their lives, only at the movie house could they escape the weather and the loneliness. For many, the theater was their first experience with air-conditioning. On occasion, the sign advertising its existence was larger than the movie marquee.

During the 1930s, the major film studios controlled all aspects of movie making and distribution when they engaged in block-booking with their own chains of theaters. This monopoly was challenged in the courts, and the system of block-booking was declared illegal in 1939. The court ruled that the double features were not that. The first film was foisted upon the public, which had no choice but to sit through this dog of a movie.

How did Hollywood come to dominate the world market? British history is instructive. Its film industry was crippled by World War I, causing the Parliament to pass the Quota Act of 1927, which mandated that movie theaters were required to show an increasing percentage of British-made films. By 1939, the quota was 20 percent. Most of the rest were American-made. Sadly, the quotas encouraged producers to make mediocre films for a quick profit. It was surprising, therefore, when the quota was retained during World War II.

Regardless of quotas in the rest of the world, by 1939 Hollywood supplied 65 percent of all the films shown in the world, and it employed 33,683 persons per month. The major studios, Paramount, 20th Century-Fox, R.K.O. (Radio-Keith Orpheum), Warner Brothers, and Metro-Goldwyn-Mayer, produced 251 films in that year alone.[4]

CATHOLICS AND JEWS

The censorship of films in 1939 resulted from a curious arrangement. In 1921 the film industry created the Motion Picture Producers and Distributors of America, headed by Will Hays, to forestall a threatened Congressional censorship because of the number of scandals involving the biggest names in Hollywood. The Production Code, which was approved in 1930, was co-authored by a Jesuit priest Daniel Lord and was administered by the Hays Office.

Three years later, the Catholic Bishops of the United States organized the Legion of Decency—the group that rated films for twenty million Americans. In an action that was probably meant to pacify the militant Legion, Joseph I. Breen, a leading Catholic layman, was appointed head of the Hays Office Production Code. The Hollywood code led most states to adopt Boards of Censors. The results were immediate. When the producers of the very popular *Thin Man* series proposed to show Nick and Nora Charles (played by William Powell and Myrna Loy) in a double bed, the Code was invoked and the two were shown in single beds, which came to be known as "Hollywood beds."[5] This leaning towards the Catholic view was odd, because most producers were Jewish and most actors were Protestant.

The Hays Office advised on the purity of pictures before they were made. Its 1930 "Code to govern the making of Talking, Synchronised and Silent Motion Pictures" was a survey of immoralities that were not to appear in motion pictures. All script and finished pictures were required to obtain a seal of approval before issuance to theaters.[6] The Hays Code was supplemented by the Legion's indexes, which were issued weekly, that classified films as A (unobjectionable for all; or unobjectionable for adults); B (objectionable in parts), and C (condemned).

The Code meant that much dialogue was "sweet talk," and so many words were taboo for the screen. And worse for lovers, there was a thirty-second limit on contact of lips during kissing scenes. In *Vanities*, which starred Paulette Goddard, Edith, who was often pregnant, got this response, "She must be either Catholic or careless." The censors mulled over this line for some time before allowing it. Another example of the result of censorship is seen in the case of one 1939 movie *Yes, My Darling Daughter*, which was banned by the New York State Board of Censors. The Board ruled that this picture would tend to corrupt morals or incite to crime."[7]

Gabler deals with the paradox of the American film industry, the "quintessence" of America, being founded and controlled by Eastern European Jews, many of whom were accused of being un-American. They seemed always to be trying to push themselves into the American mainstream, as they became victims of several waves of anti-Semitism. So pervasive was the Jewish influence in Hollywood that a 1936 poll showed that of "85 names engaged in production," 53 were Jewish.[8]

Ironically, while the political right was assailing Jews for being un-American, these Jews were doing everything possible to become real Americans. They had to confront the xenophobic attitudes of nativists, who put constant barriers before the Jews who wanted desperately to assimilate. Hollywood accepted the Jews grudgingly, because they came with money and with ideas of how to cater to the public tastes. They had the advantage of coming from the world of fashion and retailing, where "beating the competition" was paramount.

Strangely, this cutthroat competition manifested itself in high-stakes gambling—all-night poker and bridge games, sometimes at adjoining tables. Almost all Jews who mattered in Hollywood participated in this ritual. The list is a Who's Who: Irv Thalberg, Joe Schenck, Louis Mayer, B. P. Schulberg, David Selznick, Irving Berlin, Sid Grauman, Ben Bernie, Daryl Zanuck, Jack Warner and many more. Very large amounts were bet on the games, and Michael Korda exclaimed, "The mark of a man's position in the hierarchy of movies was the amount of money he could afford to lose."

Gambling was a balm for the Jewish ills. It allowed them to show their nerves and their powers of bluffing, characteristics that stood them well in the production of movies. It also was a salve for their own rejection of their Jewishness. In their frantic effort to become Americans, they had to diminish or give up their Judaism (which meant acceptance on goyim terms, that is, shaving beards, changing names, playing golf, and making their religion more Protestant).

We return to the question we asked earlier. Why did these Jewish movie producers favor films of Catholic themes? Many of these moguls "loved the Catholics," and some married them (or their children did). Louis Mayer was a good friend and an admirer of Cardinal Spellman of New York—he had a large photo of the Cardinal in his bright red vestments in the library. When Mayer was injured, he was treated at a Catholic hospital, where a priest watched over him. This had a profound effect on Mayer; he developed an affinity with the Church. But there may be another, more crass, reason for Mayer getting close to the Cardinal: he controlled the censors of the Church who could order changes in films and even ban their viewing by Catholics. The evidence supporting this view is flimsy; more important to the Jewish-Catholic link was intermarriage. Irving Berlin married a Catholic, as did Harry Cohn.

THE SUCCESSFUL HOLLYWOOD FORMULA

The chief question facing the studios was, Did art imitate life or was it an escape? Surely, in 1939 those who ruled decided it both ways. The studios kept playing follow the leader in choosing movie themes. They all had their Westerns, their good girls and bad girls, their spy dramas and, when war commenced, their patriotic movies.

Filmmakers of 1939 loved medical doctors. It began at Paramount in 1937, when it introduced us to Dr. Kildare—Jimmie he was called. In the original episode, Kildare finds a missing child with the help of a mobster (Lloyd Nolan) who is enamored of a young widow (Barbara Stanwyck). But the doctor theme did not take off until Lew Ayres showed up at MGM as Young Dr. Kildare, with surly, old Dr. Gillespie (Lionel Barrymore) offering his sagacious advice from his wheelchair. Kildare is not the usual small-town doctor; rather, he interns in a major city hospital.

By 1939, there were three dignified doctors for the viewing public to love and admire. The medical craze peaked with *Meet Dr. Christian*, starring Jean Hersholt as the venerable, sympathetic, small-town doctor, who sacrifices a personal fortune to heal everyone who comes to him. Hersholt had played *The Country Doctor* in 1936 so he had prior experience with medical roles in his career. He was so popular that the role was later revived for television.

What is more American than cowboys? Westerns were always big in the history of Hollywood. All the leading men played a cowboy at some time in their careers, including James Cagney, Humphrey Bogart, Errol Flynn, Clark Gable, and Tyrone Power. *Jesse James* marked the beginning of a great 1939 year for westerns (which culminated in the John Ford classic, *Stagecoach*—the first Western produced in color. Tyrone Power was Jesse James and he was supported admirably by Henry Fonda and Randolph Scott (who seemed to show up in every western).

As the world moved closer to war, Hollywood turned in two, related directions: spy movies and training films for the military services. The spy plots were aimed at giving Americans advice and urging them to sacrifice. In April, Warner Brothers introduced *Confessions of a Nazi Spy*, in which Edward G. Robinson in a shift from his gangster roles, played a G-man and Paul Lukas was the Nazi chief of propaganda. Because we were not at war with Germany then, some critics called the effort jingoistic. The "me too" mentality gave us *They Made Her a Spy*, and *Smashing the Spy Ring*.

1939 featured several films that were preparations for war. *Wings of the Navy* was set at the Pensacola Naval Air Training Station; and *Calling All Marines* documents the old saw that the Marines always get there on time. The war fever brought some absurd combinations of cast and plot. The worst one of 1939 was probably the six Dead End Kids in *Dress Parade*, in which Leo Gorcy and the Dead End Kids were cleaned up and sent to the Washington Military Academy. *Thunder Afloat* was as absurd; it featured Wallace Beery avenging the sinking of a tugboat, presumably by the Germans.

Just as often, Hollywood used escapism. Big-name stars were used to enhance the attractiveness of these diggings into the past. *The Story of Alexander Graham Bell* showed Don Ameche as the persevering inventor and

Henry Fonda as his assistant. Loretta Young played Bell's deaf wife. In *Stanley and Livingstone*, Spencer Tracy played Stanley as the virtuous newspaperman from New York, who is not sidetracked from his quest by a romance with Nancy Kelly. He must choose between her and his work. When he leaves her, he returns to Africa to complete Livingstone's work. Though this film was rated highly for its realistic depiction, it was degraded by the innocuous, fictional romance. Gary Cooper partook of this historical feast in *The Real Glory*— concerning the American occupation of the Philippines in 1906. Cooper as a medical doctor is called on to fight a cholera epidemic while putting together a small force of soldiers to protect Mindinao.

Escapism also gave us *Juarez* (Napoleon's attempt to establish a puppet government in Mexico during the American Civil War). Dealing with the War of the *Reforma*, The movie was an attempt to affirm the Monroe Doctrine—that European leaders should not meddle in affairs of the Western Hemisphere. The film starred Paul Muni as Juarez, the President of Mexico; Bette Davis as Carlotta, Maximilian's wife; John Garfield as Porfirio Diaz; and Brian Aherne as Maximilian, the Austrian Prince. Muni was impressive as Benito Juarez, the Zatopec Indian, who was an "Implacable foe of privilege."[9] He gained the military victory over the Austrian coalition but left his country in financial ruin. Brian Aherne was outstanding as the gentle Austrian Prince, so we become emotionally involved in the film when he is executed to the tune of "La Paloma"—the dove.

Cops and robbers was another favorite genre of the late 1930s. *They Made Me a Criminal* joined the tough Dead End Kids as prime examples. Inevitably, the cops and robbers were followed by prison films. Again, big names were involved. Ronald Reagan showed up in *Hell's Kitchen*, James Cagney in *Each Dawn We Die*, and Humphrey Bogart in *You Can't Get Away With It*.

While all these doctors, cops, and soldiers were doing their macho thing, Hollywood's presentation of women in the 1930s was not meant to destroy any stereotypes. Basinger notes that producers kept reminding women "that they had biological function relating to their role as women," and that marriage and motherhood were full-time jobs.[10] Of course, there were wonderful exceptions. Katharine Hepburn, the high-powered columnist of *Woman of the Year*, completely frustrates her husband, played by Spencer Tracy, when she latches on to a huge story ahead of him. She tries to appease him by making him breakfast (at which task she fails).

It is surprising that, with the great store of American talent in Hollywood, producers should have turned to so many European stars. The list is long: Greta Garbo, Marlene Dietrich, Charles Boyer, Peter Lorre, Maurice Chevalier, Hedy Lamarr, Louise Rainer, Francis Lederer, and (in 1939) Ingrid Bergman. The great attraction for foreigners was the Hollywood name and the almost complete absence of any competition from abroad. Americans were also enamored of foreign themes.

THE BIGGEST STUDIO OF ALL

In Culver City, California, the four white columns signified the entrance to MGM studio—the biggest in the world. It was started in the 1920s by Irving G. Thalberg and Louis B. Mayer. When Thalberg died at a very early age, Mayer took over. His motto was "Make it big." Everything about him was big, including the highest salary in the United States.

Mayer was called ruthless, benevolent, avuncular, demonic, polished, villainous, sentimental, and weepy. He was also the best in the business of making films. He used cinematographical magic, such as filming on highly polished floors to give dancers a semblance of unreality. To show that he had a sense of humor, he called his directors "The College of Cardinals." The stars that he personally signed to contracts are an incredible array of talent: Clark Gable, Lionel Barrymore, William Powell, Robert Taylor, Jean Harlow, Walter Pidgeon, Greta Garbo, Myrna Loy, Joan Crawford, Wallace Beery and Maureen O'Sullivan.

L. B. had a sharp eye for talent, wherever he saw it. When he established his MGM Studio in England, he went over to personally oversee the filming of *A Yank at Oxford*, which starred Robert Taylor. While there, he found a young Greer Garson, whom he signed for the part in *Goodbye Mr. Chips*, which won an Academy Award for Robert Donat, whose performance was brilliant and poignant. Irving Thalberg had purchased the rights to this James Hilton novel in 1924.[11]

Because he wanted a happy, wholesome or glorious ending, everyone living happily ever after (in the tulips or in the twilight), Mayer used his stars wisely. He provided them with all necessary services, including dentists, medical doctors, and even ballet schools. He gathered to MGM a coterie of child stars, signing Jackie Cooper, Mickey Rooney, Freddie Bartholemew, Judy Garland, and Gloria De Haven. But he wasn't offering happy, wholesome conditions to his children. They were inexpensive investments because they were grossly underpaid, and they were overworked and in some cases abused. When Judy Garland was reaching womanhood, the studio strapped down her bosom with wires to make her look like a teenager. It tore the tissue in her young breasts. Mayer often punished his children, and he was belligerent if they asked for more money. His only boundary was the rule that children working for studios were required to get three hours of schooling and one hour of recreation per day.

To accomplish his goals, Mayer hired the best talent for movie making. Adrian was the premier wardrobe designer, who set fashions for Hollywood and the world. Cedric Gibbons had the job of putting all the parts of a film together. He was responsible for all those extravaganzas, those lavish sets, those spectaculars.

THE TOP BOX OFFICE STARS OF 1939

The January 2, 1939 issue of *Time* listed the top ten stars of Hollywood. They were led by little ten year old Shirley Temple and followed by Clark Gable, Sonja Henie, Mickey Rooney, Spencer Tracy, Robert Taylor, Myrna Loy, Jane Withers, Alice Faye and Tyrone Power. It is interesting that there are an equal number of males and females.

One person who was not on *Time*'s list was the "Sweater Girl," Lana Turner. In the make-believe world of Hollywood, she was labeled a "can't miss" future star. No one defined "It," but Lana had plenty of it and did become a big box-office favorite, although her popularity was based more on form than finesse.

It was the age of movie magazines. They played a huge part in the success of stars, because they kept names in the limelight. Persons waited anxiously for the next issue of *Motion Picture* or *Modern Screen* or *Movie Story*. Magazine publishers encouraged fans to write for photographs of their favorite stars, and millions were supplied willingly by the studios, all with their fake autographs.

The Little Princess

Shirley Temple was a special phenomenon. She was the number-one box office draw from 1935 to 1939. She was everyone's darling; she was talented; she was vibrant; she was loved around the world by young and old. She was more popular than adult stars Clark Gable, Tyrone Power, Bing Crosby, Robert Taylor, and Mickey Rooney. She came along at the right time; she made everyone forget that it was a terrible economic time. Shirley offered an escape, because seeing her you knew everything would be alright.

Shirley Jane Temple was born in 1928. She studied dancing and ballet in Ethyl Megland's school in Hollywood. When she started acting at the age of four, she stood out in every role. Soon it was obvious that she was an adorable little girl who could act and dance.

Martha Sherrill offered a wonderful description of this "creamy fatcheeks dumpling": "She appeared as a vision in the movie houses of the Depression and altered the national atmosphere like the opening of a window on a sickroom. The breeze was exhilarating. Those tiny tap-dancing feet! Those bouncing curls! Those chubby thighs! . . . the studio heads knew what they had: an enormous talent who made everything look easy, and a girl with charm, footwork and a spooky memory."[12]

The adjectives about her flowed easily: darling, cherubic, nice, sincere, steady, reliable, serious, athletic, cute, model, adorable, inspirational, and sensational. Amazingly, all the words applied. She was a beautiful little girl, but mature beyond her years. In real life, she was actually good; she obeyed her parents, she studied hard, and she was very kind to everyone. She was given a schedule that would have tired most adults. She worked six days per week, beginning at 9:00 A.M. She had breakfast, did her schooling, took a nap and finished shooting scenes.

In 1934, Fox Studio signed her for $150 per week, but after her first film, *Little Miss Marker*, Paramount Studios offered to buy her contract for $50,000. Of course, it was refused. She reached stardom quickly. She had a stand-in at age seven. She was so much in demand from her adoring fans that Fox had to keep her isolated. She played with no children. She went to the studio school, had a private teacher, and was given a secret place to live. Fox was protecting its investment.

But it was her mother, Gertrude, who ran her life. She negotitated the salary up to $1,000 per week in 1935 (which was what the average laborer made in two years), and she controlled all financial aspects of the child's life, including endorsements, which were coming in by the thousands of dollars. Her mother dictated every move, all designed to sell her little darling. Shirley Temple made forty-three feature films, and her mother was present for every rehearsal, every scene. It was she who told Shirley to express energy, to be vivacious. Make-up artists were limited in their handing of Gertrude's precious bundle; they could not do her hair and they needed approval before completing her wardrobe. When Fox and Century Studios merged and became 20th Century-Fox, Daryl Zanuck became her boss. At that time, a poll showed that the three most popular females in America were Shirley Temple, Amelia Earhart and Eleanor Roosevelt, in that order.

The plots of her films were absurd, yet the people flocked to them. In 1937, she saved India for the British simply by asking the rebellious Khan to do so in her soft, gentle voice. Her 1939 film, *The Little Princess* was as farfetched. While she was living in an English boarding school, her life changed dramatically when she learned that her father (played by Ian Hunter) was lost in the South African Boer War. But before the last scene, he shows up alive, and it is just in time for him to be rewarded by Queen Victoria.

Shirley was always on the side of right. In her films, she fought for good causes. She was the first to perform in an interracial dancing scene, when she tap-danced with Bojangles. Although everyone put her on a special throne, she kept a good sense of herself.[13]

When it came time to give out the 1939 Academy Awards, Shirley's presence was felt. The adult nominees declared that it was unfair to put them against such a vivacious, popular national sweetheart, whereupon the Academy found its answer: it gave little Shirley a miniature Oscar.

The King of Hollywood

Clark Gable had raw magnetism. He was what women wanted and what men wanted to be. He was everyman to every woman. He was literally a giant who exuded masculinity. He was virile. He was a cynical rogue who had authority— a sense of power. In 1939 he was given an award as "The king of Hollywood."

He was born William Clark Gable, Jr., on February 1, 1901, into a plain Ohio family. Reaching adulthood, he drifted westward doing odd jobs. He went to Portland and then Los Angeles. At 22, he married thirty-seven year old Josephine Dillon, who helped him obtain minor movie roles.

In 1931 he made three films; then he became a workhorse—he made 66 movies in thirty years. But he was also a good actor, who could play a variety of roles. He was a ship's officer in *Mutiny on the Bounty*, he was a gallant lover in *It Happened One Night*, he was the hard but sensitive general in *Command Decision*. A list of his leading ladies is a history of Hollywood. They include Norma Shearer, Greta Garbo, Claudette Colbert, Helen Hayes, Jean Harlow, Carole Lombard, Ava Gardner, Loretta Young, Lana Turner, Marilyn Monroe, Myrna Loy, Grace Kelly, and Vivian Leigh.

While Gable was perfect for Scarlett O'Hara on the screen he married Carole Lombard in April 1939. How many hearts must have been broken? The two first met while making a film together in 1932, when both were married to other people; they next met at a Hollywood party in 1935, after each had been divorced. When the hostess asked all guests to wear something white, Carole responded by arriving in a white nightgown in a white ambulance, being carried in by interns, also dressed in white. Gable and Lombard danced together all evening, and when they separated she had the ambulance painted with a red heart and delivered to him. He sent her a red fire engine.

Gable had the ambulance engine souped up and drove it around Hollywood. In early April 1939, Gable drove to her home in his roadster, picked up his love, and they headed for Kingman, Arizona, where they obtained a marriage license from a startled clerk. They were married in the Methodist Episcopal Church, before the minister's wife and a high school official.

The Most Famous Teenager

He was born Joe Jule, Jr., on September 23, 1920. He grew up in vaudeville, where his parents performed. He slid naturally into motion pictures in 1933 when he signed with MGM as one of its child stars. Everyone agreed that in this group of child actor, Mickey Rooney stood out as the best actor. He played piano and drums, danced, and he gave moving interpretations in dramatic scenes.

Rooney came to Hollywood's notice as the young fisherman in the 1935 Academy-Award winner *Captains Courageous*, and in 1937, he began working in the *Andy Hardy* series, which was advertised as the life of an average American family. It became a huge money-maker as Andy got into numerous scrapes with his female co-stars Gloria DeHaven, Lana Turner, and Judy Garland. But he vaulted to stardom as the tough boy who could cry when his little friend died in *Boy's Town*.

In 1939 Mayer combined the talents of Judy Garland and Mickey Rooney in *Babes in Arms*. In speaking of his love for Judy, Mickey said, "We could have come from the same womb." Theirs was a "forever love." Rooney was the most famous teenager in the United States, and he was number one at the box office. In that year, his films earned $30 million.

THE OUTSTANDING FEATURE FILMS OF 1939

In 1939, eighty-five million Americans, or 65 percent of the total population, attended the movies at least once a week. According to Dooley, the most popular movies of that year were those in color, because only twenty were made in the whole decade.[14] There are good reasons for selecting 1939 as the greatest year in Hollywood history. A partial list reflects the output of that year: *Gone With the Wind* was everyone's favorite, but there was also *Mr. Smith Goes to Washington, The Wizard of Oz, Stage Coach, Wuthering Heights, Pygmalion, Pinocchio, Beau Geste, Good-bye Mr. Chips, Destry Rides Again, Intermezzo, The Hunchback of Notre Dame, The Hound of the Baskervilles, Mr. Lincoln, Drums Along the Mohawk,* and *Gunga Din.* 1939 was indeed the Golden Age of Hollywood.[15] These movies were an American diary of a times past.

GWTW

Gone With the Wind has been called "the greatest literary smash hit of all time." Margaret Mitchell's only book, this novel of the Civil War and Reconstruction days in Georgia, was 1,087 pages long. Mitchell was bewildered by the book's amazing success. She had been a reporter for the *Atlanta Journal* and only began the book in 1926, when she injured an ankle, which disabled her and compelled her to give up her reporter's work. Cabell Phillips relates that a Macmillan editor, who was looking for new writers, learned of the book in 1935. What she had was a manuscript of 460,000 words that the publishers thought was a valuable property.[16]

Samuel Tupper, a very close friend of Mitchell and book reviewer for the *Atlanta Journal* wrote on June 28, 1936, "It is not too much to say that 'Gone With the Wind' is among the most powerful and original novels in American literature." As she moves from casual flirtations to wife and hardened widow to a reborn woman who is rejected by her southern neighbors, Scarlett offers "adventures and wiles."

As Rhett Butler, Clark Gable is the vehicle of this transformation. Remarkably, Gable did not want the part of Rhett Butler. He said he was sick of costume parts, so he had to be cajoled to accept, and the $100,000 bonus clinched the deal. But who else could have given such a performance?

Mitchell provides just the right blend of realism and escapism. Again we quote Phillips, "There is in her story a certain vigor and modernity; she allows her characters to vomit, utter oaths and allude to bodily functions." Malcolm Cowley, writing in the *New Republic*, called the book trite and sentimental, but he added, "The book has a simpleminded courage that suggests the great novelists of the past." Southern critics praised Mitchell for her great history of the Confederacy, but they were prudishly censorious of the explicit language.[17]

Producer David Selznick had flitted from studio to studio looking for his masterpiece. This Pittsburgh native grew up in Brooklyn and migrated to Hollywood in the 1920s. His first success was *King Kong*, but he favored classic (mostly nineteenth century) novels, which led him to *David Copperfield. Gone With the Wind* would be his vehicle for success.

During the three years of preparation and filming, Selznick fired a dozen script writers and four directors, and he used every resource of the motion picture industry to complete *GWTW*. At that time, there were only seven technicolor cameras in existence, and he used all on *Gone With the Wind*. He used the old sets left over from "King Kong" for the burning of Atlanta. Although other critics found the book "banal" and "simple" and "trite," the world was captivated by this timeless classic. The production cost was enormous—more than $4 million.

When Selznick fired George Cukor as director of *GWTW*, it culminated a fiery period in the production of Hollywood's most popular movie of its time. McGilligan said it was "macho bigotry" on Clark Gable's part that brought about the Cukor's dismissal. Gable called Cukor "that fag," proclaiming, "I won't be directed by a fairy! I have to work with a real man."[18]

Cukor, the most celebrated homosexual in Hollywood in 1939, didn't have to come out; everyone knew. He had a large circle of friends who came to his big house for "lunch," and they comprised some of the most vigorous and good-looking young men in the area, and in some cases from out of town. He seemed to prefer young sailors, who were called his "seafood." Although Hollywood had its homosexual community, it was only tolerated. The homosexuals were confined mostly to fields of design, costumes, and makeup, and Cukor was called a "woman's director"—a code name to explain his homosexuality.

After Victor Fleming was made director, he called in Ben Hecht as a writer. Hecht and Selznick rewrote as David popped Benzadrine pills all day, which gave him indigestion. When shooting commenced, Fleming was in total command (his macho image pleased Gable, and they became great buddies). But six weeks after filming started, Fleming walked off the set; no one knew for sure whether it was from exhaustion or a punishment to Selznick. Sam Wood completed the film.

The cast Selznick selected was perfect: Clark Gable as Rhett Butler, the blockade runner and outcast who cavorts with prostitutes, was a unanimous choice, and Olivia de Haviland and Leslie Howard were right for their sweet and good roles. Howard, who was forty-six, had to be made younger for *GWTW*, and de Haviland, who was under contract to Warner Brothers, had to be loaned to Selznick.

But who was to play Scarlett O'Hara? The word had gone out around the world that Producer Selznick was seeking a new face for the part of the conniving, gold-digger wife. When he chose an unknown English actress,

Vivian Leigh, to play the southern belle, concern was voiced about her accent, but after she strutted on the screen, few remembered those concerns. Leigh's fiery disposition, alertness, and wonderful animation were perfect for the part. But she was also very overworked, being in 95 percent of the scenes, and every scene was reworked many times. So she applied fire and anger, some said because she was anxious to complete the film.

Blacks proved an endless problem for Selznick. First, they insisted that he delete the word "nigger" from the film, then they complained about its stereotypical Uncle Tomism (particularly in Butterfly McQueen's portrayal). They also rebelled against one scene in which they were to be seen eating watermelons.

Selznick chose a new distribution system to bring *GWTW* to the American public. Instead of releasing it to two hundred cities simultaneously, he premiered it in six selected cities, beginning with Atlanta. From there, it went to the Capitol and Astor theaters in New York; and then on to Boston; Reading and Harrisburg, Pennsylvania; Cincinnati; and Los Angeles. In all places, the prices were raised to reflect the high production costs and the very formal openings.

On September 9, 1939 there was a sneak preview at the Fox Theatre in Los Angeles. It got rave notices from the surprised movie goers. Because there was no press in attendance, the reviews did not reach the morning papers, but Selznick learned what he wanted: that he had a spectactular hit on his hands.

By the time *GWTW* was completed, Selznick was drinking heavily, losing large sums of money at gambling tables, and using pills to enable him to work his twenty-hour days. In the process, his wife left him, citing philandering as the chief reason. We wonder how he found time for all of the alleged affairs while working his brutal schedule.

When the movie premiered on December 15, 1939, the Georgians went wild. The Mayor of Atlanta asked the women to wear hoopskirts and the men to wear tight pants, bear hats, sideburns, and goatees. *Time* reported that three hundred thousand Atlantans lined the streets for seven miles to view the limousines.

The original, uncut version was over four hours, with a one-hour dinner intermission. The film opens on the family plantation in April 1861 with Max Steiner's music complementing Scarlett and her sisters as they parade around in hooped skirts. Everything is serene and happy. The Negro slaves are loveable and the place drips of old-fashioned southern hospitality. Men are drinking mint juleps, and they wear riding boots. It's all so placid, but the talk is of war. In the next four hours, the gripping chronicle unfolds. Thousands parade across the screen as we see the slow inexorable defeat of the South and the collapse of Scarlett's world. In the Old South, gallantry took its last bow. The amoral "bitch-girl" was left without husband, child or friend.

But *GWTW* is really the story of Scarlett and Rhett. He describes both of them perfectly when he tells her, "We're alike—selfish and shrewd." He's the magnificent scoundrel, and she's the wench. When Scarlett is at bottom, she weeps, "But, what will I do? Where will I go? Rhett answers indifferently,

"Frankly my dear I don't give a damn." It was a shocker. Scarlett, the heroine, the vixen, is disconsolate; Rhett, the hero, the bounder, the gentleman assures us that there will be no happy ending. But Scarlett O'Hara refuses to accept the finality of Rhett's leaving. She raises her chin and promises, "I'll think of some way to get him back. After all, tomorrow is another day."

The film's dialogue is mixed bon ton and bon mot: O'Hara declares solemnly, "If you have one drop of Irish blood, the land is like your mother." Butler tells the whole southern crowd, "The cause of living in the past is dying." And Scarlett wails at one point, "If I have to lie, cheat, steal or kill, I'll never be hungry again." And when Scarlett survives the war and the complete destruction of her genteel southern society, she plans to rebuild her plantation. She is down on her knees and is regenerated as she declares, "This will be over soon. Then I can go home to Tara."

We're Off to See the Wizard

Starring Ray Bolger, Jack Haley, Judy Garland, Mickey Rooney, and Bert Lahr, the *Wizard of Oz* was overflowing with rapturous revelry, which tells us why it became a seasonal offering for millions of American children. Based on L. Frank Baum's book *Oz*, published in 1900, the 1939 production was not the first film made: there were two silent versions, one in 1910 and another in 1925.[19]

The film premiered in New York City. Theater goers arrived at 5 A.M. for tickets. The MGM version, under Louis B. Mayer, was produced by Mervyn LeRoy. He cast Judy Garland as Dorothy, the Kansas farm girl; Jack Haley as the Tin Man; Ray Bolger as the scarecrow; and Bert Lahr as the cowardly lion. Casting was not easy. MGM tried first to obtain Shirley Temple for the part of Dorothy, but 20th Century Fox would not loan her. Next they sought Deanna Durbin, but Universal said no. Buddy Ebsen was originally assigned the role of the Tin Man, but he developed lung problems from the aluminum dust of his uniform and had to be hospitalized. Jack Haley got the part. He patterned his delivery on the voice he used to tell bedtime stories to his son. Bert Lahr, encumbered by a ninety-pound lion's suit, had difficulty going down the Yellow Brick Road to the Emerald City. Many were considered for the part of the wizard, which went to Frank Morgan.

This brilliant production was directed by Victor Fleming, whose work complemented the witty lyrics of E. Y. Harburg and Harold Arlen's melodies. Can we forget "Ding Dong the Witch Is Dead" (by the Munchkins), or "Follow the Yellow Brick Road," or "We're Off to See the Wizard," or the beautiful "Over the Rainbow"?

E. Y. "Yip" Harburg, the lyricist, was already famous for the haunting "Brother, Can You Spare a Dime," the poignant words of the unemployed veterans of World War I. Their cry of having built a "Tower to the sun" is reminiscent of "Somewhere over the rainbow." Yarburg, who was a Marxist, knew firsthand the effects of the Depression, because his appliance business was bankrupted in the 1929 crash.[20]

When LeRoy first conceived of the wicked witch, he saw her as a glamorous queen, but luckily he changed his mind. The witch's role (with her green face and red eyes) was given to Margaret Hamilton, who at one point in the film was dangerously close to being injured when there was an explosion on the Yellow Brick Road.

The good witch, Glenda, was in control of the northern portion of Oz. Knowing that the citizens of the East were very displeased with the witch, she made her move to subsume them into her kingdom, but on going to the witch's territory, she found a young girl, Dorothy, living in a house that had been blown from Kansas to Oz in a hurricane. Glenda's reaction to this surprise was to ask, "Are you a good witch or a bad witch?" Dorothy, being naive about Glenda's political intentions, said simply she was lost. Relieved, Glenda called out to the citizenry, the Munchkins, to celebrate.

The Munchkins were another innovation; there were 124 of them and many were actual midgets. They sang, "We represent the lollipop guild. We welcome you to Munchkin land." While the Munchkins reveled in a raucous celebration, the dead witch's sister walked upon the scene. When Dorothy mysteriously is seen wearing the dead witch's red slippers, Glenda, sensing Dorothy's danger, takes her to Emerald City, claiming that only the Wizard of Oz can help Dorothy to get home to Kansas.

The wizard was an itinerant con man, who controlled a large piece of Oz by using his attractive personality. He led a life of splendor by trickery. Dorothy's appearance was his undoing, as she and her companions were able to kill the wicked witch, an assignment given them by the wizard on the assumption that they would not return. Tricked by Glenda and unmasked as a mere mortal by Dorothy's dog, the wizard fled into exile riding a balloon. When Dorothy left for Kansas, she left the political struggle behind; Glenda sought to consolidate her power, but the wizard had appointed the scarecrow to be his successor.

There were rumors of much mischief by the Munchkins on the set, specifically drunkenness. But as with most moral issues of the time, if it occurred, it was covered up. Producer LeRoy was able to assemble a mixture of young (Garland was fifteen) and old actors to create a tender, sentimental love story. It all worked well. As one example, Harold Arlen conceived of the melody for "Over the Rainbow" while sitting on his car in front of Schwab's Drugstore in Hollywood.

Befitting its celebrity status, the cast of *Wizard* was heard over Ozian music at the 1939 New York World's Fair, at which Judy Garland and her costar on many films, Mickey Rooney, were seen on the stage with Mayor Fiorello La Guardia.

Mr. Smith Goes to Washington

The hero in this movie is Jefferson Smith, played by James Stewart, who confronts a major crisis of American democracy—the question raised by Lincoln: "Whether that nation or any nation so conceived and so dedicated can long endure." Producer Frank Capra, an immigrant, tried to provide an answer.

Born in Bisaquino, Sicily, in 1897, Capra's experienced a childhood marked by poverty and sickness, typical conditions for Sicilians. He came to the United States in May of 1903 at the age of six. The family settled in Los Angeles, and Francesco was put to work at a young age. By combining work and study, he graduated from the California Institute of Technology and he was attracted to the new movie industry.

From the very beginning Capra had a love affair with his adopted country. His movies reflected his populism, his love of people, and his fight for the little guy. He fought studio heads constantly, but when he began to win Academy Awards, they ceased to challenge his formulas for making movies. Pauline Kael, a leading critic of the time, called this formula "Capracorn." Another wrote of "Saturday Evening Post" populism.

Capra shrugged it off because he knew that his films were honest, patriotic, optimistic, and real.[21] He rose from the streets of Los Angeles to become the premier film director of the Great Depression. He was first named best director in 1934 for *It Happened One Night*, in which we encounter Clark Gable and Claudette Colbert trying to hitchhike a ride. Gable tries first and fails. Colbert pushes him aside with a "let me at 'em" look. She stands on the highway to adjust her stockings, whereupon a car screams to a halt almost immediately. In this film, we learn of Capra's old-fashioned prudishness, when he is compelled to put Gable and Colbert in the same motel room as single persons. His answer: he separates them with a blanket hung on a clothesline that Gable refers to as "The Walls of Jericho."

Capra won his second Academy Award in 1936 for *Mr. Deeds Goes to Town*, and his third in 1938 for *You Can't Take it With You*. By 1939, Capra was preeminent in his field, and he met the challenge with his greatest film. It is doubtful that any other movie in United States history had as much impact on American politics as *Mr. Smith Goes to Washington*.

The story begins with the death of a senator from a western state. The governor (Guy Kibbee) and the senior Senator Joe Payne (Claude Rains) conspire to appoint "someone harmless," Jeffrey Smith, a leader of the Boy Rangers. Mr. Smith is an idealistic cornball. He is totally in awe of his surroundings and totally lost in his new environment. He fumbles constantly and becomes a laughing stock. His two pieces of good luck are his secretary Saunders (Jean Arthur) and he is assigned to Daniel Webster's old desk.

James Stewart mixes innocence and anger as the lone senator fighting corruption. When they try to oust him over a "deficiency bill," he harkens back to all mythologies of our history (life, liberty, and the pursuit of happiness) as he filibusters reading the Declaration of Independence. Capra attempts to fuse other elements of our history by having Harry Carey, a famous cowboy of Hollywood films, play the role of president of the senate.

Smith does a remarkable job of dealing with where to put his hat every time his secretary, Saunders, comes into the room. He fiddles, twists it, puts it between his legs, and hides it behind his back. James Stewart had a thing about hats. He wore the same one in eleven movies claiming that it was his good luck piece.

Jean Arthur was discovered by Capra, who favored the use of strong women in all his films. This New York native, born Gladys Greene, took her screen name from Jeanne d'Arc and King Arthur. She went to New York to study acting, and upon her return to Hollywood, she accepted a part in a John Ford movie, which Capra saw. He liked her husky voice for his romantic comedies. One critic called it a "cross between sandpaper and a caress." Capra starred her in three of his best films: *Mr. Deeds Goes to Town*, (1936) with Gary Cooper; *You Can't Take it With You*, (1938) and *Mr. Smith Goes to Washington* (both with Stewart).

As the story unfolds, there is corruption in high office. The Vice President (Harry Carey) and Senator Payne collude to defeat Smith. He wanders aimlessly to the Lincoln Memorial, where Saunders finds him weeping and tells him that, "You can't quit now." She was reminding him of what he had said earlier, "I'm not licked. I'm going to stay right here and fight for these lost causes." Smith draws strength from the marble statue and returns to the Senate, where he makes one of the most emotional filibusters ever filmed.[22] The end is total chaos: Smith collapses, Payne tries to kill himself and the forces of evil are defeated (Mr. Smith overcomes the political machine).

In his biography, Capra dealt with this episode in many words. He particularly stressed the problems of filming in the "boxed-in" chamber and of creating a hoarse voice for Stewart. They actually swabbed his throat with a mercury solution each day.

But while the film was technically superb, it was not a triumph of democracy. The Ambassador to England, Joseph P. Kennedy, urged Columbia Pictures not to release the film in Europe, especially since war had already begun there. Kennedy thought the film ridiculed democracy, and would therefore imply support for the Axis powers. Capra's response was simple, "Let the voice of the people tell the Ambassador he's mistaken."[23]

Capra wrote that the issue was "Freedom of Film." *Mr. Smith* got rave reviews: *Variety* called it "Stirring drama;" the *Los Angeles Times* said it was "Hair-raising adventure;" and Hedda Hopper, with typical hyperbole, described it "As great as Lincoln's Gettysburg speech." October 16, 1939 was declared "Mr. Smith" day in Washington, and the film premiered at Constitution Hall that evening. The Hall was filled with big names—the Supreme Court justices, senators, congressmen, local officials—and except for a few technical problems (for example, the film jumping off the sound track at one point), everything seemed to go in Capra's favor until the filibuster scene. Words rang out throughout the Hall: "outrage," "insult." By the time the film ended, about one-third of the audience had left.

As Capra had correctly written, the issue was not the film, which was nominated for just about Best Everything, but freedom of film making. Senator Alben W. Barkley, the majority leader, called the film a "grotesque distortion." Another powerhouse, Senator James F. Byrnes, described it as "outrageous."

The major newspapers saw the issue as the ordinary citizen against corrupt politicians. They wrote of Smith challenging the dragons, of vindicating democracy, of holding up a mirror to democracy. The *London Daily Herald* joined in. It proclaimed, "The truth is that Democracy can stand any attack upon its weaknesses.

Joseph McBride, after interviewing nearly two hundred persons, published a very iconoclastic book about Capra.[24] McBride claims that Capra's persona was created by his writers, especially Robert Riskin, who was Capra's principal writer on each of his Academy Award winners, and who worked with Capra on nine of his best movies during the 1930s.

But McBride never quesions Capra's greatness as a director, or his superb storytelling skills. History has already rendered its judgment. In 1989, James Billington, the Librarian of Congress, included *Mr. Smith Goes to Washington* as one of the twenty-five films that make up our "National Treasury." In an oddity of history, *Mr. Smith* was the first film and the last one shown in France when World War II began and when it ended.

Stagecoach

Directed by John Ford, *Stagecoach* may be the most famous "cowboy" film of all time. This western had it all. John Wayne (the Ringo Kid) had busted out of jail and was being pursued by the sheriff (George Bancroft). Claire Trevor (Miss Dallas), the bad woman in the film, is kind to a local woman with a baby. Thomas Mitchell, who won an Oscar for his role, plays the drunken "doc."

When the stagecoach leaves town, all the main characters, except Wayne, are inside, and Andy Divine and John Carradine are driving. They are riding the Overland Stage, and they are headed into Indian country, where Geronimo is on the warpath. As we expect, he attacks, and John Wayne joins the crew for the classic chase. They are all saved by the cavalry, and John Wayne asks Claire Trevor to marry him. He sends her to his ranch and turns himself in to the authorities.

Claire Trevor, the New York-born actress, was pushed into acting when her father's tailoring business collapsed in the Depression. She preferred Broadway to Hollywood, but eventually she signed with 20th Century-Fox. Until 1939, she did nothing but B-movies, averaging eight of them per year. She claims that Zanuck thought little of her acting ability. When she completed *Stagecoach*, John Ford told her, "You're so good."

Wuthering Heights

This cult film stars Laurence Olivier (Heathcliff), Merle Oberon (Cathy Earnshaw), and David Niven (Edgar Linton) in a version of the Emily Bronte novel. Producer Samuel Goldwyn, always bent on creating lifelike sets, landscaped 540 acres into a Yorkshire Moor, and he brought in one thousand heather plants. He also hired English-language experts to perfect the accents of some of his actors.

Directed by William Wyler, this classic featured overtones of demonic behavior. Olivier was superb in his first Hollywood screen role and Oberon almost matched his performance. Alfred Newman's musical score heightened the intensity of the love and hate exhibited by the good Cathy and the morbid, meditating Heathcliff.

The moors made it all perfect. The dark clouds and the rain accentuated every line. The film opens with happy times, as the rich girl (Cathy) and the orphaned stable boy (Heathcliff) fall in love. Her father had found Heathcliff on the streets of Liverpool, but Heathcliff was never accepted by Hindley, Cathy's brother, who torments him. Cathy and Heathcliff go to their favorite mountain place, where things are special. "Nothing is real at Wuthering Heights." Cathy suggests that Heathcliff run away and "bring me back the world." She wants "dancing and singing in a pretty world."

Hindley becomes the master of the house after their father dies. Heathcliff proclaims, "There is a strong curse in me. Something that keeps me from being what I want to." And he rides off into the moors for unknown parts. Cathy is courted by Edgar Linton, her neighbor of Thrushcross Grange. When Cathy marries, Heathcliff declares, "A cold wind went across my heart—a feeling of doom." Heathcliff escapes to America.

The scene shifts, as the orphan returns a gentleman, when his investments prospered. By this time the drunken Hindley has squandered his wealth on drinking and gambling and is forced to sell Wuthering Heights to Heathcliff, his former stable boy. It is sweet revenge for Heathcliff, who was flogged by his former master and who was forced to sleep in the stable "as a miserable gypsy." Heathcliff punishes Cathy by marrying Isabella, Edgar's sister. When Isabella, feeling neglected, cries out, "Look at me, Heathcliff! I'm young, I'm pretty," Heathcliff responds, "Why doesn't your hair smell of heather?"

But now, there are portentous foreshadowings, as Cathy exclaims, "Heathcliff is not a man. He's something dark." But as she lay dying, she admits, "He was my life, my being" and "He's more myself than I am." Isabella laments, "If Cathy dies, I might begin to live." In the death scene, Cathy and Heathcliff embrace. Cathy tells him, "Don't let me go," to which Heathcliff moans, "You threw away your life for a little bit of worldliness." She begs him to take her to the moors again, and he beseeches her to haunt him because "I killed you." Wyler and Goldwyn, who made this masterpiece, won the New York Film Critics Award for Best Film of 1939.

Pinocchio—Geppetto's Marionette

Beginning in 1937, the Walt Disney Studios began to work on a story of a marionette that became a boy. This tale, whose origins are lost in Italian folklore, came to life in the 1890s in a story by Carlo Lorenzini, writing under the pen name of C. Collodi. Using artist Attilio Massino, Lorenzini gave young Pinocchio a physical shape, with a nose that illustrated what happens to boys who bend the truth. In the folktale, Pinocchio begins as a wooden figure, who is carved by Geppetto, the old master puppetmaker. When he wished to bring the boy to life, he just called on his Blue Fairy. While the old man is soaking in his tub, Pinocchio walks to him and hands him the soap.

This begins the boy's adventure that tests his courage and love for his master. He begins his odyssey, with Jiminy Cricket, against the whale, Monstro. When Pinocchio meets his test, he is declared "a real boy." The adventures include getting involved with bad boys and lying in school, for which his nose grows as wide as the classroom.

Sitting in the Disney Music Room in Hollywood, about a dozen men discussed how they could bring this story of family and love to the screen. At each meeting rough sketches (based on the Massino drawings) were hung on the wall to illustrate the plot. Next a standing figure was carved to aid the animators in making more-accurate sketches. As the artists approached the final version of Pinocchio, two clashing approaches emerged: one favored a grotesque design, but this had little support; the other was the attractive or cute version, which was used in the film. In the "final" conference, Pinocchio showed himself. He had regulation (large) shoes, a Tyrolean hat, a long nose, and a large bow tie and four-fingered hands with gloves.

When the film took shape a few modifications produced the Pinocchio we all know. The nose was made smaller, like a button (probably because Disney did not want to present to children a boy whose long nose implied that he had lied), the ears were enlarged and some hair was placed on the forehead.

This tale of bad life turned good won two Academy Awards: for best score and best song ("When You Wish Upon a Star").

THE GOLDEN AGE OF RADIO

By historical time, radio is very new. The first commercial broadcast was made on November 22, 1920 over KDKA, in East Pittsburgh, Pennsylvania. Broadcasting began with classical music, followed by the voices of George Bernard Shaw, Congressman Fiorello La Guardia, Reverend Billy Sunday and comedienne Fannie Brice. Originally, radio was rooted in vaudeville, which had a connection to burlesque, but soon it branched out into newscasting, political propagandizing (the "Fireside Chats"), quiz shows (the "Quiz Kids"), music appreciation (the "Hit Parade" and the NBC Symphony), and comedy.

Because of the tense international situation, 1939 was the year when radio news coverage became dominant. Millions of Americans sat anxiously by their table sets straining to hear broadcasts from places they hardly knew. Earlier in the decade, Gabriel Heatter, Lowell Thomas, and H. V. Kaltenborn were popular; the later 1930s saw the rise of the superb CBS team, led by Edward R. Murrow. In the 1930s, the volume of radio news more than doubled, and in the summer of 1939, a *Fortune* poll indicated that Americans believed that radio was freer of prejudice than newspapers by 50 percent to 17 percent for the press.[25]

Radio news, which was barely discernible above the static and interference, was important, but not nearly as popular as the variety and dramatic shows. The most incredible development in radio was the popularity of ventriloquist Edgar Bergen, who brought dummy Charlie McCarthy to life for millions of persons in the remotest parts of the country.[26]

In the first half of 1939, a big event in radio was broadcasting the tumultous reception that the King and Queen of England received in the United States. Reports of the World's Fair were preceded by notices of "that special relationship between the two great democratic powers." Europeans learned of the relaxed Roosevelt style that came to be called his "fireside chats." In domestic programming, Charlie McCarthy was the most popular, followed by the Bing Crosby Hour and the Jack Benny Show.

Advertisers learned early of radio. Singing commercials (Pepsi Cola hits the spot/ twelve full ounces that's a lot) propelled radio over newspaper advertising. But the real advertising money was made in the "Soaps," so-called because most of the sponsors were selling soap (Lever Brothers, Procter & Gamble and Colgate-Palmolive). The serial soap operas consumed 85 percent of network daytime programming. The big shows were on in the evening, but there was a large and growing audience of wives who kept their radios going while they cleaned house.

Soap opera had an enormous impact. Many women, particularly in rural areas, patterned their lives after characters in the soaps. They wrote to the studios asking advice about domestic problems, and the radio stations were required to keep a large staff to respond to these real-life situations.

Jack Benny—"Love in Bloom"

At the end of the 1930s, the Jack Benny Show, a Sunday night program on CBS, came into millions of homes as a family show. It made its audience comfortable, because in it Benny played a character "that included all the faults and frailties of mankind." His radio character was a stingy, vain, egotistical man, who thought he was sexy. As he said, "Every family had someone like me." When the show came on at 7 P.M., the whole nation listened. If you walked down the street at that hour in the summer, you would not miss a single minute as the sounds of the program emanated from each household. It was an

American phenomenon that has never been equalled. In that one-half hour, the United States was turned into a single community. The audience was estimated at thirty million persons.

Benny was born Benjamin Kubelsky in 1894. His family was not poor; indeed, his mother gave him a $50 violin in 1900. Benny states in the beginning that his life was not a rags-to-riches affair. He declared emphatically that he did not triumph over adversity, he did not suffer hardship. He grew up in a happy orthodox Jewish family, and he joked that his only handicap was in playing golf.

He practiced diligently, became good at playing the violin, left school and got a job in a pit orchestra in a theater. He came to his life-long occupation while serving in the navy in World War I, when he did a small part in a comedy. He gave up the musical career that his mother wanted and turned to vaudeville and radio. His first job was as "Jack Benny—Fiddle Finology." But his fiddle was only a prop, because he was a master of the opening monologue. He strutted upon the stage as if he owned it. His timing was impeccable, and he was not afraid of silence. When he did play his fiddle, he billed himself as "Jack Benny and his magic violin."

He was attractive to many women, but he married just one, Sadie Marks, and he became a loving husband and father, after they adopted Joan in 1934. He changed his name from Benny Kubelsky, and Sadie became Mary Livingstone. When he married Sadie in 1927, it was one of his luckiest moments. As his radio wife, Mary played dumb, but she too was a smart and cagey performer. In fact, Jack credits her with saving the show. She had noticed that several radio comedians were making jokes that depended on visual aspects for their punch lines (based on their experience in vaudeville). When his show reached the top in radio, he moved it to Los Angeles, because it was the center of show business.

As the 1930s began, radio centered in New York City, and from there the beams were sent westward. But there was no direct link to Hollywood, as a result of which high line charges were levied to send a program to the West Coast. This charge was eliminated once it became possible to broadcast over telephone lines. NBC headquarters was at Sunset and Vine, CBS at the Lescaze-designed studio and ABC nearby in Hollywood. This building boom diminished the Hollywood producers' fears of radio and it opened up the vast Hollywod talent pool to the networks. When the radio stars saw the growth of network programs, they moved their shows to Hollywood. By 1939, all major comedians, except Fred Allen, were broadcasting from the West. And soon the jokes took on a western flavor. We all laughed at the line about, "Anaheim, Azusa, and Cucamonga."

Unlike most comedians of his day, Benny depended more on comic situations and less on slapstick. He played up to his braggadocio and miserly demeanor. In the classic Benny episode, he was confronted by a robber who shouts, "Your money or your life." Then a long pause ensues. The anxious robber repeats his demand, whereupon Benny responds, "I'm thinking it over."

He told many jokes on himself, illustrating how pervasive his radio persona had become. On one occasion, Benny related, he checks into a hospital, where a nurse asked him for a urine sample. He protested that he had gone already, "just a few minutes ago." The nurse persisted, and Benny gave as much as he could. When she came back and saw the small amount of liquid, she looked at him with a wilted face and remarked, "You never give anything away—do you?"[27]

Benny's claims of being a concert violinist and a great screen lover were the essence of his comedy. But he also allowed himself to be the butt of jokes, which helped him to achieve his objective—the sympathy of the audience. His format, the use of a regular "family," helped him to dominate radio comedy. His radio family, or as he called them "his gang," included Don Wilson, Phil Harris, Eddie Anderson ("Rochester"), Dennis Day and his wife, Mary Livingstone. Eddie Anderson, being black, added another dimension to the program.

Dennis Day was a replacement for Kenny Baker, who left Benny to go with Fred Allen. Day, whose name was Owen P. McNulty, was hired after an audition because he made a funny response to a question put to him by Mary Livingstone. He joined "the gang" on October 8, 1939, as a comedian and tenor. On one program, he informed Jack Benny that he would not be on next week because he was going to commit suicide. Jack found out that Dennis had a quarrel with his girlfriend, and Dennis agreed to cancel his suicide, whereupon Jack picked up the telephone. "Are you going to call your girl," asked Jack. "No," replied Dennis, "Forest Lawn. I want to cancel my reservation."

Benny had a lot of company on the comic stage. The "Easy Aces," one of the first of the scatterbrain couples on radio, were a prosperous white couple who lived in a fancy Manhattan neighborhood. Mr. Ace was a New York advertising executive, and wife Jane was a stay-at-home wife. The show was broadcast without audience. The cast just sat around at a table and spoke their lines in conversational tones. The most important of the supporting actors was Marge, played by Mary Hunter. She was Jane's best friend, and she supplied many of the laughs. Ace wrote these scripts himself, but the job overwhelmed him at times, because he had to produce three shows per week, and because he was a perfectionist. For him every word needed to be just right. But he was smart enough to allow for his wife's many malapropisms, among which were "old testament houses," or "time wounds all heels."

Burns and Allen were rated highly until 1939, when the popularity of their show plummeted. George Burns and Gracie Allen played a variation on the frustated husband and dumb wife theme. Like Jane Ace, Gracie impersonated a nitwit housewife who got into domestic difficulties, from which George had to extricate her. And like Jack Benny, Burns put together a good supporting cast, which included Mel Blanc, Hans Conreid, Elvia Allman and Gale Gordon.

Fibber McGee and Molly also reached a peak at the same time. He portrayed a small-town muddler, whose antics were loveable but unsophisticated. This humor came from the heartland of the United States and was predicated on country speech and absurd happenings, which the audience readily accepted as real.

One of the most popular programs was the Chase and Sanborn (coffee) Hour. All over the United States, old and young tuned to ventriloquist Edgar Bergen. The show was an unusual manifestation of love, because Bergen's dummy, Charlie McCarthy, was invisible. It was on the air thirty minutes after the Jack Benny show in that powerful NBC lineup on Sunday evenings. The Charlie McCarthy show gave us some memorable guest appearances, particularly those of W. C. Fields. In 1939, Fields's show, which was sponsored by Lucky Strike cigarettes, was in trouble. Bergen, knowing that W. C. Fields was a top performer, put him back in the spotlight. Some of his lines were tragically humorous, being based on his real-life experiences in a sanitarium for alcoholism. Fields threw the producers into spasms of hysterical concerns, because he would constantly ad-lib lines and his improvisations were not acceptable under the codes of his time. He drank before performances, which must have altered his judgment, but it is not certain that it affected his performances. In fact, Bergen once called him "the greatest I ever worked with."

Red Skelton was a good vaudeville comedian in 1930, probably inheriting his ability to make people laugh from his father, who was a circus clown. Red followed his father in the circus, but instead turned to burlesque and pantomime. Because he was expert at several comic approaches, he earned a guest appearance on the highly watched Rudy Vallee variety show, which started him on his spectacular radio career.

These brief biographical sketches tell us that radio's heyday was very brief. The golden age of radio was one of the shortest golden ages in history.

NOTES

1. Wecter, *The Age of the Great Depression*, p. 236.
2. Brooks, *The Great Leap*, p. 21.
3. Fleischhauer and Brannan, *Documenting America*, p. 32.
4. These facts are taken from Rosten, *Hollywood*.
5. Mast and Kawin, *A Short History of the Movies.*
6. The Hays Code was published in "Film Facts," by the Motion Picture Producers and Distributors of America.
7. "Censors Ban 'Yes My Darling Daughter,'" *New York Times*, February 11, 1939, p. 1.
8. Gabler, *An Empire of Their Own*, p. 2.
9. Clark, *All the Best in Mexico*, pp. 63-66.
10. Basinger, *A Woman's View*.
11. Some of these facts are from the PBS television production, "MGM: When the Lion Roared," shown in October 1994.
12. "Dimply the Best," *Washington Post*, July 16, 1995, p. G-1.

13. Some of these views were expressed on the PBS television production of "Shirley Temple: America's Little Darling," shown in July 1994.

14. Dooley, *From Scarface to Scarlett*, p. xxii.

15. Fifty years later, the United States Postal Service honored five Hollywood legends with four twenty-five cents stamps, which depicted Judy Garland holding her dog Toto in *The Wizard of Oz*, Clark Gable and Vivien Leigh embracing in a scene from *Gone With the Wind*, Gary Cooper dressed as a French Foreign Legionnaire in *Beau Geste*, and John Wayne dressed for his part in *Stagecoach*.

16. Phillips, *From the Crash to the Blitz*, p. 337.

17. Mitchell's novel was translated into thirty languages, and sales continued strong over the years when they spurted for the fiftieth anniversary issue of the video cassette in 1989.

18. McGilligan, *George Cukor*.

19. Dooley, *From Scarface to Scarlett*, p. 391.

20. H. Myerson and E. Harburg, *Who Put the Rainbow in the Wizard of Oz?*

21. Frank Capra, *The Name Above the Title*.

22. Actually, since no cameras were allowed in the Senate chamber, Capra made an accurate copy for the movie.

23. Dooley, *From Scarface to Scarlett*, p. 595.

24. McBride, *The Catastrophe of Success*.

25. Wecter, *The Age of the Great Depression*, p. 230.

26. Wertheim, *Radio Comedy*.

27. This and many other stories are told in Jack and Joan Benny, *Sunday Nights at Seven*. The book, based on a manuscript that Jack worked on for many years but never published, was completed by his daughter.

5

Music Maestro Please

The decade of the 1930s was a golden age of popular music. It was the time of George Gershwin, Cole Porter, and Irving Berlin. For many, it was the best music ever and the most danceable. The remarkable gains of music in the 1930s resulted from the dissemination of radio. When radio was in its heyday, music made up one-half of its scheduled time. The networks provided first-class programs, both classical and popular.

THE MAESTRO

The National Broadcasting Company first offered grand opera from the Metropolitan Opera House in 1931, and in 1937, it persuaded the world-renowned conductor Arturo Toscanini to come to New York to create his own orchestra. By 1939, over ten million families were listening to the NBC Symphony.[1]

Toscanini did not come from a musical family. All of his forebears were poor, hardworking farmers. They subsisted on thick, vegetable soups that often left the boy hungry. It is not clear when he showed early signs of musical talent. He did enjoy the family get-togethers during which they would sing folksongs and arias.

Toscanini graduated from the Parma Conservatory when he was eighteen (1885), after nine years of study, during which he did much to prepare himself for conducting. He played both the cello and the piano and was so good that he was offered a post as cellist and assistant chorus master in Rio de Janeiro, Brazil. When the conductor, Leopoldo Miguez, was panned by the press, he resigned. At curtain time, it was chaos with shouting and finger pointing. Who would lead? A singer from the chorus pointed to Toscanini screaming, "You can save us. You know the score by heart."[2]

Toscanini conducted *Aida* from memory. There were bravos for Senhor A. Toscanini, and when he returned to Italy, he was a new hero. By his midtwenties, he was a leading Italian conductor. He conducted at La Scala and Paris and Berlin and most major Italian cities, and then he got the call from New York. Enrico Caruso turned out to be the middleman. He made his debut at La Scala under Toscanini, and when the manager of the Metropolitan Opera expressed an interest in him, Caruso began the negotiations. Toscanini relented, and he arrived in New York in 1908.

When Toscanini did operas, no one was immune to his criticism. He was savage, but he was always right. He could pick out one false note in the middle of an opera. He even told a German woman that she did not articulate the language well, even though he did not speak German. As Clive James said, "Toscanini had too much energy to be depressed."

During World War I, he returned to Italy. It is hard to imagine, but the foremost operatic conductor of his time conducted a military band. And he was decorated for bravery when his band continued to play at the front as the Austrians shelled his position.

In 1926 Toscanini agreed to a dual appointment with La Scala and the Metropolitan. On January 14 he conducted the New York Philharmonic for the first time, and three years later he became its permanent conductor. It did not take him long to put the Philharmonic on a par with the Boston Symphony, led at that time by Serge Koussevitzky, and the Philadelphia Orchestra under Leopold Stokowski. Once again, in 1934, he left the United States without intentions of returning.

He first conducted the entire nine Beethoven symphonies with the BBC Symphony in 1939. The Toscanini concerts were in such demand that there were requests for seventy-five thousand tickets. Because King George VI and Queen Elizabeth were to appear at one of the 1939 concerts, the upper crust of London society wanted to attend. Toscanini's diligence to his music was known to everyone but the Royal couple, who sent the maestro an invitation to visit them during the intermission. Toscanini appreciated the honor but gave them the same response he had given to King Ferdinand of Bulgaria. He could not accept, because it would detract from his concentration on the music.

On October 28, 1939 Arturo Toscanini raised his baton for the first of a nine-week Beethoven Festival with the NBC Symphony. He offered three staples: the overture to *Fidelio*, the First Symphony, and he chose his favorite Beethoven Symphony, No. 3 in E-Flat Major (the *Eroica*). Olin Downes, the music critic of the *New York Times*, reported, "He has seldom given a more impressive demonstration of his capacity to make familiar music fall so freshly and significantly upon the senses and the mind that the hearer listens to something he has known from childhood."

By this time, Toscanini was the foremost interpreter of the Beethoven symphonies. He had been conducting Beethoven since 1896, when he performed the First Symphony at La Scala. Downes called the *Eroica* the "sublime trajectory of the spirit of Beethoven." *Fidelio* and the First Symphony served as preludes to the "immensities" of the *Eroica*." Toscanini's approach to *Fidelio* as an eighteenth century opera was precise and infallible, but his treatment of the First Symphony showed a rendition more from the heart. It showed the youthful Beethoven and the memories of the youthful Toscanini of La Scala conjoining in New York for a performance of what some consider a minor work but which served as a perfect introduction to the great Symphony No. 3.

THE BIG BAND SOUND

In the 1930s, popular music was often distinguished by geography. There was Kansas City jazz, New Orleans Dixieland, country music in Appalachia and Broadway hits in New York City. But this is a simplistic typology, because there was an extraordinary amount of fusion of musical types. The itinerant blues singers from the small Texas and Oklahoma towns mixed readily with players who featured English jigs and reels. At the same time, cowboy songs were combined with polkas, Mexican tunes, banjo picking, and German march melodies. These mixtures were interlaced on the frontier and by region, and the whole smorgasbord was enlivened by black blues.

The origin of jazz is still contested. Gunthur Schuller places its start in New Orleans, where blacks played their Dixieland and blues, but many major figures in jazz and swing, including Benny Goodman, got their start in white bands, particularly the Red Nichols and Ben Pollack bands. Goodman learned two things of importance from playing in Pollack's band: Ben would feature often a small group to come out of the band to play hot jazz, which Goodman emulated later with his trio and various small groups; and Pollack liked to jam using duets (Ben and Benny), which became later Goodman and Harry James or Goodman and Gene Krupa.

Wynton Marsalis offers a unique idea on the origins of jazz (and therefore swing). He links ragtime with wind bands, which met at the turn of the century in New Orleans, to form an American version of a European style. Ragtime was a variant of "raggin"—an African music. It was decisive in changing American band music. In ragtime, the sixteen-bar strains dominated, as they did in the Souza marches. But the marches functioned in smaller ranges. Ragtime was syncopation and improvisation. In jazz, there is "collective improvisation"—all players are aware of each other's playing and they cooperate to create polyphony, in which all instruments play in different registers, and often on different melodies. When they played riffs (repeated sections), they changed the nature of Souza marches, and they launched a new form of music that Louis Armstrong and Benny Goodman picked up in their youth.[3] The blues was another variation. It had twelve bars, which some linked to twelve items to a dozen, twelve months to a year and twelve inches to a foot. It used only three cords in a 1-4-5 pattern.

There is no disputing the black influence in creating the language of jazz, which became the primary source of American musical entertainment. The black contribution stemmed from the blues, which grew out of lives of poverty and woe. There were also fortuitous factors at work in the proliferation of our dance music. The rapid technological development of radio and phonograph helped to provide a large supply of skilled musicians who could easily assimilate the innovations of Armstrong and Ellington.

Fletcher Henderson, by joining the Goodman organization, helped to develop a group of skilled white musicians and band leaders who could absorb the basic tenets of jazz and turn them into musical styles that were attractive to a vast untapped public that craved this new sound. Goodman and Miller and Shaw had taken their beat from the jazz conceptions of the blacks. The amalgamation of black and white music was cemented when the color line was broken and races mixed freely in the orchestra (for example, in the Carnegie Hall jazz concert, where for the first time the Ellington and Basie musicians played alongside Goodman's best).

There was one music that came to dominate—the Big Band Sound. It was swing music with a jazz base and was characterized by a driving beat, tight instrumentation, and solos that improvised (so much so that on subsequent renditions you never heard the exact notes twice). It was multiethnic, multicultural and multiracial. The influence of the swing band was pervasive. By 1939, records were selling by the thousands, and most homes had a phonograph to play them on. The music coming from the steel needles was scratchy but how we loved it. Band leaders were famous celebrities and their personal lives were carried daily in the newspapers.

It Don't Mean a Thing If You Ain't Got That Swing[4]

Benny Goodman may be linked with Toscanini; they both were rigid taskmasters and they both insisted on perfection from their orchestras. Benny was just as excellent doing a clarinet concerto as he was "solid" doing swing riffs on "Sing, Sing, Sing." Goodman made jazz popular; he took it out of dives and put it in hotels and theaters. He combined driving power and improvisation to create his masterpieces. For example, he took Fletcher Henderson's "Christopher Columbus" and joined it with Louis Prima's "Sing, Sing, Sing." The result was that masterly composition that highlighted solos by Goodman, Jess Stacy, Harry James and Gene Krupa.

If one event can characterize the coming out of jazz and swing, it is Benny Goodman's Carnegie Hall concert on January 16, 1938. Paul Whiteman, the King of Jazz, had played at Carnegie in the 1920s, so why not Goodman? It was a jam session with members of the Count Basie and Duke Ellington bands sitting in. The band dressed formally, but played with abandon. No more would swing and jazz be thought of as saloon music. The concert was advertised as "Twenty Years of Jazz," and how it soared! Irving Kolodin said that there were "incredible feats of expressive playing," but James Collier, a fine student of swing and jazz, said it best: "But Benny Goodman was first. It was his magical clarinet that began it." Goodman wanted to cancel, fearing that they would bomb. But the show went on, and when the promoters asked Benny how much of an intermission he would need, he answered, "How much did Toscanini have?"

The importance of the Carnegie Hall concert went far beyond the field of music; racial barriers came tumbling down. Although Goodman's band was all white, his trio included Teddy Wilson, and his quartette added Lionel Hampton. Benny decided to honor the great Negro players of his time by inviting members of the Duke Ellington and Count Basie bands to sit in. He had been playing regularly with them in Harlem, but Carnegie Hall was special. When the jam session began, there were four from Ellington's band (Johnny Hodges, Harry Carney, Cootie Williams and Walter Page) and four from the Basie group (Buck Clayton, Freddie Green, Lester Young, and Basie himself).

Benny Goodman, like Irving Berlin, came from one of the many immigrant Jewish families that gave so much to American society. Benny told us of his family in his early autobiography, *The Kingdom of Swing*. Both of Benny's parents came from Jewish ghettos (his father from Warsaw, his mother from Lithuania), which they were forced to leave because of the May Laws that were imposed by the Tsar. They emigrated separately to the United States and first settled in Baltimore, where they married. But they moved to Chicago to join the other fifty-two thousand Eastern Jews who had settled there.

Benjamin David Goodman was born there on May 30, 1909—one of twelve children of David and Dora Goodman. Benny's musical career was launched by accident, and his "choice" of clarinet was an even greater accident. The Goodmans moved often, but they settled in a cramped and dark apartment on Francisco Avenue. Two years later, when Benny was ten years old, a family from Boston moved nearby. When David Goodman learned that the boys in the new family earned money by playing musical instruments, he took Harry, Freddy, and Benny to the Lejelah Jacob Synagogue to get their instruments. When the three boys were taken to the bandmaster, named Boguslawski, there were only three instruments left. He gave the largest boy, Harry, the tuba, the next largest, Freddy, the trumpet, and that left Benny with the clarinet.[5]

Goodman was a child prodigy. At age eleven, he joined the Hull House band, which was formed by Jane Addams in the former home of Charles J. Hull. It was one of the settlement houses where immigrant families went to become Americanized. Benny enjoyed the emphasis the house had on music, dance, and drama.

Goodman was raised on the classics. He studied under a very strict German—Franz Schoepp—but like all young music lovers, he was totally captivated by the New Orleans sound that had just reached Chicago. Being too young to go to the Dixieland clubs, he learned his hot licks by accompanying sounds on old phonograph records. Despite his age, Benny gave an excellent account of his musical progress. Listen to Bud Freeman, "There was a kid in the band playing clarinet; he was no more than thirteen years old. He played the clarinet so beautifully—it was not to be believed. He had the technique of a master and a beautiful sound to go with it. His name was Benny Goodman."[6]

If Benny became a virtuoso on the jazz clarinet, it must have begun with his sojourn in the classics. This grasp of his instrument enabled him to be a strict and demanding leader. His work with Schoepp was also discernible in his clarinet playing—Benny was always cool and clear. He was miles from Le Jazz Hot, and although he appeared to have raw talent at times, he always regulated his flawless vibrato, for which some critics called him mechanical. But it was this attention to playing flawlessly that enabled him to become the King of Swing at the age of twenty-six.

Although he was in the public spotlight for most of his adult life, Benny Goodman was a very private person, who refused to talk about his poor and difficult childhood in Chicago. If he had scars, he did not talk about them; rather he believed that a man should make it with ability and without excuses. This showed in his music; he could not tolerate mediocrity—it produced anger and impatience. Goodman's life was always music, or as Firestone wrote, in *Swing, Swing, Swing,* his craving for perfection made him the most demanding of orchestra leaders in the 1930s, and it created a number of enemies, including some of his best musicians and arrangers.

During the 1920s, Goodman was very busy playing in jazz bands. There was a great demand for musicians who could read music and play it hot. By this time, Benny had given up on high school and had started playing in the illicit world of moonshine whiskey. Whites and blacks intermixed freely as they were carried away by the syncopating melodies. Goodman played with as many black musicians as white. This undoubtedly shaped his notions about integration that he carried with him when he formed his own bands.

Goodman mixed with many who became names later. He played "dime a dance" in a band with Glenn Miller, and when Ben Pollack took his band to New York City, they gave a commission to John Hammond, a great fan and music critic, to make some records with a new singer, Billie Holiday. And it is a little-known fact that Goodman played in the pit orchestra for the Gershwin musical "Girl Crazy," with Ethel Merman.

Fletcher Henderson made an enormous contribution to Goodman's success. Henderson was a college graduate, a fine pianist and an accomplished arranger. When he realized that his talents were being wasted on a mediocre band, he turned to some innovative examples of genius: he featured brassy horns rather than the violins, banjos, and pianos of the bands of his day; and he discarded the arrangements that were available from the tin-pan-alley stores in favor of personalized arrangements that emphasized hot solos. These solos were taken by persons who became legends in musical history, beginning with Louis Armstrong, Benny Carter, and Coleman Hawkins.

In the mid-1930s, Henderson was forced to disband his orchestra. It was not a good time for black jazz; bookings were slow and recording companies often discriminated against its players. John Hammond, a friend of Benny Goodman, told Benny of Henderson's marvelous arrangements, and an alliance was formed that literally changed the direction and shape of the Big Band sound. It was Henderson who convinced Goodman that he should hire Gene Krupa and Jess Stacy, and it was Henderson who revived a moribund Goodman band with a new beat and excellent arrangements that melded brass and reeds in improvised jazz. According to Schuller, Goodman's soloists were no match for Henderson's seasoned black musicians.

Goodman's rise was not automatic. In Lansing, Michigan, the Goodman band performed before just eighteen people, and it got no better in Denver on the swing West. But then the miracle happened: at the Palomar Ballroom in California ten thousand persons jammed the place. As Benny said, "They were blowing the roof off." The band's success was based on solid fundamentals. But Benny was his own taskmaster; he used up to fifty to sixty reeds per day to achieve the perfect sound (which, according to him, he never achieved). And there were rules: no smoking, no chewing, and no crossing of legs (man or woman). The regimen was grueling. They played hundreds of one-night stands, often five nights in a row.

The year 1939 marked the end of Goodman's great band era, although he continued to play and record and to travel all over the world bringing American jazz everywhere. The first band, 1935-36, was good but not as famous as that of 1937-39. Goodman, himself, thought that the 1938 group was "the greatest of any of his bands." These bands recorded on the Victor label.[7] By that summer, Harry James left Goodman, and so did Gene Krupa, Jess Stacy, Teddy Wilson, and Ziggy Elman. Each departure was agonizing for Goodman. He was especially grieved to lose Teddy Wilson, who had been with him since 1935. Wilson was a consummate pianist, who could soar on "Sing Sing Sing," and could deliver a graceful solo as part of the Goodman trio on "The Man I Love." He was an integral part of the chamber jazz that Goodman-Krupa-Wilson offered. Wilson was an improviser who was stylistically perfect, but who could switch to dirty jazz when the jamming began. When Lionel Hampton joined the trio, making it a quartette, he totally overshadowed Wilson's quiet, business-like approach to music. Hampton was loud, wild, histrionic, and popular with Goodman's public. Without doubt, this weighed heavily in Wilson's decision to leave Goodman.

Benny, with a new arranger and new sidemen, signed with a new recording company—Columbia, which was bought by CBS in 1938. It was good timing, because total record sales in 1939 reached fifty million—five times greater than in 1932. Most of these sales were the big band, swing sounds of Goodman, Miller, Shaw, and Dorsey.

The new band was clearly a different sound, which flowed from the new combination of CBS music director John Hammond and arranger Eddie Sauter.

Sauter was unusual; he slept on the floor and he spoke Japanese, but he was a good trumpet player as well as arranger. The music Sauter arranged for Toots Mondello, Adrian Rollini, Nick Fatool, and Jimmy Maxwell was different from and perhaps inferior to the sound produced by Harry James, Gene Krupa, and Jess Stacy for Victor Records.

Sauter, who was born in Brooklyn, was, like Goodman, trained in classical music. Sauter studied at the Chicago Music College, Columbia Teacher's College, and Juilliard. He liked Caruso records, but he loved the sounds of bands he heard as a teenager. He went from flugelhorn to drums to trumpet to arranging, first with Charlie Barnet then Red Norvo and in 1939 to Benny Goodman. His musical education made his arrangements not just different but complex and difficult to play. He was no Fletcher Henderson, who was self-taught. Goodman thought his music was too busy and too classical for swingtime. The prime example of this was "Clarinet a la King," a composition in six sections, the first and last of which developed the same theme (very classical).

Charlie Christian

In 1939 the Goodman sextet made its first recording, "Flying Home," which Lionel Hampton appropriated later for his theme song. This record introduced Charlie Christian, who many consider to be the greatest jazz guitarist ever. Christian was born in the tiny town of Bonham, Texas, but he was raised in Oklahoma City. He learned his guitar from his blind father, also a guitarist. As a teenager, young Charlie Christian played in his father's string band, mostly in nonblack neighborhoods. This Oklahoma-Texas region produced many names in musical history, including Jack Teagarden, Coleman Hawkins, "Hot Lips" Page, and Ben Webster.

Christian's playing companions were not ignorant musicians; they had some awareness of classical harmony, some having had experience with concert bands and symphony orchestras. Having mixed freely with banjo and mandolin players in Oklahoma City, who were plucking in western (country) style, Christian's own playing must have been influenced by these ballads and moanful styles.

Before joining Benny, Christian was working in Kansas City when he heard a record by the Andy Kirk Orchestra, called "Floyd's Guitar Blues." In it, Floyd Smith used an amplified electric guitar. The exact origins of the electric guitar are uncertain. Eddie Durham claimed that he developed the first such instrument, but many others were experimenting with it in the 1930s, including Les Paul.

Once again, John Hammond, that master locator of musical talent, was involved in bringing Christian to New York City (he was an early discoverer of Billie Holiday). One evening at a Beverly Hills restaurant, Hammond sneaked Christian onto the band stand, and when Goodman called for "Rose Room"

Christian played an amazing improvisation for many minutes. Benny disregarded the rubelike dress of the Texan and made Christian his regular guitarist.[8]

Although Easterners were surprised by Christian's virtuosity, they forgot that Texas and Oklahoma were guitar country, especially blues guitar. Christian brought this blues guitar to jazz with amazing talent when he joined the Benny Goodman Sextet at age twenty-three. Until he joined Goodman, Christian traveled the United States with good musicians such as Mary Lou Williams, Oscar Pettiford, and Eddie Durham. He abandoned his father's string band (which included two brothers) that had played all over Oklahoma.

At first, Goodman assigned Christian to the rhythm section, where he provided strong support. But soon, he was given an opportunity to show his magnificence as a solo player on the electric guitar on recordings such as "Flying Home" and "Star Dust, " which were spectacular examples of his "horn-like" playing, his clean style, and his amplified melodic "bell-like" tones. All this came from a technique that was relatively new for its time. Schuller compares his style to that of Django Reinhardt, the talented Belgian-born guitarist. But Reinhardt developed from a European French-Spanish, gypsy style, rather than from American jazz. Sextet members were required to solo; but a solo with an acoustic guitar was impossible, so when Christian ran his long series of notes on his amplified guitar, he soared above the group. Henceforth, the guitar moved to the front of the orchestra. Christian's contribution to music was attenuated by his tragic death at age twenty-six.

Goodman's rank in music is secure. He is the standard by which to evaluate others. He had the best sidemen, the best soloists, the top arrangers. He hired more great jazzmen than anyone, with the possible exception of Duke Ellington. Goodman reigned supreme at improvisation, with large bands and small groups. Benny Goodman played his clarinet with incredible brilliance, and he was brilliant at all speeds, and he elevated the performances of those he played with.

But no man is an island. Benny acknowledged his debt to Lester Young, Basie's great tenor sax man. And Goodman condensed all that was good of Paul Whiteman, Ben Pollack, Red Nichols, and Fletcher Henderson and made it popular and acceptable. He did this by being a great musician and an astute manager of musical talent. He mixed his classical and New Orleans experiences to create a new complicated jazz of counterpoint and rhythm.

Goodman's status as an individual is far more controversial. He was petty; he was mean. He slighted his best friends continuously. He insulted even those he admired. Many of his best sidemen left "for personal reasons." Some attribute his social failings to his poverty in his growing up years. This is food for psycho-historians.

"Tuxedo Junction"

He was born Alton Glenn Miller in Iowa but was always known as Glenn. His father, who was a carpenter, moved the family to Nebraska, where they lived in a sod house. Glenn loved music, which began with the mandolin, which he hated, so he soon switched to trombone. When he tried to obtain work, he was forced to compete with Jack Teagarden, who also played trombone, so Glenn, at twenty-two years of age, started arranging for the Ben Pollack band, whose players included Benny Goodman, Jack Teagarden and Jimmy MacPartland. When Pollack's band broke up, Glenn played and arranged for Red Nichols' Five Pennies. In 1935, he agreed to help Ray Noble, the famous British conductor, form a band for a New York appearance in the Rainbow Room. Miller was versatile to the nth degree, playing jazz trombone while providing interesting arrangements in many styles of music.

When Noble succeeded, Glenn Miller thought about forming his own orchestra. As he said, "I am tired of arguing about arrangements." He wanted to hear his own sounds. But the 1937 Miller orchestra was a flop, in part because it sounded too much like Benny Goodman. Glenn and Benny were roommates and good friends, although Glenn was five years younger.

Miller suffered all the misfortunes of the Great Depression and more. There was little money for low-paid musicians; they played one-night stands and went by auto, because they could not afford a bus. There was much drinking, and often only half the band showed up for an engagement. Worse, he and his wife Helen could not conceive a child.

But he refused to relinquish his life's dream. Miller's early experience prepared him well for achieving the kind of mass appeal he finally garnered. Unlike the Dorseys, who were confined to the East, Glenn confronted Chicago jazz, but his dreams lay elsewhere: he wanted a mainstream music that would fuse eclectically the best beats of Hollywood and Broadway. Miller chose to make a break with black jazz. In fact, he was closer to Gershwin than Armstrong, because he (Miller) had studied with the same teacher—Russian-born Joseph Schillinger.

By April 1938, Miller put together a new band, with a five-man saxophone section, four trombones, and four trumpets, which opened with a clarinet lead. It included Tex Beneke, who handled many of the vocals; Hal McIntyre; Paul Tanner; Al Klink; and Wilbur Schwartz, who played clarinet over saxophones. One sax played one octave, another played an octave lower and the clarinet or another sax played the melody. Newcomer Schwartz became the key to the later success. It was an idea that Ray Noble had rejected: using a clarinet and tenor saxophones to introduce melodies, but this was the new Miller sound. George T. Simon, the music critic, called it the "plunger brass, boo ah, boo ah sound."[9]

The "overnight success" began in March 1939 when the band played at Frank Daley's Meadowbrook in New Jersey and at the Glen Island Casino in New Rochelle, New York, a gig which lasted all summer, where announcer

Hugh James would introduce Glenn Miller "beside the beautiful waters of Long Island Sound." Gradually Miller gained national acceptance, particularly after the band started to broadcast ten times per week at the Meadowbrook. His group became the "most danceable band" in the business. The place was packed every night, where police held back crowds. His first big hit was "In the Mood," but in that first year, he also recorded "Stairway to the Stars," "The Lady's in Love With You," and "Little Brown Jug."

The band also acquired a contract to make records on the RCA Victor label, but the early 1939 records achieved few sales. If the popularity of his music was spreading, it was due almost exclusively to his radio broadcasts. He started the Chesterfield Hour in December, when he was still imitating Goodman, but he was mixing it up with his slow, very-danceable selections. His repertory would nearly always include songs like "King Porter Stomp" and "Bugle Call Rag," as well as his "Moonlight Serenade" and "Sunrise Serenade." These were to become his sign on and sign off songs—selections that were easily recognized the world over.

When Miller was booked to play the Capitol Theater in Washington, the price for his band was ten times that of New Rochelle. His bookings went high hat: he played the Hotel Pennsylvania in New York and the Paramount Theater. No matter where, the bobby-soxers screamed

In time, Miller offered less Goodman, and he created a music that was meant for a young, white population. Whereas Bill Sauter was providing Benny Goodman with more complicated and complex arrangements, Miller was making his music simple, smooth, and danceable. He stuck to the distinctive reeds the muted brass, and the four-trombone sounds. He knew that the marketplace of song was not jazz, but slow swing, which explains his preference for Debussy's "Reverie," "Danny Boy," and "My Last Goodbye." By the end of 1939, Miller had evolved a unique sound that was far removed from the world of jazz—in fact, most jazz books give short shrift to the music of Miller. But he had earned public acceptance: the *Downbeat* magazine poll voted his band second to Benny Goodman.

Miller was an astute businessman. He was extremely opinionated, but he was an efficient leader and a good friend to his band members. He pressured his musicians constantly to play better, and quickly got rid of those who did not meet his high standards. His shows were just that—shows. He was keenly aware of the visual effects of the music. So he had his trombonists move their instruments from left to right while the trumpeters were moving theirs up and down. Occasionally, they used hats to cover horns and reeds while they were put in motion. His craving for perfection led him to inspect his musicians for shined shoes, combed hair, and for just the right amount of handkerchief sticking out of their lapel pockets.[10]

On August 1, 1939 the Miller band recorded "In the Mood." It was a very lucky day for Glenn. It became one of the best-known recordings in the world, because it has been used in countless movies and television productions to signify World War II. The band wasn't impressed with the song—they thought it was square and a bad tune. In fact, Artie Shaw turned down the tune earlier as being "too simple." Many of the musicians in that recording session became names later. Ray McKinley was on drums, Tex Beneke on sax, Billy May was trumpeter and arranger, and Mel Powell played piano. All of them went on to start their own bands.

On September 27, 1939 he made his first recording on the Bluebird label, and shortly after, he recorded "Moonlight Serenade," which became his theme song. Glenn attributed his huge success to the "juke box," which in 1939 offered up to twenty-four selections for five cents each. By that time, there were over three hundred thousand boxes nationwide, and Miller's songs often commanded up to six of the total selections.

In December, Miller began his three-times-per-week broadcasts for Chesterfield cigarettes, and on this show, he began his famous medleys: "Something Old, Something New, Something Borrowed, Something Blue." Typical of these was the wonderful combination of "My Melancholy Baby," "Moon Love," a new version of a Tchaikovsky concerto, "Stompin at the Savoy," (borrowed from Benny Goodman), and "Blue Moon."

Glenn Miller became a legend in American musical history. When his band took off in 1939, he broke all attendance and sales records, surpassing those of the Goodman orchestra. One person characterized this time as "Moonlight, Memories and Miller."[11]

Here is what Schuller says about the Miller sound: "Its famous reed section sound was a musical phenomenon for which one is hard put to find many parallels, certainly in Western music. For while all great composers have their special sound—an amalgam of specific harmonic usages, voice-leading and instrumentation—it is hard to think of anyone with a sound so unique, quite so mesmerising—and, more astonishingly, so resistant to becoming tedious."[12]

A final word on "Tuxedo Junction." It was a real place in Alabama—a honky tonk "where people go to pass the night away" (mostly blacks). The place was memorialized by Erskine Hawkins, but the song could not catch on until Glenn Miller provided his slow, rhythmic beat. It sold so many copies that when Miller bought a ranch in California, he named it "Tuxedo Junction."

TD and Brother

Tommy and Jimmy Dorsey made over a hundred records between 1928 and 1935. These were not distinguished jazz pieces, and Schuller claims that they were poor soloists because they had never been exposed to the early work of Louis Armstrong, Duke Ellington, and the other great black innovators. In the Dorsey band, Tommy was the leader and Jimmy was the featured soloist on clarinet or saxophone. Jimmy Dorsey was the more admired technician, and he did make a mark later in his Latin-American period (1939-1941), when he produced the very popular "Maria Elena," "Malaguena" and "Six Lessons From Madame La Zonga."

Their father, the boys' first music teacher, gave them a solid technical foundation. Each day, when he returned from the coal mine, he would test little Tommy on techniques of playing the cornet. But playing in Pennsylvania and along the East Coast limited their exposure to real jazz. They missed the Chicago-Kansas City experience that helped Goodman and Miller.

Tommy Dorsey was difficult to play for, a trait he acquired from his father; he was no-nonsense. His marvelous talent for playing and directing soon produced a string of hits: "Boogie Woogie," "Marie," "I'll Never Smile Again," and "Song of India."

During 1937 and 1938, the Tommy Dorsey band played mechanically: each song was introduced by Tommy's trombone, followed by a vocal (usually Jack Leonard), and completed by one or more solos—musicians called it the "Mickey Mouse" style. Sy Oliver changed the image of the orchestra completely. Joining the group in 1939, Oliver gave Dorsey his first real jazz sound. Oliver played, sang, and arranged several of Dorsey's greatest hits, including "Opus No. 1" and "We'll Git It." These reflected Oliver's work over many years with the Jimmy Lunceford band. Oliver's talent raised Dorsey's performance to unprecedented heights.

Oliver energized the soloists to new levels; they played with more enthusiam, with more focus, and with a much better beat. To achieve his new sound, he substituted a baritone saxophone for the bass clarinet, a feature most black bands had used for years. Whites preferred the softer tones of the clarinet.

Dorsey featured soft, beautiful harmony combined with his muted trombone—it was the kind of music that gave him the title, "The Sentimental Gentleman of Swing." He presented an array of musical offerings, including "The Clambake Seven," "The Dixieland Band," "The Pied Pipers," and the Modernaires." This is one reason why his band kept getting larger, until it numbered twenty-nine members.

Let's "Begin the Beguine"

He was born Arthur Arshawsky, but he burst upon the musical stage as Artie Shaw. He gave us all the puzzling aspects of his confused life in his autobiography—*The Trouble With Cinderella*. His life was certainly controversial—perhaps because of his brilliant mind and innovative ways. He was hindered in the beginning by a lack of skill in his clarinet playing, which is remarkable, because he became a great jazz clarinetist. His skill was so improved by the end of the 1930s that he challenged Benny Goodman for the top place in several polls. The answer that Shaw gave to this enigma was that he was determined to make himself the greatest clarinet player alive, and towards that end, he practiced seven or eight hours per day for four to five years.

Shaw began as an iconoclastic dreamer who started out in the mid-1930s to create a new kind of jazz band, which included only his clarinet, a rhythm section and a single trumpet, saxophone and trombone. He failed miserably and in disgust he decided to challenge the musical world on its terms. He created his Goodman-like orchestra with his own group within a band—the Grammercy Five—a name that came from his New York telephone listing. He achieved distinction by having Johnny Guarnieri shift from piano to harpsichord for the pounding, driving renditions of "Summit Ridge Drive," "Cross Your Heart," and "My Blue Heaven."

By 1939, he was no longer imitating Benny Goodman, and he was playing the upper registers of his instrument flawlessly. Moreover, he sought new musical expressions and concepts in his own playing and for the cohesion of his band. He became a seeker of substance and quality—aspects that he achieved with good arrangements from Jerry Gray and great work from his new drummer Buddy Rich, who was only twenty years old at the time.

Having studied the techniques of black drummers Jo Jones and Sid Catlett, Rich brought a new anima to the rhythm section. He and Gray effectively altered the band's performance from the moment they linked up their talents. In January 1939, Rich and Gray produced "Lover Come Back to Me," and in that year Artie Shaw achieved a new pinnacle when his band was voted number one, capturing the title from Benny Goodman, but Benny was still voted the number one clarinetist.

Shaw's ego was almost as large as his clarinet playing; he acquired and disposed of many wives. He claimed credit for many successes that were due almost entirely to Jerry Gray's excellent arrangements. Gray, who was inconspicuous as a violinist, became renowned for his arrangement of the Cole Porter tune, "Begin the Beguine."

Here we confront one of the puzzles in Shaw's musical journey. He tended to eschew the popular tunes that made him famous and rich to pursue some exotic notions about how music should be performed. He consistently turned to African-like drumbeats and tom toms on such numbers as "Nightmare," "Jungle Drums," "Traffic Jam," and "Hindustan." He did not abandon this search until he enlarged his band later to play his more symphonic pieces, such as "Concerto for Clarinet." George T. Simon wrote that Artie Shaw was an "unusually bright, articulate, imaginative musician . . . who has always taken his music, and often himself, very seriously."[13]

Because he openly imitated Benny Goodman, Shaw created a musical controversy. Goodman the King of Swing; Shaw the upstart. Shaw was no match for Goodman's virtuosity on the clarinet, but how he could pick his vocalists and his sidemen. Who can forget Shaw's recordings with Lena Horne, Billie Holiday, and Helen Forrest. And what a band: Billy Butterfield and Roy Eldridge on trumpet; George Auld and Tony Pastor on Saxophone; and that driving, pulsating rhythm section led by John Guarnieri on piano and Buddy Rich on the drums.

Shaw used his talents well, and he had a penchant for spotting good tunes (for example, "Begin the Beguine," "Frenesi," and "Back Bay Shuffle"). He was able to combine a good melody with his exceptional rhythm section. He was noted also for following Duke Ellington in initiating the Latin sound in jazz.

Meet the Duke

As the blues permeated the swing sound, blacks were well represented in the Big Band era. But Edward Kennedy Ellington—the Duke—towered over all the rest. Ellington was born in Washington, D.C. on April 29, 1899, and began playing the piano at a very early age. After starring in his own local jazz combo, he left Washington for New York City in 1923 to play in the Wilbur Sweatman jazz band in Harlem. Soon his extraordinary musical talent was evident to Irving Mills, a musical publisher, who signed Ellington to a recording contract.

With this as a starting point, he expanded his combo to fourteen men and moved to the Cotton Club, where he began to compose and play his incredible repertoire of wonderfully smooth and intensely wild and frenetic style of music. Compare "Mood Indigo" and "Ring dem Bells." Or "Sophisticated Lady" and The "Mooch." As he explained, "We put the Negro feeling and spirit in our music." In 1935 his music took another turn when he asked Juan Tizol and other Puerto Ricans to join his band. It changed the Ellington style, beginning with "Caravan." What is remarkable about Ellington is that he composed those wonderful melodies, played the piano, led the orchestra and did all of the orchestrations.

In 1939 the Duke recorded nearly fifty tunes, yet he was in a state of dejection over musical trends. He saw the rise of Miller as "creative stasis." Swing was at its peak in 1939—but Ellington was not a major player. He chose not to imitate Shaw, Miller, or Goodman. Rather, he would ride out this wave of popular bands that was distorting the true essence of jazz. Having said that, he proceeded to imitate Miller's In-the-Mood approach on some of his recordings. The pull of the marketplace was too powerful to ignore.

But Ellington's creative urges returned. In the spring of 1939 he composed the elegant "Serenade to Sweden" during the orchestra's second European tour (it was based, in part, on the theme from "Moonglow"). The work seemed anachronistic—it was melodious and harmonic—at a time when all Europe was praying for peace but preparing for war. At least Ellington was at peace with himself, and the fantastic reception given him by the Swedish people told him that he never had really deviated from his unique musical journey. For the first time in his career, he was feted by his critics and his public as a serious creative artist—a reputation he could not enjoy in the U.S. music world dominated by Miller and Goodman.

The 1939 band was aided by the addition of Ben Webster, Jimmy Blanton, and Billy Strayhorn (what a Dickensian name!). For Ellington, Blanton's bass-playing had the biggest impact because of the importance of the rhythm section in the Ellingtonian scheme of music. It was essential for classic jazz, but Blanton brought much more than rhythm to his playing—he used his instrument for bass runs and for solo purposes by alternating bow and plucking pizzicato. Equally important was Strayhorn's contribution as composer and arranger; he brought a fresh admixture of talent and energy that enhanced the orchestra's potential, so much so that Duke soon considered him his soulmate.

The Ellington and Strayhorn collaboration has been called unique in musical annals, particularly because they were both pianists. Strayhorn, who was raised in Pittsburgh, studied classical music extensively before joining the Ellington band at the age of twenty-four. At first, he worked only on the lyrics for Ellington's tunes that required vocals, but soon Strayhorn made his name in music for "Take the A Train."

Ellington saw jazz as a restless thing that was always probing, innovating, and searching for new ways of expressing musical forms. Its heart was the repetition of riffs, and its soul was constant improvisation. Even though the band might have played "Don't Get Around Much Anymore," "Mood Indigo" and "Sophisticated Lady" every evening before a different audience, the sounds were always new. Ellington, born on the edge of a new century, created the incomparable sounds that established him as a leading composer and placed him at the front of arrangers. Amazingly, he scored all his music in his own flowery handwriting. He scored with great precision; all the parts were written out note by note. The only exception was the role of the drummer.[14]

By the end of 1939, Ellington was recognized by the cognoscenti as "the most original musical mind in America." But it was the racial character of Ellington's music that led many to call him "unrecognized royalty." If one scans records that offer collections of the greatest selections of the swing era, Ellington is either passed over or given a small role. Ellington, who was a very proud man, tried to diminish his disappointment over the neglect of his music. He once said, "I am a pedestrian minstrel." And on another occasion, when asked about his early work, he replied, "That was before my time, You know. I was born at the Newport Jazz Festival, in 1956."[15]

In the 1930s the swing bands were supreme. The music of Goodman, Miller, and Shaw was the popular music of the time, not that of Ellington or Lunceford. Even the Kay Kysers, the Orrin Tuckers and the Sammy Kayes benefited from the swing craze. In a more conventional time, these schmaltzy, mediocre bands could not have survived. As Schuller wrote, they "plagiarized and trivialized the musical innovations and styles of the leading black musicians, reducing the content to a banal, lowest common-denominator of accessibility."[16]

Sadly, this did not concern the average person who wanted only to dance to the tunes of the time. Ellington's rich arrangements may have been ignored by some, but they established him as one of America's greatest composers, some say America's premier composer.[17]

Louis

Louis Armstrong was the great jazz anomaly. He qualified as a crooner, because he sang in low, gentle tones, and he could sing in a sentimental manner, but he was also one of the greatest jazz trumpeters. It was said he could hit one hundred consecutive high Cs and he could also reach a high E-flat.

Born in New Orleans in 1901, he got his first commercial job at age seven, when he blew a horn from atop a wagon to announce its presence in the neighborhood. The owner of the wagon later gave Louis $5 to purchase his first trumpet. At age eleven, he was sent to the Home for Colored Waifs, because he fired a pistol on New Year's Eve, and it was in that home that he perfected some of his playing techniques.

Armstrong seems to have invented syncopation, from which swing evolved. It began with the ragtime form, where strong beats are where they are not supposed to be. It was an uneven count, not 1,2 divisible by four. In the 1920s Armstrong helped to evolve the jazz style by working with Jelly Roll Morton and Bix Beiderbeck. It was a fusion of the New Orleans and Chicago styles. The New Orleans style sprang from funerals, for which small combos played in march cadence and used simultaneous improvisations, whereas Chicago jazz was indoors and stressed solos.

When Armstrong moved to Chicago and New York after 1924, he studied and worked with King Oliver and Fletcher Henderson, and soon he was the first trumpeter of jazz. He was so amazed at his popularity that he put out a pamphlet on "125 Jazz Breaks for Cornet," which sold for $1—a tidy sum in 1927. In the 1930s, Armstrong had to confront discrimination everywhere he went. White announcers refused to introduce his band, and he was denied the use of restrooms, forcing him into the humiliation of relieving himself in alleys. When he got his first passport in 1931, he tasted the delicious idea of equal treatment. Returning to the United States, he smiled through all the hurts. In one of his movies, he had to sing "Jeepers Creepers" to a horse.[18]

He overcame adversity by being the king of the trumpet. Wynton Marsalis states, "Louis is Jazz." Armstrong's playing companions make up a trumpet hall of fame: Bix Beiderbecke, Red Nichols, Bunny Berrigan, Harry James, Rex Stewart and Charlie Shavers.

Those who followed owed him for the skills he generously offered. Some techniques, however, they could not imitate. He was the primary exponent of combining singing and playing in harmony, which came to be called "scat vocalizing," in which the human voice imitated the sound of the instrument. In the 1930s, this approach was used extensively by the Mills Brothers.

CROONERS AND THRUSHERS

The Big Band era was memorable for the variety of its musical sounds. Each band had a unique style, a theme song by which you could recognize it and vocalists who could deliver the wide range of ballads and blues that were integral parts of the music of that time. Who can forget the flawless diction and the phrasing of Lena Horne, Ella Fitzgerald, Helen O'Connell, Helen Forest, Jack Leonard, Art Lund, and the youthful Frank Sinatra. O'Connell shot into prominence in 1939 with her rendition of "Green Eyes," with Bob Eberly and the Jimmy Dorsey Orchestra. How we swooned to the suggestive rhythms of "Those cool and limpid green eyes!"

Der Bingle

Of the crooners, one name dominated. Beginning in 1931 and continuing until his death in 1977, Bing Crosby was able to mix jazz, cowboy, religious, and patriotic renditions in such a way that his name showed up on several lists of crooners and jazz singers. He moved freely with Louis Armstrong and Count Basie, as well as with Woody Herman. In doing jazz, Bing was often like another instrument. He used his consummate phrasing skill and vocal trills to improvise on the basic melody (scat singing).

But Crosby was just as accomplished on Irish, Hawaiian, and novelty tunes, and the classics of Cole Porter. In 1939, when Sinatra was doing vocals for Tommy Dorsey, the band leader told his young balladeer to listen to Bing Crosby and to pay attention to the words, as Bing did. And when Irving Berlin went to Crosby with his new "White Christmas," Bing put his ever-present pipe in his mouth and calmly told Berlin that "you have nothing to worry about."

Lady Day

Billie Holiday was an important figure in American popular music; she was one the first great female singers of jazz. Her influence was wide: there are elements of her style in Helen Forrest, Anita O'Day, Frank Sinatra, Nat King Cole, and even Dinah Shore. Billie's songs were an outlet from her marital disappointments, violence, drugs, alcohol, and racial discrimination that haunted her throughout her brief life.

Billie was always known as "Lady Day," a name given her by saxophonist Lester Young (in turn, she called him "Prez" for President). Her voice reflected the pain of her life, the sorrow, the love-gone-wrong, the heartache. In her pure voice, we were emotionally involved in her tragic memories. She brought the best qualities of jazz to popular music—"the precision of jazz" and the "vibrant intensity of the blues." Like Ella Fitzgerald, Billie's singing was inclined towards instrumental-like techniques.

Holiday's childhood and adult life produced the blues that she sang. Her travails were laid out passionately in her autobiography, *Lady Sings the Blues*, which was ghost-written for her and which is a mixture of fact and fiction, undoubtedly influenced by her drug use.[19]

She was born Eleanora Fagan in Baltimore, Maryland, in 1915, and she started singing professionally at age fifteen. She made her first recording in 1934 with the Benny Goodman band, and she moved constantly. Her personal life was tempestuous; it began with her illegimate birth and a father who abandoned her, and it progressed to failed marriages and her own strange fruit—opium, which she found in 1939 and that was followed quickly by heroin.

April 1939 was the high point of a life that was clearly marked for tragedy—when Billie Holiday recorded "Strange Fruit." It was to change her life, but not for the better. Until that time, she had sung briefly with Benny Goodman, Count Basie, and Artie Shaw. She was convinced that she would never find her niche unless she struck out on her own as a soloist, because the unknowing public was getting its thrills from mediocre (mostly white) vocalists. (She forgot that Artie Shaw had given her just the start that she sought and that she left him abruptly).

John Hammond helped her to obtain an opening at Josephson's Cafe Society club in Greenwich Village, where she found stardom of a sort. It was in that club that Lewis Allen, a school teacher and poet, came to a performance. He offered her his haunting, metaphoric poem, "Strange Fruit," which he had set to music. It went so sensationally well that he helped to put her rendition on a phonograph record. It was like nothing before, although there were intimations of Bessie Smith's blues recordings. It was blues at its best—funereal, dirgelike, slowly recitative, but its subject was shocking—the lynching of blacks in the South.

It was no Hollywood tune, so Brunswick, Holiday's regular recording company, refused to publish it, but the new Commodore Records grabbed it eagerly. It was a feast for liberals but anathema to disk jockeys. The BBC in England banned it, but most Americans were unaware of it. "Strange Fruit " was a powerful statement of a grievous wrong that American society was ignoring. It was gutsy to sing it, and Billie did it with feelings of sorrow for her people. The moving document was sung in B-flat minor after a muted-trumpet opening by Frankie Newton and a statement of the theme by Sonny White (her lover at the time).

On the same day that Billie recorded "Strange Fruit," she also did three other songs. Two became her trade marks: "Fine and Mellow" and "I Got a Right to Sing the Blues." "Fine and Mellow" was perfect for the timbre in her voice and the tragedy in her lyrics. She sang nothing but slow blues and melancholy melodies, which reached the depths in "Gloomy Sunday." It was reported that several persons committed suicide on hearing it.

Although it was reported that she had an IQ of only 81, she was a very complex person. She was kind, generous, sympathetic, and a friend for life, but she was depressed, suffered from inferiority, and wanted to be detroyed. Clarke describes her as "a walking zombie" who was "punch drunk." She begged her lovers to "use me" and to "beat me." Amazingly, Holiday rose above this miserable existence to produce songs that achieved legendary status. Americans, who love an underdog, took her to their hearts.[20]

Ella

In 1935, a very young girl made her first recording with the Chick Webb band. It was not a hit, but it demonstrated her extremely wide range of voices and control that was to make her "The First Lady of Swing." It was a title she earned easily with her talent and grace. She had perfect pitch, an amazing range, and a voice "tinged with honey."

She was born in 1917, just two years after Billie Holiday, with whom she was often compared. Her first stage experience was embarrassing. As a shy teenager she was coaxed into entering the weekly talent show at the Apollo Theater in Harlem. She was scheduled to dance, but after watching two sisters perform in spectacular fashion just before her turn came, she developed stage fright. The MC, sensing her difficulty, asked her to sing, whereupon totally unprepared she did an imitation of the popular Connie Boswell song "The Object of My Affection." She won the first prize of $25 (a very large sum for a teenager), and she was on her way.

Because of the Apollo appearance, she was discovered by Chick Webb, the drummer and band leader. Because she was an orphan, Webb adopted her and guided her over the difficulties in her growing-up years.

Her first phonograph record, which she made for Decca in 1935, was reviewed by music critic George Simon in *Metronome* magazine, who predicted correctly that "Miss Fitzgerald should go places." In late 1938 she made a record that would stamp her for life. Until then, she survived on jazz, but the swing version of a nursery rhyme, "A Tisket, A Tasket," became a million-dollar seller, and it became one of her most enduring trademarks. Between 1935 and 1939, when Webb died, she sang on at least one side of every record that his band cut.

TIN PAN ALLEY

On Armistice Day 1939 singer Kate Smith, the darling of American popular ballads, introduced Irving Berlin's "God Bless America" to her radio audience. Its patriotic theme and sentimental lyrics touched the soul and the nerve of the nation. Berlin wrote it in 1918 but did not publish it. This simple song was to become the "second national anthem of the United States."

Berlin, who was born Israel Baline, was a Russian immigrant who landed at Ellis Island in 1893 and who remarkably, lived until September 22, 1989. His nine hundred songs reflected the dreams of all Americans in the twentieth century. They were fiercely patriotic and slightly sentimental, but as Jerome Kern said, "Irving Berlin is American music."

When Berlin's father died, fourteen-year-old Israel left home and took a job as a singing waiter. In 1907, he wrote his first song, "Marie from Sunny Italy," and he signed his name I. Berlin. From then he became Irving Berlin. During World War I, he was drafted into the army, where he was commissioned to write musical revues. In one, his song echoed his feelings about army life. He wrote, "Oh How I Hate to Get Up in the Morning." Upon discharge, Berlin started his own musical publishing company, and he started writing musical scores for Broadway and Hollywood. His first motion picture score was "Top Hat" with Fred Astaire and Ginger Rogers, from which we got "Cheek to Cheek."

One final note about Berlin. In 1939 he wrote "White Christmas." It was not released until 1942 in the movie *Holiday Inn.* Bing Crosby's version of this song became the largest selling Christmas song of all time. It may seem odd that a Jew should write of Christmas, but Berlin had plenty of exposure to Christian things after he married Ellin Mackay, a Roman Catholic, who was the daughter of Clarence H. Mackay, the president of the Postal Telegraph Company.

ON BROADWAY

The Depression changed Broadway markedly. The financial troubles of that era spawned a number of psychological, pathetic dramas that mirrored the crippling blow the absence of patrons and customers had produced. But by 1939, Americans felt better about their economic lives, and this more positve disposition was reflected in the theatrical offerings on Broadway. Altogether seventy-six nonmusicals were produced (the lowest number in the decade) and fifteen musicals. They gave Americans plenty of time to enjoy a feast of superior singing, dancing, and acting.[21] They could view Maurice Evans as Falstaff in Shakespeare's *Henry VI*, part I; Katharine Hepburn in *The Philadelphia Story;* and Katharine Cornell and Laurence Olivier in *No Time for Comedy.* Reflecting the increasing bouyancy of the year, musicals accounted for roughly 20 percent of all theatrical offerings. The two biggest hits, *DuBarry was a Lady* and *The Streets of Paris*, continued the trend of presenting unreal worlds in a slapstick fashion.

The year 1939 was also notable for the number of performers whose debuts presaged their later stardom: Broadway-goers came to notice Gene Kelly in *One for the Money*, Danny Kaye in *The Straw Hat Review;* and Abbott and Costello in *The Streets of Paris.* Others having brief stints in first productions included Lena Horne in *Blackbirds*, Desi Arnaz beating a congo drum in *Too Many Girls*, Phil Silvers coming from burlesque to play in *Yokel Boy* and Betty Grable just showing up for *DuBarry was a Lady.*

The Negro theater was in a state of eclipse for much of the 1930s only to be revived by the very controversial *The Swing Mikado* and *The Hot Mikado*, which premiered in the spring of 1939. These twin productions were an unusual episode in Broadway programming. *The Swing Mikado*, the all-Negro production of the Chicago Federal Theatre, was a 1938 jazzy version of the Gilbert and Sullivan musical. On May 1, 1939 it opened at the 44th Street Theatre on Broadway.

Producer Michael Todd had offered to buy the show, but when he was refused, he presented his own competing version, *The Hot Mikado*, at the

Broadhurst Theater, with Bill Robinson as the emperor decked out in gold finery. The ever-flamboyant Todd, who used a spectacular erupting volcano and a forty-foot waterfall as props, set his tickets for his show at $3.30, three times the price of the Chicago *Swing Mikado*. Todd won the competition despite the higher prices, and his show was presented in the Hall of Music at the New York World's Fair. Todd sold his show to the Fair, where it was offered to fair goers for from forty to ninety-nine cents.

In 1939 Jerome Kern returned to Broadway with his musical *Very Warm for May*, a story about a group of college students who take over a summer theater in a barn and make it a success. Unfortunately, the show fared less well—its Alvin Theater production lasting only for fifty-nine performances. Despite Kern's music and the book by Oscar Hammerstein and direction by Vincent Minnelli, the plot could not sustain the music, which was vintage Kern and included the wonderful "All the Things You Are." *Swinging the Dream*, a musical version of Shakespeare's *A Mid-summer Night's Dream*, was a bigger flop, lasting only thirteen performances. It was the story of a Louisiana governor in New Orleans who had no purpose other than to allow a great cast of musicians to show their stuff, led by Louis Armstrong, Maxine Sullivan and the Benny Goodman Sextette (including Benny with Lionel Hampton, Fletcher Henderson, Charles Christian, Nick Fatool, and Arthur Bernstein). One decent tune survived the production: "Darn that Dream."

During the year, many musical comedies were divorced from the problems of the real world. On December 6, 1939, the last show of the year, *DuBarry was a Lady*, arrived on Broadway at the 46th Street Theatre. It ran for 408 performances, making it one of the hits of the decade. The mixture was just right: comedian/singers Ethel Merman and Bert Lahr joined with the music of Cole Porter. The plot involved a night club attendant (Bert Lahr) who won the Irish Sweepstakes' $75,000 prize and who attempted to win Ethel Merman with his new status. The title comes from a dream scene in which Lahr is Louis XV of France and Merman is his DuBarry, his "mistress in name only." Despite all his grandiose plans, he gets nowhere with DuBarry. In the dream, twenty-three year old Betty Grable makes her Broadway debut singing "Do I Love You?"

The plot is convoluted by a triangle in the dream and in real life, and the music is replete with bawdy references and double entendres. For example, Bert Lahr, in singing "It Ain't Etiquette," got off these lines:

> If you thought you were gypped at the Fair last year
> And that Grover is just all wet
> Don't suggest what he can do with the Perisphere
> It ain't chic, it ain't smart, it ain't etiquette.

Federal Theatre

This music program brought talent and good cheer to millions who craved it and resulted in the production of 5,300 original works, as it supported fifteen thousand persons. Musicians, who performed a total of 150,000 programs for one hundred million persons, were able to keep their professions alive. With WPA help, they later settled into some of our finest symphony orchestras. The North Carolina Symphony Orchestra began as a WPA organization. By 1939, there were 270 symphony orchestras in the United States, most receiving support from the WPA.[22]

The federal role began when Harry Hopkins, head of the Federal Emergency Administration, saw some unemployed musicians in the streets begging with violins in hand. With the help of then Governor Franklin Roosevelt, a temporary relief program was established. The federal program followed quickly, under which unemployed musicians were sent all over the United States giving vaudeville shows and legitimate theater, and artists were paid to decorate federal buildings.

This episode in the cultural history of the United States was directed by Hallie Flanagan, who, like her new boss, had settled in Iowa, where she taught a course at Grinnell College. Her success there won her an appointment with the famous 47 Project at Harvard University, where she worked under George Baker. When Harry Hopkins began his theatre project, he promised to put three million people to work. He had to find work for thirteen thousand employees and directors. For this task, he chose Flanagan as his assistant.

Flanagan saw the problem as "Men Not Working." She set out to preserve the skills of the workers, and in the process preserve self-respect. This emphasis on human values begged the main question: was the emphasis to be on relief or on the quality of theatre? Flanagan told a story that suggested she could do both. An old violinist from Tampa, Florida, approached her and said, "Do not judge what we can do in six months by the way we play tonight. Our hands are still too calloused for the bow."[23] It turned out that the only employment the artists could find was doing road work. Flanagan proposed that the proceeds from an amusement tax be used to finance theatrical activities in twenty-five to one hundred cities, which would provide free performances. Such a plan would duplicate the taxes of Bulgaria, Chile, Denmark, Estonia, Greece, Iceland, Latvia, Romania, and Yugoslavia. But Senator Claude Pepper said, categorically, that the Congress was not ready for "so advanced a plan."

Flanagan considered the Broadway stage the main street of American theater, so she was very anxious to find a person qualified to head the New York City project. She found her man in Elmer Rice, the forty-three year old playwright and stage director. His own plays had changed with the Depression, from portraying the American scene to reporting on social and political themes.

Rice clearly wanted the job, because he told Flanagan, "Even if we had twenty plays in rehearsal at once, with thirty in a cast, that would keep only a fraction of them busy." But Flanagan needed Rice, so she tossed out an idea: they could do living newspapers, by which she meant having actors use the stage to dramatize every-day events. Rice jumped at the chance, as he cried: "Yes! And I can get the News-paper Guild to back it!"[24] In accepting the job, Rice made Flanagan promise that no performances would be censored. So enamored was he of this assignment that he worked seven days per week for the $260 that the job paid.

Rice set very high standards for the Federal Theatre. He promised work, not relief, and he demanded courtesy, consideration, and high standards of excellence from his professionals. He believed firmly that his shows could continue on their own even if the federal program was terminated. Rice was forced to hire from the welfare rolls, which limited employment possibilities. One person who applied for work was so tense that he beat his head against he wall, and a clown who was hired was so excited that on the opening night of the show, he suffered a stroke and never recovered.

Some dramas were written especially for the WPA, but for many royalties were paid. Some of the biggest names in drama, however, allowed their works to be performed for a token payment. George Bernard Shaw charged only $50 per week, provided that the ticket prices did not exceed the fifty-cent maximum. The brusque Shaw wrote that he "was not making a public-spirited sacrifice; I am jumping at an unprecedentedly good offer."

Sinclair Lewis went one better. Turning down a large contract for the right to produce one of his novels for the stage, he offered it to the WPA, because he supported its efforts and he knew that it would be played in a nonpartisan way. The last point was particularly important, because the novel was *It Can't Happen Here*, the life of Huey Long. Its message frightened many American, who did not believe that it could happen here.

In addition to the "living newspapers," the Federal Theatre presented a great variety of shows, including children's theater, puppets, marionettes, Negro drama, dance drama, classic drama, foreign language shows, vaudeville, religious drama, opera, and documentaries (for example, those concerning VD).

Roosevelt and the Democrats could not help Hallie Flanagan, because the New Deal was in trouble. The President was in the final months of his second term, and there was a growing antipathy against welfare and relief programs. Republicans were joined with conservative (mostly southern) Democrats, who were anxious to wrest control of the Democratic Party from the liberal wing.

Although many of the charges against Flanagan and the relief agencies could not be substantiated, there was agreement that WPA funds had been used inappropriately (illegally?) in some states. And so, the full House was not in any mood to debate the merits of the WPA Federal Theatre. But the Senate was more friendly. It concentrated its investigation on the jobs issue, which was Flanagan's strong suit, because 90 percent of her employees were taken from the relief rolls.

When the theatre budget was threatened, Hollywood responded with big guns. James Cagney, Edward Arnold, Pat O'Brien, George Jessel, Tyrone Power, Orson Welles, Raymond Massey, and Lionel Barrymore all spoke or wrote in favor of continuation. Certainly, the most colorful person to come to the aid of the Federal Theatre was Tallulah Bankhead, who, at the time, was starring in *The Little Foxes*. While the bill was being debated, Tallulah provided entertainment for the legislators. She was chosen by the Federal Theatre Project to lobby in support of the bill, because the glamorous actress was no stranger in Washington. Her father, William B. Bankhead, was Speaker of the House, while her uncle, John H. Bankhead, was the senior Senator from Alabama.

Tallulah was a show by herself: she hugged her uncle and begged all to come to the aid of the unemployed actors. Miss Bankhead knew that there were communists in the Federal Theatre Project, but she urged the appropriate committees of the Congress not to kill the program, because it was the primary source of employment for the hundreds of persons involved.

Throwing her femininity around, she told the senators in her deep, throaty voice that they simply must do somethmg for the unemployed actors, to which her uncle offered a rejoiner: "These city folks in Congress never vote to do anything for the farmers."

Goaded into action, she tossed her hat aside, baring her reddish-brown hair that flowed to her shoulder, and plopped herself on a table, being sure to show her long, beautiful legs. Getting the attention of the congressmen, she proceeded to give a lengthy exposition on the costs and benefits of the WPA program, as she read her prepared statement. Unlike her southern compatriots, she sped through the text. Her arguments were solid: the theatre provides a 10 percent federal tax on admissions; it employs actors and musicians, who know no other work; and it brings respite from the drudgery of living to millions. Reaching a dramatic crescendo, she screamed, "Actors are people." Then the Alabama sweetheart sat down at the end of her reading and cried.

William Brockman Bankhead, who was appointed Speaker of the United States House of Representatives in June 1936, was sometimes known, outside of Washington, as "Tallulah's daddy," but inside Washington, the Bankheads were an Alabama dynasty. His brother John was a Senator, his father, also named John, was a Senator; and House member. The Bankheads had been in Washington politics for more than seventy years.

William Bankhead, who was a University of Alabama Phi Beta Kappa and a fullback, got a law degree from Georgetown University and became an apprentice lawyer in Manhattan. He rose in politics with a stint in the state legislature, then as city attorney, and finally as representative from the Seventh District of Alabama. When he entered the House of Representatives, he looked like a leading man in a dramatic production. His suave manner made him one of the best-loved men in the Congress, and it was perfect for his job of keeping decorum in the House, where 435 representatives were cultivating their own little fiefdoms. He used a mellifluous voice (tinged with his Southern accent) in a dramatic manner to win many a fight through conciliation. A story illustrates his very calm demeanor. While campaigning for Al Smith, a member of the Ku Klux Klan threw eggs at him, whereupon he turned to the sponsor of the meeting and declared, "Sir I have been treated discourteously."[25]

But the bugaboo of communism reared its head. Senator Claude Pepper suggested a formal oath of allegiance. Not sufficient. The wrangling went on until midnight June 30, 1939, when opponents carried the vote. The new bill authorized funding for the writer's, music, and art projects only.

All across the country, theaters ran until midnite of the last day. In New York, "Pinocchio" shut down, as "bells claim our grief." The stagehands took down the sets and laid Pinocchio away in a pine box which read: BORN DECEMBER 23, 1938; KILLED BY ACT OF CONGRESS, JUNE 30, 1939.

OFF BROADWAY

George M. Cohan wrote stirring American music. Who is not moved patriotically by his "It's a Grand Old Flag" or "Over There"? His songs are "made in the USA." They called him the "Yankee Doodle Boy," a title that pleased him, because for fifty years he had touted America. But the "man who owned Broadway" and who wrote "Give My Regards to Broadway" as well as ninety-one plays and nearly three hundred other songs refused to allow his life to be produced on the stage or screen. He refused offers of $100,000 from Hollywood studios for his biography. Perhaps he feared the unknown, dark side of his life. He was egotistical, proud, and, when necessary, ruthless. He fought his actors, his unions, and his producers.

It shocked the musical world, therefore, when in 1939 Cohan happily gave his permission for his biography to be produced by a relatively obscure Drama Department at The Catholic University of America in Washington, D.C. This tight Yankee allowed the production free of charge. The link between George M. Cohan and Catholic University was Dr. Josephine McGarry Callan, who was hired in 1937 to join Father Gilbert V. Hartke, Walter Kerr and Leo Brady to establish a new drama department.[26]

Callan, a native of Baltimore, lived in Chicago, where her parents, Josephine du Pont and John McGarry, were prominent politically. When Brady learned of her connections, and wanting strongly to do Cohan's life, he approached Callan to make the overtures. Fortunately, Cohan was to be in Chicago for an Irish-American meeting, which her parents would attend. Callan contacted her father, who, surprisingly, got Cohan's approval for the production.

Written by the twenty-one-year-old Brady and the twenty-seven-year-old Kerr, "Yankee Doodle Boy" opened in December 1939 at Catholic University, with Cohan in attendance at the opening. The musical, by the school's Harlequin Players, was acclaimed by the national press, and it thrust the new department into the theatrical spotlight. The reviews from drama critics were positive, but, more important, it got a rave review from Mr. Cohan himself.

The musical mirrors Cohan's life. He was born on the third, not the fourth of July, 1878, into a family of vaudevillians in Providence, Rhode Island. When the production opens, George M. is shown as a child in a bunk backstage surrounded by vaudevillians; he waves a flag and sings "I'm a Yankee Doodle Dandy." The biography moves through his childhood quickly to the time when he joins his parents and sister as part of "The Four Cohans." From there, it was just a few steps to fame as a song-and-dance man, playwright, and composer.

MEDLEY OF MUSICAL FRAGMENTS

The King of Western Swing

Bob Wills was one of many white fiddlers from the southwest who played country music that was based on Irish jigs. In 1930 he formed his first musical group—"The Light Crust Doughboys Band"—which was successsful as an advertisement for a local flour company. It made Wills a living, but he was anxious to create his kind of music, so he struck out for Tulsa, Oklahoma, where he found his musical home. He named his band "Bob Wills and the Texas Playboys."

Because Wills had never studied music, he did not know that he shouldn't combine a fiddle band with a jazz band. He put together five fiddles, jazz guitar, steel guitar, saxophone, and rhythm section. By 1935 he was the "King of Western Swing," and his sidemen were earning $100 per week. Western swing was a mixture of white country and black blues, with occasional "hollers" thrown in. Hollering is best understood in a song that Wills wrote early in his career that later became "Rose of San Antone." Anytime in the middle of this tune, Wills would holler "Ah hah." At other times he would scream, "Never never."

The tunes of the Playboys made little musical sense, but it made Wills rich and famous. By 1938 he was playing more swing like Goodman and Miller and less of the country and blues. His was the most famous band in the southwest. When he recorded "Rose of San Antone," Irving Berlin asked Wills to provide music and lyrics for publication by the Berlin company. Bing Crosby's recording of the song was a sensation.[27]

"Down in de Meddy"

But if it can be said that American music reflected its culture, then the goldfish-eating craze spawned a song that defied comprehension. It was first heard by Saxie Dowell while he was visiting in the South as a member of Hal Kemp's dance orchestra, which toured college campuses for their gigs. Dowell was fascinated by an old nursery tune called "Down in de Meddy." He thought the college kids would take to it, knowing the success of "A Tisket, A Tasket."

Dowell rewrote the lyrics and added some "boop poops," causing jazz musicians to fume and music lovers to develop stomach problems. It came out as "Three Little Fishes" and was sung in "fish language:" "Down in the Meddy in an Itty Bitty Poo" (translation: Down in the Meadow in a Little Bitty Pool.) The verse ended, "And They Twam (swam) and they Twam all Over the Dam." The chorus was sung: "Boop Boop Dittem Dattem Whattem Chu."

Unbelievably, this song set records for sheet music sales in the summer of 1939, and it was recorded by Guy Lombardo, Kay Kyser and Paul Whiteman, as well as Hal Kemp. More startling, Mildred Bailey, a jazz singer plugged the song on the radio.

NOTES

1. Wecter, *The Age of the Great Depression*, p. 234.
2. Taubman, *The Maestro*, p. 26.
3. "Marsalis on Music," PBS television, October 23, 1995.
4. Schuller's monumental study of the *The Swing Era*, which resulted from his listening to thirty thousand phonograph records, must be considered authoritative, although he has many dissenters, this section relies heavily on his writing.
5. Collier, *Benny Goodman and the Swing Era*, p. 18.
6. Collier, p. 22.
7. Collier, p. 195.
8. Schuller, *The Swing Era*, p. 563.
9. He discussed his early work with Miller on the Ed Walker "Options" radio broadcast on National Public Radio, December 11, 1994.
10. Some of these notions were gleaned from the PBS television production, "Glenn Miller—Musical Hero," shown on March 12, 1993.
11. There is no doubt that Miller's death in the service of his country in 1944 added to his legend. He stands for the nostalgia and the fond memories of a time when it seemed that the country was more united than at any other time since.
12. Schuller, *The Swing Era*, p. 661.
13. Editor of *Metronome* and writer, RCA Records, 1956.
14. Ellington studies received a tremendous boost in 1986 when Mercer Ellington donated his father's scrapbooks, records and thousands of items of memorabilia to the Smithsonian Institution.
15. Leonard Feather, on the dust cover of "Duke Ellington's Greatest Hits."
16. Schuller, *The Swing Era*, p. 199.
17. John Haase may be in this camp. See his biography of the Duke, *Beyond Category*.
18. Some of this information is taken from the Smithsonian Institution exhibition, "Louis Armstrong: A Cultural Legacy," which was shown in July 1996.
19. *The New York Times Obituaries Index*, p. 360.
20. Clarke, *Wishing on the Moon*.
21. Green, *Ring Bells! Sing Songs!* p. 175. The following section draws heavily from Green's book.
22. Ellis, *A Nation in Torment*, p. 513.
23. Flanagan, *Arena*, p. 82.
24. Quoted in Ellis, *A Nation in Torment*, p. 516.

25. *Current Biography*, 1940, p. 47.

26. This version is based on a May 31, 1990, story in the *Catholic Standard* by Norman McCarthy.

27. The A&E television series "Biography," which featured Wills on March 14, 1996, credited him with being a forerunner of the Rock and Roll revolution, because "Bill Haley and the Comets" began as "Bill Haley and his Western Swing Band."

6

Nothing Could Be Finer

FINE ARTS AND GREAT DEPRESSIONS

100 Percent Americanism

American painters, who had gone to Europe to live and to absorb avant garde styles, came home in the Depression to a spiritual awakening that became a wave of patriotism. Each artist emphasized a regional approach. Each considered his region to be the most American. The four major regionalists were Grant Wood of Iowa, John Steuart Curry of Kansas, Charles Burchfield of Ohio, and Thomas Hart Benton of Missouri. It is significant that all these men were from the Middle West; they rejected the styles of the eastern schools that clung more to abstract impressionism.

They championed a new "American Scene," made most explicit by Wood's *American Gothic,* showing the old farm couple with a pitchfork. His simplicity of psychological designs was combined with childlike panoramas, smooth landscapes and angularity of features. Benton sought to revive the backwoods folklore (manifested by his sympathy for the hillbilly and the Negro sharecropper). Curry specialized in the "farm genre of Kansas." His art sprang from a love of the soil, depicted by windblown, sun-drenched plains. Georgia O'Keeffe wove her delicate strokes to fashion abstract forms of her southwestern region.[1]

The return to reality in America was to paint factories, farms, dams, and life in real terms, including the depiction of poverty and personal losses. This folk art was simple, often was untutored and often was the product of weekend painters. In 1939 a cunning and shrewd grandmother from upstate New York exhibited her wares for the first time. This Mother Moses soon became known as Grandma Moses.

Grant Wood

Grant Wood personified everything that was American in art, although he got there by a circuitous route. In the 1920s he was painting impressionistic pictures in southern France, but by 1939 his style was literal, the color was clear, the outlines sharp. For his objective style, he chose homely subjects and a mechanical approach.

Wood was born on a farm at Anamosa, Iowa, a son of Quakers. His father died when Grant was only ten years old, which forced the family to move to Cedar Rapids. Grant did odd jobs to help support the family, and, in the process, he learned many hand skills. He decided to learn a craft and use it as a means of pursuing an art career. He was almost nineteen years old when he enrolled in the Handicraft Guild of Minneapolis, where he took courses in woodworking and metal crafts. He paid his way by working nights as a watchman. Two years later, he moved to Chicago, where he continued his work and study. By day, he was a jeweler; by night a student at the Art Institute.

World War I disrupted his life's plan. Although he stayed in the United States painting for the Camouflage Division, after the war, he went to Paris, where he joined the Bohemians and became one. After painting nondescript fuzzy, veiled landscapes with hundreds of other would-be impressionists, he realized that he wanted to paint Iowa. Returning home, he began his professional career as a painter. He painted *Woman With Plants*, then his classic, *American Gothic*, which was exhibited at the Century of Progress Exposition in 1930. It depicted the gaunt Iowa farm couple standing in front of a Gothic farmhouse.

In 1939 Wood painted *Parson Weems' Fable*, of a uniformed George Washington being scolded for chopping down the cherry tree. This fanciful depiction of a national folk tale was second best in the Carnegie Exhibition in Pittsburgh—the first prize going to a grim landscape of some shacks by a stream with a Negro family standing forlornly in what the painter, Alexander Brooks, called *Georgia Jungle*.

Thomas Benton

Thomas Hart Benton, the Kansas City social realist, was most identified with the American heartland. Born in Missouri, he was named after his great uncle, who was Missouri's first Senator. When his father was elected to Congress, young Thomas accompanied him to Washington in the fall and returned in the spring.

His father decided that Tom should become a lawyer, but the son did not cooperate. Instead of books, he preferred to walk and talk to the town folk and to draw them. He began drawing murals at a very early age, running the gamut from freight trains to battleships to Indians. The freight train mural ran up the stairway of his home at an angle so that the large, black smoke trailed it down the entire wall.

At seventeen, he got his first job as a professional artist; he drew cartoons for the Joplin, Missouri, *American*. This first effort only served to whet his appetite for something bigger. He left small-town life for the big cities: Chicago, Paris, New York. But after sampling the Bohemian life, he longed to return to Missouri and to paint "Missouri types." Instead, as he traveled to Texas, Mississippi, Ohio, Arkansas, and Tennessee, he came into contact with a variety of real American types. He painted a series of *American Portraits*, and he developed a deep interest in all things American.

He traveled by backpack and by knapsack, he went leisurely on foot, and he went up and down the Mississippi and Ohio Rivers. He studied workers in the oil fields of Texas, in coal mines, in steel mills, and in shipbuilding plants. Wherever he went, he took a supply of drawing materials. Benton related all these experiences in his autobiography, *An Artist in America*, which he illustrated. He had to draw the great panorama of the United States, which led him to painting murals. Soon, his murals were in demand by museums, and in 1933 he received a commission to do a mural for the Indiana exhibit at the World's Fair in Chicago. Benton was pleased with his progress, but he longed to do a mural of Jesse James and Frankie and Johnny and Prendagast as very realistic conceptions of Missouri's history. Other Missouri painters, who were avant-garde, were appalled. But as Thomas Craven has shown, Benton was never a modern painter.[2]

There was one other side to Benton's art: in 1929 he began producing a number of black-and-white lithographs on stones, the first one being *The Station*, showing a train at rest. In the next decade, he drew horses and anything with smoke showing. A later lithograph shows a horse galloping ahead of a steam locomotive racing across the plains, with smoke trailing from the engine across the entire picture. It was a masterful comparison of a horse in the flesh and an iron horse that Benton lamented was replacing it.[3] He painted Jesse James and Huck Finn, which one critic called "cornball."

Benton's art was in dynamic tension: his murals were complicated by contrasts—units were juxtaposed to indicate the intensity and rawness of America. Benton belonged to no school; his eclectic drawings featured raw individualists, rough humor, and a sentimental view of westerners. He drew all things in representative fashion, but by 1939 a New York exhibit of his works indicated that his drawings were undergoing change. Among the 1939 paintings were nudes from Greek mythology, some still lifes, and some uncharacteristic landscapes. Benton seemed to add much more color and texture to these paintings.

Edward Hopper

Edward Hopper believed that Americans should be weaned from the French. For him, the frontier was the American self, and with its perspective; he painted lonely individuals and buildings without people. He favored sun and shadows and slanting light. His 1939 *Women on the Move* showed the starkness of social isolation.

The Left-Wing Moderns

Stuart Davis was captivated by the thought of fusing everyday objects with his abstract drawings. Typical of these was his eggbeater series, which were not eggbeaters at all. They only served as vehicles for his purposes. He also rendered such mechanical objects as gasoline pumps and telephones. Almost anything served as models for his abstract treatments. Davis's attempts to tell his story were particularly hard to grasp, because his forms came not from the precise thing he viewed, but rather from the environment of colors and shapes abstracted from reality.

Davis arrived at his discontinuous theory gradually. He went to the Henri School of Art in New York, then he drew for the Army Intelligence Division in World War I. This experience convinced him that his naturalist piantings were useless, because the camera could produce better results. He struggled vainly to produce formless paintings, which led him to Paris. Returning to the United States, he settled in Gloucester, Massachusetts, where he could do his impressions of marine life.

Although he was always a left-wing artist, the Depression set off in Davis a radical response. He formed an artists' union, whose purpose was not just to enhance their economic stability but also to promote the artist in American society. When it became more obvious what Hitler's intentions were in the field of art, Davis formed the American Artists Congress to oppose Hitler's views of culture.

Although he engendered an enormous amount of controversy in his time, he was given the commission to paint a very large mural in the Communications Building at the New York World's Fair. To symbolize the development of the communication industry, Davis painted a huge spiral, signifying the universe and a seashell hinting at the origins of sound. The overall scene conveyed total disorder. A man is seen rising to confront the objects of sound and communication that surround him: he sees the sign language, a printing press, an early telephone instrument, a carrier pigeon, a human ear, radio towers, and some mail.

The Lyrical Armenian

One foreign artist built bridges between the two art worlds. He was the Armenian-born Arshile Gorky. Unlike other immigrants who came to New York, he was anxious to make friends with young American painters. He particularly sought out those who wanted to break from realism and regionalism that survived in the 1930s. He was the link between Paris and New York. Behind his lines one sees Paul Cezanne and Vasily Kandinsky. Gorky was generous of his time, but he could not escape being a melancholy loner. Yet he was successful in shifting his own styles of painting; he moved from cubism to surrealism to abstract expressionism, and he had a great impact on Willem de Kooning and Jackson Pollock.[4]

Arshile Gorky was known as the "lyrical Armenian." A native of Khorkom, Vari, in Turkish Armenia, he studied in the Polytechnic Institute in Tblisi, which became a part of the U.S.S.R. He arrived at Ellis Island in 1920 after watching his mother starve to death after their village was overrun by the Turks. He captured the love and mourning of these episodes in his painting *Portrait of the Artist and his Mother,* completed in 1926 after ten years' work. He settled in Providence, Rhode Island, where he continued his studies in the Rhode Island School of Design and the New School in Boston. He also studied and taught in New York City.

Gorky's first show in 1932 marked him as a leading abstract expressionist in the United States. During the New Deal, he was part of the Federal Art Project, for which he completed murals for the Newark, New Jersey airport and for the Aviation Building at the New York World's Fair.[5]

World War II made the United States the capital of modern art. Millions of frightened persons scrambled to get out of Hitler's way as tanks rolled across Poland, including some of Europe's most creative artists. Quickly, Marc Chagall, Salvador Dali, Max Ernst, Fernand Leger, and Piet Mondrian landed at American ports, and they completely transformed American art.

A WPA FOR ARTISTS

The cultural history of the Great Depression was marked by a unique proposition: that the federal government had an obligation to preserve the talents and livelihoods of unemployed artists and actors. In the process, the artistic results of their ventures would be made available to a mass audience that had no previous exposure to such esthetic activities. Although foreign (mostly European) governments had a long history of support for the arts and the theater, the New Deal was the first such aid in U. S. history.

The previous chapter stressed that the WPA was an integral part of the cultural and social history of the Great Depression. It was predicated on the idea that all Americans were entitled to useful jobs, including artists. The Federal Arts Project, which began in 1935, provided a subsidy for the resurgence of American painting. It employed five thousand easel painters, sculptors, graphic artists, and muralists at subsistence wages. In hundreds of communities across the United States, classes were conducted in the history and fundamentals of art. More than a million works of art were rendered for government buildings, schools, and hospitals, as a means of preserving a vital part of our cultural heritage, which contributed greatly to an intense desire for fine arts in the large cities and the rural communities.

The FAP employed persons of every art style, but three major schools emerged: the abstractionists, the regionalists, and the social propaganda school. The latter's best exponent was Ben Shahn, whose art depicted the Sacco-Vanzetti case, scenes of hungry children, and barren landscapes.[6]

The WPA Arts Project, which was set up by Holger Cahill, a passionate follower of folk art trends, replaced the system of private patronage that existed before the Depression. The church, the states, and the rich had traditionally been the sponsors of art, but now it had a new patron. It sponsored an unprecedented murals program, which showed up at airports, hospitals, government buildings, the New York World's Fair, and in schools. The artists were paid $23.88 a week in all 48 states. Most of the murals had historic or heroic themes, but some featured labor themes.

Despite its wide support, the program was attacked as "frivolous" and as "left-wing." The last charge stemmed from mountain of class-conscious paintings that came from artists who turned from the frivolity of the 1920's to the serious themes of the Great Depression. As with the writers' project, many participants went on to fame. Those whose reputations rose included painters such as Moses Soyer, Jackson Pollock, Willem de Kooning, Joseph Hirsch, Ben Shahn, Philip Evergood, Jack Levine, and William Gropper.

The Federal Arts Project achieved prodigious results. In New York City, certainly the art capital of the United States by 1939, Audrey McMahon, the Regional Director, reported that between 1935 and 1939 over fifty-two thousand works of art were produced and more than 616,000 children and adults received art instruction.[7]

Despite the output, critics were not pleased with the direction of American art in 1939. The emphasis on regionalism and social criticism, they believed, produced a sterile, stale, and tired art. It was only imitative, not creative.

DEGENERATE ART

While Americans were struggling to determine the precise role of government in the arts, the Germans supervised art as they did the economy, education, and other aspects of life. Art was part of the *Kultur*, which was to be an amalgamation of physical strength and ideology. These were to be the ethos of the Third Reich.

Hitler, who was a painter, compared his tasks as Fuhrer to those of the ancient Greeks. Whether Hitler had talent as a painter is immaterial; he attempted to shape the course of modern art, which he called "degenerate art," "Jewish," and "Bolshevik." He preferred military subjects to nudes (although we learned later that he had done some very explicit female nudes as a young man).

Germans viewed the military as affording "the opportunity to be creative." For Hitler, art was racially motivated and timeless; German art had to be classical. German artists had to receive their inspiration from the "weltanschaung" of the National Socialists. In 1937 he decided to highlight the degenerate nature of modern art by sponsoring two exhibits. In one, he showed the people true German art, with battle scenes and portraits of himself. The other show backfired on him. It turned out to be the largest and best-attended exhibition in history. The 650 objects were viewed by over three million persons.

Hitler's anti-Semitism showed up in the placement and description of objects in the exhibit. A label pointed to *German Farmers—A Yiddish View*, although very few of the paintings were Jewish. To complete his picture, the Negro often became his symbol of degenerate art. Some paintings were purposefully decadent, some beautiful, some ugly, some realistic, some abstract. The 1937 exhibition included numerous propaganda shows to teach the people to despise this art.

Between 1937 and 1939, Hitler's raiders took sixteen thousand art objects from European museums. These included paintings by Matisse, Gaugin, Van Gogh, Chagall, Picasso, and Braque. They discussed how to dispose of their treasures. Sadly, hundreds of paintings by Klee and Kirchner were burned in public, and in an act of utter hypocrisy, they sold the most valuable ones at auction in the same year. They stated that they wished to "make some money from this garbage."

While Hitler was dismissing expressionist art as garbage, Americans were struggling to define its nature. Was it a new way of looking at the canvas in geometrical, abstract ways or was it an action-oriented approach that tended to diminish the importance of form? Five noted works of "degenerate" art were put on exhibit at the Museum of Modern Art in New York City in August 1939. The paintings include *Valley of the Lot at Vers* by Andre Verain (1912); *Street Scene* by Ernst Kirchner (1913); *The Blue Window* by Henri Matisse; *Around the Fish* by Paul Klee and a sculpture of *Kneeling Woman* by William Lehmbruck. These expressionistic works were not removed from German museums for racial reasons, because two of the artists were German. Rather, the *New York Times* of August 8 blamed "Hitler's Taste."

By 1939 the group of angry painters who inhabited New York City were trying to untangle the many antagonisms that their styles engendered. It was Mark Rothko against Jackson Pollock. The hard-drinking Pollock crowd believed that art should not be discussed, because it came from the sub-conscience, but others saw art as having a social conscience (Barnett Newman ran for Mayor of New York in 1933 on the "artists' ticket").

But superseding this controversy, the expressionists held a naive belief that art led to the salvation of society. They thought that art defined the culture and was a powerful force for good. Whether their work was violent or despairing, it would lead to redemption.[8]

The Blue Rider

In 1939 Vasily Kandinsky, the Russian mystic, completed the last of his series of "compositions," titled *Composition X*. *Compositions I-X*, with their swirling waters and their phantasmagoric depictions of the dead, were abstractions of the end of the world. Kandinsky, who worked with the German expressionists of the early twentieth century, was a founding member of the *Blaue Reiter* (blue rider) school that was formed in 1911. These expressionists distorted shapes and used colors in arbitrary ways, eliminating the true subject and substituting expressive shapes and colors.

In Kandinsky's abstractions, the titles tell us nothing about the subject, but only serve as identification marks, which explains why they are called compositions or improvisations. The goal of the German expressionists was "to express emotion and experience with large and simple forms and clear colors."[9] The German expressions became "rigid, ponderous and coarse," in contrast with the French, which were more fluid and refined. In German hands, the paintbrush became dark and melancholy. But Paul Richard affirms that Arshile Gorky's visions, Jackson Pollock's "swirling skeins," and Willem de Kooning's abstractions would have been impossible without Kandinsky's Compositions.[10]

Kandinsky was an academic at the University of Moscow, where he taught law and economics. After visiting the forested North, he returned to Moscow with unrealistic notions of gaudy folk art, which he was able to compare with the classics in the Hermitage. He lost his interest in economics and got a job in a printing establishment. At the age of thirty (1896), he made his life's choice.

When he commenced painting, he attempted to combine nineteenth-century realism with impressionism and an Art Nouveau style (*Jugenstil*). Gradually, there was a coalescence of styles that led to his own abstractionism. He became a dreamer who saw objects dissolve before his eyes. Thus, in *Composition IV* (1911), there is a fusion of Cossacks riding, lightning bolts, and lovers in the grass, and *Composition V* is about the resurrection. As Kandinsky progressed from *Composition I* to *Composition X*, the images of Monet are fused with the music of Wagner, both of which are incorporated into his Siberian folklore. His compositions became more blurred: what was a horse in *I* became a line in *VII*. *Composition VI* is an abstract painting of Kandinsky's vision of the Biblical flood. He attempted by his colors to arrive at the spiritual essence of inanimate things, which allowed him to combine roses, onions, horses, and swords.

World War I was completely disillusioning for him, as was the Russian Revolution, which led him to paint what some called his masterpiece—*Composition VII*. It is the draining experience of war, shown in rising arcs and circles and framed by diagonals. It is spontaneous and contrived; it is of the present and the hereafter. But the whole thing is a contradiction, because the painting seemed to take him away from his earlier notion that one can find food for the soul in colors. The last three Compositions have less life, and as Richard wrote, "the dancing has gone stiff."

Pablo Ruiz Picasso

In November 1939 a very large exhibition opened in the Museum of Modern Art in New York City of 360 of Picasso's works, which covered forty years of the artist's life. The catalogue described the artist's work as "fecund and versatile and genius." The earliest picture, *Moses*, was dated 1888 and some were painted in 1939. Nearly one-half of the items came from American museums, and it is fortunate that the paintings that were borrowed from European museums arrived before the outbreak of war.

The exhibition was shown by periods. First, the Blue and Rose Periods, then the Negro Period, leading into the Cubist, Realistic and Classical Periods. These works of art wound their way through three floors, with the most recent on the top level. Their most striking feature was the great variety of media and styles. It seemed that Picasso himself never knew just where his creativity would turn. He worked in oils, watercolors, sculptures, collages, tapestries, and graphic media, and he did illustrations for ballets and books. But in the exhibition, there were mostly oil paintings.

Picasso's *Guernica* offered the stark grimness of the slaughter of the Spanish Civil War. The picture is a very large painting composed of a central theme with two wings that simulated a triptych, all hung together by triangles. The result is a violent, explosive depiction of the outrage he felt over the mass bombing. Viewing the scene, one sees a "carnage of dead, dying, and mutilated animals and human beings."[11] In the center, there is a severed arm holding a broken sword, the symbol of defeat; on the right, a figure falls in flames; and on the left, a bull (the Spanish symbol of brute force) rises over a fallen woman who clings to her dead child. Above the arm there is a grotesque horse's head, which in its hideous way tells us of the ugliness of war. Canaday states, "There is every reason to believe that it [*Guernica*] will remain one of the masterpieces of our century."

Pablo Picasso, who was the best-known modern artist of 1939, was born in Malaga, Spain in 1881. His father, who was a drawing instructor, instilled in the young Pablo a sense of discipline in the classics. By his "teen" years, he was adept at putting meaning into his drawings, but soon they became more unrealistic and more "fantastic." Brenner said that he "went off the deep end" doing things that looked like "machines, weird animals, lobster dreams and telephone booth scratchings." But at the same time, she called him the "Mississippi of the Moderns."[12]

He studied at the Beaux Arts school in Barcelona, then Madrid and Paris, where he settled into the high life of the Left Bank. In the ensuing years, he and George Bracque became the Siamese twins of modern art. They lived together, studied together, and developed the style of Cubism together.

For his views, Picasso was criticized, analyzed, and envied, because he was rich and famous, and he was a super salesman. Gertrude Stein said he looked like a bull fighter, and he was just as tenacious. There is no easy way to understand Picasso, because he set the prevailing styles in art and then he resisted them. He painted out of anger (*Guernica*) and he painted out of depression (the blue period). His works were called Spanish and French, but Picasso's description was, "I paint what I see." Yet, what he saw changed constantly. He saw Cezanne and he saw African sculpture. When he went to Rome, he saw and emulated "classic" art. When he returned to Spain, he saw the horrors of the bombing of Guernica.

Though the critics marveled at his versatility, the public made no sense of his scrawls and scribbles. They had to learn that in Cubism the artist laid out the painting from several angles and from the inside out. In this way, he achieved a spatial geometry and multiple images of the same object.

Two 1939 paintings by Pablo Picasso fueled the controversy over modern art. The first was *Still Life With Glass and Fruit,* dated February 2, 1939. It looked like a classical still life, but the red and yellow carafe had definite sexual overtones, which were punctuated by triangles that were pointed upward. The second Picasso was the Dora Maar portrait, *Woman With Green Hat*, completed on October 29, 1939. It depicted Maar, a surrealist photographer whom Picasso had met in 1936, in a particularly grotesque way. He presented this beautiful woman as a kind of Spanish queen on a wooden throne with a green hat that is supposed to represent her crown. But her face is distorted as Picasso painted her with a large nose, a low forehead, and an out-of-place ear. Again Picasso injects a sexual theme into a nautical background. What does it mean? Or should art just be, not mean?

In the Depression, most American artists stuck to their regional, realistic themes, while ignoring the abstract styles of Europe. But when immigrant artists settled in New York City, they quickly adopted the cubist-impressionist-surrealist, avant-garde abstractions that formerly had been in Parisian salons. The American art scene that had grown feeble in the Depression era was now charged with a new vigor, but it was still seen as a curse by much of the American public.

While art-loving Americans struggled to accept this strange art, the artists themselves had to adjust to life in cities that had no sidewalk cafes and no real debate about the future of American art. Their egos renewed old European rivalries and created new tensions in the United States. Dali, for example, was derided for his "crass commercialism." In an ironic twist, these expatriates looked down on American artists. Most did not learn English and they seemed not to care about the problems of daily American living.

Four Mexican Muralists

The years following the Mexican Revolution saw a rebirth of popular, native culture. Artists celebrated the revolution by looking backward to the time before the Spanish invasion and forward to a new art that would accent the uniquely Mexican culture. They wanted to excise the sterile art that was imposed on them by the royal Spaniards. For them, the future of art was in the masses. Out of this creative explosion, there emerged four painters who set out to fuse painting and architecture, which they accomplished through their murals.

The four who were at the forefront of this movement are Jose Orozco, David Sequeiros, Rufino Tamayo, and Diego Rivera. They not only blended their art with architecture, but they also united art with their politics. They became the chief artistic exponents of the radical societal changes that were being discussed by members of the PRI, the *Partido Revolucionario Istitucional* (Institutional Revolutionary Party). They were openly communistic in their sympathies. As this Mexican School took form, Rivera helped organize the "Syndicate of Painters, Sculptors and Intellectual Workers." He showed his leftist leanings early by painting Emiliano Zapata, the leading advocate of land reform, in the mural at Cuernavaca.

In 1922 the four men began a project to paint the heroes of Mexico's past. Ironically, they broke with that past by eschewing any formal (classical) training. Rivera, who was best known in the United States, went to Europe after the 1917 revolution, but he found nothing there to excite his creative interests. Returning to Mexico, he jumped for joy—everything around him was subject for a mural. He painted native festivals, marketplaces, crowds of people in the squares, craftsmen at work, and women at home.

In the 1930s the influence of these muralists spread across the United States as they completed works in faraway places such as Dartmouth College and New York City. Jackson Pollock rhapsodized about the Mexican school. He said Orozco was the person to see, and he participated in the Museum Of Modern Art's experimental workshop on Sequeiros; and when the museum sponsored an exhibition of Matisse, it was dedicated to Rivera.[13]

THE KRESS COLLECTION

In the midst of controversy concerning old and new painting and sculpture, Samuel H. Kress announced that he was donating his collection of 375 paintings and 18 sculptures to the National Gallery of Art in Washington, D.C. He had made his fortune in his five-and-dime stores that operated as S. H. Kress.

The collection represented major Italian painters from the thirteenth to the eighteenth centuries. It was called the largest private collection in the world and included the works of Fra Lippo Lippi, Andrea del Sarto, Correggio, Bellini, Carpaccio, Giorgione, Giotto, Titian, Tintoretto, and Veronese. When combined with the Mellon Collection, which was the heart of the National Gallery of Art, the addition of the Kress collection made the United States one of the greatest repositories of Italian art in the world.

Kress wrote President Roosevelt on July 1, 1939, to announce his decision. He praised the President for his interest in art, and he included a copy of his letter to the Board of Trustees of the National Gallery. In it, he noted that he had striven to keep Italian paintings in the United States that would otherwise have been returned to Europe. Roosevelt responded: "Not only are the treasures you plan to bestow on the National (sic) incalculable in value and in interest, but in their bestowal you are giving an example which may well be followed by others of our countrymen, who have in their stewardship art treasuries which also happily might find a home in the National Gallery."[14]

ARCHITECTURAL STYLES

The bitter rivalries of the art world were mirrored in architecture, where radical designs were anathema. Again, the conflicts stemmed from ideas brought here by immigrants, which challenged the old, classical views of design and construction.

During the Depression, American architects began to break away from imitational styles. One reason was economic: builders could no longer afford the lavish ornamentation of the past. The Chicago Century of Progress World's Fair of 1933 and the New York and San Francisco World's Fairs of 1939 presented structures that were modernistic and plain by historical standards. They were in the new "International Style," and they provided functional space. Only on the federal level did designers adhere to historical styles, but many of the new public buildings were feeble, barren copies of classical architecture.[15]

While the United States has benefited from the teachings of old world (European) architects, the primary source of the American style was North America. The skyscraper was the first example of innovative American architecture. As early as 1893, Europeans who came to Chicago for its Columbian Exposition were astounded at the visions of the tall buildings. However, skyscrapers alone did not delineate the American impact. Our factories, with their continuous process systems, were favorites of both the communists and the Nazis, who commissioned Americans to bring these innovations to Europe. The primary interest was not aesthetics, but the concept of mass production.

The Influence of Bauhaus

Walter Gropius was the founder and director of Germany's Bauhaus. Born in Berlin into a family with a long tradition of architecture and painting, he decided at an early age to choose architecture as an occupation. While enrolled at the *Berlin Technische Hochschule*, he designed his first buildings. These won him an appointment as Chief Assistant to Professor Peter Behrens, his former teacher.

In 1910 Gropius temporarily abandoned teaching to practice architecture. He won several commissions as he achieved his fame by using new building materials, including concrete, aluminum, stainless steel, and polished glass—a technique which came to be known as the International Style. Its early exponents were Le Corbusier, Mies Van der Rohe, and J. J. Oud. They saw the new approach as a fusion of the imagination and industrial techniques—a linking of art and crafts and industrial production. They worked with everyday objects such as lamps and chairs.

After World War I, Gropius was made director of the *Staatliches Bauhaus*, where he introduced new methods in teaching art by destroying the artist's prejudice against the use of practical objects in art. The Bauhaus fostered a new respect for the machine and its products. Paul Klee and Vasily Kandinsky worked there; and Max Breuer, the father of modern furniture design, was on the staff.

Gropius was concerned with the human condition, so when the Bauhaus was taken over by the Nazis in 1934, he went into exile. He went to England first, but in 1937 he established permanent residence in the United States. He settled in Lincoln, Massachusetts, and joined the Harvard University faculty as Professor. He and Marcel Breuer designed a number of residences, and in 1939 he designed the Pennsylvania exhibit at the New York World's Fair.

The lasting contribution of the Bauhaus architects was in education. They developed a basic course that spread across the land from small colleges to major universities. This new pedagogy destroyed the old French school in favor of one that featured a peoples' approach.

Some abhorred the Bauhaus school, among them Philip Johnson. He went to Harvard University in 1939 at age thirty three. It was there that he became enamored of socialism and Nazism and was a strong supporter of Huey Long and Father Charles Coughlin.

He had no particular style—some called him an "architectural whore," but he was the best promoter of his own works, which were often described as sculptures, not buildings. The best example was probably his "glass house."

ARCHITECTURE UNDONE

The Unbuilt Saarinen and Wright

The most celebrated case of an unrealized plan involved the competition in 1939 for a gallery of art on the mall in Washington, D.C. The Finnish-born father-and-son team of Eero and Eliel Saarinen, who won the competition, designed a very modern structure on a prime piece of Washington real estate that now houses the Air and Space Museum. Because the plan was deemed to be too "radically modern" in concept, the gallery was never built. Instead, a classical building was erected, in the style of the structure of the Federal Reserve System. The rejection of the Saarinen plan led to a bitter controversy among American architects. It was opposed by the conservative Commission of Fine Arts, which had its roots in the early twentieth century.

The failure to proceed with Saarinen's plan is particularly puzzling because of President Roosevelt's silence on the subject. Earlier, he had endorsed the modernistic views of Edward Bruce, who had filled the jury with his supporters.

In the debate between the conservative realists and the modernists, the Congress stood down politically. It avoided controversy by not funding the project.

In the debate, the modernists raved about the superiority of the newer designs, but conservatives insisted that any designs preserve tradition and the elegance of the past. The plan for the Jefferson Memorial was greeted with vehement protests from the ultramodernists. They called it a sterile expression of the past, which had no connection to the United States and to Jeffersonian principles. Defenders of the design emphasize that the monument was the work of John Russell Pope—one of our best beaux-arts architects. Anyone who has stood on the land under moonlight to look at the statue of Jefferson and the dome reflecting on the river might well side with Pope.

The unfortunate result of the hardening of the two positions was that the United States lost a major Saarinen plan that would have completely transformed the Washington mall. The rejection of Saarinen was a continuation of the principles set in 1901 by the McMillan Commission, which established Washington as a conservative architectural place.

Unbelievably, this nonbuilding happened to Frank Lloyd Wright also, over a hotel-apartment complex that would have been built on the corner of Connecticut and Florida Avenues, a place that now is dominated by the curved Washington Hilton Hotel. Wright's design included fourteen glass, marble and bronze towers that rose to different heights, which gave it its name—Crystal Heights.[16]

Rising above the oak trees in one of the busiest locations in the nation's capital, it would have included twenty-five hundred apartments, each with a fireplace, and access by elevators. Plans included also a one-thousand-seat movie theater, an art gallery, bowling alleys, retail shops, and a four-hundred-foot bar. Wright's genius also showed in his placement of a parking garage below the entire structure, which, he claimed, could park eight miles of vehicles in twenty minutes.

The rejection of both the mall plan and Crystal Heights meant that two of the greatest architects of their time have no representation in Washington, D.C.—a fact that grieved them greatly.

AND DONE

The American Fountainhead

Frank Lloyd Wright was the towering figure overshadowing other twentieth-century architects. His output was staggering, and his life was equally full. He had good and bad luck, wives and lovers, drama and tragedy, controversy and rejection. At one point, he was bankrupt, homeless, and without an architectural commission, at which time he left his wife to live with a European beauty.

He was born in Wisconsin in 1867, but he moved to Chicago in the 1880s. Although he was born in the Victorian era, his life spanned the period of

America's industrialization. It was a time of new technologies—electricity, new steel, reinforced concrete, and mass production techniques. These fostered a new architecture: buildings with steel frames that could support floors without load-bearing walls. He grew up with the surging manufacturing, transportation, and construction sectors of the economy and he matured in Sandburg's Chicago. His employer and mentor there was Louis Sullivan, the father of modern American architecture.

When Wright left Sullivan's office to work on his own, he too had to confront the romantic/futurist controversy. He had the talent and a strong will, and he knew that the time called for innovational ideas about architecture. By 1939 he was able to meld successfully the new designs with their historical ancestry. Philip Johnson once called Wright "America's greatest nineteenth century architect," a statement that he probably regretted later.

Fallingwater

Benjamin Forgey might have best characterized Fallingwater when he labeled his article about it, "A River Runs Through It."[17] It was conceived by Wright in 1935 but not completed until 1939. It was certainly the most famous private home in the United States. In addition to that wondrous setting in southwestern Pennsylvania, Wright had the advantage of building a home for Edgar and Liliane Kaufman, the owners of the Pittsburgh department store bearing their name. Their son, Edgar, Jr., had apprenticed with Wright in his Taliesin, Wisconsin studio, and it was he who introduced his parents to Wright. The Kaufman family was probably more sympathetic to Wright's high fees and to the final cost of construction, which exceeded the original estimate by a factor of four.

The family had been using the waterfall area for summer activities, and they were anxious to have a house built nearby. When Wright showed them the plans, with the living area directly above the water, they were stunned; they were not prepared for this bold design, but they accepted it without change. This decision preserved one of the architectural masterpieces in this century. Wright combined the international concepts of the Bauhaus with those of his love of nature. He literally joined man's work and God's.

Fallingwater is part of the Western Pennsylvania Conservancy, which was founded in 1932 to protect and preserve natural areas in that state. Wright's plan for the home was totally consistent with the conservation objectives. In fact, it is the only home of such historical significance that retains all of the original furnishings and art works.

Fallingwater may have been Wright's masterpiece. It is both creative and commodious. It is spacious and uplifting. Although the art work was sometimes foreign, most of the building materials came from nearby Pottsville. The flagstones used for flooring were quarried on the property, and the hills themselves were the materials for cantilevering the main structure. To enable the

Kaufmans to enjoy their falls to the fullest, the windows facing them fold in such a way as to disappear when opened. This sprang from his love of Japanese teahouses, with their sliding screens and open fireplaces.

To achieve his result, Wright utilized cantilevered members that were immediately challenged by his peers. Would the reinforced concrete support such a structure over the cascading water? For Wright, the cantilever was not a matter of engineering but of philosophy.

Secrest notes that Wright's designs were the product of his nineteenth-century sensibility (he did spend the first thirty three years of his life in that century), and she is not sure he ever accepted modernism, with its mass production and impersonal life-style and work ethic. This might explain why Wright designed not only Fallingwater, but all the furniture and accoutrements of living in the place. He created every element of landscape, building, and furniture as an integrated whole.[18]

NOTES

1. Pagano, *Contemporary American Painting*, p. xv.

2. Craven, *Thomas Hart Benton*.

3. Jo Ann Lewis, *Washington Post*, May 8, 1995.

4. No one knows why this strange person with a drooping mustache that highlighted his moroseness changed his name from Vosdanig Adoian to Arshile Gorky. Why did he adopt the name of a Russian writer? The only clue is that Gorky means "the bitter one." He gave his birthday as 1904 and 1906 and he said it was in April, except when he said it was in October.

5. Bolino, *The Ellis Island Source Book*, pp. 271-273.

6. Malone and Rauch, *War and Troubled Peace*, p. 278.

7. "WPA Art Project Produced 52,344 Works Since Its Inception in 1935 to This Year," *New York Times*, May 21, 1939, p. G5.

8. Kingsley, *The Turning Point*.

9. Canady, *Metropolitan Seminars in Art*, Portfolio 3, p. 27.

10. Richard, the art critic of the *Washington Post*, described these compositions in the February 5, 1995 issue.

11. Canaday, *Metropolitan Seminars in Art*, Portfolio 6, p. 13.

12. See her sketch of the man and the exhibition in the *New York Times*, November 12, 1939.

13. Clark, *All the Best in Mexico*, p. 27-137.

14. "Kress Gives His Art Treasures to National Gallery Collection," *New York Times*, July 13, 1939, p. 1.

15. Malone and Rauch, *War and Troubled Peace*, p. 279.

16. Crystal Heights almost came to fruition. Entrepreneur Roy S. Thurman and his financial backers thought the Heights would be "the greatest building of modern times." But when, on January 16, 1940, the District of Columbia Zoning Commission rejected the plan, in part because it would have violated the 110-foot height restriction, he called the Commission "this moronic bureaucracy." Wright said "The pillars of ancient Rome are against him." There was a deeper, unspoken, aspect to Wright's rejection: that he was

a communist and therefore not worthy of creating a building on federal lands. See the *Washington Post*, July 4, 1992.

17. Benjamin Forgey, "A River Runs Through It," *Washington Post*, September 7, 1994, p. C-9.

18. Secrest, *Frank Lloyd Wright*.

7

Science in the World

John Brooks wrote, "It is surprising how many developments that have made obvious marks on the country and the rest of the world since then had their beginnings in 1939."[1] The list includes television, nylon, and, most importantly, atomic energy. These developments were catalogued in the clearinghouse for ideas on the future of science at the New York World's Fair, whose theme was "The World of Tomorrow," meaning the tomorrow of science.

The basic industrial processes, which were the basis of the mass production system of 1939, were displayed at the Fair. One of the most popular scientific exhibits was the display of lightning by the General Electric Corporation. GE built and wired ten million volts of lightning, which jumped across a thirty-foot gap with a very realistic crack. In another area, at the "The March of America," the company reproduced a street, with appropriate lighting, for the year 1891, and juxtaposed it with a street of the future.

Westinghouse Electric chose to show Americans of the year 6939 what 1939 was like. It placed a metal time capsule in the ground, which contained such things as coins, books, photographs, an alarm clock, fabrics, a can opener, the Lord's Prayer printed in three hundred languages, the alphabet, magazines, films, a speech by Franklin D. Roosevelt, and a statement by Albert Einstein. Westinghouse also displayed a robot that performed twenty-six different operations, including walking, talking, and smoking a cigarette.

Chrysler Motor Company presented a pagaent of transportation that started with Lady Godiva on her horse and ran to rocket travel of tomorrow. In between, the viewer could see the 1831 British-built John Bull locomotive, covered wagons, steam and diesel engines, and an interplanetary rocket ship—a hint of the world of tomorrow—which took off several times per day to an imaginary location.

In a related effort, F. Trubee Davison, head of the American Museum of Natural History, released two six-foot balloons, each filled with dirt from the fair grounds and inflated with helium. When they achieved an altitude of sixty thousand to eighty thousand feet, they burst scattering the dirt into the stratosphere. There were hints of things to come in other fields. For example, there was a mechanical heart, designed by national hero Charles Lindbergh, suggesting the possibility of a machine that would allow open-heart surgery; and in the Hall of Medicine, several advances in the fight against infection were displayed.

QUANTUM AND ASTRO PHYSICS

Splitting the Atom

The road to atomic energy led from a basic principle of physics: matter can neither be created nor destroyed but only changed in form. From this came Einstein's idea that matter could be converted into energy, and that an increase in mass led to an increase in energy. In the 1930s, research in physics was concentrated on tying nuclear forces to quantum mechanics. Experiments all over the world aimed at penetrating the nuclei of atoms to release their radioactive isotopes. It was found that an atom of lithium could produce a million kilowatt hours of electricity.[2]

In keeping with his racist policies, Adolf Hitler separated general physics (meaning non-Aryan) and German physics. After the Austrian Anschluss, all of its physicists were classified as Germans. One of those Austrian physicists, Dr. Lise Meitner, was a leading analyst at the *Berlin Kaiser Wilhelm Institut*. She was working with Otto Hahn and Fritz Strassmann on nuclear fission, but when it was learned that she was a Jew, she was locked up in her laboratory. Her colleagues went to Hitler to stress that the Germans had achieved many more Nobel prizes than any other nation and to plead that there was no such thing as German physics, but he angrily charged that she was a "white Jew," and he ordered her arrest.

She stole across the Dutch border disguised as a tourist and went to the Swedish seaside town of Kungalv, near Goteborg, where she would be near two other noted physicists, Niels Bohr in Copenhagen and Otto Hahn, who fled to Stockholm. They were pursuing research that was suggested by Einstein's theory of relativity: a body in motion has a greater mass than one at rest, the variation being the speed of light. The German physicists were splitting atomic nuclei, making new elements and creating large amounts of energy in the process.

On December 22, 1938, Otto Hahn published a paper on these results in *Naturwissenschaften*, but he did not believe his own work. As he said, "After the manuscript had been mailed, the whole thing once more seemed so improbable to me that I wished I could get the document back out of the mailbox."[3] At least half of the world's physicists were dismayed and confused at the possibilities. Hahn said it would be "contrary to God's will," and Bohr believed that such a device could not be built. Even Einstein was not sure that fission could produce an explosion.

On February 2, 1939 Leo Szilard wrote Joliot-Curie from the United States: "When Hahn's paper reached this country about a fortnight ago, a few of us at once got interested in the question whether neutrons are liberated in the disintegration of uranium. Obviously, if more than one neutron were liberated, a sort of chain reaction would be possible. In certain circumstances this might then lead to the construction of bombs which would be extremely dangerous in general and particularly in the hands of certain governments."

The subject became urgent when Otto Hahn and Fritz Strassmann, of the *Kaiser Wilhelm Institut* in Berlin, split atoms, using a methodology derived from Fermi. They had bombarded a small piece of uranium with a stream of neutrons in such a way as to split the uranium atom into two parts, causing a violent burst of energy. It was neither seen nor heard, but their calculations showed that the experiment had let loose two hundred million volts. They identified two elements in the process—barium and kryton. The barium element was surprising and exciting, since its atomic weight was only 137, compared to 238 for uranium. It showed that a bomb could be made that was twenty million times more powerful than TNT. This experiment tended to confirm Einstein's $E=MC^2$, that a very small amount of mass (M) can be converted into a large amount of energy (E). The amount of energy released is equal to the mass times the square of the speed of light (C).

These awesome results created the fear that Hitler would get control of this means of mass destruction, which led to a major migration of European physicists to the United States. Lise Meitner left Sweden, Fermi left Fascist Italy for Columbia University, Edward Teller went to Washington's George Washington University, and Bohr joined Einstein at Princeton. In the United States, where scientists cherished their academic freedom, experiments on fission were conducted in open laboratories. The Meitner results were reconfirmed in the Pupin Laboratory at Columbia University on January 25, 1939. When the test was completed, the oscilloscopic needle registered exactly two hundred million volts. It was clear by then that if uranium could be broken down into its isotopes and U-235 extracted, a bomb could be produced.

When the experiments on nuclear fission were announced in January 1939, the foreign-born physicists (Leo Szilard, Eugene Wigner, and Edward Teller of Hungary; V. F. Weisskopf of Austria; and Enrico Fermi of Italy) began to talk about the possible military uses of atomic energy. They spoke of restricting publication of their findings, which at the time was anathema to American scientists. In the spring, the group, led by Szilard, sought the help of Niels Bohr to cease all publication of data by a voluntary agreement. American and British physicsts agreed, but F. Joliot of France refused.

Niels Bohr, who was leaving Copenhagen for the United States to work at Princeton's Institute for Advanced Study, reached New York on January 16, 1939, where he found a cable affirming the astounding potential of atomic energy. He informed U.S. scientists, including Fermi. They confirmed the positive results with fission at a meeting on January 26, 1939, in Washington, D.C., whose results were published in the February 15, 1939, issue of the *Physical Review*.

In 1928 the University of Michigan began an annual Symposium on Theoretical Physics, where the world's leading nuclear physicists gathered. In 1939 Werner Heisenberg, winner of the 1933 Nobel prize, came to Ann Arbor to lecture. He was met there by Enrico Fermi and Max Dresden of the Stanford Linear Accelerator Program. Until then, the scientists had scrupulously avoided any political discussions, hoping that they could keep their science unblemished. They had been able to limit their conversations to two topics: physics and music, which they loved passionately.

Dresden came to Ann Arbor from Holland to complete his Ph.D. with Enrico Fermi. Because Dresden worked as a waiter at the homes of University of Michigan professors, he was privy to many of the details of the changing world of physics. He remembers the "tense conversation" between Fermi and his wife and Heisenberg. The Fermis said the only thing any self-respecting scientist could do was to leave Italy or Germany, because they insisted that there could be no "scientific integrity" in either country.[4]

According to Dresden, Heisenberg angered those present by his "refusal to address the moral issues they raised." Heisenberg's only response was that the Nazi regime was "bad for Germany." He had earlier criticized Hitler's statement that Einstein's theory of relativity was "Jewish science." But as a German, he felt he had an obligation to stay and work to change the system. Heisenberg's decision was a powerful factor in stimulating the American effort to create an atomic bomb; American scientists knew that Professor Heisenberg was capable of bringing the German uranium project to a successful conclusion.

But the thought that Hitler might build an atomic bomb was deeply troubling. German physicists recommended that they proceed to construct a uranium machine in secret, but Dr. S. Flugge, an anti-Nazi physicist, informed the world by publishing the results of German research in the July 1939 issue of *Naturwissenschaften*, which circulated quickly through the scientific community. The Nazis were infuriated at the "leak" of their secret work, so they forbade the export of uranium ore from Czecho-slovakia and ordered an embargo on all news about uranium research.

Enrico Fermi, who headed the American effort to build an atomic bomb, was born in Rome on September 29, 1901, to Alberto and Ida De Gattis. Enrico took an interest in science, which he nurtured by buying books at used-book stalls. He increased his scientific knowledge quickly when an engineer friend of his father offered to teach him. He soon surpassed his teacher, who encouraged him at age seventeen to apply for a scholarship in Pisa, which he won easily. Three years later, he earned his doctorate in physics on the theory of X rays. His oral defense was so erudite that his examiners could not fully comprehend his theories.

Enrico needed better teachers, which he found in Gottingen, Germany. There, he met Max Born and other scientists, who competed with him later in producing an atomic bomb. But being the only Italian in his class, he returned to Italy, where he met and married Laura Capon. As Fermi's fame spread, the Chairman of the Physics Department at the University of Rome, who was also a senator, convinced the government to create a chair for Fermi. His research was considered so infallible that he was given the name of "the Pope."

Between 1932 and 1938, Fermi spent his time teaching and doing research in nuclear physics. When he learned that Frederic Joliot and his wife, Irene Curie, had created a radioactive form of aluminum by using alpha particles, Fermi analyzed the results and arrived at a new theory—that more radioactivity would be produced if neutrons were used instead of alpha particles. Neutrons had been discovered by English physicist James Chadwick.[5] Fermi decided to test this theory. Working with three of his colleagues, Fermi bombarded all ninety-two elements with neutrons. More than sixty elements became radioactive, but when the neutrons were slowed down, using paraffin, the radioactivity increased up to one hundred times. For this discovery, Fermi received the Nobel prize.

The political situation in Italy troubled Fermi, because his wife Laura was Jewish. When Mussolini signed the Rome-Berlin pact in 1936, he adopted some of Hitler's anti-Semitic policies (probably reluctantly). Although his wife was exempt from the policy that could deport her, because she was married to a Catholic, Fermi contrived to remove his wife and two children from this dangerous political climate. He took them to Sweden in December 1938 to receive his Nobel prize, but instead of returning to Italy, they sailed to the United States, arriving in New York on January 2, 1939.

Leo Szilard was one of four Hungarian physicists who fled Europe because of Hitler's racist policies concerning research (the other three were Eugene Wigner, Dennis Gabor and Edward Teller). Szilard, who was born in Budapest, left there after World War I to study physics. He came under the influence of Max Planck and Max von Laue, both Nobel prize winners.

At Berlin, his teaching was a heady experience. He offered a seminar with Gabor, Wigner, and John von Neumann, and they were all under Albert Einstein. Despite cavorting with these giants of the physical world, Szilard never completed projects, and he had difficulty finding employment. He had great ideas, but he was a loose cannon. And they said he was lazy, because he loved to sit in a bathtub for two hours each morning while he contemplated a variety of theoretical notions. But he was always around when great events were taking place.[6]

Leo Szilard met Einstein on a visit to Berlin. When the Nazis took power there, Szilard went to Vienna, where he led the efforts to find jobs for displaced Jewish scientists. He learned of the possibility of splitting the atom from Hans Bethe, and he was determined to find out which element would exhibit a chain reaction. Szilard hoped to duplicate the German process. He visited Fermi for his reaction. Fermi thought that there was a remote possibility of the emission of neutrons, and when pressed for his definition of remote, he replied, "Well, ten percent." Szilard believed that a 10 percent chance was not a remote possibility, especially if Hitler took the uranium deposits in the Belgian Congo for these purposes.

In 1938 Szilard came to New York carrying the idea of the bomb with him, but it was not comprehensible to anyone who listened. Morgan calls this "surely one of the most extraordinary episodes in American history: a handful of immigrant scientists peddling their idea for an atom bomb to a skeptical government."[7]

The expatriates in the United States decided that Roosevelt must be warned. Most had no influence in Washington, and they had difficulty with English. Few physicists realized the implications of this research, but Fermi was adamant. He must warn the United States. But how? Even with his Nobel Prize, he was received coldly. The Army and Navy were fighting to increase their budgets for conventional weapons, the State Department was more interested in the the European situation, where peace was in its last days, and it considered uranium a useless metal.

Fermi and Leo Szilard contacted Alexander Sachs, a Jewish refugee from Lithuania, who was an adviser to Roosevelt. Sachs recommended that they draft a letter to the President and that they have Einstein, the most notable of the emigres, sign the communication. They were certain that Einstein, the long-haired scientist who was known throughout the world, would not be ignored. Sachs promised to deliver the letter personally to the President.

On July 12, 1939 Szilard and Eugene Wigner went to see Einstein on Long Island, where he was vacationing. Szilard telephoned Einstein urging that they meet. First, Fermi and Szilard had to locate him on Long Island. On a very hot day, they sought the address they were given. They thought he had said Patchogue, but he really said Peconic. Reaching Peconic they were so hopelessly lost that Szilard thought they ought to quit. Miraculously, a small boy volunteered to take them to Einstein's house.[8]

Einstein agreed to write the letter if Szilard would write a draft. These scientists spoke broken English and wrote the same. Not being sure how the American bureaucracy worked, Szilard did not know how long to make the letter. Their solution was to write two drafts—one short and one long. Einstein preferred the longer one.

On August 2, Szilard returned to Long Island with Teller. Einstein dictated the letter in German, which Teller translated. The letter was hand carried to Washington, where Sachs delivered it to Roosevelt. He said it was his proudest moment. The letter read:

From Albert Einstein
Old Grove Road
Peconic, Long Island
August 2nd, 1939

To F. D. Roosevelt
President of the United States
White House
Washington, D. C.
Sir:

Some recent work by E. Fermi and L. Szilard, which has been communicated to me in manuscript, leads me to expect that the element uranium may be turned into a new and important source of energy in the immediate future. Certain aspects of the situation which has arisen seem to call for watchfulness and, if necessary, quick action on the part of the Administration. I believe that it is my duty to bring to your attention the following facts and recommendation.

In the course of the last months it has been made probable that the work of Joliot in France as well as Fermi and Szilard in America—that it may be possible to set up a nuclear chain reaction in a large mass of uranium, by which vast amounts of power and large quantities of new radium-like elements would be generated. Now it appears almost certain that this could be achieved in the immediate future.

This new phenomenon would also lead to the construction of bombs, and it is conceivable—though much less certain—that extremely powerful bombs of a new type may thus be constructed. A single bomb of this type, carried by boat and exploded in a port, might very well destroy the whole port together with the surrounding territory. However, such bombs might very well prove to be too heavy for transportation by air.

In view of this situation you may think it desirable to have some permanent contact maintained between the Administration and the group of physicists working on chain reactions in America. One possible way of achieving this might be for you to entrust with this task a person who has your confidence and who could perhaps serve in an unofficial capacity.[9]

Sachs handed the letter to FDR on October 10, reading it aloud. It was too long and the President was bored. He said any action at that time was premature. Sachs persisted, asking if he could meet again on the topic. The President assented. They met at breakfast, where Sachs reminded Roosevelt that many leaders had rejected new ideas as impractical only to find that another country eagerly embraced the invention. He used the example of Robert Fulton, who took his designs of a steamship to Napoleon, because the United States was not interested.

Roosevelt was convinced. He called General Edwin Watson and told him that this letter required immediate action. Not long after, Roosevelt appointed a committee, led by Lyman J. Briggs, Director of the National Bureau of Standards, to study the possibilities. The committee met first on October 21,

1939. The team received a $6,000 grant from the U.S. Navy to research the subject. They gave the project the code name "Manhattan District."

Later, working under the stairwell at the University of Chicago Stadium in the old squash court, Fermi and his team achieved a chain reaction by bombarding uranium atoms. This prepared them for placing the atom smasher in a bomb that was being built at Oak Ridge, Tennessee, and Hanford, Washington. It is fitting and proper that when the 100th element was discovered—the eighth created by man—that it was named for Fermi: Fermium.[10]

The "Impractical" Cyclotron

In a related action, Professor Ernest O. Lawrence of the University of California was awarded the Nobel prize for physics in 1939. Lawrence, a native of South Dakota, received academic degrees, including a Ph.D. from Yale and an LL.D. from the University of Michigan. He taught physics at Yale until he moved to the radiation laboratory at the University of California at Berkeley.[11]

Lawrence's work on the cyclotron was difficult to comprehend, and it was deemed "impractical." It involved using a uniform magnetic and an alternating current field to accelerate heavy nuclear particles (i.e. protons and helium nuclei) to propel them around and around until they achieved a very high velocity, enabling them to crash into matter with sufficient energy to shatter an atom.

Early research by Rolf Wideroe on particle accceleration used the linear, repetitive approach, but in 1929 Lawrence originated the circular resonant machine (the cyclotron), which was augmented by 1939 to produce the proton cyclotron. This was not considered an invention, because it did not have an immediate practical application (although the later development of atomic energy for commercial use was dependent partly on Lawrence's discovery).

The Nobel Prize Committee spoke of his dedication, ingenuity, and contribution to the physical sciences, and it only alluded to his work in medicine, where he was experimenting on finding an inexpensive salt that could be made radioactive and serve as a cure for cancer. It put him in the same class as other great scientists, such as Faraday and Fermi. The Committee called the cyclotron a "Rube Goldberg contraption of steel, copper and aluminum weighing 220 tons and used to study one of the tiniest units of the physical world."

When Lawrence received his award, he was designing a new two-hundred-million volt cyclotron that was to cost over $750,000 to build. He needed to depend on private donations to carry on his work of atom smashing.

Hubble Nebulae

On May 8, 1939 Dr. Edwin Hubble, of the Mount Wilson Observatory near Pasadena, California, reported that he had discovered "a fundamental pattern underlying the structure of the universe in photographs of extragalactic nebulae that covered three-fourths of the sky at a distance of seven to five hundred million light-years.

His photographs, which were reported at a symposium on galactic and extragalactic structure at the dedication of the eighty-two-inch telescope at the McDonald Observatory, Texas, suggested that the cosmos grew in an orderly, not a cataclysmic fashion. The photos, which were taken with the world's most powerful one-hundred-inch "cosmic eye" telescope, show a "smooth and continuous progression along a definite sequence." The results seem to challenge the "big bang" theory of creation.

This assembly of the world's leading astronomers and astrophysicists in the Big Bend country of Texas were able to see through the darkness of outer space where, in the eons of time, countless universes were being created or were dying. Each nebula is a stellar system comparable to our galaxy, the Milky Way, which is about one hundred thousand light years in diameter and contains about one hundred million suns. A light-year is about 6,000 billion years distant.

Hubble summarized his findings: there was a dearth of data on the appearance and development of spiral structures, which are associated with the presence of super-giant stars. The incipient spirals were comprised of obscuring and luminous materials, which developed into embryonic universes, having elliptical shapes. According to Hubble, these incipient spirals are like the wings of an embryo bird, which contain millions of giant stars. These are part of the fundamental basis of the universe and the cosmic system.[12]

DEVELOPING TELEVISION

Scientists pursued research on the transmission of moving images for many years. James C. Maxwell, of Edinburgh, Scotland, made a startling discovery: electricity and magnetism, when joined, produced light (we call this now the electro-magnetic spectrum). What he gleaned from research was that currents and magnetism, when produced in a vacuum, travel at the speed of light. Radar and television flowed directly from Maxwell's work.

Alexander Graham Bell patented plans for a television set in the 1880s, and continuing his search for such a device, Herbert Ives, of Bell Laboratories, announced a research program for transmitting motion pictures by television. Ives demonstrated a television screen in his office that showed a dancer strutting on the roof of the Bell skyscraper in New York (the image in bright sunshine was easily seen on the small screen).[13]

An American from New York, Charles F. Jenkins, the inventor of the movie camera, transmitted the first moving images by television on June 13, 1925, using vacuum tube amplifiers and photoelectric cells.[14] By 1928, there were 15 stations broadcasting a grainy picture using mechanical scanners. It was done by turning a wheel that sent light through a wire. These wheels were very large and therefore impractical.

Philo T. Farnsworth, a twenty-one-year-old engineer from Utah, conceived of an electronic system for scanning images when he was in high school. It used an image bisector and occilator, a process that he patented. He gave a demonstration of his television system in the Philadelphia Museum of Science in 1934, but he received no monetary advantages, because he was in a patent dispute with RCA. He won his case when his high school science teacher testified that he remembered Farnsworth presenting the basic designs in his class. In October 1939 Farnsworth won his case. RCA was ordered to pay him royalties for cross-licensing agreements, but he never received his fortune because World War II shelved TV in favor of radar. Farnsworth became an alcoholic.

But the real father of television was Vladimir Zworykin, a student at the St. Petersburg Institute of Technology before World War I. As his interest in putting sight to radio piqued, he went to France to study under Paul Langevin. When Zworykin returned to Russia, he kept experimenting for the Russian Wireless Telegraph and Telephone Company. Fearing for his life in the Russian Revolution, Zworykin immigrated to the United States. After drifting into many jobs, he settled at Westinghouse in East Pittsburgh, where he plunged into researching his "iconoscope"—which was a crude television camera. In 1929 Zworykin's demonstrated a cathode-ray television receiver at the meeting of the Institute of Radio Engineers in Rochester, New York. Because he worked for RCA, it meant that it could produce a commercially feasible television system, however, the Wall Street crash delayed the exploitation of this system.

In the 1930s, experimentation continued, but the first major breakthrough did not occur until 1936, when a coaxial cable was laid between New York and Philadelphia by the American Telephone and Telegraph Company and the Philadelphia Electric Storage Battery Company (Philco). Immigrants made major contributions in the field of electronic engineering.

During the 1930s, both CBS and NBC inaugurated experimental television stations, which carried the X designation in their call letters (for example, NBC was W2XAB). These stations carried local and national news. The CBS inaugural was more of a gala: it featured Mayor James Walker, George Gershwin, and Kate Smith, who sang her theme, "When the Moon Comes Over the Mountain." The signals were of insufficient sharpness and quality; the fuzzy pictures stemmed from the small number of lines making up the picture. In 1931, RCA raised the number from 60 to 125 lines, and it built a TV antenna on top of the Empire State Building, the world's tallest structure at the time. The number was raised again in 1935 to 243 lines (less than one-half the current 525 lines).

A major milestone was reached in 1938 when Dumont began manufacturing television receivers on its assembly line. It was a propitious time, because Dumont was preparing for the much larger audience that it was anticipating would attend the New York World's Fair. The Farnsworth, Dumont, General Electric, Philco, and Zenith radio companies were all experimenting with telecasting, but it was RCA and its president, David Sarnoff, that "was consistently in the lead."

Born near Minsk, Russia in 1891, Sarnoff was brought to the United States at age nine. He attended public high school in Brooklyn, New York, and studied electrical engineering at Pratt Institute. When he was only fifteen years old, his father died, so he became the "man" of the family by working at the Marconi Wireless Telegraph Company for $5 per week, and he became a telegraph operator two years later after he taught himself the Morse code.

In 1912 while serving as wireless operator on the *S. S. Beothic*, he gained fame when he was the first person to pick up the distress signals coming from the sinking *Titanic*. Staying at his post for seventy-two hours, he dispatched information about the rescue operation and the list of survivors, and, for his steadfastness, he was promoted to chief radio inspector and assistant chief engineer. When the Marconi company was absorbed by the Radio Corporation of America (RCA) in 1919, he became general manager—a title that he kept. He rose quickly in the new company to Vice President in 1929 and President in 1930, when he was not quite thirty-nine years old.

Sarnoff had a reputation as a sharp-witted executive, but for some, he was "brutal, stubborn, and even vicious when the occasion required." Sobel relates the story of how Sarnoff hobbled into an elevator with his leg in a cast when he encountered President Harry Truman. Seeing his condition, Truman remarked, "Well, General, I guess now for a while you'll have to kick people in the ass with the other leg, won't you?"[15]

As early as 1915, Sarnoff wrote that radio was a means of carrying music into the homes, but no one listened. In the 1920s, however, RCA became the leading producer of radios in the United States, which justified Sarnoff's insistence that RCA establish the National Broadcasting Company (NBC) to ensure that RCA could sell all those radios. Radio sales amounted to more than $83 million by 1924.[16] When radio broadcasting became established, Sarnoff never forgot his love of music (he had sung soprano in a synagogue). He allowed the Metropolitan Opera to broadcast over NBC, served on its Board of Directors; and in 1937, he convinced Arturo Toscanini to come to the United States to conduct ten symphonies on NBC.

In the 1930s, his company allocated a million dollars for the development and commercialization of television, which had an unpleasant side effect that cost Sarnoff his friendship with Major Edwin Howard Armstrong. Armstrong was raised in Yonkers, New York. He attended Columbia University, where he worked for years in one of its laboratories and where he showed himself to be a very original thinker. One of his first discoveries was regeneration—a process that amplified long-distance radio signals. He built a tower in his back yard to test his apparatus. It succeeded, but his regenerative feedback system for amplifying radio signals was involved in a long patent litigation with Lee de Forest, an early pioneer in the development of radio. When the United States Supreme Court refused to review his case, it effectively denied Armstrong a patent for his achievement.

Hurt and psychologically wounded, the intrepid Armstrong pressed on in a new area of research. He discovered multiplexing—which allowed a single FM station to transmit several signals over the same FM wave, which he patented in 1933. It was the beginning of stereo broadcasting.[17] Armstrong, with his little box, met with Sarnoff to demonstrate his radio signal, which was totally free of static. He expected David to accept and to use the new system. But at this time, RCA was too involved with television, and as Sarnoff said, "This is not an invention—it's a revolution." For FM to be adopted, it would have meant scrapping all existing radio sets in the country. Sarnoff did not believe that the American people were ready for such "an unprincipled extreme."

Armstrong thought that classical music, live news and dramatic productions would be serious competition for soap operas and comedy shows that dominated the radio waves in AM stations. But Sarnoff saw FM as a threat to RCA. This enraged Armstrong, who decided to establish his own FM station. He built a powerful fifty-thousand-watt station at Alpine, New Jersey, with call letters W2XMN, by selling his holdings in RCA stock to pay for the construction costs.

The venture failed. Armstrong's dream of wedding FM to classical music collapsed when the anticipated growth of FM sets failed to materialize. Sarnoff approached Armstrong and offered him a million dollars for his patents. Sarnoff wanted to join FM sound to television, an innovation that would come years later.

When RCA recovered from the effects of the Great Depression, it turned to creating new products and exploiting new markets. In 1939, for the first time, its revenues exceeded $100 million, and its profits reached 7.4 percent of revenues. Although the company did not become the leader in radio manufacturing, it earned a greater percentage of profits through advertising as NBC accounted for one-third of RCA's total revenue. It benefited by a shift from print advertising to radio. By 1939, radio advertising was over 10 percent of the total. Most of the gain came from musical shows.

At the October 20, 1938 annual meeting of the Radio Manufacturers Association, Sarnoff announced that "television in the home is now technically feasible," and that RCA and NBC would install a limited, commercial telecasting service in the New York area when the World's Fair opened in April 1939.

Behind Sarnoff's use of the word "limited" was a major technical dispute: how should the industry specify the density of the scanning lines and how many picture frames should there be per second? This meant that unless all sets had the same specifications those locked into one station would be unable to pick up telecasts from other stations. Standards had to be frozen for a reasonable time to allow TV to develop. Since RCA led the field, it was no surprise when the FCC chose its recommended standards.

RCA's announcement of the development of television came in full-page ads in local newspapers on March 1, 1939. The company advised those who wished to purchase the new television sets that while there would be meager offerings in the beginning, NBC promised to create a nationwide television network in the near future. This announcement was aimed at freezing the development of FM in place, at blocking the creation of a competing system by CBS, and at winning early FCC approval.

RCA's move set off a wave of competitive actions. Philco changed its name to the Philco Radio & Television Company, and Zenith declared that its television receivers were the best available. Its May 1939 advertisement stated, "Radio Dealers! Zenith has television sets." And it added, "Zenith is ready—But Television is Not."[18]

When Sarnoff opened the World's Fair exhibit, there were about two hundred receivers in the New York metropolitan area, but within days, sixteen other manufacturers were offering sets for sale, including Philco, Crosley, Farnsworth, and Dumont. Sarnoff told his Victor Corporation to prepare to produce TV receivers, and shortly after, RCA was offering four models for sale at prices of $200-$1,000.

When the World's Fair opened, the RCA exhibit allowed hundreds of thousands of visitors (this writer included) to see television for the first time. When the cameras were turned on, viewers, who were eight miles away, saw hundreds of workers at the curbside eating lunch. Moments later, a bugle sounded and the Stars and Stripes went up the mast to officially open the ceremonies.

Sarnoff dedicated the RCA exhibit, and those present heard him declare that RCA was "launching a new industry, based on imagination, on scientific research and accomplishment," but hundreds more saw Sarnoff on one of the many receivers scattered throughout the Fair grounds, as well as about a hundred special guests at the RCA Building in Manhattan. Remarkably, some persons saw the proceedings in their homes on nine-inch sets they had purchased for $625.[19]

The ten-inch picture was poor, but the experiment was deemed a success by the company, which proclaimed that it would be a vital part of the lives of Americans in the near future. But skeptics abounded. No one was more pessimistic than Professor Chester Dawes of Harvard University who declared that television's appeal was limited, because "It must take place in a semi-darkened room, and demands continuous attention."

The year 1939 offered an expanded menu of entertainment for TV viewers. During the Fair, NBC presented television from Radio City, and there were broadcasts of several sports events, including the Columbia-Princeton baseball game, the Lou Nova-Max Baer boxing match, and a football game between

Fordham University and Waynesburg College. After the Fair closed, the Macy Thanksgiving Day parade was featured.

Despite all the enthusiasm, radio broadcasters feared what Harvard economist Joseph Schumpeter once called "creative destruction"—that this new medium would destroy their golden calf. But Sarnoff, ever a visionary, did not wish to be accused of withholding or delaying such an astounding industrial innovation. Hollywood producers panicked with the appearance of talking pictures and they knew, especially, how the phonograph was injured by the advent of radio broadcasting.

ENIAC

During World War II, two scientist, J. Presper Eckert and John W. Mauchly, developed a digital computing machine, which they called ENIAC (electronic numerical integrator and computer). Originally, it was called a mechanical and numeral integrator, yielding the acronym MANIAC, which was discarded for obvious reasons. They said they had conceived of the idea while drinking coffee in a Philadelphia restaurant. We learned later in a lengthy lawsuit that their work was heavily dependent on research done by another scientist, Dr. John V. Atanasoff.

John Atanasoff was born in Hamilton, New York, in 1904. He received an electrical engineering degree from the University of Florida, a master's degree in mathematics from Iowa State University and a doctorate in physics from the University of Wisconsin. He returned to Iowa State to teach mathematics and physics.[20]

Atanasoff said the idea for a computer came to him while he was drinking bourbon in a roadhouse in Illinois in 1937. He jotted on a cocktail napkin all of the principles of computing for his new system. With a $650 grant, he and his graduate student (Clifford Berry) built an analog computer called a laplaciometer—the first desk calculator. But it was insufficient for his complicated mathematical processes, because he needed regenerative memory— whose idea came to him in that Illinois tavern.

Within months he and his assistant constructed an electronically operated device that used the base two (binary, digital) system, instead of the usual base ten. It weighed seven hundred pounds, had a mile of wires and three hundred vacuum tubes. They called it the Atanasoff-Berry Computer (ABC). Its primary innovation was the condensers that allowed him to regenerate memory in case of electrical failure. This crude prototype of a computer used a mechanical clock, but all computing was done electronically, using vacuum tubes. The data were entered by punch cards. The entire project, which cost $1,000, was recorded in a thirty-five page manuscript that university lawyers sent to a patent lawyer for filing in 1939. Iowa State University held up the patent because of a quarrel over property rights to the computer.

When World War II began, Atanasoff was called to Washington to do research for the Navy, so the patent was never filed. He abandoned his work on computers and became director of the underwater acoustics programs at the Naval Surface Weapons Center at White Oak, Maryland.[21]

THE WONDER WORLD OF CHEMISTRY

Ersatz Fibers

By the time the Germans unified their country under Bismarck, the English and French had claimed a large part of the world's resources in Africa and Asia. This was especially true of natural dyes and rubber. The German answer was to develop ersatz products. There was an expectation that rayon would replace silk, but in 1939 twice as much silk was produced as rayon. This research helped to produce synthetic dyes, and synthetic rubber and paved the way to the production of popular synthetic fabrics.

Synthetic fibers revolutionized the economic geography of the textile industry. No longer would the United States be dependent on Asian supplies of silk, rubber, or dyes. In the Great Depression, while output was falling in most American industries, the value added for chemicals rose, due in part to the growth of synthetic fabrics. In the 1930s, rayon production grew 158 percent, and cellulose acetate products grew 7,100 percent (from 200,000 pounds to 14,400,000).[22]

Chemical fibers replaced natural ones. Du Pont led this revolution. By 1935 it had gained 80 percent of the market, previously held by natural silk. Its development of rayon in sheet form made cellophane a new leader in wrapping material. But it was Du Pont's research on synthetic fibers in the late 1930s that gave it one of its biggest successes.

Du Pont was very active in promoting a large line of synthetic products, including lucite and neoprene. Its research on giant molecules, which began in 1928, was directed at improving the quality and durability of multifilament fibers. Dr. Charles Stine, who was the director of chemical research at Du Pont, was very interested in organic substances of high molecular weight. He learned that a young instructor at Harvard University, Dr. Wallace H. Carothers, who worked under Roger Adams at the University of Illinois, was described as one the most brilliant persons ever to obtain a doctorate at that university. Stine enticed Carothers to move his research to Du Pont, with the pledge of the company's ample resources. Carothers, who taught at Illinois until 1926, moved to Du Pont in 1929, where he continued his work on polymerization by condensation.

Six years later, Carothers discovered one superpolymer with unique properties, which offered promise. He learned that certain polyesters, when subjected to cold stretching, assumed an arrangement of molecules that were similar to natural silk. It was a protein-like polymide substance that is a combination of coal and water. It was insoluble in common solvents, and it had a very high melting point—260 degrees—which made it ideal for ironing. In the next forty-four months, he and his research team spent $8.6 million to put the fiber through its pilot-plant stage. They coined the word nylon, which was their expression for any long-chain synthetic, polymeric amide that could be formed into a filament. The research on nylon turned to commercial production. The work of spinning, finishing. dyeing, and knitting which first was called "Fiber 66," took five years.[23]

On October 27, 1938, Du Pont announced its intention to build a plant at Seaford, Delaware—this expensive, intricate plant was completed as Project 3873 on August 15, 1939. The company declared that nylon was "something new under the sun," but it was more than a new fiber; it had unusual properties that gave it versatility; and, significantly, the new plant had sufficient capacity "to throw about 7,500,000,000 Japanese silkworms into technological unemployment." Within a year, American demand for natural silk fell by 10.4 million pounds (18 percent).[24]

The product was one of the most important developments in the company's history. It was the world's first synthetic fiber that was comparable to natural fibers: it was strong and resilient and could be used in thousands of industrial articles. The commercial development of nylon opened the way for the family of synthetics that followed.

Although hosiery seemed a promising field for nylon, early experiments were discouraging and the results uncertain. The first pair of nylon stockings made (now stored in the company's Hall of Records) brought snide remarks from merchandisers who were called to the plant to examine them. Du Pont secretaries became guinea pigs, as did the Rockette dancers from NBC. When nylon passed all tests to determine the stresses and strains placed on the hosiery by an active woman's daily schedule, it was ready for market. The response became legend. American women bought sixty-four million pairs in the first year of production, and women in the entire world awaited their chance to buy.[25] Nylon joined ice cream, hot dogs, and baseball as American institutions. Its economic significance was considerable, because at the time, hosiery manufacturers were facing wildly fluctuating silk markets due to Japan's absolute monopoly of silk.

Though more expensive, nylon wore longer and was more sheer—a quality that endeared it to the women (and to the girl watchers). Although it was most appreciated by women, who could now wear seamless hosiery, it soon became a product for everyone. Various forms of nylon, like plastics, were used in toothbrushes, fishing lines, surgical sutures, wigs, clothes, upholstery, and parachutes. Lammot Du Pont, head of Du Pont Corporation, said in 1939, "Progress elements of business have long recognized that the cure for many of our economic ills lies in a consistent and honest application of the doctrine of giving more for less."[26]

The nylon exhibit at the New York World's Fair was a headline performer. The five million visitors to the Du Pont exhibit "saw the new nylon hosiery on living models, heard tales of promising new plastics and chemicals that would lighten the burdens and ease the discomforts of mankind." There was at least one minor crisis: the clinically dressed young lady showing off her nylons sustained an awful run in her stocking before a large audience. But the show received spontaneous applause, and the viewers left with expectations of wonders to come.

The Wonder Drugs

There were two fortuitous developments in the field of medicine that were timed perfectly for the war that followed them. These drugs saved countless lives and came to be called "wonder drugs." In 1922 Dr. Alexander Fleming discovered lysozyme, a bacteria-dissolving enzyme that is found in body secretions, especially in tears and saliva (which is why animals lick their wounds) and egg white. Bacteriologists had been working on thyrothricin, which comes from the soil, to kill pneumococci and streptococci. But thyrothricin had a major disadvantage—it was found among millions of bacteria, fungi, and worms.

It was found by accident in 1928 while Fleming was vacationing in Scotland. He had been growing staphylococci on petri dishes, and one day he noticed a green mold on one of his culture plates. There was nothing between the mold and the microbes. What he had discovered was the ideal chemotherapeutic agent, which he called "penicillin," which was the Latin word for mold. He pondered a question: why was there no staphylococci on the clear areas of the dishes? Other research showed that penicillin grew on cheese and bread and in the soil. When Fleming applied his culture to microbes, they all died. He knew that he had discovered something, and in June 1929 he published his results.[27]

But as good as penicillin was, it had to be available inexpensively to become a wonder drug. The chief deterrent was its instability and erosive qualities. Fleming decided that prospects were not bright, and for years the drug lay dormant. Many felt that the sulfa drugs, which were just being developed, were the answer to infections. In 1939 Dr. Howard W. Florey was working on lysozymes, the most potent microbe killer known, when he read Fleming's paper on penicillin. He obtained some penicillin from the Sir William Dunn School of Pathology, he made a concentrate that was one thousand times stronger than the original. When it showed no toxic effects, it was injected into experimental mice that were infectious. The results were astonishing. Even the mildest, crude preparations of the culture, which was 99 percent impure, stopped the growth of bacteria.

Because Florey had no more penicillin, it took a few months before he could test it on a human subject, who was a policeman dying of a staphylococcus blood infection. The sulfa drugs, which were tried first, could not help because the infection had spread to his face and scalp. After five days on penicillin, he showed improvement and began eating again. But when the penicillin supply was exhausted, the microbes began to multiply, and he died. A second case ended similarly, but then there were several successes.

The war in Europe increased the demand for penicillin. To meet this demand, Florey organized a team of bacteriologists, pathologists, and chemists to solve the problem of supply. They learned how to grow the mold in quantity, but they did not succeed in obtaining the correct chemical formula. Later researchers learned how to make crystals of penicillin salt, which were effective against most cocci, but not against tuberculosis.

100 YEARS OF PHOTOGRAPHY

1939 marked the centennial of photography.[28] Although photographs were grand, photographers were constantly debating whether they were artists or scientists or merely technicians. The debate intensified when photography was excluded from the 1904 St. Louis Exposition (as it was to be excluded in its centennial year in the 1939 New York World's Fair). One critic stated categorically, "Photographers can never be artists," and another asserted, "The hand of the painter is incurably mechanical; his technique is incurably artificial." Painters declared that they were the guardians of fine arts, while photographers were only instruments users.

For the first time, in 1935 the Farm Security Administration (originally the Resettlement Adminstration) created a photographic division to document everything and anything American. For the 1939 issue, three thousand photographers submitted about fifteen prints each. These were reduced to five thousand and then to five hundred by Edward Steichen, who received a Guggenheim Fellowship for his outstanding efforts in publishing the 1939 and 1940 volumes.

In his *U.S. Camera*, 1939, Steichen published some of the photos that were shown at the International Photographic Exposition in New York City, marking the centennial. In it, he used the word "documentary" to describe his presentation, by which he meant pictures that "tell a story." These photographs of immigrants and migrant workers, the very old and the very young did indeed have a story to tell—it was about the hardship and the heroism of the time. It was about the grimness of the farm life and the wretchedness of the urban. Ben Shahn described these photos as "pictures that cried out to be taken."[29]

Dorothea Lange captured the essence of the human and financial disasters that hit farmers by concentrating on the plight of women and children.[30] One photograph shows a young, wrinkled mother holding a baby in a tent, while her daughter, also grim looking, places her chin on her mother's shoulder. What the photograph doesn't say is that the woman had sold the tires from her car to buy food for the children.

Lange, who was born in Hoboken, New Jersey, in 1895, had a very unhapppy childhood: she contracted polio at age seven, and her father abandoned the family five years later. This sadness contributed to her boldness. She smoked when few women dared, and her clothes were outlandish, which were accentuated by her limp. She wore large, primitive jewelry and outfits that looked like costumes. She announced at age eighteen that she had chosen photography for her life's work, despite not owning a camera. She studied at Columbia University, where she learned the "Photo-Secession" school that aimed at obtaining no frill images.[31]

Lange married a painter, Maynard Dixon, who specialized in western scenes. He took her to the mountains of Arizona and to California, and it was this experience that marked a change in Dorothea's instincts concerning photography: from emphasizing portraits to melding soft human forms and realistic landscapes. As she said, she wanted to know "more about the subjects than just faces." But her boldness remained. She would climb on top of an automobile, throw a black cloth over her head and camera, which, combined with her black slacks, made her look devilish.[32]

When her marriage to Dixon ended, she immersed herself in the suffering of the people in the Depression. She was obssessed—driven by "personal turmoil." Her photos changed drastically as she covered the unemployed, the maritime strikes, and May Day demonstrations. Following in the steps of Louis Hine and Jacob Riis, she attempted to record the impact of economic hard times on the American people. Between 1935 and 1939 she was employed by the Farm Security Administration, which was created to document the need to give assistance to the poor. Farm tenancy had replaced slavery, making white and black farmers equally vulnerable. Poverty increased as the soil was overplowed and undernourished. As Henry Allen wrote, "She could be cross-indexed through a thousand social-science files as victim, survivor, minority, Southerner, farmer worker, senior citizen."[33]

When her work with FSA was completed, she and her husband, Professor Paul Taylor, of the University of California at Berkeley, collaborated on a book of her experiences. *An American Exodus*, published in 1939, which combined her photos and his text, was not a big seller because the economy was recovering and the American public was losing interest in the Depression.

In the Introduction to the *U. S. Camera* 1940, published in 1939, Steichen ignores the false dichotomy of art/science and summarizes the state of photography: "At the close of the first hundred years, as shown here, it is good to record that no *ism*, no particular theory, or no particular photographic process dominates the scene. In integrity and directness of approach, present day photography bats a high average. Photographers are increasingly using the camera as a medium capable of a vivid presentation of life."

GETTING AROUND

On the Ground

By 1939, there were twenty-six million automobiles on our crude highways, and billboards defiled the American landscape. But the cars were very different: they were large, heavy, long-hooded, and as Brooks states, "They have something of the prehistoric look of an anteater."[34]

American automobile producers were completing their transition from the plain, bare-bones "tin lizzies" offered for years by Ford to the stylish coupes, touring sedans, and broughams. The 1940 Oldsmobile marketed in September 1939, had a semi-automatic clutch—the earliest type of automatic transmission. The larger cars had straight-8 engines (eight cyclinders in line); smaller cars had convertible tops and rumble seats.

Some of the extraordinary achievements in automotive safety and comfort were on display at the New York World's Fair, where 1919 and 1939 vehicles were exhibited together. The improvements were remarkable. The 1939 vehicle had 85 horsepower and 3,025 pounds compared with the older car's 31 horsepower and 2,215 pounds. More important for comfort, the 1919 car was open, whereas the 1939 model was closed and much more spacious. The 1939 automobiles had long hoods, powerful engines, large sixteen-inch tires, and new shifters, which served as intermediates between the floor shifter and the automatic transmission. Cord offered an electric shifter, which was operated by push button.[35] More important for Detroit, city streets were becoming crowded with these humpback vehicles.

At a meeting of the World Automotive Engineering Congress in New York, Edwin L. Allen, an automotive engineer, predicted that the American car of the future would be shaped like a teardrop, with the point at the rear. That car would have a single button to open all doors. The interior would give the "impression of entering a commodious room." It would not be necessary to crawl over seats or humps in the floor. Allen predicted that the seats would be moveable chairs and a portion of the roof would be translucent to admit the rays of the sun. Another engineer foresaw, correctly, that the running board was soon to be gone.

And in the Air

In 1939 the United States had eighteen domestic air carriers, whose 276 airplanes carried a million passengers over 35,492 miles of airways.[36] On June 1 an event that was linked to the celebration of the World's Fair presaged a much more important milestone in aviation history. Forty-two passengers, seated in the four-engine DC-4, were treated to a flyover of the fairgrounds, before putting down at Floyd Bennett Field in Brooklyn. It was the last leg of a coast-to-coast flight.

This "flying pullman" was an engineering marvel: it was all metal, had a wing span of 138 feet and a height of 24 feet, and it was an investment of $2 million for the Douglas Company. Each of the four Pratt and Whitney engines generated 1,450 horsepower. With a cruising range of 1,425 miles, it could easily make the coast-to-coast run with two stops.

At 12:01 A.M. on December 2, 1939, an airliner landed at the newly opened New York Municipal Airport (now La Guardia Field)—a $40 million investment. Mayor La Guardia and three thousand spectators were present at North Beach to greet the plane in a steady downpour. The first passenger off the Transcontinental and Western flight handed the mayor a bouquet of flowers. The Mayor greeted the passengers, "I am glad to welcome you to New York." Soon after $40 worth of commemorative stamps were sold to collectors.

The airport, which was declared to have fantastic potential, was the eastern terminus of four airlines. In addition to Transcontinental, the others were United, American and Canadian Colonial. This potential was obvious when in ten minutes, a second plane landed, an American Airlines flight from Fort Worth, Texas. It was estimated that initially there would be 115 takeoffs and landings per day from La Guardia, although the capacity was for 700. The airport benefited from having thirteen million candlepower of lights, so that by day or night the planes could fly on "visible pathways" provided by radio range beacons.[37]

Advertising brochures suggested that this airport, which was only twenty-seven minutes from Grand Central Station, was a worthy competitor for the trains. Tickets would be available at offices in downtown Manhattan, as well as the rotunda of the administration building. This is in marked contrast to the approach taken in 1929 by the Transcontinental Air Transport and the Pennsylvania Railroad, which started air-rail service between the coasts.

Surprisingly, until then New York did not have a major commercial airport, although many important flights did take off from Floyd Bennett Field, a five-minute drive from the Belt Parkway in Brooklyn. It was dedicated on May 23, 1931, and for the remainder of the decade, it struggled to increase its commercial business, but it suffered from the competition of the Newark Airport. Bennett Field had the longest concrete runways in the world and few obstacles in its path, making it ideal for test flights. Several coast-to-coast records were set in flights that originated there. Wiley Post, Howard Hughes, Jacqueline Cochran, Amelia Earhart, and Douglass "wrong way" Corrigan, used Bennett field for their historic flights.

SUBMARINE DOWN AND UP

Because Oliver F. Naquin, a native of New Orleans and a 1925 graduate of the U.S. Naval Academy at Annapolis, had done postgraduate work in engineering at the University of California at Berkeley, he was assigned as a research scientist to work on and develop a submarine dehumidification system.

Soon after, he was made Commander of the submarine *Squalus*, which sank during a trial dive off the coast of Portsmouth, New Hampshire on May 23, 1939.

The crew comprised fifty men, five officers, and three civilian observers. The new submarine left port for the open Atlantic Ocean just after 8 A.M. Its mission was to obtain periscope depth of sixty feet in sixty seconds at a speed of sixteen knots. When he gave the order to dive, the lights on a panel in the control room turned from red to green, indicating that all valves had closed. But as the submarine nosed down at a ten-degree angle, the engine room began flooding. One valve had failed to close.

Naquin was faced with a terrible decision of command, because twenty-six men were trapped in the flooding compartments. He had little time for his decision, because the sub was going down. He gave the order to seal the watertight doors, dooming the trapped men. When batteries began to short circuit, Naquin ordered the electricity cut off to prevent an explosion. The *Squalus* settled on the ocean floor, 240 feet below the surface, with thirty-three survivors but without heat or light. Soon radios were blasting out the news special, and the print media had an "Extra" on the streets. Reporters and journalists crowded into Portsmouth to report this amazing rescue attempt to the world.

Naquin marked his position with smoke bombs and an orange bouy. These were seen by another submarine—the *Sculpin*, which radioed the position to the rescue team. Naquin also told his men to bang on the ship's hull with sledgehammers, using Morse code.[38]

The following day, deep-sea divers arrived from Washington, bringing with them an experimental rescue bell from Groton, Connecticut. The divers lowered the bell 240 feet onto the deck of the *Squalus*, fastened it to the hatch and brought survivors to the surface in dives lasting about two hours each. The crew was below for thirty-nine hours.

Naquin praised his crew, who, he said, were not fearful and did not complain about the bitter cold. The three navy divers who rescued the men received the Medal of Honor for gallantry. The Navy later concluded that mechanical failure had kept an induction valve open. It commended Naquin for "Outstanding Leadership."

The operation produced at least one hero. After the survivors were removed from the *Squalus*, the salvage ship *Falcon* attempted to raise the sunken craft. One set of lines was tied to a buoy with a three-inch hawser; the other thirty-one ropes could be reached from the ship's railing. The turbulent seas, which tangled the hawser, were too heavy to launch a small boat to correct the problem, and matters worsened when the communications on the *Falcon* went dead.

At this point, Alfred W. Pickering, a thirty-seven-year-old diver from Camden, New Jersey, who was a veteran of three submarine disasters, suggested that he swim to the line and cut it. The idea was approved only because

Pickering was a strong swimmer. Looking out at the waves, he stripped, held the knife in his teeth and jumped into the twenty-foot waves. By bobbing through the white caps using a powerful overhand stroke, he reached the buoy, more than thirty yards away. His main worry was to keep from being thrown against the hull of the ship, but with a few jabbing cuts he sliced through the heavy hose. Barely ten minutes after the start of his exploit, he was back on board the *Falcon*. He shrugged off the episode as "nothing," and his chief reward was a cup of coffee with rum, which he sipped between his quivering teeth. His bravery allowed the rescuers to cap the lines and fasten them to buoys for riding out the northeaster. All was ready now to salvage the submarine.

On July 13 the bow of the *Squalus* shot straight out of the water in the salvage operation. Then it fell back in as the chain supporting the submarine broke. It settled back at the ocean's bottom, 240 feet below. Fortunately, three pontoons were still attached to the vessel with a part of the chain, making another attempt at recovery a bit easier. A similar difficulty was experienced with the stern section, which was raised 85 feet before dropping off. Eventually, the ship was salvaged, and the gray ship was taken to the Portsmouth Navy Yard for repair and refueling.[39]

Far from New Hampshire, a second submarine, the *Phoenix*, sank without a trace off Cam Ranh Bay, French Indochina on Thursday, June 15, 1939. French naval authorities ordered an extensive search using naval units and airplanes, but because the ship's dive took place in one of the deepest waters of the South China Sea (it was estimated to be lying at 302 feet) and because the vessels had no life-saving equipment, the search was abandoned after two days and the four officers and fifty-nine crew were declared lost.[40]

The submarine departed from Toulon for the Far East before going down. She was of the *Redoubtable* class, one of the most successful in the French navy, which was known for its ability to make very long cruises. This was attributable, in part, to her large size—1,500 tons, 302 feet long—and to the twin, 6,000 horsepower engines.

The French made note of the absence of rescue diving bells, such as those that allowed the United States Navy to rescue part of the crew of the *Squalus*; they had been considering the purchase of this equipment from the United States, but the crew found itself with only the Davis Lung, which was totally inadequate for rescue.

While the Americans were rescuing the *Squalus*, the British submarine *Thetis* left Liverpool Bay with 103 persons on board, including seven civilian experts, four submarine captains, several naval engineers and one engineer from Vickers-Armstrong—the builder of the vessel. When it dived to the bottom out of control, 99 men died. A public inquiry revealed that the two forward compartments flooded quickly sending the vessel down, but it also learned that the 103 on board were nearly twice a normal complement of 53 for that ship. The overloaded vessel used up its oxygen much more rapidly and prevented any successful rescue of the crew, which was tapping signals against the bulkheads until 2 A.M.

Four men escaped through a hatch, leaving the question, why did not more use that escape route? One possible answer was that each time the hatch was opened, two tons of water entered the submarine. Because the hatch was opened twice, four tons gushed in, and this amount of water would have flooded the electric batteries and produced deadly chlorine gas.[41]

Because the Bay was shallow, when the nose of the *Thetis* hit bottom, it was buried forty feet in the sand and the aft end protruded eighteen feet above the water line. Angry parents of the crew asked why the Admiralty had not cut a hole in the vessel to allow for escape, to which it replied that there would have been need to cut through the outer shell and the inner bulkheads, and the rising tide did not allow enough time for this dual operation.

The loss of three late-model submarines by three naval powers within a short time inevitably raised the question of sabotage. Was it chance that the *Squalus* off Portsmouth, the *Phoenix* off Saigon and the *Thetis* off Liverpool had gone down so close in time? Or was it a "spectacular coincidence"? Naval authorities in all three countries dismissed sabotage of a submarine, because the chance of a person getting on board to damage the essential parts was very remote and the chance of a member of the crew risking his life did not seem credible.

THE K2 DISASTER

The 1939 American Karakoram mountain climbing expedition to K2, the second-highest mountain in the world, was a catastrophe. It began as a scientific project to remap the mountain, to obtain medical data on the effects of altitude on human biology and to explore the changing climatic conditions at levels above 28,000 feet. But the Italian mountain climber, Fosco Maraini, described the events of the climb as "one of the worst tragedies in the climbing history of the Himalayas."[42] This expedition is a tale of mismanagement and bad luck.

The team leader was Fritz Hermann Ernst Wiessner, who was born in Dresden, Germany, of well-to-do parents. His father, Hermann Ernst, had real estate holdings, but his passion was art and architecture. He was, in fact, a professor of art. Dresden was a wonderful place to pursue interests in art and culture.

Fritz Wiessner inherited this love of beauty, especially the love of nature and outdoor sports. His father took him on long walks along the Elbe River, that winds towards what was then the Austro-Hungarian border. He developed into a short, powerful man who turned to mountain climbing, and he had the physical attributes that were necessary to tackle mountains anywhere in the world. Although he had a "baby-face," he was tough, strong-willed, and stubborn. He did not take advice well, which was not an ideal situation for a person who was to command a team of Americans, who were accustomed to informal rules and democratic behavior.

Wiessner chose his team from among the many persons he had climbed with earlier. The second member of the team, and the deputy leader, was Eaton O. "Tony" Cromwell, of New York City, who some called a playboy. He was the oldest member of the team, with the most climbing experience, but he lacked qualifications for the grueling trek to Karakoram. Chappell Cranmer, the youngest team member at twenty, had learned climbing in the hills of New England when he was a student at Dartmouth College and in the Colorado Rockies, which was his home. Fritz seemed to be more impressed with the prominence of Cranmer's family than his lack of experience. George Sheldon was a classmate of Cranmer's at Dartmouth. His whole climbing experience was all on the Tetons of Wyoming. Dudley F. Wolfe, another member of the team who was later implicated in the great tragedy of Karakoram, was part of a rich Colorado family who made their wealth in silver. Dudley knocked about doing interesting things: he drove an ambulance in World War I, joined the French Foreign Legion, won several boat races, got interested in skiing and finally in mountain climbing. He too had little experience. Jack Durrance and Sherpa guides, Pasang Lama, Pemba Kitar and Sidur Kikuli, completed the team.

Wiessner was prepared to lead the group to K2, but he was not a professional climber—he had never used guides, and he had never led an American team. They chose to climb the second-highest mountain in the world, whose altitude was 28,253 feet, compared to 29,029 feet for Mount Everest, and they elected to get to K2 from Srinagar in what is now Pakistan through Karakoram. The climbers started by rail across India in the one-hundred degree heat. After repacking the load in Rawalpindi, the six men motored to Srinagar, which was to serve as the first staging area. They left Srinagar on May 2, 1939 for the Karakoram. They crossed their first glacier twenty days later moving on to the Baltoro glacier, which runs westerly for about forty miles.

On June 3 Wiessner, Cromwell, and Kikuli made a reconnaissance at 19,000 feet of Sella's Peak. It was there that they decided, confirming an analysis by Charles Houston, who had tried K2 earlier, that the best route to K2 was by way of the Abruzzi Ridge. The problem with the ridge was that it wasn't: it was a series of rocks, many loose and subject to rock falls.

Wiessner established Camp IV at about 21,000 feet—an altitude at which there is considerable physical deterioration. Dudley Wolfe and Wiessner did not seem to mind the altitude, but they were destined to spend over a month at this perilous level. When Camp IV was secure, plans were made to go higher to form Camp V, but a hurricane-force wind intervened. It was two degrees below zero Fahrenheit and the wind reached eighty miles per hour. It was nearly as bad at Camp II, causing one climber to record, "It is far too windy & dangerous to relieve oneself at our eagles' nest privy."

Despite several additional mishaps (e.g. tents blowing away), Wiessner pushed on setting up Camp VII by July 22. By this time, the team was in poor physical condition. Cranmer was ill, as was Jack Durrance, and a guide, Pasang

Lama, had an injured kidney and chest bruises. With the frostbite and the missing tents, Fritz decided to split up the party—a prelude to disaster.

Facing a multitude of problems below, Wiessner decided to leave Dudley Wolfe alone at Camp VII, which was at nearly 25,000 feet. He and guide Lama descended towards Camps IV, V, and VI, which they found abandoned. Arriving at Base Camp, Fritz exploded at Tony Cromwell, threatening him with a lawsuit for putting the whole crew in a perilous position.

But the problem at hand was Dudley Wolfe, alone at Camp VII with a torn tent, no food, and without the skill to descend to Base Camp. Two Sherpa guides, Tsering and Dawa, and porter Pasang Kitar were sent up on a rescue mission; they all vanished in the wind, haze, and snow.

What went wrong on K2? The first answer is that Wiessner chose to go along a difficult and dangerous path with a weak team. Cranmer, Cromwell, and Wolfe were from rich families, but all lacked the skills and temperament to conquer K2. Some challenged Fritz's leadership record, especially his decision to go on with the climb when it was obvious that the team did not have the strength or skills needed to succeed. By the time they had reached Camp IV, everyone except Fritz and Dudley Wolfe favored terminating the project. Dudley's loss was more baffling, because he was unprepared to assault the top of K2. There were rumors that the two men had struck a financial deal that would allow Dudley to reach the summit first in exchange for financial assistance for those who could not pay their way. This allegation was never proved.

NOTES

1. Brooks, *The Great Leap*, p. 4.
2. Brown and MacDonald, *The Secret History of the Atomic Bomb*, p. 15.
3. Manchester, *The Glory and the Dream*, p. 211.
4. "The Race for the First Atomic Bomb," *Michigan Alumnus*, May/June 1992, p. 26.
5. Beard, *Our Foreign Born Citizens*, p. 224.
6. Lanouette and Szilard, *Genius in the Shadows*.
7. Morgan, *On Becoming American*, p. 166.
8. Manchester, *Glory and the Dream*, p. 214.
9. Taken from Williams and Cantelon, *The American Atom*, p. 12.
10. For the technical minded: Fermium is a particle having a half-integral spin and obeying the exclusionary principle and the Fermi-Dirac statistics. Professor Hall Crannell, who teaches physics at the Catholic University of America, told me that the half-integral spin really does not spin and that the exclusionary principle has a greater applicability than Fermi thought.
11. Heilbron, *Lawrence and His Laboratory*.
12. "Hubble Shows Scientists How the Universe Evolved," *New York Times*, May 8, 1939, p. 1.
13. Settel and Laas, *A Pictorial History of Television*, p. 29.
14. *Fifty Years of Popular Mechanics*, p. 188.
15. Sobel, *RCA*, p. 42.

16. *Current Biography*, 1940, p. 713.

17. Lyons, *David Sarnoff*, p. 212.

18. Quoted in Sobel, *RCA*, p. 132.

19. Lyons, *David Sarnoff*, p. 216.

20. Atanasoff's work was recognized by Mollenhoff in his *Atanasoff: Forgotten Father of the Computer* (1988).

21. In 1941, John Mauchly stayed in Atanasoff's home for five days, where he learned of the Iowa State computer. Mauchly linked up with J. Presper Eckert to build ENIAC, with a huge government grant. Later they started UNIVAC Corporation, which was purchased by Sperry. The Atanasoff prototype was recognized as the father of the modern computer in a law suit between Sperry Rand and Honeywell, during which the federal judge voided a claim by Sperry Rand because its model had been derived from Atanasoff's ABC invention.

22. Haynes, *American Chemical Industry*, p. xvi.

23. There is one sad element to the nylon story: on April 27, 1937, Wallace Carothers committed suicide at the age of forty-one. This brilliant chemist never saw the fulfillment of his dream.

24. Haynes, *American Chemical Industry*, p. 366.

25. *Du Pont*, p. 106.

26. *Fifty Years of Popular Mechanics*, p. 247.

27. Kaempffert, *Science Today and Tomorrow*, p. 57.

28. This history is taken from McCausland, "100 Years of the American Standards of Photography," pp. 11-18.

29. Fleischhauer and Brannan, *Documenting America*, p. 51.

30. Her most noted picture is on the cover of *Dorothea Lange*, Masters of Photography, (Macdonald, 1985).

31. *Dorothea Lange*, p. 6.

32. These personal aspects of her life are documented by her son, Daniel Dixon, in his *Dorothea Lange: A Visual Life*.

33. Henry Allen, "Come Back Dorothea," *Washington Post*, May 21, 1995, p. G 1.

34. Brooks, *The Great Leap*, p. 11.

35. *Popular Mechanics*, December 1938, p. 240.

36. Brooks, *The Great Leap*, p. 28.

37. "La Guardia Field Begins Operation," *New York Times*, December 2, 1939, p. 1.

38. "Squalus Worker Risks Life in Swim," *New York Times*, September 1, 1939, p. 14.

39. The *Squalus* was rebuilt and recommissioned as the *Sailfish*. During World War II, it sank seven enemy ships.

40. "French Submarine With 63 on Board Sinks in the Far East," *New York Times*, June 17, p. 1.

41. "99 Dead on Thetis, New Count Shows," *New York Times*, June 4, 1939, p. 1.

42. Kauffman and Putnam, *K2: The 1939 Tragedy*, p. 11.

8

Sports Notables

The world of 1939 gave us a full schedule of sports personages, but the three most notable were Lou Gehrig, Ted Williams, and Joe DiMaggio.

THE COMINGS AND GOINGS IN BASEBALL

The Iron Horse Stops Running

In 1939, when baseball was celebrating its centenary, the New York Yankees won the World Series for the fourth straight time—an all-time record. Led by Joe DiMaggio and Lou Gehrig, the Yankee Bombers were invincible. But the air of unconquerability was shattered by the fall of Gehrig. It is ironic that Lou Gehrig, the robust Iron Horse of baseball, one of the greatest sluggers on a great New York Yankee team, whose name was associated with strength, should be struck down with a crippling disease in 1939 that killed him in June 1941. The disease, amyotrophic lateral sclerosis, now bears his name.

When he joined the Yankees, he was given still another name—Buster—by his teammates. It was a term of endearment, because he was the most popular member of the team. They admired his modesty, his honesty, and his quiet performance. Gehrig's physique was the envy of his teammates: he was six feet one inch tall, 205 pounds with wrestlers shoulders and football-player legs.

Henry Louis Gehrig (always known in baseball as Lou or Larruping Lou) was born in a poor, congested neighborhood of upper Manhattan at 1994 Second Avenue, near 102nd Street—one of four sickly children. Three died in childhood, but Lou survived to play baseball, basketball, and football.

When young Lou was growing up, both his parents worked at Columbia University—his mother as a cook and his father as a handyman. Eventually, he became a student at the university, where he was a star on the baseball team (his teammates there called him Heinie). When he hit a ball completely out of the stadium onto 116th street, a Yankee scout signed him. Gehrig started his baseball career under manager Miller Huggins in June 1925. One day, Huggins summoned young Lou from the bench and told him to "take Wally Pipp's place at first base today."

For the next fourteen years, the clean-living, milk-drinking, Wheaties-eating son of an immigrant handyman started every game the Yankees played. His record of 2,130 consecutive games stood as one of the most durable of athletic feats.[1] But he was not just durable, he could hit. His worst year came in 1938 when he hit "only" .295 and had 29 home runs and 114 runs batted in (a performance that would put him near the top of the batting statistics in the 1990s).[2] His career totals are impressive: a .341 batting average, 494 home runs, 1,991 runs batted in, and 2,721 hits. One statistic is a flashing light: in 1931 he batted in 184 runs! It's still a record.

The only love of his life was Eleanor Twitchell, the daughter of a well-to-do restauranteur from Chicago. Although Gehrig was thoroughly pre-occupied with baseball, she got his attention, and they were married on the day of a game on September 29, 1933. The boy from Second Avenue married the girl who lunched at the 21 Club. When the Yankees played away from home, Gehrig, who attended Columbia University, chose to stay in his hotel room to read when he was not playing baseball.

Gehrig started that last spring training very slowly, but he thought he was only getting rusty. In his first twenty-eight at-bats in 1939, he had just four hits with no homers and one RBI. When he got a hit, he could barely run; he missed throws and fumbled ground balls. One episode is very telling. The Yankees were playing the Washington Senators, and Joe Krakauskas, a mediocre pitcher, was on the mound against Gehrig. Krakauskas threw one inside pitch and was astonished to see the ball go through Gehrig's arms. Gehrig saw the ball, but he could not move away from it.

On May 2, 1939, he told Manager Joe McCarthy that he was taking himself out of the lineup. Lefty Gomez, the relief pitcher and Yankee clown, tried to console him, but his humor was feeble. He said, "Hell Lou, it took 15 years to get you out of a game; sometimes I'm out in fifteen minutes." When Gehrig went to the bench, he knew better than anyone that he was not hitting and was hurting the Yankees on defense.

The Hall of Fame Library in Cooperstown, New York has a handwritten, undated letter written by Gehrig to his wife that says much about the decency of this man. It seems to allude to that Tuesday May 2, when his consecutive-game streak ended. "My sweetheart," he wrote, "and please God grant that we may be ever such—for what the hell else matters—the thing yesterday I believe and hope was the turning point of my life for the future as far as taking life too seriously is concerned. . . . How would this affect you and I . . . you are the bravest kind of partner . . . my inferiority grabbed me and made me wonder and ponder if I could possibly prove myself worthy of you."[3]

Gehrig went to the Mayo Clinic in Rochester, Minnesota, on June 13, 1939, to find out why he could not grip his bat any longer. He stayed until June 19. After a week of tests, he learned the terrible news: his paralysis attacked the spinal cord, his muscles were wasting away, and he was dying. The debilitated Gehrig accepted his fate. He said, "If this is the finish, I'll take it."

On July 4, 1939, 61,808 fans packed Yankee Stadium to say goodbye to Henry Louis Gehrig. The Yankees chose to parade the 1927 team and the 1939 team before Lou in pre-game ceremonies. They were to signify his first and last championship teams. John Drebinger called his farewell address "as amazing a valedictory as ever came from a ball player."[4]

When he strode to the microphone, he could not speak for a long time. He had prepared a speech, but he decided against using it. Babe Ruth ended his feud with Gehrig (they had not spoken for seven years) by hugging him and whispering in his ear. The feud had resulted from something Mrs. Gehrig said to Mrs. Ruth. Reassured, Lou said, "You have been reading about my bad breaks for weeks now. But today I consider myself the luckiest man on the face of the earth. I've got an awful lot to live for."

As John Kiernan said, Lou Gehrig lived the old maxims: "Early to bed and early to rise make a man healthy, wealthy and wise." And "A penny saved is a penny earned."[5] The Yankees could no longer count on "Old Reliable" Lou. They had lost their "Iron Horse." When he left, he held twenty-five league or World Series records.

When Gehrig contracted his paralysis, he received many offers of soft jobs with large salaries—in night clubs, in hotels, and even from Hollywood, but Lou, who came from a poor family always believed you worked for what you got. Mayor La Guardia, aware of Gehrig's disablement, summoned the slugger to his office. "How would you like to be a Parole Commissioner?" he asked Gehrig. "Gee, Mr. Mayor," he answered, "but I don't know anything about law." The Mayor told him the job required only common sense, and he promised to send Lou some books and reports.

Before accepting, however, he asked for three months to think it over, and he studied books and reports on crime and prisons and he visited jails. *Scholastic* magazine wrote, "It is the luckiest thing that ever happened to the youngsters of New York to have men like Gehrig—honest, conscientious, human and public spirited—going to bat for youth."[6]

Gehrig studied the material, after which he told La Guardia that he would take the job. He was sworn in on January 1, 1940. As he interviewed prisoners for possible parole, his only complaint was that they insisted on calling him Commissioner. As he said, "I was Lou on the field and I will always be Lou."[7] When Gehrig assumed his role as Parole Commissioner, a young man, Rocco Barbella, was brought before him. After they talked for a while, Gehrig returned him to reform school. Later he was to win a boxing championship as Rocky Graziano.

Enter "The Kid"

Teddy Samuel Williams (a name that he hated) made his major league debut in 1939. From the beginning, he was known as "The Kid," but he was also known as the Splendid Splinter, Thumping Ted, and, as Casey Stengel called him, "That Williams Fella." Sportswriter Grantland Rice once described Williams as "A great big kid with an inferiority complex," Al Wesson labeled him an "evangelical swatter," and Edwin Pope wrote that "Williams is a complicated man: irascible, charming, articulate, profane, friendly, hostile, absorbed, irreverent."[8]

But Colonel Egan, a Boston sportswriter, gave him the unkindest appellation of all: he called Ted "T. Wms. Esq."—apparently to knock some of the cockiness out of him. Many considered Williams a loudmouth nuisance. It was more than that: Williams was a foul mouth, and it went with his foul temper.

Ted Williams was born on August 30, 1918, in San Diego, California to May and Sam Williams. His mother was part Mexican-American part French. Imagine the following he would have had among the Hispanics of California and the rest of the United States if that had been common knowledge. We would have been comparing Italian-American DiMaggio and Hispanic Williams!

His mother was a fanatical Salvation Army worker, who was known as "Salvation May" and "Angel of Tijuana," because she walked the streets for long hours in search of funds for her cause. When she appeared with the Salvation Army band, little Ted had to stand beside her. He was miserable, and he said he "never got over it." This zeal made her a part-time mother for Ted, which may explain why he spent most of his waking hours at the North Park ballfield near his home. Ted says that he knew exactly when his craving for hitting began: it was when he was ten or eleven years old, and he had just learned that Bill Terry of the New York Giants had hit .401. Ted didn't know what it meant, but he knew it was something special with the bat and that he wanted to do it.[9]

Lanky Ted Williams often loped around the base paths after he deposited the baseball in the stands for a home run. He would jump up and down like a little kid. How he loved to hit. He was a zealot for baseball as his evangelical mother was a zealot for the Lord. She was enthusiastic and emotional—characteristics that she passed on to son Teddy. But Ted's mission was not religion, it was hitting. The son was fanatical about every aspect of putting the Louisville slugger to the ball. His cry was always the same, "Give me a bat. Let me at the ball." And then he would exclaim that this particular pitcher was a lamb, meaning that Ted was going to murder his best tosses. As every pitcher became a lamb for Williams, he earned a new nickname, "The Lamb."

It is clear that Williams never wanted to be anything but a ball player. His mother relates that when he was three he would take a very large baseball cap and pull it over the side of his head, he would drag a bat that was bigger than he, and he would announce that he was gonna be a "Babe Wooth."

When Ted was eleven years old, he spent most of his time at the playground near his home. Rod Luscomb, the playground director, commented that Ted had a wonderful swing and that it was unchanged from then until he went to the big leagues. When Ted played for the San Diego ball team, Manager Lefty O'Doul, of San Francisco, a pretty fair hitter in his day, told Ted, "Don't let 'em change you, kid. Stay as sweet as you are."

If Ted had to rank his favorite activities, he would probably list batting first, then fishing, and finally eating. His appetite was legendary. An old high school teammate, Roy Engle, his catcher at Hoover High, remembered one day when the team was to play a doubleheader in Pomona one hundred miles away. Ted's breakfast was strawberry shortcake and a malted milk, but because of the two games to play, he had no lunch. Instead, he consumed thirteen ice-cream bars and eleven bottles of pop. He has been known to order a second dinner right after eating a first. Amazingly, Ted kept his six-foot, three-inch frame at 180 pounds. Those who have seen him fidget nervously in the field and at the bat can easily understand how he kept himself a "splendid splinter."

The Red Sox nearly lost Williams to the Yankees! Bill Lane sold him, but refused to pay a bonus. Luckily, Eddie Collins flew to California and paid Williams' mother $2,500 (mainly out of his own pocket). Ted reported to Sarasota in 1938, but was sent to the minors for spouting off. When manager Joe Cronin gave him an order, the exuberant nineteen year old answered, "Okay, sport!" Cronin called him a fresh punk and sent him to Minneapolis. As his teammates ridiculed him, he was overwhelmed with sadness, but he covered it with braggadocio, "I'll be back and I'll rattle them off the fences."

His father, Sam Williams, was not a major figure in Ted's life, and it is ironic that Sam Williams abandoned the Williams household in 1939, the year Ted was called up to the majors by the Boston Red Sox. With a part-time mother, an alcoholic father, and a brother (Danny) who got involved with the wrong crowd, perhaps these domestic conditions explain Ted's brooding, temperamental, and explosive demeanor, and it may also explain why he could not adapt to family life, and why all three of his marriages ended with divorce. Seidel asks, "How could a ballplayer so controlled, precise, and patient at the plate, turn into a monster of temperament, precipitateness, and verbal disarray away from it?"

The answer is that Williams was a master technician of hitting. If you doubt that, read his book, *My Turn at Bat*. He was an average runner and a better-than-average fielder, particularly when taking balls off the left field wall at Fenway Park in Boston. Like Babe Ruth, Ted Williams began as a pitcher-outfielder, but Ted liked hitting too much to remain on the mound and on the bench between pitching turns. Williams once said that hitting a baseball is the most difficult thing in sports. Professor Robert Adair, of Yale, tells us why. A good fastball is coming at the batter at 97 miles per hour. At that speed, the pitch takes 0.4 seconds to reach home plate, and Adair calculated that the batter has .17 second to decide whether to swing at the pitch.[10]

The Williams stance was classic: He stood in the batter's box with feet about fifteen inches between his insteps. His left was six inches from the back of the box. When he started his swing, he took a step of from eight to ten inches with his right foot, the toe pointing towards the shortstop. Then came the crucial part: he followed the ball right to the plate and didn't start his swing until the last fraction of a second. During the swing, he gave a forward movement of his hips to increase his power, he followed the ball with head down and eyes fixed, and he used his wrists to achieve a tremendous snap of the bat. His perfect eyesight enabled him to watch the ball if it curved going over the plate. He defied convention by abandoning a level swing in favor of hitting a little above level.

From the beginning, Williams declared war on the press, even on those who treated him fairly. When he broke in as a rookie, there were seven daily papers in Boston, whose reporters were hungry for any quotation or rumor about Williams. They did not have to wait long. Williams was constantly popping off, giving reporters and fans "the finger," and even spitting on the field on more than one occasion.

He was ready to hit, but he was ill prepared for the Boston writers. When they needed a story, they trapped him. He fidgeted at questions, and he didn't care about the effects of his answers. He believed that the writers were insulting him. In one sense Williams was right. Dave Egan, a writer with a law degree from Harvard, kept needling him by comparing everything Williams did with DiMaggio's exploits. Egan wrote for the *Daily Record* under the byline of "The Colonel," and what everyone in Boston wanted to know each day was "What did Ted do," and "What did the Colonel write?" But what Ted did not know was that on many days Egan was too drunk to write his column, so it was dubbed by other reporters in the Egan style.

In 7,706 times at bat, Williams claimed that did not tip his hat once to the hungry fans who idolized him regardless of his immature antics on the field, but Linn tells us that in 1939, when Ted played right field, he would lope out to his position after hitting a home run, raise his hat high over his head and smile at his idolizing fans (mostly young boys in the stand). Williams was a rarity: he hit best when he was angry. When he drove a ball out of the park, it was an act of defiance. When some fans did boo him, he simply tried harder, and he usually showed his mettle under pressure.

In his first season with the Red Sox, Williams developed his insatiable appetite for information about opposing pitchers. He went to the veterans like Jimmie Foxx, Joe Cronin and Doc Cramer. He took in their views, but he never deviated from his idea that you never swing at a bad pitch, even if the game were on the line. He was criticized for this, but he maintained that if he swung at bad balls, it would widen the strike zone against him. And besides, he had the word of the great Rogers Hornsby that he should always "get a good ball to hit."

In 1938, Williams played for the Minneapolis Millers. He was sensational, winning the triple crown. The Red Sox management, who had been watching him, made its move. They released regular right fielder Ben Chapman, even though he batted .340 that year. Manager Joe Cronin disliked Chapman, so he (Cronin) was going in 1939 with The Kid. When Williams reported to Sarasota, Florida, for spring training in 1939, he was put in the outfield with Joe Vosmik and Doc Cramer. Ted was given Chapman's number 9; he first used number 5, the same as DiMaggio. In one of those oddities of life, DiMaggio started with number 9 and was switched by the Yankees to Number 5.[11]

When Williams joined the Red Sox in 1939, he was six feet three inches and weighed 175 pounds. He looked liked a bean pole. He was a "splendid splinter." He opened the season at Yankee Stadium on April 19 against pitcher Red Ruffing—a future Hall of Famer. When Ted swung, the bat was perfectly level to the ground, but Ruffing struck him out in his first at bat. In the fourth inning, however, Ted crashed the ball against the center field wall for a double. It was his first hit, and he would finish with 2,653 more. The game was also notable for one more fact: it was the only time Williams played on the same field with Lou Gehrig.

The 1939 season was a wonderful year for Williams, although he was not chosen for the All Star game for the only time in his playing career. He was batting only .280 at All Star time, but he was leading the league in runs-batted-in. He finished the year with a league-leading 145 RBI's—the first rookie to ever accomplish it. As Williams said, "I can't imagine anyone having a better, happier first year in the big leagues."[12]

One unreported aspect of William's first year was his generosity. He overcame his shyness by offering to help those in need, provided that there was no publicity (later, when he started the Jimmy Fund for research against cancer in children, he could not keep it a secret). Williams loved to do things for children. On one occasion, he rounded up a group of kids and took them all to the Revere Beach amusement park, where he ate with them, rode the roller coaster and bought them souvenirs.

As a long-ball hitter, he loved to hit the high fast balls when he first came to the Red Sox, and as a consequence he struck out sixty-four times. He soon learned that it was up to the hitter to narrow the strike zone, and he seldom struck out thereafter. He always preferred to take a bases on balls than to chase a bad pitch, and he went on to set a record for most consecutive years with 100 or more base on balls. When the 1939 season ended, he was batting .327 and had a league-leading 344 total bases, and Babe Ruth called him "rookie of the year," a designation that did not exist then.

Williams finished the 1939 season with 31 homers, fewer than he thought he would hit. Two factors accounted for the underperformance: the treacherous Fenway Park wind, which often blew in from right field; and the long distance to the wall. The Red Sox management could not alter wind patterns, but they moved in the wall. The foul line was only 302 feet from home plate, but it curved sharply to 404 feet at the bull pen. It was shortened to 380 feet for Williams.[13]

With or without closer fences, Williams was destined to become one of baseball's greatest hitters. But even experts can be wrong about this. Here is what Joe McCarthy, the Yankee manager said about Williams: "I hear the Red Sox think pretty well of Ted Williams. Well, he led Joe Gallagher [a Yankee player] in batting average, but he was in a short park. . . . That Williams is a nice hitter, all right. Takes a good cut. But when you figure out the parks they played in I still think it makes our man look like the better hitter."

The Yankee Clipper

If Ted Williams was the new idol of the Boston fans in 1939, by then Joe DiMaggio had already created a part of his legend. He was always identified as an Italian American, who personified the American dream. His decency and popularity were his symbols. Throughout the 1930s, DiMaggio's clean successes were contrasted with "Mussolini's dubious achievements." Which is why *Life* put DiMaggio on its cover on May 1, 1939, with an article stressing DiMaggio's Italian ancestry. This magnificent symbol of Italian Americanism was compared with Mussolini's attack on Albania. *Life* ridiculed his "easy victory," calling it "simple rape."[14]

Joe DiMaggio was the son of Giuseppe and Rosalie DiMaggio. Joe's father was born on a small island northwest of Palermo, Sicily. He was one of the thousands of Italian immigrants who flooded the United States between 1880 and 1914—many of whom were WOPS (those who came With Out Papers). As an islander, it was natural for Giuseppe DiMaggio to spend his days as a fisherman, as his father and grandfather had done. But life off Sicily was hard, and he was hearing about the better things in the United States. He joined his *paisini* in the San Francisco area, where following his American dream, he came to own his own boat.[15]

Young Joseph took up that most American of all sports, baseball, because baseball had a clean image, and through it he could escape the stereotype of the "dago," violent carrier of Italian ethnicity. In 1936, he reported to the Yankees' spring training for the first time. While reporters marveled at his big bat and his loping stride in the outfield where few balls eluded him, DiMaggio struggled to become a true American. He was always in the shadow of Benito Mussolini. But DiMaggio stood tall as a "son" of Italy. He was everything Mussolini wasn't. DiMaggio was tall, muscular, poised, quiet, graceful, capable. Diggins called him "Italy's Horatio Alger."[16]

Joe DiMaggio was always the "Yankee Clipper." What an apt title for so graceful a ballplayer! But it also signified the sea and his island heritage and San Franciso upbringing. Ironically and to his father's dismay, DiMaggio hated the smell of fish. Joe turned to baseball, where as Casey Stengel said, "He made the rest of them look like plumbers."[17]

DiMaggio had an uncanny ability to follow the flight of the ball as he sped towards the fence. His action was natural and totally unrehearsed. Sports writers compared him to Tris Speaker. Joe was the consummate outfielder, whose greatness could not be disputed. The only question arose when comparing him with ballplayers of old. Cannon agreed they were good, but as he said, "In this time there is not another ballplayer who is DiMaggio's equal. He is a ballplayer without a flaw. There is nothing he does not do well and no one has more style."

Some who did not appreciate fully the grace and elegance of the Yankee Clipper complained that DiMaggio lacked charisma or color. True. He did not rant or rave at umpires; he did not complain about third strikes; and he never grandstanded or showboated before his public. He had no vile temper and he was no hater of sports writers. If this was lack of color, Jolting Joe accepted it silently and stoically. He felt deeply about the game and his personal life, but for him these were private matters.

He led the major leagues in hitting in 1939 (and in 1940). He flirted with a .400 average all season, and finished with .381. On September 3, when Britain and France declared war on Germany, DiMaggio was batting .408.

Establishing Baseball Folklore

In 1939 baseball celebrated its centennial, in the same place where Abner Doubleday scratched out baseball foul lines with a stick. His crude diamond for playing "Town Ball" is still a marvel, because by some incredibly crude calculations, he hit on just the right distance to first base—a distance for which the ball and the base runner usually arrive at the same instant.

Americans claim baseball as their own, but the British argue that it evolved from their game of rounders or cricket. In fact, Henry Chadwick, who moved to the United States in 1837, originated the scoring system then in use. For this, he was called the "Father of Baseball."[18]

Abner Doubleday, who later distinguished himself as a Union general at the Battle of Gettysburg, established the game of baseball as we now know it by setting out four bases, reducing the number of players to nine and devising rules for playing.

Ford Frick was a sportswriter who became famous for writing Babe Ruth's *Book of Baseball*. In 1934, Frick was named President of the National League, and he began immediately to strengthen weak teams and to promote the idea of a Hall of Fame. He knew that Americans desired legends.

Baseball provides a surfeit at Cooperstown, New York, about twenty miles north of Oneonta. On June 10, 1939 Grover Alexander, Ty Cobb, Eddie Collins, Walter Johnson, Nap Lajoie, Connie Mack, Babe Ruth, George Sisler, Tris Speaker, Honus Wagner, and Cy Young were present at the dedication of the new "Hall of Fame" building and were the first inductees. To the strains of "Take Me Out to the Ball Game," they agreed to be photographed, and this lifesized photo is now on the Museum wall.

Kenesaw Mountain Landis, the Commissioner of Baseball, made the dedicatory remarks. Named for the Civil War Battle, Landis was made

commissioner after the Black Sox scandal of 1919. He was given absolute
power to clean up the game, which he used to drive the gamblers out of
baseball. It is said that Judge Landis saved the game, but he did not favor
owners. He blamed them of "covering up" players to retain monopoly rights. He
alluded to these in his dedicatory statement: "I should like to dedicate this
museum to all America, to lovers of good sportsmanship, healthy bodies and
keen minds. For those are the principles of baseball."

When the plans for the baseball museum were announced, the Library of
Congress began to search its volumes for books on the origins of the game. The
Library found a "A Little Pretty Pocket-Book," dated 1787 that described a
game similar to baseball in verse:

> Base-Ball
> The Ball once struck off,
> Away flies the Boy
> To the next defin'd Post,
> And then Home with Joy.[19]

The artifacts put in the museum in 1939 and after capture the spirit of this
great American game. When it opened, the museum's holdings were confined to
baseballs, bats, gloves, uniforms, and film, but modern technology allows the
directors to offer quizzes, statistics and other esoterica of modern baseball.

On July 22, 1939 before the scheduled game between the Boston Red Sox
and the St. Louis Browns, about four to five hundred persons participated in a
pageant, "The Cavalcade of Baseball." The history of baseball was traced from
the time when Abner Doubleday introduced a game of ball between boys, which
became the national pastime.

Leroy and the Monarchs

President Roosevelt stressed the democratic aspect of baseball—"The symbol
of America as melting pot." But he did not say that the great black players could
only play in the Negro League. Four out of five persons polled said that they
favored integration of the Negro and Big Leagues, but the owners in 1939 were
not interested.

The Negro National League was formed in 1920 in Kansas City. The local
team, the Kansas City Monarchs, was located at 18th and Vine Streets at the
center of culture, and they were truly kings. Hoping to be assimilated into one of
the white leagues, their behavior was impeccable. Off the field, players wore
coats and ties at all times. They were celebrities, and they ranked with preachers
and entertainers in the social stratum. They engendered enormous civic pride.
Even the taxi drivers wore ties out of respect for the Monarchs. This was
remarkable for a city that was wide open; there was plenty of jazz, gambling,
liquor, burlesque, and easy women.

Out of Kansas City, life was quite different. The players slept in a bus and ate on the road. It was their home. They played cards, sang songs, told jokes, camped and fished along the highways. As they traveled through Oklahoma, Arkansas, Missouri, Indiana, and Ohio, their chief worry remained: where to use the bathroom. One player observed, "People clapped for you in the field, but then you couldn't buy a sandwich."[20]

Throughout the 1930s the Monarchs played eighty games per year barnstorming across the South. They had to innovate to stay alive. They inaugurated night baseball six years before the major leagues, and they used every gimmick to attract crowds, including having Jesse Owens race against horses and trains before gametime.

Although they clowned around, they were great ball players. After the American Negro League was formed in 1937, the Monarchs won five of the next ten world series. When the games were played at Comiskey Park in Chicago, fifty thousand persons showed up. They came on the "City of New Orleans" train from Memphis and on the New York Central trains from the East. One fan declared, "Ain't seen nothing like it since."

The Negro Leagues featured some players that baseball enthusiasts could only dream of seeing against the best of the majors. Josh Gibson was called the "Black Babe Ruth," Walter "Buck" Leonard was said to be the equal of Lou Gehrig, and "Cool Papa" Bell was the equal of anyone in baseball

Gibson, the greatest catcher the Negro leagues ever produced, was the saddest story of all. Trapped within his black skin, he turned to excessive eating and to alcohol and drugs. Mark Ribowsky described Gibson's life as "The Power and the Darkness."[21] Like Babe Ruth, to whom he was often compared, Gibson had an enormous appetite, which undoubtedly was partially responsible for his early death at age thirty-five. Ribowsky does not specifically make the connection between the horrible conditions that Negroes faced in playing in white towns against white teams, but Gibson's death stands as bleak testimony to the tribulations of black ball players.

Leroy "Satchel" Paige, who signed with the Kansas City Monarchs in 1939, never warmed up, yet he had great control. His philosophy was simple: never waste pitches. He turned batters into knots with his variety of deliveries. He might use no windup on one pitch then use his hesitation windup on the next one. He also threw his "B-ball," "wobbly ball," "dipsy doodle," or his "tittie pitch." He always said keep the ball around the knees so they wont hurt you. When he wasn't pitching, he sang and played the ukelele.

Some who began in the Negro Leagues made it to "the big show," including Jackie Robinson and Leroy "Satchel" Paige. Paige came to the majors very late in his career, but there was still enough of the blinding speed to make us wonder how good he would have been if he had come up earlier. We could see those arms, legs, and eyes all moving in seeming contradictory motions as he pitched for the Cleveland Indians. And we know how great Hank Aaron was (he broke

Babe Ruth's home run record) and Willie Mays made it to the Hall of Fame with the third highest home run total.[22]

PIGSKIN PARADE

Tom Harmon, A Life of Legend

Tom Dudley Harmon, a native of Gary, Indiana, was one of the greatest players in the history of football at the University of Michigan. When he enrolled at Michigan, he was one of the best all-around athletes in the land. At Horace Mann High School in Gary, he was captain of the basketball team, he pitched three no-hitters for the baseball team, and he was a 9.9 sprinter and a champion hurdler.

Between 1938 and 1940, he was a triple threat. During these years, he scored a record thirty-three touchdowns—breaking the old mark of thirty held by Red Grange of the University of Illinois. As a tailback on the old single wing formation, Harmon was the man to stop if a team wished to beat Michigan. He handled the running, kicking, and passing and also played defense. In his time there was no unlimited substitution rule, which gives us the specialists of today. In 1939, most teams had a right-handed offense, which meant that they attacked the left side of the defense, where Harmon played. Few passed to his side of the field, because Harmon was nearly six feet tall and around 190-195 pounds. They preferred to throw towards Bob Westfall, who was only five feet six inches tall.

The 1939 Illinois-Michigan game was memorable for what Grantland Rice called Fritz Crisler's "important mistake." In an interview before the game, Crisler, Michigan's coach, stated that Harmon was a better back than Red Grange. All week long during practice Bob Zuppke, the Illini coach, kept telling his players that "Crisler says Harmon is better then Grange." Rice wrote, "When Illinois, an inferior team with a far inferior record, met mighty Michigan, Tommy Harmon thought he was playing against twenty or thirty tartars. Every time he took the ball he was tackled by eight or nine men." The final score was Illinois 16-7.[23]

In spite of his one poor day, Tom Harmon was voted to the 1939 All-America team. In the backfield with him were Paul Christman, of the University of Missouri, at quarterback; Banks McFadden, of Clemson University, at fullback; and Nile Kinnick, of Iowa joining Harmon at the other halfback post. Kinnick was named the leading college football player of the year, but he was to die in combat in World War II. As great as Tom Harmon was in 1939, he was even better the following year, when he won the Heisman trophy.

The Game That Closed a Stadium

The University of Michigan football team of 1939 was awesome. Led by some of the most outstanding players in Michigan history (Al Wistert, tackle;

Ed Frutig, end; Bob Westfall, fullback; and Forrest Eveshevski, blocking back), the Wolverines overwhelmed opponents. But the offense relied on the exploits of Tom Harmon, who set several scoring records in his three-year career.

But one of his games had a lasting impact on Big Ten football. It was the Michigan-Chicago game held at Stagg Field in Chicago in 1939. At half time, Michigan was leading 55-0, and there was talk of shortening the quarters in the second half. But Michigan Coach Fritz Crisler, who had been an All-American football player at the University of Chicago, had a different solution. He told the team that any player who was on the field when Michigan failed to quick kick on first down would never again play a game at Michigan. True to the coach's demand, Michigan punted on first down every sequence when it had the ball, but they still scored 30 more points in the second half, on interceptions, punt returns and fumbles.

Robert M. Hutchins, the twenty-nine-year-old President of the University of Chicago, suspended football the next day. These abandoned football lockers were made famous when they became the site of the "Manhattan Project" to develop the atomic bomb in World War II.

Undefeated and Unscored On

The Duke University football team achieved a remarkable record in 1938. It is hard to imagine any team coming closer to perfection. It won its first nine games by a combined score of 114 to 0. It was undefeated, untied and unscored upon by Davidson, Colgate, Georgia Tech, Wake Forest, North Carolina, Syracuse, Virginia Tech, North Carolina State, and Pittsburgh.

This achievement got it an invitation to the 1939 Rose Bowl game against Southern California, which stood in its path towards a perfect season. Duke scored first on a field goal, and with a minute left it was still Duke 3 and Southern 0. But woe betide: with forty-one seconds remaining, the Trojans scored a touchdown. Before a mostly partisan crowd of ninety one thousand, the Trojans had gone sixty-one yards for the score. Final score, Southern California 7, Duke 3.[24]

Southern California traveled through the air for its victory, but the mighty Trojans had to rely on a substitute back and a sophomore end to put down the Iron Dukes from North Carolina, using four straight passes by the unheralded duo (quarterback Doyle Nave and sophomore end antelope Al Krueger, who was from Antelope, California).

For three quarters, neither team could penetrate beyond the other's 35 yard line. It was a battle between what the Duke coach called the Trojans "four teams" and Eric "The Red" Tipton—Duke's one-man offense. But in the final quarter, Duke drove to Southern California's 15 yard line; the drive was spearheaded by a twenty-three yard pass from Tipton to George McAfee. Because the last quarter was nearly over, the Blue Devils were very content to allow their place-kicking star, Tony Ruffa, to try a field goal on fourth down. He booted it straight and true, and the Carolinians started to celebrate.

The teams jockeyed back and forth and suddenly the Trojans were moving towards the Duke goal line. With the ball on the Duke 35 yard line, U.S.C. coach, Howard Jones, did something strange: he took out first-string quarterback Ransdell and substituted Doyle Nave, who was a better passer. It was clear by then that Jones was going for a victory.

Nave threw four passes sucessfully, the last across the field to Kreuger for the touchdown. The game was over, and the Blue Devils could contemplate a long, tiresome train ride to Durham. Duke went the way of two other great undefeated teams—Notre Dame and California—who were beaten by the more spectacular Trojans, but Duke coach Wallace Wade could have been criticised for his overly conservative game plan. He relied too much on the great foot of Red Tipton, who often punted on third down. His lame excuse was that Southern California had too many horses (Trojan, we presume).

For whatever it means, not a single member of the Duke University team made the 1939 All-America selections, and Duke was not voted the number one team; instead, that honor went to Tennessee, which was undefeated, untied and unscored on in nine games.

THE BROWN BOMBER WENT DOWN

The fight game in the United States was not noted for strict adherence to the Marquis of Queensberry rules of boxing. It was dominated by crooked managers and fighters who did not recoil from the thought of throwing a low punch or putting a thumb in an opponents eye. For good reasons, the public was suspicious of the sport. Joe Louis restored the public's confidence in the integrity of prize fighting. He never fought a dirty fight, and he certainly never threw a fight; there was never a frame up in the Louis repertoire. Jimmy Cannon called Louis "an honest man in a league of burglars."[25]

Joseph Louis Barrow, who chose the ring name of Joe Louis, was the most successful champion of his time, and he was the youngest person ever to win the heavyweight boxing crown—he was champion of the world from 1937 to 1949. One of thirteen children, he was born and lived in a one-room shanty near the cotton fields of Lafayette, Alabama. His father, Munn Barrow, who was a sharecropper, died when Joe was four, so his mother took in washing to support her family. Three years later, she married again, and the family moved to Detroit.

Joe was a slow learner and was often embarrassed in school, which may help to explain why he turned to boxing, but the family certainly needed the seven dollars he earned in his first fight. When he wasn't in the ring, he worked as an iceman to build up his muscles for boxing, which was his first love. He carried blocks of ice to homes in Detroit—a time before air-conditioning, Joe would take a fifty pound block on his back up as many as four flights of stairs. This helped him build up his body into the powerful six-footer he became.

His beginning in the ring was not auspicious: he was knocked down several times in early bouts. Although showing some promise, Louis was a poor defender in the ring; he needed a manager. When Louis won the 1933 Golden Gloves, John Roxborough, a Detroit lawyer, was impressed enough to sign him to a professional contract and assign him to Jack Blackburn—a very shrewd handler of new fighters.

Louis learned much from Blackburn, who saw that the young, untrained boxer had tremendous possibilities that could be tapped. He taught Joe to use his natural gifts and his superb body. Blackburn's efforts were so successful that Joe earned the title of "Brown Bomber," and it brought him to the attention of Mike Jacobs, who had tried unsuccessfully to sign up another promising fighter, James Johnston. Blackburn and Jacobs steered the young Louis towards a championship fight with James L. Braddock, and on June 22, 1937, the Brown Bomber knocked out the champion in the eighth round. He had reached the top of the boxing world in just three years.

Joe was probably looking forward to his rematch with Max Schmeling, the German who had knocked him out in 1936. The fight achieved international importance, because Hitler had boasted of the superiority of the German over the "inferior Negro." Louis, always reticent in the ring, came out for the first round like an enraged tiger. He was merciless, as he beat Schmeling to the floor under an incredible barrage of blows. When the fight was stopped in the first round, the German was on the canvas looking up at Louis with eyes that were pleading for mercy. Louis had his full revenge.

Louis, no intellectual, spent his spare time playing his jazz records (he favored the music of Jimmy Lunceford). "When he plays a record he dances around the room with a phantom partner, grinning from ear to ear. He sleeps 12 to 14 hours a day. When not in training he drinks four quarts of milk daily and eats enormous in-between-meal snacks."[26]

Louis was a soft-spoken, gentle man out of the ring, but in it he was ferocious. He sent one opponent to the hospital with a concussion, but he said matter of factly, "I am sorry that happened. But they come to beat me up. I have to go back at them the same way." For this, he was called the "Alabama Assassin." He was also called "Shuffling Joe," but he could deliver lightning strikes and hammer blows to the body as fast as any fighter in history.

For Louis, prize fighting was a sacred occupation—a way to raise his people out of their depths, a way to achieve the promises of the Declaration of Independence. Malcom X said that Joe Louis had "coalesced the masses of Negroes." Louis disdained retaliation for illegal punches, even when provoked. The most striking time came in the fight against Max Baer, when Baer hit him after the bell had sounded. The average fighter would have retaliated, but not Joe. He just looked at Baer with utter disgust, and he proceeded to get his kind of revenge—in the ring.

In 1939 he was at his peak, and he was once again on top of the boxing world in the heavyweight class, having defended his title four times. In January, Joe Louis defended against a light heavyweight, John Henry Lewis, in Madison Square Garden. It was the battle of the same sounding names. They were each twenty-five years old, but John Henry had more ring experience. Shufflin' Joe was the heavy favorite (10 to 1), despite John Henry's record of ninety-two victories in ninety nine fights. John Lewis was a boxer and fast and shifty on his feet, which promised to give the champion trouble. It was scheduled to go fifteen rounds. Reporters noted that Louis had trouble with Tommy Farr (the dodger) and Bob Pastor (the elusive one). They escaped Shufflin' Joe's lightning strikes by running away from Louis.

It was up to the Brown Bomber to chase and tag John Lewis; the public paid $16.50 to see Louis deliver his well-known hammer blows. They said that Lightning Joe's wallops were harder than any fighter since Jack Dempsey. Though the public hungered for Joe's offensive show, his managers told him that against John Henry he would need to improve his defense. John Henry, who never reached his full potential, was still a good fighter. He could hit, he could dodge and weave with his feet, and he could confuse Louis as much as Bob Pastor.

The fight began with Louis hitting John Henry with several rights and lefts to the head and jaw and John Henry went down. He got up to be greeted with more punches to the body and head. John Henry went down a second time. He hopped up at the two count. It was his last mistake. The Brown Bomber was at his usual ferociousness. Down for the third time. At the count of five, the referee stopped the fight. It lasted two and one-half minutes. There was no more talk of artful dodgers in the ring against Joe Louis.

In 1939 it was four fights and four knockouts. Fight experts were ranking Louis with Jack Dempsey and Gene Tunney on the all-time lists. John Henry Lewis was beaten in January in 2:39 of the first round. Jack Roper lasted only 2:20 minutes. The comment about him was that he was a competent electrician.

Fight number three, on June 28, 1939, was something more. The headline read, "Louis Knocks Out Galento in the Fourth." But it was not Joe Louis at his best. Louis expected a tough fight, but he did not expect to be on the canvas in the third round. John Roxborough and Julian Black, Louis's managers, were not surprised at the challenger's strong showing.

Tony "Two-Ton" Galento, the tavern keeper with the rotund figure from Orange, New Jersey, was considered a clown by many, because he had extremely unorthodox methods for training, which included drinking beer. At one point, Galento said, "I'll flatten dat bum with one punch." His looks were deceiving; he could stand up and slug as well as any fighter in his day. This was his strategy against Louis. He would give up his clownish capers in the ring, and instead fight without fear. His record was deceiving: he had been fighting for eleven years and had been beaten twenty-two times.

It was clearly the best of four fights in 1939. In the first two rounds, the challenger stooped over throwing his left to Louis's face. He and the champ traded hooks and crosses, but in the third round, the unthinkable happened: Louis was lying on the deck. He sprang up and avoided Galento's roundhouse punches until the round ended. When round four started, Louis looked more than determined; he had that "finish-him-now look." Galento, thinking he had the champion's number, waded in. Abandoning his crouch, which had confused Louis, Galento decided to challenge Louis on his terms, by waging a stand-up battle. He walked into an unrelenting barrage of left hooks and right crosses. It was like practice on a punching bag. Louis did not miss.

Galento's face was unrecognizable. He had cuts over both eyes and over his lip, and his entire face was swollen. Referee Arthur Donovan stopped the fight momentarily to inspect Galento. Sadly, he allowed the pummeling to continue. Soon it was over. Louis hit Galento so hard that the challenger was spun around ninety degrees, and at this point Donovan declared Louis the victor in a technical knockout. It required twenty-three stitches to put Tony's face back together, But he wasn't impressed with the champion: "He is not as good as they rate him." History says otherwise. Max Schmeling and James Braddock were the only others to deck the champ during his spectacular career.

As Joe Louis racked up victory after victory, the question arose as to who of the past champions could defeat him. Jack Dempsey had his opinion, "My man would be Gene Tunney." Tunney had retired in 1928 as undefeated champion. Dempsey, the Manassa Mauler, believed that a smart boxer like Tunney would stab Louis consistently with his left jab and finish him off "with a right cross."

Some say that Louis was just an ordinary boxer and that his record was improved by fighting a long list of mediocre opponents. But no fighter in history ever had as many fights as Louis. He took them all on. They came in all styles: some just stood there, like Galento; some couldn't move, like Carnera; and some tried to hide, like Wolcott. Joe's response was, "They can run but they can't hide."

Louis put his heavyweight crown on the line against all comers. For him, all opponents were alike. He never ducked, which is why on December 22, 1939 when the National Boxing Association issued its rankings for heavyweights, Joe Louis headed the list again, followed by Tony Galento, of New Jersey, who decked Louis to the canvas earlier that year. Max Baer, who was champ in 1934, was rated sixth best.

By 1939 Louis was a large success: he had earned over one million dollars, which he invested in a restaurant, two homes, a farm, and apartment houses. He also indulged himself with a large Buick and several $100 suits. But his worth was to his people. He became a symbol of decency. He spoke out against the lynchings and mutilations of blacks. Until Louis, blacks had little hope of becoming heavyweight champion, because whites remembered the reign of Jack Johnston (1908-1915), who was arrogant, flamboyant and who flaunted his many white women in public.

MISTER ZERO

Boston had two phenomenal rookies in 1939. The first was Ted Williams; the second was Frank Brimsek, who came to be known as "Mister Zero," because of the number of shutouts he achieved (ten) in his first year of goal tending for the Boston Bruins of the National Hockey League. Brimsek won the Calder Trophy as Rookie of the Year, and he was given the Vezina Trophy as top goalie of 1939. He also was the first rookie in history to be named to the All-Star team.

Brimsek, a twenty-two-year-old native of Eveleth, Minnesota replaced Tiny Thompson in the opening game when Thompson was injured. He never returned in goal. Brimsek was scheduled to be sent down to the Bruin's farm team in Providence, but he was so sensational as a goalie that Thompson, an All-Star, was sold to the Detroit Red Wings.

As good as Brimsek was, he only won the Rookie of the Year honor by four points—seventy points to teammate Roy "The Rifle" Conacher's sixty-six. The left winger led the league in goals scored, but this mark did not stand up next to Brimsek's shutouts and fewest goals allowed.

These two sensational rookies led the Bruins to victory in the 1939 Stanley Cup championship. The team's split the first two games, but Boston came back to win three straight—the last at home before 16,891 screaming fans in the Boston Gardens. It was their first championship since 1929 and only their second overall. Manager Art Ross compared the two teams: in 1929, the Bruins had one great line—Cooney Welland, Dutch Gainer, and Dit Clapper. Now, he said, "We have three good lines. The Kichener kids are tops in my book."[27] He was referring to his Kraut Line of Bobby Bauer, Woodie Dumart and Milt Schmidt, all of whom came from Kichener, Ontario.

The Boston Bruins eliminated the New York Rangers in the first round of the National Hockey League playoffs that started on March 21, 1939. In spite of the overwhelming superiority of the Boston club, it was a titanic struggle. The Bruins won the first three games, but New York captured the next three.

It came down to a seventh game, which was in Boston before a capacity crowd of 18,981 frenzied fans. The two teams punished each other for 108 minutes—48 after regulation play. Mel Hill scored the winning goal, with assists from Bill Cowley and Roy Conacher. Amazingly, it was the third time that Hill had provided the clincher in the series. It earned him the title of "Sudden Death" Hill. Remarkably, four of the seven games, including the first and last, went into overtime.

The games of March 30 and March 31 were particularly odious. On March 30, as sports writer Austen Lake told it, there was an "atrocity scene," during which the "hairy apes" of New York ganged up on Boston defenseman Eddie Shore and "gouged and garrotted him." They broke his nose. The following evening, the "Boston burghers" came to the Garden loaded with vegetable matter, beer cans, pipes, and pieces of metal—all good for heaving at the Rangers. Others just threw newspapers or magazines or game programs. Each time the ice crew cleared the rink of debris, another volley cascaded from the gallery (somehow these people were known as "gallery gods"). Lake, in his cute way, stated that all the pipes and scrap metal thrown on the ice was "cast in the spirit of innocent merriment."[28]

The Bruin victory over New York gave the team the right to meet the Toronto Maple Leafs for the Stanley Cup. The Bruins were heavy favorites, because they beat the New Yorkers, who many considered the second-best hockey team. Toronto, which finished third in league competition, beat the Montreal Canadiens in Series C and the Detroit Red Wings in Series D to earn the right to face Boston.

The Toronto series was anticlimactic. Boston won the series by four games to one, and it won the final game by that score. It was sweet revenge for the Bruins, who had been eliminated in the first-round playoffs by the Maple Leafs for four straight years.

The Bruins' results in the season and in the playoffs gave them a commanding lead in All-Star positions. In addition to Brimsek, Boston placed Eddie Shore at right defense and Aubrey "Dit" Clapper at left defense. They were known as "the dynamite trio," and they were teamed up with Sylvanus Apps and Gordon Drillon of the Toronto Maple Leafs and Toe Blake of the Montreal Canadiens. Art Ross of the Bruins was rated top coach. He called his 1939 Bruins "The greatest team I have seen in thirty-seven years."

NOTES

1. On September 6, 1995, Cal Ripken, of the Baltimore Orioles, broke Gehrig's record, a record which most thought would never be broken.

2. Robinson, *Iron Horse.*

3. Quoted by William Guildea in his *Washington Post* story of August 6, 1995.

4. "61,808 Fans Roar Tribute to Gehrig," *New York Times*, July 5, 1939, p. 1.

5. John Kieran, "Journey's End," *New York Times*, June 22, 1939, p. 29.

6. October 30, 1939, p. 35.

7. "Gehrig Considering Offers for New Job," *New York Times*, October 10, 1939, p. 28.

8. Pope, *Ted Williams*, p. 8.

9. Linn, *Hitter*, p. 3.

10. Adair, *The Physics of Baseball.*

11. Linn, *Hitter*, p. 97.

12. *My Turn at Bat*, p. 53.

13. I remember being in the stands at Fenway Park one raw April day when Williams hit a ball to right center field that was heading about fifty feet over the fence when a northeast gale blew in, caught the ball in flight and dropped it into the glove of the opposing right fielder, who was standing near the wall watching the flight of the ball. We can only imagine how many home runs Williams would have hit if he had played in a domed stadium.

14. Moore, "Understanding Joe DiMaggio as an Italian American Hero," 1989.

15. Cinel, *From Italy to San Francisco.*

16. Diggins, *Mussolini and Fascism*.

17. Hollander, *Great American Athletes of the 20th Century*, p. 40.

18. Rosenburg, *The Story of Baseball*, p. 7.

19. "The Doubleday Claim," *New York Times*, April 23, 1939, p. 2E.

20. This comment and some of this brief history are taken from the PBS special, "The Kansas City Monarchs," shown on April 17, 1996.

21. Ribowsky, *The Power and the Darkness*.

22. Merkin, *Leagues Apart*.

23. Rice, *The Tumult and the Shouting*, p. 197.

24. On October 1, 1939, Duke beat Davidson, 20-6. It was the first time Duke was scored on in the regular season since 1937.

25. *Esquire's Great Men and Moments in Sports*, p. 13.

26. *Current Biography*, 1940, p. 524.

27. *Boston American*, March 15, 1939, p. 27.

28. *Boston American*, March 31, 1939, p.48.

Part III

IT HAPPENED OVER THERE

9

Wars "Good" and Bad

United States journalists and essayists portrayed the Great Depression as if it were a purely American circumstance, but the effects were world wide and were much more devastating in the undeveloped world. Because Americans were content to isolate themselves from the devastation in the rest of the world, they were unable to prevent the totalitarian tide that brought war. These events did happen "over there," but, as we soon learned, we could not escape their consequences.

SPAIN: WAR AS A PRELUDE

The Spanish Civil War of 1936 to 1939 was a popular resistance to an attempt to bring about a military coup by the fascist leaders of Italy and Germany. It so aroused the intellectuals of Europe and the United States that many actually fought on the Republican side. In Europe, André Malraux and George Orwell took up the fighting with mixed emotions, and in America there was Hemingway.

In July 1936 Generalissimo Francisco Franco set out from Morocco with a small army of over seventeen thousand men to conquer Spain. His objective was to eliminate the Popular Front (communist) government. In the next three years, he increased the size of his fighting force to 750,000 men.[1] The Spanish Revolution was an attempt to collectivize the economic system. Dolgoff asserts that while the fighting progressed, agrarian and industrial collectives were instituted all over Spain, and it was because of these popular changes that Franco encountered so much opposition from the "forces of democracy."[2]

Who was this general who consorted with Hitler and Mussolini? Franco was born in Galicia in northwestern Spain in 1892, the son of a naval officer. At fourteen years of age, he entered military school at The Alcazar in Toledo, where he received an ordinary military education. He graduated three years later with his commission and was asssigned to fight the Riffs in the Spanish Moroccan war, during which Lieutenant Franco was wounded and decorated for bravery.[3] At first, Franco was hesitant to join the rebellion; he was cautious, loyal, and unwilling to confront the greatest issue of his time. When he decided to rid Spain of corruption and communism, he depended on voluntary contributions, but in time he simply took what he needed to continue fighting.

The loyalists, who controlled most of the gold reserves in the Bank of Spain, recruited an even larger army in two places: Catalonia and Castile. The loyalist troops, although larger in number, suffered heavier losses—the figure has been estimated at about seven hundred thousand. This figure does not include civilians who were executed by both sides and those who were killed in bombing attacks.

According to the Dupuys, this war saw ferocious fighting, dreadful losses for both armies with "no appreciable result."[4] Madrid was bombed and destroyed under a twenty-eight-month siege. The most obvious outcome of this conflict was to provide a proving ground for the Soviet, German and Italian armies. These countries provided thousands of "volunteers"—actual numbers are impossible to obtain. Estimates are that the Germans and Russians supplied an equal number, about fifty thousand troops each. When fighting began, soldiers were mere mobs, but as the war progressed, each side became more efficient at killing people.

The war began on July 18, 1936, as a military revolt in Spain and Morocco against the socialist government. Franco flew to Morocco to take command of the thirty thousand troops, who began their journey towards Madrid. In September, the war became international: Russia chose to support the Loyalist (socialist) government, whereas Italy and Germany aided Franco by providing Junker dive bombers and light tanks.

The Soviet propaganda machine helped to enlist many American "volunteers," including the Abraham Lincoln Brigade, which was part of the International Brigade. Thomas estimates in his *The Spanish Civil War* that twenty-eight hundred Americans fought in the struggle for democracy against the forces of fascism, and Germany and Italy sent fifty-six thousand troops to Spain. Many historians claim that the Lincoln Brigade was under the control of the American Communist Party, because the Republicans received considerable aid from Soviet Russia.

General Emilio Mola, leader of the insurgents in northern Spain, left his mark on history when he declared that he had four columns converging on Madrid and a "fifth column" in the city—a term to be known as a synonym for subversive actions. As the war progressed, it got uglier. Nothing typifies its sordid aspects as much as the bombing of the Basque village of Guernica on April 25, 1937. The world was shocked as Franco's Luftwaffe pilots bombed the northern city causing large losses to civilians. There was a world outcry against this massacre.

By the fall of 1938 Franco controlled most of Spain, and in January 1939 the rebels took Barcelona, which had been the victim of a naval blockade after the Loyalist government moved there. Mussolini, who promised to withdraw troops from Spain, but who kept forty thousand soldiers there, helped Franco take Barcelona. Loyalist troops fled across the French border, where they were kept in confinement.[5]

Franco's armies swept past Montserrat to the hills near Barcelona, where the fight for Barcelona was ferocious. It was Spain's largest port and an important industrial region. German planes bombed the city continuously, and artillery pounded it from the ground. Men under fifty-five were conscripted to dig trenches, and women took over the normal occupations of the city. Loyalist fighters tried to destroy the attacking bombers, but the Spaniards were greatly outnumbered. In February, Franco marched into the city, as two million persons offered no resistance. The fall of Barcelona meant the disintegration of the army's morale. As if to write an epitaph on the war before it was over, in March, British Prime Minister Neville Chamberlain and French Premier Edouard Daladier announced that the governments of Britain and France were recognizing the government of Generalissimo Francisco Franco as the true government of Spain, thereby removing recognition of the Loyalist government.

Madrid was the last stop for Franco. On March 28, 1939, Madrid and Valencia surrendered. Spain's thirty-two-month war, which caused an estimated 1 million deaths, was over. When the end came, it was snowing heavily and Madrid was out of fuel and food. *Time* reported on April 3 that the 1 million Madrilenos were "half-starved" and that two thousand persons were dying daily of hunger and disease. The city was dying too. No trains or buses moved; nothing ran. The people could only hope for a quick, honorable, and a "merciful" peace. But Franco gave word from his headquarters in Burgos that he was still demanding "unconditional surrender"—he wanted to see white flags over Madrid.

In early May 1939 Mussolini promised that his troops would withdraw from Spain by the end of the month—a promise he kept. He indicated that the Italian Black Shirts would not occupy any part of the Iberian peninsula. He left it to Count Costanzo Ciano to give the balance sheet of dead and wounded: 3,327 dead, 11,227 wounded. The Italian role began after July 25, 1936, when Franco requested assistance to fight the communists. In time, Italy sent one hundred thousand men to the Spanish front.[6]

Franco's *Movimiento Nacional* replaced the democratic, military, Catholic Republic with an authoritarian, atheist government. He rejected the English-French ideas of liberty and equality and replaced them with Falanges based on "bread and justice." The Falange sought a return to authority in place of anarchy. Franco agreed with the Nazi argument that the Jews were the boil on the body of democratic societies, because they created Bolshevism (Marx was a Jew), and Lenin had planned the Spanish Civil War years before it began.

Franco's fight was meant to remove Spain from the clutches of international communism. Intellectuals divided along philosophical lines. T. S. Eliot refused to comment on the war, but Ezra Pound, who cozied to Mussolini, saw it as a battle of monied interests. His assessment was that, "Spain is an emotional luxury to a gang of sap-headed dilettantes."[7]

A Divided Church

Americans were passionate in their concerns for the outcome of the Spanish struggle, because it was communist inspired. Many Americans joined the cause of the Spanish Republic believing it had democratic roots. Spanish Republicans insisted that theirs was a democratic fight against the forces of fascism. Americans, who believed in the force of law, thought that the Republican government was a legal one.

American Catholics were uneasy about Spain, because they could not reconcile the Church's teachings with its behavior. How were they to understand that most of the working poor hated the Spanish Church, which they said exploited them? And how were Catholics to reconcile the actions of bishops with the teachings of the encyclical of Pope Leo XIII "On the Conditions of Labor"? The Bishops, they were sure, had contributed to the slaughter, and so many Catholics left their faith behind to fight alongside the communists. *Life* on July 12 called the rulers of Spain (which included bishops) "irresponsible, arrogant, vain, ignorant, shiftless, and incompetent."

President Roosevelt's sympathy was for the Spanish Republic, but he was compelled to follow a course that injured the Loyalists. Two main factors yielded this result: first, all the polls indicated clearly that the majority of Americans were anxious to stay out of any European wars, and second, the Roman Catholic bishops saw the struggle as a "holy war," and they were vehemently opposed to aiding the Republicans, who were receiving help from Soviet Russia.

The opposition of the Roman Catholic hierarchy was most intense in the matter of repeal of the embargo on shipments of war supplies to belligerents. Congressional leaders warned the President that lifting the embargo would mean the loss of the Catholic vote, on which many Democrats depended. But not only were Catholics not a monolithic vote, but they were in the mainstream on this issue; only about one-fourth of Americans favored amending the neutrality acts. Even the liberal, international newspapers (the *Washington Post*, *New York Times* and *Christian Science Monitor*) were in favor of rigidly adhering to the laws as they were.

The Catholic press was elated over the outcome. No Catholic magazine supported the republic. The Diocesan newspapers were generally pro-Franco, but even the *Catholic Historical Review*, a journal of scholars, printed favorable articles of Franco. According to Guttman, only 39 percent of Catholics were sympathetic with the nationalist cause (compared to 9 percent of Protestants).[8]

But if 61 percent of Catholics did not support Franco, it shows a greatly divided Catholic Church, and it indicates that Roosevelt's policies based on fears of losing "the Catholic vote" were misguided.

"THE POPE, HOW MANY DIVISIONS DOES 'HE' HAVE?"[9]

Pius XI was elected Pope in 1922. As Monsignor Achille Ratti, he had risen from peasant stock to parish priest to prince of the church. When he became Pope, the long-standing enmity between the Roman Catholic Church and the Italian State had begun to wane. The time was ripe for an official reconciliation. There was one struggle the Pope could not avoid. He had to deal with Benito Mussolini—*Il Duce*. By using bully tactics, Mussolini controlled every aspect of business and labor. The original fascists detested the state and the church, but he soon realized that he needed rapprochement with the Vatican for legitimacy. Pius XI knew that Italy had never before faced an atheistic government, so on February 11, 1929, he negotiated a peace.

The Concordat reaffirmed the Italian Constitution that the Catholic and apostolic religion was the sole religion of the state. It reduced the number of bishops, but Vatican City achieved political independence. The Lateran Accord was a great victory for the fascists, because it healed rifts between the Vatican, the state, and the king. It did not, however, remove the essential conflict between Catholicism and fascism.

In the winter of 1938-39, the Pope suffered three heart attacks, leaving his eighty-one year old body sapped of its vitality. As he lay on his death bed, he wrote a letter to all bishops warning them of the dangers from both sides of the political spectrum. On the morning of February 10, 1939, near dawn, the Swiss Guards in their medieval uniforms held their halberds tightly in the cold Roman night. The Pope's attendants prepared him to leave this world. He said his last confession feebly and received absolution. They washed his face, hands, and feet and anointed him in extreme unction (the last rites of the church). The sacristan touched the Pope's eyes with oil and prayed, "Send him, O Lord, help from thy place, and defend him out of Zion." At 5:31 in the morning, Pius XI whispered, "We have so much to do," and gave up his soul. Pope Pius XI was buried in a triple coffin in a crypt under Saint Peter's.

Almost two months later, the conclave to select a new Pope convened. The sixty-two cardinals were ushered into San Domaso Court, and the heavy bronze door was sealed with its six keys. Under a century-old tradition, when the votes were taken, the results of each secret ballot were told by smoke coming from the chimney in the Sistine Chapel. Black smoke meant that no cardinal had obtained the required majority; white smoke signaled a Pope had been elected. At 5:28 P.M. on March 2, 1939, a puff of white smoke rose from the chimney, and the people of Rome ran to St. Peter's Square. It was one of the shortest conclaves in history, lasting only two days. The crowd in the square pushed forward to be nearer the balcony.

Forty minutes later Cardinal Caccia-Dominioni strode to the microphone. His purple cassock blew in the wind as he spoke. His words went out over loudspeakers in the square to radio networks everywhere, *Nuntio vobis guadium magnum: habemus Papam* (I announce to you a great joy: we have a Pope). He continued speaking, and his voice raised for dramatic emphasis, *Eminentissimum ac Reverendissimum dominum meum, Dominum Cardinalem Eugenium Pacelli.* He announced to the most eminent and most reverend Lord that Eugenio Cardinal Pacelli, the Secretary of State, was the new Pope. The crowd roared and broke into song.

Pacelli took the name of his predecessor and therefore became Pope Pius XII. The tall, lean cardinal walked out on the balcony of St. Peter's wearing a red ermine cape. It was his sixty-third birthday. He raised his hand and gave the *urbi et orbi* blessing (to the city and the world). Pacelli was no stranger. He was born in Rome, and as a Vatican diplomat, he was known widely to Catholics and non-Catholics alike. The world knew him as a scholar and linguist who spoke nine languages. Having served as papal nuncio to Bavaria, he knew Germany, and he was anxious to mediate the dispute between Germany and Poland, but he was bound by the Lateran Treaty, which forbade the Pope from dealing with "temporal conflicts." He could only use his office as a moral force.

The world knew the Pope but may not have known how simply and frugally he lived. He ate little, and, strangely for an Italian, he drank little wine. He did succumb to some worldly things, such as his fully equipped gymnasium, his motor vehicle, and his electric shaver. His first day as Pope was typical. He arose at 6 A.M., shaved, celebrated Mass, had coffee and rolls, then worked a full day, with time off for a brief walk in the Vatican garden.

THE DICTATORIAL POWERS

Once in a Thousand Years

During the First World War, the Allied nations believed that they were fighting to make the world safe for democracy, but when victory was achieved, the democracies were tottering, making possible the rise of dictators in Germany, Turkey, Italy, and Spain. One was Adolf Hitler, who was born in Brannau in 1889. He was a short Austrian, a Roman Catholic altar boy whose mother wanted him to be a priest. He loved music, especially Wagner, and he expressed this love by singing in the choir. When the great inflation of 1923 wiped out the wealth of the German middle class, he blamed the Jews. He spoke in the streets, incited riots and attempted a coup d'etat in Munich, for which he was given a five-year prison term. It was there that he dictated *Mein Kampf.*

Hitler was a psychologist's dream. He did not eat meat, he did not smoke, and he was a neat freak. Women adored him; they fought for invitations to Berghof, his retreat in the Bavarian Alps at Berchtesgarten (eagle's nest), three-thousand feet above sea level and about fifteen miles from Salzburg. He could grasp the moment and he moved people. He once got on a platform and said nothing for sixty seconds. When he spoke, it was electric. Fromm diminishes the importance of economic and political factors as explanatory causes of Nazism and prefers to state categorically that "Nazism is a psychological problem."[10] He chooses words such as "Neurotic" and "mad" and "mentally unbalanced" to describe Hitler and is not willing to accept German imperialism or economic expansion as necessary conditions. He quotes Lewis Mumford: "In overwhelming pride, delight in cruelty, neurotic disintegration—in this and not in the Treaty of Versailles or in the incompetence of the German Republic lies the explanation of Fascism."[11]

The Nazi ideology was accepted passionately by the lower strata of the German middle class, particularly by shopkeepers, craftsmen, and white-collar workers. For them, the call for blind obedience to the Fuhrer and hatred for racial minorities was an opportunity to exalt the Nordic race. They perceived this as a battle between the strong and the weak. They empathized with Hitler, their leader, who came from this class—a nobody, an outcast who was born outside of the German mainstream.

A contemporary called Hitler a great medicine man and said there was no use in mocking him. He was the product of the savagery of his time; it gave him the power to cast a hypnotic spell over the German people. The word "will" appeared incessantly in Hitler's speeches and writings. The *Triumph of the Will* was the only documentary of Hitler that was made in his time. He was obsessed with and expected the German soldier to carry out his will, because the will of the German soldier could overcome all foes (he called them all "peasant armies"). He spoke these words to Rauschning in 1939: "No matter what you attempt, if an idea is not yet mature, you will not be able to realise it. I know that as an artist, and I know it as a statesman. Then there is only one thing to do: the work goes on. It matures, sometimes it dies. Unless I have the inner, incorruptible conviction . . . I do nothing . . . I will not act; I will wait."[12]

The Nazi principles flowed from *Mein Kampf*. It is the work of the conscious and the subconscious, not the ravings of a maniac. It is Hitler's Book of Revelations. It rejects communism and class struggle and substitutes a kind of Darwinian biological determinism, leading to racial purity. For him, it was an eternal verity. Humans were engaged in an endless struggle to improve the races, which required that inferior peoples be eliminated. In pursuing this process of racial selection, he praised the "militant Nordic section," which "will rise again and become the ruling element over these shopkeepers [the British] and the pacifists [the French]."[13]

"Uncle Adolf" was a lover of children (except Jewish ones). He fawned on them, dealt with them on their level, and they adored him. He seemed to be the perfect leader. One of his admirers said that a person like him came along "once in a thousand years." Others called him a miracle of twentieth-century efficiency. In addition, Hitler had charisma. He strutted, he boasted and he was electric. He looked ordinary (like Charlie Chaplin's version of him), but he had the capacity to move people. So fanatical was his following that when he walked by, they cried, "Hitler is our Savior. Hitler is our Lord."

The Depression gave Hitler his long-awaited chance, because it shattered the good fortunes of the republican government. There were over four hundred riots, with Nazis triumphant as the army made a deal with Hitler.[14] When Hitler became President and Chancellor, everyone called him "Fuhrer" (leader). His economic program was simple. He froze wages, threw out unions, retained private property, but interfered with business on a massive scale. The first four-year plan concentrated on road building, construction of public buildings, improvements in canals and land reclamation (He chose four-year plans, because the Russians whom he detested, were using five-year plans). The second four-year plan (1937-41) was aimed at war. German scientists were told to produce synthetic fibers, rubber, and gasoline from coal.

The spending of $80 billion on armaments brought economic recovery. Between 1933 and 1939, Germany produced 30 panzer divisions, 70 motorized divisions, 140 infantry divisions, and it greatly multiplied the number of planes for the Luftwaffe. In 1935 Hitler ordered national conscription and created the youth corps (he said it was to study and build gliders!). Then he seized the Rhineland and had the Siegfried Line built—twenty-two thousand fortified positions on the French-German border.[15]

Weinberg suggests that Hitler's fight was a war of eugenics—an attempt to promote Darwin's principles of natural selection and evolution. It was a defense of ideal specimens of Germans and an elimination of the subhuman species (Jews, blacks, Gypsies, the handicapped, and the infirm).[16] To promote his policy of mass murder, Hitler began by selecting a large group of misfits as his aides. There was the porcine Herman Goering, the rat-face Joseph Goebbels, the weird Rudolph Hess, the relentless Heinrich Himmler and the pompous Joachim von Ribbentrop.

Goering was a World War I flying ace who was credited with shooting down twenty-two allied planes. He took over the "Flying Circus" when its leader, Manfred von Richtofen (the Red Baron), was shot down. Goering was a very early supporter of Hitler and was wounded in the 1923 putsch in Munich. When Hitler took power, Goering was given a number of important posts in the Nazi Party. He was head of the Gestapo, President of the Reichstag, Air Minister, Commander of the Luftwaffe, Reich Commissioner of the four-year plan and Reichsmarshall of the Greater German Reich. In 1939 he was given an order to defeat the British in the preparation for Operation Sea Lion (the invasion of Britain).

Goebbels, a sardonic, brilliant Rhinelander, less than five feet tall, failed at everything until Hitler gave him a platform as Minister of Propaganda. For him, war was the climax to fifth-column activities, which accounts for his transmitting his messages into twenty-seven languages. He recognized the power of music for indoctrination. His favorite song was "Bombs Over England." On several occasions, he lined major streets and buildings with hundreds of Nazi flags. When he suggested that Germany burn all books by and about Jews, he confirmed what Heinrich Heine had said: wherever they burn books, they will burn people too.

Heinrich Himmler, the chief of the secret police, was born in Munich, the son of a school teacher. As Hitler's personal bodyguard, he savagely eliminated all of the Fuhrer's rivals. He believed in the occult, in Lucifer and in the existence of the Holy Grail, which was the subject of Wagner's opera *Parsifal*. Himmler enlisted Otto Rahn as an investigator to do genealogical research on Caucasians. The Germans were seeking a genealogy free of Jews. In March 1939, after Himmler learned that Rahn had a Jewish grandmother, his body was found murdered on a mountain slope in Austria.

Rudolph Hess was third in the Nazi hierarchy, but he was on the fringe of power. He was a vegetarian who was always ill (which probably soured Hitler on him). Hess, who was his personal secretary, was used for a variety of tasks, including taking dictation of *Mein Kampf.*

Joachim von Ribbentrop was considered a fool by almost every German, except Adolf Hitler. Ribbentrop was thought to be industrious but unintelligent, and he was boring, officious, and pompous—just the right mixture of characteristics for rising in the Nazi Party. He was known for "the trappings of statesmanship rather than by its substance."[17] Bloch asks, how could such a "non-entity" survive as Hitler's foreign minister for six years? He answers that Ribbentrop was the consummate "yes man." But he was expert at taking any of *der Fuhrer's* wildest schemes and enlarging it into a grand plan. In this way, this little, oafish man, the great collaborator, came to personify the evil that was Hitler's.

Ribbentrop was cognizant of his inferior class standing, so he remedied this inferiority by literally purchasing a title—he was thereafter to be known as von Ribbentrop. The ambitious Ribbentrop continued his social climbing. He married Anna Henkell, the daughter of a wine manufacturer, who supplied the spark to his career. The Ribbentrops, being well-off, supported the Nazi Party, and it was then that he first met Adolf Hitler. Ribbentrop was able to play his one trump card: he used his friendship with von Papen to negotiate a settlement between Hitler and President Paul von Hindenburg under which Hitler would become Chancellor. Serving as middleman at his Berlin-Dahlem villa, Ribbentrop kept the parties talking even after negotiations had broken down.

Il Popolo d'Italia

Benito Mussolini, the son of Alessandro Mussolini and Rosa Maltoni, was named after Benito Juarez, the Mexican socialist leader. As a boy Benito was sent to a Catholic boarding school, where he first exhibited bully tactics. During World War I, he became a patriot; he served in the army, was wounded and was sent home to resume his writing. Postwar conditions were desperate, and Mussolini seized the opportunity. Into the void of chaos, strikes, and disorder,

Mussolini created the Fascist party on March 23, 1919. He formed the *fasci di combatimento* (bundles of combat), and he declared his program to be "Law and Order," which meant saving Italy from the communists.

Benito was "obsessed with atheism, republicanism, antimilitarism, and the principle of social revolution."[18] After trying a career as a teacher (emulating his mother), he found his real calling, as a journalist for a socialist labor weekly— *L'avvenire del Lavotore* (The Future of the Worker). He quickly disputed editorial policy, causing him to launch his own paper—*Il Popolo d'Italia* (The People of Italy) to champion the grievances of World War I veterans.

In the beginning, they were a few hundred, but as they strutted down the main streets with their black shirts and fatigue caps, they enlisted thousands in their fight to put down political unrest and to suppress the socialists. They used gangster tactics, breaking strikes, wrecking socialist clubhouses, and they were implicated in the disappearance (murder?) of Giacomo Matteotti, the most anti-fascist deputy in the government. Mussolini said he made the streets safe; his answer was, "I have sent all the gangsters to America."

Massock describes the birth of the new party very graphically: "Fascism was born in a brawl with a club in its hands, and a club and a chopper have remained the insignia of its mystery. The first fascists attracted the favor of the employers in a labor struggle by their skill and determination in street rioting. . . it has been a combination of every illegal menace with every illegal brutality that has kept him hitherto in power." It was said that the thirty million Italians were controlled by thirty men for the benefit of three hundred thousand.[19]

In 1937 after Mussolini visited Hitler, Italy passed laws stripping Jews of their civil rights. The following year, Hitler visited Italy and Mussolini adopted the German goose step. With growing popular support and the army behind him, Mussolini marched on Rome. The King offered no resistance; Rome and Italy were Mussolini's. He ordered mandatory military training for all persons between eight and thirty-two years of age. It was to be the beginning for this second Julius Caesar.

A Softening of the Brain

A dictator's sex life is not germane unless it affects his policies and his people. In 1939 a rumor spread across Rome that Mussolini had fathered a child by a very young woman who had been quartered in his villa. Housemaids and diplomats speculated that Il Duce was very abrupt with Prime Minister Chamberlain during his Rome visit because of the imminent birth.

Mussolini always had a roving eye for a woman with a good figure, especially one with blond hair. He was not one to sublimate his sex drive; like many of his aging fascists of lesser rank, Mussolini exhibited his sexual virility. But the whispering was that this energetic exertion was leading to a "softening of the brain." The subject of these accusations was a young lady he met at Terminella, a small resort area near Rome. She was the daughter of a medical doctor and the wife of one of his flyers. He used to drive to the place for a day or two of skiing and found her to be an easy conquest. Who could refuse the most powerful man in Italy? Even the husband, who knew of the liaison, could not protest. The flyer husband was promoted and sent to Ethiopia! The young lady soon learned that Mussolini was her pot of gold. She obtained a villa in a fashionable suburb of Rome, which she furnished lavishly, and she was given charge accounts in all the luxury shops.

Taking Tirana

On April 7, 1939, Easter Sunday, a large contingent of Italian troops assembled at the ports of Bari and Brindisi for the invasion of Albania, forty-five miles across the Adriatic. King Zog I, the tribal chief who had seized power, was as amazed as most Europeans that the landing took place. Mussolini announced that his "friendly" troops were taking over the country to "re-establish order, peace and justice." They confronted the Albanian army of thirteen thousand, which was armed with ancient rifles and daggers. In just hours, the fascist Black Shirts achieved the steep mountain climb to the capital, suffering only twenty-one killed and ninety-seven wounded.[20]

Taking Albania defied logic, because it was the poorest and most backward of all the independent nations of Europe. Its living was grim. The villages were squalid; the port was very primitive; and the capital city, Tirana, was modern in name only. The one million persons who made up the population were hopelessly poor. They subsisted on a backward agriculture that featured a goat's cheese and crude bread. They raised their crops with hand tools, wooden plows made from forks of trees and water buffalo. They slept in mud huts that had no furniture. Each week they made their way down the mountains from their villages to Tirana with their donkeys and packhorses to exchange their crops and hand made items for clothing and the other necessities of life. There were no trains, no oil, and only a few minerals.

Such was the country that the great Mussolini sent his troops to conquer. For the world it was incredible, but he explained that southern Italy was over populated and nearly as poor as Albania. The dictator needed a safety valve, and he needed it nearby. Earlier he had taken Ethiopia and Djibouti, Ethiopia's neighbor on the West. Djibouti had only 250,000 persons, but it had 8,880 square miles.

Italy's stance was military puppetry. David Brinkley relates one aspect of the comic nature of the Italian military might. The military attache in Washington, General Adolfo Infante, was given a $500-per-month budget to obtain information about American war plants. While attending a movie, he discovered that the newsreel provided much detail about U.S. production of tanks and planes. He was given the authority to purchase the newsreel and ship it to Rome. When he enquired about purchasing other newsreels, he was told that the cost of shipping them to Italy was too high. "Couldn't Infante simply go downtown to Loew's Palace Theater, buy a ticket, sit in the balcony, and take notes."[21]

Assaults on Party Cadres

Throughout 1937 and 1938 the Communist party leadership in Russia engaged in a wave of repression that eliminated former members of defunct opposition groups. "By the beginning of 1939, 110 of 139 members and candidate members elected at the XVIIth Party Congress in 1934 had been arrested." Many of them perished in the purge.[22] The purges removed the intelligent classes, the military, and the factory operators. Radzinsky reports that on an average day in 1937 or 1938, Stalin issued the death sentence to more persons than were executed by the Tsar in all of the nineteenth century.[23]

By the middle of the year, only 7 of 136 party secretaries were still functioning. Almost all the others had been arrested and shot. Virtually none of the oblasts (autonomous republics) of the U.S.S.R. escaped this purge, which is why by the mid-1930s, most non-Soviet opposition parties had gone underground. Few were immune to this wave of terror.

Experiments in Investigation[24]

As the new Pope prayed for the conversion of Russia, conditions could not be worse in the "workers paradise." Solzhenitsyn detailed his own arrest and the arrest of millions of Russians in the years from 1937 to 1939. His arrest was "the easiest imaginable kind." He was a captain on a narrow salient on the Baltic Sea, when his brigade commander asked for his pistol and shouted, "You are under arrest!" There were absurd, fantastic reasons for making arrests. They were made on the "strength of false denunciations." Those arrested were educated persons and peasants. The agricultural workers were accused of being "agricultural wreckers," who sowed weeds in Russian fields.

They took only Solzhenitsyn's political notes and his map case. He described how they put him in a punishment cell that was a closet in a German peasant house. When he was shoved in after midnight, he was the fourth person imprisoned there. The other three moved over, giving him enough space to lie on one side, half between and half on top of the others.

A few were freed, but mass arrests continued. Thirty thousand Czechs fled the Germans in 1939 to be with their Slavic relatives in the U.S.S.R. Because a few of them had been spies, they were all sent to northern prison camps. The West Ukrainians and the West Byelorussians received similar treatment. In 1939 there was a "reverse wave" of arrests. These were the 1-2 percent of persons who had been arrested but not yet convicted. They were freed, and Solzhenitsyn calls this "giving back one kopeck change from a ruble.[25]

Living conditions in the camps in 1939 were hellish. The kerosene lamps burned away and smoked the air. Electric lights burned red at half voltage, and the hinged panes used for ventilation were kept shut, being opened only for trips to the toilet. The prisoners' sheets were always damp and the walls were as moldy as their daily bread. No vegetation grew; anything that might have grown was covered over with concrete and asphalt. But the height of Russian inhumanity was their regulation that forbade lifting up one's head during walks. The rule was "Look at your feet!"

Joseph Vissiarionovich Stalin (formerly known as Dzhugashvili) was the architect of this political terror. As the Bolshevik Tsar of the largest country on earth, he "broke all records" for killing people. Stalin's cruelty exceeded that of Caligula, Nero, Tomas de Torquemada, and Ivan the Terrible. Stalin's totals for the years 1936 to 1939 were "immeasurably greater." Using what he calls "cautious estimates," Roy Medvedev reports that four or five million Russians were subjected to political repression and that four to five hundred thousand (mostly high officials) were summarily shot. He claimed that these purges were aimed at breaking up an anti-Soviet underground movement, but they also destroyed the relatives of "enemies of the people," many of whom were only twelve to fifteen years old. When the quotas for industrialization were not met, Stalin created the system of Gulags—the labor camps. If a factory worker was ten minutes late for work, that person received a three-five year prison sentence. The penalty was as severe for stealing a potato.

Stalin was a man of many faces (his was also pockmarked). Like Hitler, he was short at five feet five inches, and he was as devious. In justifying his killings, he said casually that "death solves all problems." He was strong, but he lacked any moral principles and convictions. He was a murderer with charisma, who did not love or respect his people. It was said that the only person he ever loved was his daughter Svetlana, and she defected later. He made a show of conviviality, preferring a drunken atmosphere and violent dancing, in which he participated. For foreign visitors, Stalin presented another side. He was charming, generous, tender, and gentle. Like Hitler, he would go into his garden to pick a rose for his guests. Many foreign correspondents returned home to write glowing reports of the Russian leader.

F. F. Raskolnikov, a hero of the October Revolution and Commissar of Naval Affairs, was a Soviet diplomat in the 1930s. In 1939 he wrote in his diary: "The fundamental psychological trait of Stalin, which gave him a decisive advantage, as the lion's strength makes him king of the jungle, is his unusual, superhuman strength of will. He always knows what he wants and, with unwavering, implacable methodicalness, gradually reaches his goal."

Raskolnikov was alarmed at the destruction of the best party members and, after being followed by NKVD agents, was declared "an enemy of the people." In July 1939 he wrote "An Open Letter to Stalin." His words were firm and bristly:

Stalin, you have begun a new stage, which will go down in the history of our revolution as the 'epoch of terror'. . . with the help of dirty forgeries you have staged trials, which, in the absurdity of the accusations, surpass the medieval witch trials you know about from seminary textbooks. . . . You have defamed and shot long-time colleagues of Lenin, knowing very well that they were innocent. You have forced them before dying to confess crimes they never committed, to smear themselves in filth . . . you have plundered those whom you murdered and defamed, appropriating their feats and accomplishments to yourself.[26]

This letter appeared in a paper that was published by White Russian emigres, but it passed unnoticed. Raskolnikov died in September 1939. According to the French newspapers, he either committed suicide by jumping from a window, or he was thrown out.

The economic consequences of the purges were appalling. The five-year plan that placed so much emphasis on heavy equipment manufacturing was decimated by the liquidation of plant managers and Party members. By 1939 the metallurgy, electrical, and chemical industries were without competent managers.

Another Master Race?

After World War I, Japanese-American relations deteriorated steadily. For almost twenty years, the two countries adopted conflicting foreign policies in Asia. The Japanese seemed bent on asserting their dominance over China, which ran counter to the American doctrine of an "open door policy."

Americans considered the Japanese to be inscrutable, incomprehensible and unpredictable. But Otto Tolischus wrote that they were not unfathomable if you used their own words: "The best sources of that knowledge are the Japanese themselves. Like the Nazis, the Japanese have not been backward in declaring themselves. Like the Nazis, they, too, pursued two lines—an official line advancing limited aims with conciliatory gestures to confuse and divide expected opposition so that the intended victims could be swallowed one by one, and a propaganda line stating the true aims."[27]

The "true aim" of the Japanese was a "glorious hundred years war." Lieutenant Colonel Tatsuhiko Takashimo wrote in February 1939, "History teaches us that such great tasks take at least one or two centuries to accomplish. . . . Now we must exert all the national strength, fully comprehend the true secret of Imperial Japan, so lofty in human history and unparalleled in the world, and fighting with total force over the whole world, firmly establish its structure and without any negligence bring it steadily to completion." The rule of China is the first step toward the rule of the world.

The Japanese claim is centuries old and has its basis in Shinto, "The Way of the Gods." It penetrated all aspects of Japanese existence, its thoughts, traditions, and political and social institutions. Shinto imbued the Japanese with the notion of a superior race and led them to believe that the gods supported their idea of world conquest. In its most basic form, Shinto preaches that the Japanese people are children of the gods and that the emperor is divine. The

Japanese considered themselves to be the highest beings in the cosmos, a master race, hence they deserved to rule the world. It is through Shinto that the Japanese arrived at *Mikadoism*, the emperor as god. This unique position proceeded from his direct lineage from the Sun Goddess—the highest deity in the Japanese Pantheon.[28]

Hirohito's Role

In 1939 Emperor Hirohito was the High Priest of Japan. He was god of the universe. Unfortunately, his reign was an undiminished evil, which is ironic because his name means "Radiant Peace." As a follower of Shinto, he became a puppet of the military clique that controlled Japan.

The modern Japanese plans for conquering the world date to the ambitious scheme conceived by Premier Baron Giichi Tanaka in a memorial, which was first published in 1931. It was his design for world domination. It would begin with the conquest of Manchuria, followed by taking possession of China and the rest of East Asia and Oceania; winning India, Central and West Asia, and Europe; and overcoming the United States. He wrote that the surrender treaty would be signed in the White House. To buttress the planks of the new world order, Lieutenant Colonel Tatsuhiko Takashima proposed a national education policy. It would rise above the "petty theories of Adam Smith, Kant, Hegel, Marx, Clausewitz, etc."

Lurking behind these words were unspoken ones concerning the tyranny of the white races. The Japanese believed that Americans and Anglo-Saxons were arrogant, self-centered, unintelligent, and supported a shallow life style. By these pronouncements, the colored people, who formed the bulk of the world population, were to be freed of oppression and taken into the nirvana of equality and peace for all humans.

As Japan gobbled up Asian territories, Secretary of State Hull warned that its drive for Asian domination might trigger an American embargo of goods that were vital to Japan's armament industry. The American threat of embargo threatened Japanese sources of supply, because European supplies were cut off by the arms race that Hitler had forced on other nations. The biggest issue was scrap steel and oil. Almost all of Japan's aviation gasoline and nearly all of her steel came from the United States. Japan's imports of steel scrap rose from 690,000 tons to 860,000. Although both of these figures were below the peak of more than one million tons in 1937, they indicate a continuing buildup of steel reserves.

The Battle for China

The *New York Times* headline of September 24, 1939 proclaimed that "Japan Risks All to Win in China." Its four million square miles made it the second largest land mass in the world, and in 1939 it had 450 million people—one-fifth of the world's population. In 1937 the Japanese bombed Shanghai—the largest city in China, with a population of 3.5 million. It began on July 7, when there was a skirmish between Japanese and Chinese soldiers on the centuries-old Marco Polo bridge, which crossed a dry river bed in an area near Shanghai. This altercation gave Japan the pretext to attack China, which was the actual beginning of World War II for the Chinese. The Japanese invaded from the south, with two divisions, leaving a trail of atrocities. They beheaded thousands of civilians, for which they were censured by the League of Nations. The Chinese withdrew with very heavy losses.

In the same year, in a very provocative act, the Japanese sank an American ship, the *Panay*, in a river south of Nanking. They unleashed their air squadrons to bomb soldiers and civilians. The Chinese defense of the city was futile, and it surrendered in just days. As John Wiltz wrote, the Japanese "reinforced a newly-acquired reputation for brutality by giving themselves over to an orgy of looting and murder—the "rape of Nanking.""[29] Over three hundred thousand Chinese were killed, butchered, and raped in one week; the Japanese celebrated in the streets.

The Chinese retreated westerly, with a scorched-earth policy. They burned the ground, killed animals, and destroyed their factories. They dug up and carried away steel railroad ties. They left nothing for the Japanese. In one of the most astounding migrations in world history, thirty million Chinese moved two thousand miles from the East. They carried books and other elements of their culture for preservation, using the rivers where possible. They moved their capital to Chungking—one thousand miles away—which the Japanese started bombing immediately.

Communists on the March

When Sun Yat Sen, the President of China, died, the communists began plotting their efforts to take over China. Chang Kai-shek, a fervent anticommunist resisted, precipitating the long struggle for the control of China. The nationalists drove the communists to take their Long March, which lasted from 1934 to 1936.[30] When Shanghai fell, the Nationalist and Communist governments of Chang Kai-shek and Chou En-lai agreed to stop fighting and to form a united front against the Japanese. Under the agreement, the communists agreed to give up their policy of land confiscation and agreed to follow the more-democratic policies of Sun Yat Sen.

Mao Tse-tung began his rise in the Communist Party in 1937 at Yenan in Northern China. He controlled an area of thirty thousand acres with a million persons. As the Chinese fought the Japanese, the communists expanded eastward and southward. By the fall of 1938 the Chinese were in retreat as the Japanese captured Canton and Wuhan, forcing the National government to move to Chungking. When 1939 began, the Japanese held the entire eastern third of China.

There was a grim aspect to the movement of Japanese troops in China. In what was called a failure to maintain discipline, there were documented records of looting, raping, and indiscriminate killing of Chinese civilians. Not only did it create an anti-Japanese feeling amongst the citizenry, but it was a complete breakdown of military organization. In one area, which had changed hands several times, a local resident complained, "Japanese, too many killed; Kuomintang, too many taxes; Communists, too many meetings."[31]

After his forces had been at war against China for nearly a year and a half, the Emperor of Japan, Hirohito, decided to sample the rations that his soldiers in China were enduring. He and the Empress, who was eight months pregnant squatted before a low table to eat a bowl of boiled rice and barley, some powdered bean paste, and pickled radishes. For lunch they consumed a cereal, gruel, bean noodles, pork, boiled spinach and salty pickled plums. For their main evening fare, they dined on boiled rice and barley (again), side dishes of dried fish, carrots and boiled lotus roots. As *Time* of January 30, 1939, told us, "One day of war-fare was enough for the Son of Heaven."

Clearly, the food was not enough to cheer up the boys at the front, so the military brass sent hundreds of geishas, wrestlers, chorus girls, magicians, actors and prostitutes to China. Incredibly, the Japanese soldiers turned to writing heroic poems to commemorate the experience! And a Japanese magazine held contests to publish the best of the soldier-poets.

How did Americans react to the Chinese situation? The Gallup polls showed a sizeable shift of sentiment in the United States. The September 1937 poll asked if we should take sides with Japan or China. The results: 43 percent voted for China, 2 percent for Japan, 55 percent were undecided. But the June 1939 poll, which asked the same question, showed very different results: 74 percent voted in favor of China, only 2 percent for Japan and 24 percent remained undecided.

THE PALESTINIAN QUESTION

As conditions in Germany worsened for Jews, many sought to escape. Some crossed borders illegally, others tried to book passage out of Germany. When the existence of concentration camps became known to world leaders, they looked for a place where refugees "could be admitted in almost unlimited numbers," to use Roosevelt's phrase.[32] In what became a surrealistic exercise, the heads of government mentioned Ethiopia (Roosevelt's choice), Madagascar (Hitler's nominee), Russia (chosen by Mussolini), and Alaska (Stalin's choice). Many other locations were suggested, but all were rejected by Hitler or Jewish organizations. All the places were totally unsuited for Jews who were merchants, shopkeepers or businessmen. They preferred Palestine, which was their Zion.

The British White Paper on Palestine

On May 7, 1939 the British introduced a White Paper on Palestine, which had the effect of barring U.S. Jews from acquiring land in Western Palestine and restricting Jewish immigration to Palestine, especially from Europe. The British were willing to admit fifteen thousand Jews per year for five years and no more.

The British White Paper was sent to the League of Nations on May 22, 1939. The Council of the League declared that it was not in accordance with interpretations made in 1937 and was therefore unworkable. The point of controversy was the terms of the Mandate for Palestine, which stated that Palestine should be placed "under such political, administrative and economic conditions as will secure the establishment of the Jewish national home."[33] But the British reminded the League that its declaration of policy for 1937 contained the statement that "there is an irreconcilable conflict between the aspirations of the Arabs and the Jews in Palestine, that these aspirations cannot be satisfied under the terms of the present mandate." The British were embarrassed by the almost-universal condemnation of the plan, so they quickly offered forty thousand square miles of land in British Guiana for Jewish refugees.

In 1939 the Zionist movement was controlled by Europeans and the Palestine Yishuv. American Jews were restricted to making substantial financial contributions towards the creation of a Jewish state. The advent of war reduced the power of European Jews and brought American Zionists to the front of the movement. Dr. Solomon Goldman, President of the Zionist Organization of America, visited President Roosevelt before the white paper was issued and asked him to instruct Ambassador Joseph Kennedy to urge the British to postpone the plan. In relating the details of the meeting to David Ben-Gurion by letter, Goldman stated that he felt that "In Roosevelt we had a sincere friend who no doubt wanted to do much more for us, were he not hindered by the political situation."[34] But Schechtman called the statements of the Roosevelt Administration "doubletalk," because each time the State Department made promises to the Jews on Palestine, it watered down the version for the Arabs.

When World War II began, there was little mention of the Jews in the press. This was a war against Nazi Germany. The Jews set about to rectify this neglect. They proposed to field an all-Jewish army of Palestinians to fight under the English flag against Hitler. It never materialized.

The New Diaspora

The origins of Hitler's anti-Semitism is complex. The Nazi party, before he became Chancellor, did not have an anti-Jewish plank, and even when he rose to power, one survey indicated that only 13 percent of party members were "paranoid anti-Semites."[35] Hitler wrote about the Jewish problem in *Mein Kampf*, but some analysts have adopted a Freudian approach to explain his maniacal attitude towards Jews. Some ascribe his anti-Semitism to the time when his mother died after she had been treated by a Jewish physician. For a layman it called forth Oedipal conflicts. Others believe that the hatred stems from his father, Alois, who was the illegitimate son of a Jewish mother.

When Hitler took power in Germany, he started a program of sterilization and euthanasia to rid the country of undesirables. At first, he concentrated on the mentally ill and on habitual criminals. By the end of the 1930s, German physicians were writing of the need to "cultivate" genes. Lifton, in *The Nazi Doctors*, stresses that throughout history a corrupt superego has been the norm, not the exception. Those with strong Freudian superegos were able to excuse slavery and racism and most wars.

Whatever the origins, Hitler's hatred of Jews was extraordinary, and he was the principal advocate of unbending anti-Semitism in the Nazi government. For him, ideology was insufficient; it had to be converted into reality, which meant the slaughter of Jews. In January 1939, the German High Command began to speak of the need for a radical solution of the Jewish question, by which it meant the removal of all Jews living on German territory. Germany was willing to negotiate the matter of Jewish property rights, but it was clear that the departing Jews were not going to be allowed to remove much.

On January 30, in an address to the Reichstag, Hitler issued a most ominous threat to Jews:

In the course of my life I have very often been a prophet, and I have usually been ridiculed for it. During the time of my struggle for power it was in the first instance the Jewish race which only received my prophecies with laughter when I said I would one day take over the leadership of the State, and with it that of the whole nation, and that I would then among many other things settle the Jewish problem. Their laughter was uproarious, but I think that for some time now they have been laughing on the other side of their face. Today I will once more be a prophet. If the international Jewish financiers outside Europe should succeed in plunging the nations once more into a world war, then the result will not be the bolshevization of the earth, and thus the victory of Jewry, but the annihilation of the Jewish race in Europe.[36]

In the fall of 1939 Heinrich Himmler, the head of the SS (the German elite bodyguards), was appointed by Hitler to create the Reich Commission for the Consolidation of Germandom, an agency that would coordinate all policies pertaining to population in all areas controlled by Germany, including Jews and non-Jews. It was the beginning of the final solution.

On February 13, 1939 the German government announced its plan. The report began by stating that the plan applied only to Jews, and it defined a Jew as one who had three or four Jewish grandparents or one who had two Jewish grandparents and had become Jewish in recent years or one who married a Jew.

The essence of the plan was to allow Jews to be wage earners while they were awaiting emigration. These would leave first according to annual quotas, and dependents would follow after the wage earners were established in their new homes. The Germans hoped to move 150,000 wage earners per year out of Germany and to follow with up to 200,000 relatives and dependents.

Jews who were held in concentration camps would be released for emigration. Jews who had no skill or trade would be retrained in agriculture or as artisans. Those Jews who were given work would be separated from Aryans in the Reich. Those unable to work would be supported by funds obtained from the sale of property taken from Jews. The process of emigration would be paid out of a trust fund created by taking one-fourth of Jewish wealth. Jews who left Germany would be allowed to take all personal belongings except art objects, jewelry, and other similar valuables.[37]

There was a fraudulent aspect to the German proposal, because the government, while it paraded about in the community of nations with high-sounding plans, was also doing everything it could to drive Jews from Germany. It destroyed Jewish culture and Jewish religion and it made Jewish life unendurable.

A Leading Industrialist Deserts

In December 1939 the Nazi government in Berlin announced that pursuant to the law of July 14, 1933, which provided that all the property of a person whose actions or speech were inimical to the state and nation could be confiscated, the "moveable possessions" and real estate of Dr. Fritz Thyssen, formerly of Muhlheim in the Ruhr, were confiscated by the state of Prussia. It declared that no legal appeal could be made against the action.

This seizure was the final break between Thyssen and the Third Reich. Thyssen, a very wealthy industrialist whose support had helped Hitler to become Fuhrer, left Germany soon after war broke out. With his family, he made his way to Switzerland. He left behind his Rhineland industries, including factories and mines, which became a part of Herman Goering's four-year war plan.

Fritz Thyssen inherited his wealth from his father August Thyssen, a hard-nose, no-nonsense businessman who created an industrial empire in the period of German economic expansion from the end of the Franco-Prussian War to World War I. His estate included coal mines, rolling mills, iron foundries, railroads, and power stations. Fritz set out to enlarge his father's holdings. Within a year, he had absorbed several other companies to create the *Vereinigte Stahlwerke* (United Steel Works), which was the largest steel trust in the world, reaching out to Brazil, Russia, and India. When Thyssen's firm was bankrupted, he joined the National Socialist Party. He said that the liberal, classical economics (British economics) had produced bankruptcy and that only the Nazis could bring the nation out of its doldrums. Thyssen admitted later that he had given a million gold marks to the party.[38] He was rewarded by being appointed economic dictator of Germany.

The real breach came when Thyssen objected to Hitler's treatment of the Jews and Catholics. Fritz Thyssen had many Jewish friends and business associates, and he was raised in a devout Catholic family. He told Hitler that he would always "keep allegiance to my faith," and personally he thought that racial persecution was an unnecessary and stupid policy that would lose Germany the good will of the world. Thyssen believed that Germany should always remain a capitalist, anti-Bolshevik nation, and when Hitler approved the German-Soviet Pact, Thyssen was appalled. He decided that he must leave Germany.[39]

In a letter of December 11, 1939 Thyssen told the German people "I shall call upon the conscience of the world and shall let the world pass judgment," and he added, "I believed in you, Adolph Hitler, the Fuhrer, and the movement you led. I believed with all the ardor of one passionately German." And he pleaded with Hitler to "listen to me and you will hear the voice of the tormented German nation that is crying out to you: Turn back, let freedom, right and humaneness rise again in the German Reich."

And a Minister Returns

In 1939 Dietrich Bonhoeffer, the German Protestant theologian, made his way to New York City with the help of American friends, who thought his life was endangered by his sermons and writings. Bonhoeffer assumed an important role in support of ecumenism in Nazi Germany—a role he learned from his father, Karl Bonhoeffer, who was a Professor of Psychiatry and Neurology at the University of Berlin.

But after only a month in the United States, he returned to Germany. He wrote to his American sponsor, Reinhold Niebuhr, "I will have no right to participate in the reconstruction of Christian life in Germany after the war if I do not share the trials of this time with my people." In the same letter, he asserted, "Christians in Germany will face the terrible alternative of either willing the defeat of their nation in order that Christian civilization may survive, or willing the victory of their nation and thereby destroying our civilization."[40]

Bonhoeffer's journey of conscience began when he studied theology at the Universities of Tubingen and Berlin, after which he attended the Union Theological Seminary in New York City as an exchange student. Returning to Germany, he accepted an appointment as lecturer in theology at the University of Berlin.

Despite his absence of two years during which he served as pastor of a church in London, Bonhoeffer became a leading spokesman for the Confessing Church, the focus of German Protestant resistance to the Nazi regime. In 1935 he organized and assumed the leadership of a new seminary of the Confessing Church at Finkenwald in Pomerania. This church is credited with shielding one thousand Jews from the Nazis.

In 1937 he wrote in the *The Cost of Discipleship* that suffering was the true badge of a Christian disciple and that every person is called separately to stand alone. But we are all frightened of solitude, so we join societies that emphasize material things. From that time, Bonhoeffer's sermons and writings became increasingly political in nature, and in 1938 his brother-in-law, Hans von Dohnanyi, introduced him to a group of Germans who were plotting the overthrow of Adolf Hitler. Bonhoeffer was able to work continuously for the German resistance movement, which took a stand against Bishop Ludwig Mueller, who acquiesced in all matters of Nazi policies.[41]

Voyage of the Damned

The United States got its first taste of the refugee problem near its borders when the ship S.S *St. Louis*, of the Hamburg-American Line, filled with middle-class Jews, was refused permission to land in Caribbean ports. The odyssey of the ship says more about the world's attitude towards Jews in 1939 than any other event. The American decision not to accept the refugees from the *St. Louis* mirrored the feeling in the United States towards immigrants. The *St. Louis* sailed from Germany with 937 passengers.[42]

These refugees carried passports stamped with a red "J." When they paid for their passage, they received landing certificates that allowed them to land in Cuba. According to Richard Ketchum, "734 of them had also been assigned quota numbers by the U.S. Immigration Service, which meant that they could enter this country between three months and three years after arrival in Cuba."[43]

Leaving behind the fear, brutality, and the stigma of the red "J," they began their voyage on the "pleasure Palace." They danced, played games, entertained themselves, and ate the good food aboard. Captain Gustav Schroeder was sympathetic; he knew what indignities they had endured under the Nazis. Schroeder wanted to make amends. He provided soft chairs and string quartets. But as their past persecution became a memory, the reality of being Jews struck them. Before reaching Cuba, Captain Schroeder received a telegram concerning the validity of the landing certificates the refugees had purchased. Schroeder was not aware that Cuban President Federico Laredo Bru had signed a decree eight days before the *St. Louis* left Hamburg nullifying the immigration documents because they were purchased in wholesale lots and sold illegally. Bru said that the Jews needed to obtain new visas approved by the State, Labor, and Treasury Departments of Cuba. Hopes faded.

The *St. Louis* arrived in Havana Harbor on May 27, 1939, and it was greeted by a large welcoming party, which had hired small boats to circle the incoming ship. It all appeared joyous, but none of the passengers was allowed to go ashore. At night searchlight beams swept the waters around the ship. The Jews were prisoners.

On June 2, with passengers weeping along the rails, the *St. Louis* left Havana harbor. Captain Schroeder, still hoping for a favorable resolution of the impasse, headed for the coast of Florida straits with 907 passengers. Thirty persons had been authorized to leave the ship in Havana: seven were Cubans or Spaniards, and twenty-three had their documents validated in Europe by paying an additional $500.

The attitude of the Cubans was part anti-Semitism, part greed. The Cuban officials were contending to see how quickly they could obtain money from the desperate Jews. Next to the deplorable behavior of the Cubans, the American actions also had a stench about them. The passengers on the *St. Louis* had valid entry permits, yet the Roosevelt Administration remained silent, even as the *New York Times* ran daily accounts.

On June 5 the ship was off the Florida coast. On the following day, the Cuban government announced that it would not permit the 907 Jewish refugees to land at any Cuban port. Lawrence Berenson, of the National Coordinating Committee, who was negotiating for the refugees, was surprised by the declaration, because he had come close to the amount that Cuba was demanding ($453,000). Berenson offered $443,000, which included a $200,000 deposit, $40,000 to be paid by the refugees and $203,000 to be raised by New York Jewish organizations. But his other condition probably killed the proposal: that the Cubans also admit 98 from the French liner *Flandre* and 154 from the British *Orduna*.

These persons escaping German persecution, who had sailed from port to port, headed back to Europe, which meant Germany and certain death. On June 12, 1939, The Netherlands government offered to take 194 of the refugees who were heading back to Europe. As the *St. Louis* moved closer to Hamburg, the passengers became more and more unstable. Young adults patrolled the decks to keep the older passengers from attempting suicide. The little children played a grim game. They barricaded the deck and formed a line. Ketchum relates what happened next. A small child in line requested permission to enter.

"Are you a Jew?" he was asked.
"Yes," the child answered.
"Jews are not admitted!"
"Please let me in," the child pleaded. "I'm only a little Jew."[44]

Captain Schroeder, who was the most decent German in this episode, told later how in his anguish to save the Jews he considered grounding the ship on the coast of England while awaiting instructions from Hamburg. The passengers wanted assurance that he would not return them to Germany. He answered, "I give you my word that I will do everything possible to avoid going back to Germany. I am only too well aware of what they would do to you."[45] They thanked him for his honesty.

As the *St. Louis* neared Antwerp, where the passengers were to disembark, the Jews stood tall along the railing of the ship. In the final disposition of passengers, some were more fortunate than others. The largest number (288) went to England, 224 were assigned to France, 214 stayed in Belgium, and 181 were sent to Amsterdam.

Those sent to England, the lucky ones, appeared to be safe, but as soon as war was declared, they were classified as German nationals and enemy aliens, and they were interned. For the others, safety was only temporary. When the Germans invaded Poland and conquered Belgium, Holland, and France, the Jews of the *St. Louis* knew they were to die in the gas chambers.

THE RUSSO-GERMAN ALLIANCE

In 1939 the Russians and the Germans began meeting frequently about common economic and political problems. Kennan relates that on July 26, 1939, Russian and German representatives sat in a private restaurant in Berlin to discuss how to carve up Eastern Europe. Russia was assured that Germany was prepared to pay for Russian neutrality. The two sides were bidding for Russia's favor in the battle for Poland.[46]

This surprising incident stunned the world. What did it mean? How could these evil forces of the left and right have anything to discuss? Charles E. Bohlen was sent to Moscow as Second Secretary and Consul to cover these affairs. He learned that in July the Soviets had placed a large order for German turbines and were considering additional orders for antiaircraft guns and machinery. The ominous part of the agreement to trade was that it appeared that the Nazis and Soviets had agreed in principle to settle their long-standing differences.[47] The German radio announced on August 21, 1939, that Ribbentrop would go to Moscow to sign a nonaggression Pact with Stalin. The negotiations were so secret that even the German high command was unaware of their existence.

This political and economic marriage was linked to territory. Bohlen learned that a secret protocol was part of the ten-year pact, which provided that western Poland was to be in the German sphere of influence and eastern Poland, Estonia, Latvia, and Bessarabia in the Soviet. The Germans also insisted that the two nations agree not to join any alliance that would jeopardize the other.

Hitler was pleased with the arrangement, because he saw it as a "new distribution of the world." As he said, "Stalin and I are the only ones who see the future."[48] He promised to shake hands with Stalin on the Russian-German border, then he added, later "we shall crush the Soviet Union."

The key section was Article I, which proclaimed that the two countries would "desist from any act of violence, any aggressive action, and any attack on each other." "In case one of the parties to this treaty should become the object of warlike acts by a third power, the other power will in no way support this third power."

This alliance demonstrated that Hitler and Stalin had much in common. Alan Bullock describes them as having "Parallel Lives."[49] Both were ruthless men who were on special missions, and both were willing to use realpolitik to achieve their ends. Both had their fanatical followers, and each had a twisted sense of his place in history.

The nature of Soviet propaganda changed immediately, which only confused the Soviet populace. Viktor Kravchenko, the director of a factory in Siberia, remembered that suddenly the Minister of Cultural Relations discovered the marvels of German culture—Moscow was buzzing with news of German drama, but the United States was still pictured as Uncle Sam sitting on money bags.

The Pact Heard Round the World

The leftists of the world were appalled at the Nazi-Soviet Pact. In Paris, physicists Frederic and Irene Joliot censured Stalin, and Arthur Koestler, a communist for seven years, saw it as the death of his Utopia. Koestler compared the Russian behavior to that of the medieval church, which he said had "soiled and compromised Christianity." As he said, "No death is so sad and final as the death of an illusion."

According to Wolfgang Leonhard, Arthur Koestler's break with communism came in two phases. In March 1938, when he learned of the trial of Nikolai Bukharin, he was deeply troubled by this absurdity, and he decided to make a break with communism. Knowing that the war in Spain continued, he had to be obtuse and circumspect. He stated three carefully crafted sentences that were aimed directly at the Stalinists: "No movement, party or person can claim the privilege of infallibility. . . . Appeasing the enemy is as foolish as persecuting the friend who pursues your own aim by a different road. . . . A harmful truth is better than a useful lie" (taken from Thomas Mann).[50] These events disillusioned him, causing him to leave the Party by 1939. The Nazi-Soviet Pact was the end of his socialist leanings.

Enrique Castro Delgado, the Spanish representative in the Comintern, was one of the organizers of the Fifth (Communist) Regiment in the Spanish Civil War. When the Republican Army was defeated in 1939, Delgado went to the U.S.S.R. He heard voices that repeated: "Stalin is right. Stalin never errs." Then he thought from the heart: "I am a Spaniard. Germany helped Franco gain power. . . . An airplane, a Messerschmitt extinguished the life of my brother Manola. . . . Hitler wants to dominate Europe . . . I am shocked by my thoughts . . . But from Almeria to Guernica, from Badajoz to Barcelona I hear the words 'but . . . the dead . . . the dead . . . the dead.'"[51]

In France, the August 23 agreement also had a major impact, because the Communist party there was the largest outside of the Soviet Union and because there were thousands of anti-fascist emigres from Germany, Italy, Spain, and the Eastern European countries who had escaped to France. The French Communist Party had become a major political force during the period of the Popular Front (1936-1938). The success of the French communists was noted at the Eighteenth Party Congress in Moscow in March 1939. France was seen as a shining example of how the Communist Party could succeed in the anti-fascist struggle. The August Pact was especially shocking to these French communists. Since the

Pact made the French communists allies of the Nazis, and because this created a danger of fifth-column activity.

THE "GOOD" WAR[52]

Although he came to accept it, the start of World War II was a shock to Neville Chamberlain. He had always believed that peace could be obtained if England and Germany collaborated. Because he had no real army to back any belligerent positions, he chose appeasement. When Hitler chose war, Britain and France began an ideological war against Hitler. Chamberlain embarked on a verbal campaign of rectitude, hoping to convince the German people that they should overthrow the Nazis. He spoke directly to the German people, telling them that the war was not against them but against the tyrants who ran their government.

Whereas Chamberlain chose to emphasize what was right, Hitler exhibited his might. His objective was labor and raw materials. His method was to demoralize nations from within. He sent agents as students, as tourists, and as spies. In each country, he established subversive Nazi organizations. At the same time, Himmler made plans to eliminate the opposition by stealth and by murder.

The United States, which was a signatory to the Kellogg-Briand Treaty, was one of fifteen nations to renounce war and to disarm. All the parties to the great debate over whether the United States should enter World War II came to agree that Hitler (and Mussolini and Tojo) represented evil forces and that fighting them constituted a just war. Russet described it well, "Participation in the war against Hitler remains almost sacrosanct, nearly in the realm of theology."[53]

In the first weeks of the war, thousands of British and French soldiers suffered very painful wounds or death on the war front by detonating hidden German mines. The haughty French drove hundreds of pigs in front of the troops to locate mines. It was a new kind of minesweeping. Continuing their use of animal power, the morally strict French recruited one hundred thousand pigeons along the Maginot Line to carry messages through German artillery barrages. The November 6 *Time* called it "Pigeons in, Men out."

Sea Battles and Blockades

The battle for the Atlantic became the battle for supplies. When war began on September 3, 1939, Germany had fifty-seven U-boats, but only twenty-two were suitable for patrolling the Atlantic Ocean (they were 740 or 517 tons). The rest were the smaller (250 tons) "Dugouts," which had been built in 1935 as the basis of Hitler's new submarine force and which were intended strictly for coastal work or for training purposes.

The war on the Allied shipping lanes was conceived by Grand Admiral Erich Raeder, who was a close confidant of Hitler's. In 1939 Raeder developed a secret supply organization, the *Etappendienst*, which set up a communications network in all major ports of the world for reporting the disposition of merchant ships. This would enable his U-boats to prey on Allied shipping with accurate information about location of vessels.

At the same time, Raeder conceived of a program to build a fleet of battleships of one hundred thousand tons each (the Z Plan Fleet). Both Raeder and Hitler were enamored of the glamor of these large ships. Several battleships were built, although the largest were seventy-five thousand tons. These included the *Deutschland, Admiral Graf Spee, Admiral Scheer, Leipzig, Koln, Emden,* and *Schlesien.*

Despite the British having the three largest battleships afloat—the *Hood, Renown* and *Repulse*—and numerical superiority in number of fighting ships, the Germans had the best of the supply battle from September 3 until the end of 1939. The British lost 137 merchant ships, totaling 460,134 tons, whereas the German losses were only 21 ships of 122,415 tons. French losses were even smaller—11 ships of 48,038 tons.[54]

Life on a U-boat lost its glamour because of the incredibly close quarters. When the vessel left port, it had to take on provisions for the forty-six man crew to last for weeks. Fresh food, which was consumed early in the voyage, made passage in many corridors impossible. It is best to quote a U-boat commander on living conditions. "The air would be heavy with odors—the penetrating dungeon-smell from the bilges, the whiff of Diesel oil and of unwashed humanity, the smell of cooking, of Colibri (eau-de-Cologne used by the crew to remove the salt encrusted on their faces by the seas which broke continuously over the bridge) and a generous contribution, despite air purifier." He added, "The submarine would be in motion, violent motion—corkscrewing, pitching, yawing, rolling, adapting herself to the surge and swell of the water. In heavy seas it would not infrequently heel through an angle of almost sixty degrees; sometimes a sleeper would be catapulted out of his bunk."[55]

During the 1930s, Germany built three pocket battleships: the *Deutschland, Admiral Scheer,* and *Admiral Graf Spee.* These ships were the best in the world; they were speedy, light, and carried heavy guns. They were the size of English cruisers, but maneuvered like battleships. German science provided new metals and new welding techniques to achieve this technological supremacy. Churchill wrote that by August 1939, Germany had sixty submarines for coastal and ocean service and that it expected to have an additional seventy-four in service by December; this total exceeded the combined numbers of France and Great Britain.[56] The Allied superiority on the sea and the German superiority under it, led them to revert to a strategy that was used in World War I—blockade and counterblockade.

Sinking the *Athenia*

On that first day of war, twenty-six-year-old Oberleutnant Fritz-Julius Lemp, Commander of U-30, was cruising 250 miles off the coast of Ireland when he sighted a passenger liner, whose bearing was just right for a torpedo attack. The submarine commander dreamed of being the first to sink a British ship in the war. Because the liner was off the normal shipping route and because it was zigzagging, he assumed that it was a troopship. When he sighted the British flag, he ordered four torpedoes to be fired, one of which struck midship. The 13,581-ton S. S. *Athenia* exploded and sank with the loss of 128 lives; it was the first such loss in World War II.

The ship sailed on September 2 with 1,103 passengers, the majority of whom were Canadian and American citizens. Captain James Cook and the crew of 315 were sure that the Germans would not attack an unarmed passenger ship, because the Germans adhered to the 1936 Hague Convention Submarine Protocol, under which a submarine could not sink a merchant vessel until the passengers, crew, and ship's papers were put in a "place of safety."

Of the 1,103 passengers on board, 292 carried American passports. Many of them reported that the submarine circled the sinking ship without attempting to pick up survivors. Churchill was especially angered because the ship had left port on September 2, before war was declared, and the submarine was clearly waiting "to pick up its prey on route." The next day, Churchill announced that 125 passengers and crew members were missing, A Swedish ship, the *Southern Cross*, rescued 376 persons, who were transferred to the *City of Flint* and a British destroyer. Churchill deplored the inhuman action of the German captain, who after hitting the *Athenia* abaft, "the submarine came to the surface and fired a shell which exploded on C deck."[57]

At first, the German government denied that the ship had been sunk by a U-boat. No U-boat had reported the incident, and even Lemp made no mention in his wireless report to the Naval High Command. But at the end of September he told Commander Donitz verbally that he had sunk the *Athenia*. The German High Command continued to deny responsibility; they ordered Lemp to remove the page in the log concerning the sinking and to substitute a page with the details expunged. The Germans claimed that Winston Churchill had a bomb placed on the *Athenia* that would sink her so as to draw the United States into the war. When there was outrage throughout the world over the sinking of the *Athenia*, the Germans contended that it was sunk by a floating mine, but when the Admiralty announced that no mines had been laid in that area, the Germans were compelled to acknowledge the sinking.

U-boat commanders were stung by the ferocity of the comments against the sinking of the *Athenia*. They heard "dastardly attack," "unpardonable outrage," and "horror and disgust " thrown at them. They set out to silence their critics. Hitler, fearing that the sinking of the *Athenia* would drive Americans away from neutrality, issued a special order: "Passenger ships until further notice will not be attacked even if escorted."

The order was not a simple one to follow. When the commander of U-48 came upon the British steamer *Browning*, he asked his executive officer for advice. The answer: put the passengers in lifeboats and sink the ship. The passengers were already in the lifeboats when the captain realized they were hundreds of miles from land and there was little hope of rescue. He undid the order, putting all passengers back on the ship, with the only condition being that they not wire the sub's position.[58]

Scapa Flow

A more spectacular and daring episode occurred when Lieutenant Gunther Prien, Commander of submarine U-47, successfully entered the well-guarded, main anchorage of the British fleet at Scapa Flow and sank the battleship *Royal Oak*. Scapa Flow, which commands the Pentland Firth near Scotland, is approximately eight miles by five miles and is fifteen fathoms deep. The tide runs ten knots, and the area is surrounded by the most treacherous waters off the British Coast. Twice in World War I, U-boats tried to penetrate Scapa Flow, but each time the submarine was sunk.

On the night of October 13-14, 1939, when Lieutenant Prien made his daring attack, the British were certain that their round-the-clock patrols and other defenses made the anchorage impenetrable. Using information obtained by reconnaissance planes, the Germans attempted to enter Kirk Sound, because it is one of the smaller entrances to Scapa Flow.

Prien chose the night of October 13, because the weather forecaster promised complete darkness and favorable tides, but the forecast was wrong. The sky was lit brightly by the aurora borealis. Prien started out in spite of the handicap. Staying on the surface, he steered the U-47 through the channel inside the Flow. When he reached the main anchorage, he was surprised to find it empty. He did not know that the entire fleet had put out to sea hours earlier, but just ahead of him he saw the silhouettes of the *Royal Oak*, a 29,150-ton battle wagon, one of Britain's twelve capital ships and the H.M.S *Pegasus*, a very old aircraft carrier.

Prien surfaced in the bright natural sky and fired his five torpedoes. Only one made a hit, as it struck the bow of the *Royal Oak*. Now Prien made a daring move. Stalled in the middle of the sound, he ordered his torpedo tubes to be reloaded with his spare charges. There was no response from the British defenses. Firing from the same angle, Prien unloaded the salvos from torpedo tubes at the battleship. They all hit the target, as the *Royal Oak* was blown apart. More than 800 of the 1,200-man crew perished, but it was no time to celebrate. Commander Prien needed every skill he possessed. He bucked the heavy tide, skirted the sunken ships, and headed towards the open sea. Unseen, the U-47 returned to base. Even the British admitted reluctantly that it was a magnificent bit of seamanship.[59]

Scuttling the *Graf Spee*

In early December 1939 the British learned that Brazilian authorities were permitting the sale of fuel to Nazi freighters that stopped at Brazilian ports. The British, suspecting that these freighters were being used to refuel Nazi U-boats, sent a task force to follow the freighters to their rendezvous points.

The *Admiral Graf von Spee*, the German pocket battleship that was launched in 1936, had more armament than any cruiser, had a top speed of twenty-five knots and could sail for 12,500 miles. It terrorized commercial shipping all over the world as it sank ships off Africa, France, and Uruguay. It came to a dramatic climax on December 13, 1939, when three British men-of-war encountered it off the Brazilian-Uruguayan coast. Captain Hans Langsdorff wasn't concerned. His ship had a 3-to-1 advantage in firepower over the three cruisers combined. They would not dare to approach. But approach they did, using smoke screens.

On the bridge, Langsdorff gave the alarm. He was confident as the British cruisers closed in. He knew his best strategy: attack the heavy cruiser first, then the two light cruisers would be at his mercy. He identified the heavy cruiser as the *Exeter* (8,390 tons) and the light cruisers as the *Ajax*, which he sighted first, and the *Achilles* (7,030 tons). The *Graf Spee* aimed its big turrets on the *Exeter*, and used its smaller guns to hold off the light cruisers. But the British were not cooperating; the task force commanded by Commodore Harwood of the *Achilles*, put up a smoke screen, came out into the open long enough to fire off some salvoes, then darted behind the cover. Langsdorff decided that he had to get his two reconnaissance planes into the air, but the British foiled this attempt by knocking out the first plane, which was elevated on the catapult.

The cruisers kept aiming shells from all directions, removing the *Graf Spee*'s advantage. But the relentless shelling paid off. She struck the *Exeter*'s superstructure, causing the ship to withdraw from battle. Langsdorff turned next to the light cruisers, which surprised him greatly. They kept up a merciless barrage of shelling for fourteen hours, forcing the captain to run for cover to the nearest port, which was Montevideo. As the *Graf Spee* headed towards Punta del Este, the *Ajax* and the *Achilles* circled and hit at the *Spee*'s bow, causing her to take on water. Limping, she backed into Montevideo harbor, dropping anchor.

The British next played their propaganda game. They announced that a major naval force was close enough to the harbor to provide reinforcements for the *Ajax* and the *Achilles*. Using radio and the press, they may have convinced Langsdorff that a sizeable force was closing in on the *Spee*.

Uruguayan officials boarded the ship to determine how long the *Graf Spee* should be allowed to stay. The Hague Convention of 1907 permitted a belligerent ship to remain in a neutral port for twenty-four hours, unless it was damaged. It could not, however, repair any armaments. After inspection, Uruguay gave the captain four days to make his ship seaworthy. As the workers removed the steel plates with welding torches, they found thirty-six bodies, which they carefully placed in swastika-wrapped coffins and buried ashore.

Thousands of Montevideans lined the coast for the expected battle. What would the German ship do? The fight that everyone waited for never took place. On December 17, the *Spee* got out in the river, dropped anchor, and the crew went over the sides into barges. Captain Langsdorff stepped into a motor launch, carrying a long, thin cable. With his officers by his side, he saluted and pressed the button on the end of the cable. Black smoke shot straight upward coming from midship; orange flames spread over the superstructure. Then the ship shuddered and sank to the bottom. Kapitan Langsdorff and his crew reached safety, but before abandoning ship, Langsdorff sent an acrid message to the British and the Montevideans. In it, he protested their refusal to allow him to remain in the harbor long enough to make all repairs, which "makes it necessary for me to sink my ship near the coast and save my crew." Three days later in Buenos Aires Captain Langsdorff wrapped himself with the flag of the Imperial Navy and put a bullet into his head.

THE WINTER WAR

During the Russian Revolution, the Finns declared their independence, but in 1939 Russia signaled its intention to regain the territory lost after 1917. Stalin spoke of respecting "the integrity and inviolability of our frontiers." But, he added, "Only Soviet Russia could be the guarantor of the border states, including Finland." Later, Foreign Minister Molotov told the world that the Alands belonged to Russia "for more than a hundred years."

The Soviets made demands on all three of the Baltic States (Estonia, Latvia, and Lithuania) and Finland for the acceptance of Soviet bases and troops to be stationed in those countries. The three Baltic countries, having been abandoned by the Germans, quickly accepted, but the Finns refused.[60]

President Roosevelt, in a press conference, read in a very grave voice that the United States deplored the attack on Finland. American hostility to Russia, which reached new heights with the German-Russian Pact, soared even higher. Senator William King, of Utah, spoke for the people when he announced, "My country will no longer grasp the bloody hands of Stalin."[61]

The new Ambassador to Russia, forty-six-year-old Laurence Steinhardt, was transferred from Lima, Peru. Although he was appointed in the spring of 1939, he did not arrive in Moscow until August 8, 1939. As he watched negotiations, he shared the view of most observers that nothing would happen, especially with the coming of the cold northern winter. Finland returned "to the tempo of normal life." Those who had evacuated cities in October returned home. As Vaino Tanner wrote, "We trusted firmly the Soviets' love of peace, proclaimed constantly for twenty years."[62]

Russia sent a new proposal to Helsinki: it offered to exchange Soviet territory for Hogland and four other islands on the approach to Leningrad, and if accepted, it would lead to a solution of the other main issue, the Alands. Finnish military leaders recommended accepting the Soviet terms, because the islands Russia sought had little military value.[63]

While the Finns and the Russians talked, the Russians amassed a total of 1,564 airplanes of all types to carry out its mission of destruction. Besides the Stuka, Heinkel, and Donier bombers, it had the Messerschmitts for fighter cover. On November 30, 1939, early in the morning, the Soviet Union launched a sudden attack against Finland. The attack, by land and sea, came as troops crossed the Finnish border at several points. In this campaign, the Russians used Tupelov commercial planes for dropping paratroopers into Finland. Within hours, Soviet planes, using bases in Estonia, bombed Helsinki. The bombing was indiscriminate, because there were few military targets near the drop zone. It was a brutal attack against civilians.

According to Moscow, the long night of November 29-30 began at 2 A.M., when Finnish soldiers invaded Russia. To punish them for this aggression, the Red Army, counterattacked at 8 A.M. The forces were very uneven: the Soviets had two million soldiers and 5,000 airplanes against two hundred thousand Finnish men and 150 airplanes. But even with ten-to-one odds, the tough Finns were more than a match for the Russian war machine.

The real war began with formations of bombing planes over Finnish cities. The Russians were not able to deliver. They came in under overcast clouds over the capital at Helsinki for their bomb run aimed at the railroad station, freight yards and navy yard, but they succeeded in hitting only apartment houses, the new Olympic Stadium and women and children. When fliers were shot down by Finnish antiaircraft guns, they were attacked by a mob of Finnish women, who slaughtered them with axes and pitchforks.

Comrade Molotov accused the Finns of "provocational shelling," and he demanded that troops withdraw immediately. The Finnish government contacted all border stations and found no such artillery fire, but it ordered its troops to withdraw a half mile from the border. The December 11 *Time* called it the "U.S.S.R.'s grotesque impersonation of a bear being bitten by a rabbit."

The Russian soldiers in Finland were ill-prepared for the *talvisota*—the winter war with its heavy snow and the forty-below-zero weather. A blinding blizzard grounded all Soviet planes, and tanks met formidable barriers. The Russian soldier's weapons, feet, and food froze. Many of them froze to death in grotesque positions. It looked like a sculpture garden. Engle and Paanenen relate a story of a Finn who was found with six bullet holes in his chest. He was taken to a tent where the dead were being stored. The next morning an orderly who was on duty lit up a cigarette only to hear, "Hey, give me a cigarette." It was the "dead" man. The cold had saved his life; in its absence he would have bled to death.[64]

The Finns attacked in the windy blizzard. They were nearly invisible with their white capes, white caps, and grey-green uniforms. Their machine gun emplacements offered the Russians a constant staccato of shells. The Russian version of the German blitzkrieg was not working. The Finns sabotaged all services to discomfort the invaders. They filled wells with dirt and removed all edible animals in their path. The Russian troops in the Karelian region were pathetic, miserable beings, sacrificed by Stalin. They lacked proper boots for fighting in the high snows, and several had frostbite.

The Congress considered severing diplomatic relations. Senator Arthur Vandenburg, the powerful Michigan advocate of a bipartisan foreign policy, spoke of selling military supplies to Finland and loaning money for the purchases.[65] When Foreign Minister Molotov made an anti-Roosevelt speech, Congressman John McCormack of Massachusetts, urged repeal of the embargo and the recall of Ambassador Steinhardt from Moscow. When the President was asked about McCormack, he replied, after a pause, "I have never believed that poor manners should beget poor manners." It was the kind of rebuff that had no precedent in American diplomatic history.

Americans wanted desperately to help the Finns, and Herbert Hoover, who had led humanitarian efforts during World War I, volunteered to serve as Chairman of the Finnish Relief Fund, a private organization. The response was immediate. Money and clothing began to flow into the Fund office, leading Hoover to announce that he hoped to raise between four and five million dollars. While Americans were attending their "Help Finland" rallies, the Finns were defending their country, and doing fairly well at it. Michigan led the movement to help the Finns, because that state had the highest percentage of Finns and children of Finns in the United States.[66] The *New York Times* of December 22 reported that in the Borough of Queens, New York, a half-day holiday was declared to celebrate the Soviet closing of their exhibit from the World's Fair.

The Red Army forces were greatly superior, and the Finnish fortifications were insufficient to counter that force. The Finns had improved island fortresses in the Gulf of Finland during the summer, but without outside aid the small nation was doomed. On December 17, the Soviets launched a major offensive for Viipuri. Russian casualties were very high. The Finns also halted a major Russian drive around Lake Ladoga. The great disadvantage in manpower seemed less important, but sadly, the favorable Finnish outcome made Americans less eager to help. Helsinki was still anxious to sign a peace agreement with the Soviets, and the Allies, who were in a war, were determined that the Soviets would not seize Narvik and its iron-ore fields. On December 19, the Allied War Council met to draft a strategy for aiding Finland and for protecting its iron ore. The Council agreed that an expeditionary force should be sent to Finland.

The Kremlin offered to initiate trade talks. Moscow sent an emissary to Helsinki with a new proposal. He told the Finnish government that if an agreement could be reached on Hogland and four other islands, ostensibly the Alands (*Ahvenenanmaa*) on the way to Leningrad, it would "facilitate the solution of other outstanding issues." When Finland repeated its position of neutrality, they withdrew their offer. On March 11, 1940, Molotov presented a peace plan that the Finns accepted late that evening. It ceded about one-tenth of Finland to Russia. The Kremlin announced that hostilities would cease on March 13 at noon, Moscow time. The war had lasted 105 days.

NOTES

1. "Franco's Victory Won at Huge Cost to Spain," *New York Times*, February 26, 1939, p. 5E.

2. Dolgoff, *The Anarchist Collectives*, p. 44.

3. Preston, *Franco*.

4. Dupuy and Dupuy, *Encyclopedia of Military History*, p. 1033.

5. "Spanish War Seen Near Its End," *New York Times*, January 28, 1939, p. 5.

6. Massock, *Italy from Within*, p. 166.

7. Quoted in Guttmann, *The Wound in the Heart*, p. 28.

8. Guttmann, *The Wound in the Heart*, p. 200.

9. This Was Stalin's response when he was asked if he was concerned about the opposition of the Roman Catholic Church to his policies.

10. Fromm, *Escape from Freedom*, p. 208.

11. Mumford, *Faith for Living*, p. 118.

12. Quoted in Fuller, *The Conduct of War*, p. 226.

13. Rauschning, *Hitler Speaks*, p. 229.

14. This history is based on Shirer's *The Rise and Fall of the Third Reich*.

15. Some of this information is gleaned from Frank Capra's "Prelude to War," a War Department Film, 1943.

16. Weinberg, *The World at Arms*.

17. See Kai Bird's book review of Michael Bloch's *Ribbentrop* in the July 11, 1993 *Washington Post*.

18. Massock, *Italy from Within*, p. 13.

19. Massock, *Italy From Within*, p. 29.

20. "Albania," *Timecapsule/ 1939*, p. 106.

21. David Brinkley, *Washington Goes to War*, p. 39.

22. Medvedev, *Let History Judge*, p. 192.

23. Radzinsky, *Stalin*.

24. I have taken the liberty of paraphrasing the Subtitle of Aleksandr Solzhenitsyn's *The Gulag Archipelago*, "Experiment in Literary Investigation" (1974).

25. *The Gulag Archipelago*, p. 76.

26. Medvedev, *Let History Judge*, p. 256.

27. Tolischus, *Through Japanese Eyes*, p. 2. Tolischus, who received a Pulitzer Prize in 1939 as a foreign correspondent in Berlin and London, spent the next three years trying to understand the Japanese mind. The section that follows owes much to his research.

28. Tolischus, *Through Japanese Eyes*, p. 38.

29. Wiltz, *From Isolation to War, 1939-1941*, p. 60.

30. Lindsay, *The Unknown War*. Because this book has no pagination, we can only cite the "Introduction" as a source.

31. Lindsay, *The Unknown War*, no pagination.

32. Thomas and Morgan-Witts, *Voyage of the Damned*, p. 16.

33. "Palestine Policy of Britain Scored by Mandates Body," *New York Times*, August 18, 1939, p. 1.

34. The letter was dated April 6, 1939 and is quoted in Schechtman, *The United States and the Jewish State Movement*, p. 22.

35. Marrus, *The Holocaust in History*, p. 12.

36. Baynes, *The Speeches of Adolf Hitler*, I, p. 735.

37. "Orderly Settling of Jews Planned," *New York Times*, February 14, 1939, p. 12.

38. Payne, *The Life and Death of Adolf Hitler*, p. 223.

39. He gave his reasons in letters to the Nazi leaders, which were published in the April 29, 1940, issue of *Life*.

40. Bill Broadway, *Washington Post*, April 8, 1995, p. H7. The definitive biography is Bethge's, *Dietrich Bonhoeffer*.

41. On April 9, 1945, Dietrich Bonhoeffer and four other conspirators were marched to the gallows, where death came in seconds. He was thirty-nine years old.

42. The exact number of persons aboard the *St. Louis* was in dispute. Thomas and Morgan-Witts, authors of the *Voyage of the Damned*, state that "937 refugees" awaited their fate, but the *New York Times* repeatedly published a figure of 907 until it corrected this to 711 on June 13, 1939. The 907 total comes from subtracting the 30 persons who left ship at Havana.

43. Ketchum, *The Borrowed Years*, p. 116.

44. Ketchum, *The Borrowed Years*, p. 120.

45. Thomas and Morgan-Witts, *Voyage of the Damned*, p. 120.

46. Kennan, *Russia and the West Under Lenin and Stalin*, p. 327.

47. Ketchum, *The Borrowed Years*, p. 186.

48. Shirer, *Midcentury Journey*, p. 147.

49. Bullock, *Hitler and Stalin*.

50. Quoted in Leonhard *Betrayal*, p. 184.

51. Leonhard, *Betrayal*, p. 18.

52. This is the title of Studs Terkel's oral histories of World War II (New York: Pantheon Books, 1984). The recollections of the men and women who fought suggest that a war is good when you win it. One reader objected to the use of this phrase, because, as she said, "There is no such thing as a good war."

53. Quoted by Lindberg in *War Within and Without*, p. xvii.

54. "Merchant Ships Sunk in War," *New York Times*, December 29, 1939. p. 3.

55. Busch, *U-Boats at War*, p. x. Translated from the German, this book is a useful account by a person who served in the U-boat Branch of the Kriegsmarine.

56. Churchill, *The Gathering Storm*, p. 424.

57. *New York Times*, September 17, 1939, p. 5.

58. Hughes and Costello, *The Battle of the Atlantic*, p. 12.

59. Snyder, *The War*, pp. 173-74.

60. Kennan, *Russia and the West Under Lenin and Stalin*, p. 337.

61. "Finland," *Timecapsule/1939*, p. 113.

62. Tanner, *Winter War*, p. 45.

63. Jakobson, *Diplomacy of Winter War*, p. 41.

64. Engle and Paananen, *The Winter War*, p. 44.

65. "The International Situation," *New York Times*, December 3, 1939, p.1.

66. The largest body of materials on Finns (mostly letters to Finland) were contained at Soumi College, Houghton, Michigan.

10

The USA on the Edge of War

1939 did not go well for anti-fascists. Franco finished taking Spain in March, about the same time that Hitler took the rest of Czecho-slovakia and possession of the seaport of Memel from Lithuania. Mussolini invaded Albania on Good Friday, and in December the Russians occupied Finland. Appeasement did not work.

Roosevelt, trying to employ rational approaches with irrational men, urged Hitler and Mussolini to give up the use of force for ten or twenty years. On April 15, 1939, Roosevelt sent similar messages to Hitler and Mussolini. The President told them that the "tide of events" had reverted to "the threat of arms," and that three nations in Europe and one in Africa had lost their independence. Then he challenged them. "Are you willing to give assurance that your armed forces will not attack or invade the territory or possessions of the following nations: Finland, Estonia, Latvia, Lithuania, Sweden, Norway, Denmark, The Netherlands, Belgium, Great Britain and Ireland, France, Portugal, Spain, Switzerland, Liechtenstein, Luxembourg, Poland, Hungary, Rumania, Yugoslavia, Russia, Bulgaria, Greece, Turkey, Iraq, the Arabias, Syria, Palestine, Egypt and Iran?"[1]

Hitler mocked the letter. In a speech to the Bundestag, he read the name of each nation slowly in a derisive tone, and each time those in attendance roared at the performance. William L. Shirer called it his most brilliant speech. Hitler spelled out the German efforts for keeping the peace. Speaking in the Berlin Opera House on April 28, he blamed England and France for the unsettled conditions of Europe by their alliances with Poland and other countries, which, he claimed, were strangling Germany. He sneered at the British and French claims that he was planning to gobble up all of Europe, by censuring them and the United States for their imperialist policies in Europe and Latin America. His sarcasm heightened when he said he would refrain from invading the United States, and then he addressed the President directly, "Mr. Roosevelt! I fully understand that the vastness of your nation and the immense wealth of your country allow you to feel responsible for the history of the whole world and for the history of all nations. I, sir, am placed in a much smaller and more modest sphere."[2] Then he reminded the world of his accomplishments. He had brought order to Germany, increased industrial production, reduced unemployment, and rearmed the nation.

It was clear that Germany would attack Poland if the United States did nothing. In spite of our having a "broomstick" army, Hitler feared the American industrial might. Although repeal of neutrality would not subdue Germany, Hull and Roosevelt believed that it might slow down Hitler's schedule of conquest, and it might buy time for the Allies. Typically, FDR saw it as a "save the world" move. He and Hull had to convince the recalcitrant legislators that amending the neutrality acts was the only viable, immediate alternative to Hitler's land grab.

In that hot summer of 1939, the two hundred thousand federal workers went about their business in discomfort. The wise ones left the sweltering heat, including the President. The rest tried to escape the heat by dressing down, meaning light and white. It was the age of white hats and white suits and white wing-tip shoes.

Those who came from other climes must have thought that God used his leftovers to make such an ungodly city. It was a giant slum, with shacks and houses of every description that had no plumbing; it was attracting low-income people by the hundreds each day; it was the largest city with outdoor plumbing in the western world; it was "first in war, first in peace and last in the American League." Many thought it was last in other things.[3]

Most members of Congress discovered what most Americans had already learned: the coolest place in town in the summer heat was the air-conditioned movie theater. Since the RKO and the other movies downtown had air-conditioning, the Congress insisted that cool air be drawn into the House and Senate chambers and even into their offices across the street.

Americans expected their congressmen to put in a full-day's work for a full-day's pay, since the cool chambers now permitted them to work longer hours in comfort. But, as Brinkley stated in *Washington Goes To War*:

Congress in 1939 was still carrying on in the leisurely and genteel manner of the days of McKinley, in a setting of marble stairways, horsehair sofas, polished brass spittoons, snuff boxes on the senators' desks, potted palms, Oriental rugs, leather chairs and Havana cigars. There were even a few members still affecting frock coats, wing collars and black string ties. It was a gentlemen's club with but one woman senator—Hattie Caraway of Arkansas, who sat in the chamber every day knitting.

AMERICAN PREPAREDNESS

Broomsticks and Floating Tubs

When World II began, America's military might was described as an Army with broomsticks and a Navy of floating tubs. Roosevelt had to change things quickly. The strength of active-duty Army was increased immediately by one hundred thousand, but not many young men were anxious to enlist; they saw that the regular Army was a group of derelicts. Not even the unemployed could be convinced to fill the new quota. They could read about the invincibility of the German war machine, which cooled any fervor they might have had for enlisting.

Perret describes the ludicrous situation of the "best" American tanks. These twelve-ton vehicles had no periscope, which compelled the commander, if he wished to see the terrain ahead, to stand on the shoulders of the driver. Because there was no intercom, he used his feet to direct the course of the action—a kick in the back meant foreward, a kick in the right shoulder was a signal to go right and a kick to the left shoulder was a left turn. These problems paled next to the main disadvantage of the American tank: it used machine guns as tank destroyers. Later, when 37 mm cannons were added, the total firepower was still less than that of the German and English fighter planes.[4]

The Navy was in slightly better shape, but most of its ships were decrepit tubs. It had the advantage of keeping a large Pacific fleet, based in Hawaii, and a smaller Atlantic strike force. The main Atlantic defense was probably the British fleet, which was the largest in the world.

When war came in Europe, the United States found itself with substantial unused industrial capacity. There were still millions of hard-core unemployed, many jobless for years. In agriculture, farmers were bearing the pain of large surpluses of wheat, cotton, rice, and corn. But the possession of idle materials and productive capacity was advantageous in a time of impending war. When Germany made its bold, ridiculous claims on Austria, Czecho-slovakia, and Poland, when it cast aside democracy, and when it started its campaign of racial genocide, the United States was a limp, sleeping giant.

Preparation for war, which was already in full swing, sped up once war began. President Roosevelt issued a proclamation on September 8, 1939, declaring a limited national emergency. He ordered that the regular Army be increased to 227,000 men, the Navy to 105,000, and the National Guard to 235,000. The War Department, reacting to the emergency, announced that it was organizing a new, active-duty corps of five mobile divisions of fifty thousand soldiers each, which were designed to prevent enemy incursions anywhere in this hemisphere. It also established a new Caribbean Department at Puerto Rico, and it ordered the reinforcement of the garrison at the Panama Canal. As a further deterrent against attack, the strength of the Army Air Corps was to be doubled by 1941.

The Navy, which would be crucial in repelling an invasion, proposed a ten-year building program, to allow it to go on the offensive against enemy fleets and enemy shipping should they venture towards American shores. The subsidy to the American Merchant Marine was also viewed as a necessary condition for guaranteeing military transportation in case of war.

The President's proclamation included protection for what he called "our neighborhood"— the whole of the Western Hemisphere. He was fearful of a German victory that would menace the bridge to the United States (Iceland and Greenland), the Americas, the Caribbean area, and the Panama Canal. He sought agreements with Caribbean leaders for cooperative efforts to guarantee the security of these islands to keep the Nazis from establishing footholds that could be used to conquer a South American country and the Panama Canal. The question of how to deal with fifth-column activities was not considered.

Lucky Lindy

Charles Augustus Lindbergh, the tall, handsome, gallant aviator, was America's greatest hero. Born in Detroit, his family moved to Little Falls, Minnesota—an unlikely place for a flying hero. The son of a Swedish-American congressman who ran for governor on the isolationist ticket, Lindbergh inherited his father's hatred for war. The congressman had voted against America's entry in World War I, and young Lindbergh, who was a teenager, was won over to the antiwar cause.

When his parents split up, Charles, who was called "Slim," was raised by a domineering mother, who was a school teacher. It is said that Lindbergh would race across the Minnesota fields chasing birds and longing to emulate their flight. When he got his chance to fly, he knew his choice was a right one. His flight to Paris in 1927 made him "The Lone Eagle" and "Lucky Lindy." He was idolized, adored, fawned on, and was constantly in the glare of the American press.

Because of his knowledge of airplanes, he was given a commission as a Colonel in the United States Army Air Corps. In October 1938 Herman Goering presented him with the highest medal it could give to a foreigner—"The German Eagle." Lindbergh was pleased with the award, and he seemed not to notice the events of Kristallnacht. In 1939 Lindbergh returned to the United States, where he was employed as a technical consultant to the Air Corps.

The headlines of October 1939 announced: LINDBERGH GIVES U.S. NAZI AIR DATA, and LINDBERGH BARES NAZIS' AIR POWER and LUCKY LINDY AIR SECRETS STIR CAPITOL. The rumor was that Lindbergh was hobnobbing with the Nazis in Berlin and that he was a German spy. In reality, he was actually performing a spying mission for the United States. He made a special visit to Germany, during which he was able to make an intensive study of the Luftwaffe.

Hitler and Goebbels, Lindbergh's "friends in Berlin," gave him the rare opportunity of viewing the best of German armaments and the leading German research laboratories. Lindbergh confirmed that Germany had more and better fighting planes than any other country. Equally alarming for America's industrial health, Lindbergh told the War Department that Germany was far ahead of the world in the mass production of airplanes and was about to challenge the United States in the sale of commercial airplanes.[5]

Though Roosevelt was always a Navy man, he believed that airplanes were the antidote to Hitler's poison. FDR was grateful for the information that Colonel Lindbergh had brought him about European aircraft. Lindbergh's estimates were alarming. He wrote that Germany could produce thirty to fifty thousand planes per year, and that German aircraft strength was greater than the combined air forces of England and France—a fact that reinforced his isolationism. Lindbergh gave what was described as "the most accurate picture of the Luftwaffe, its equipment, leaders, apparent plans, training methods, and present defects" ever encountered. Although he gave this detailed information to the Air Corps, he still did not favor our entry into the war. So glowing was Lindbergh's assessment of German air strength that Chamberlain was said to have been influenced by it to choose appeasement rather than war.

When George Marshall learned of these alarming assessments, he told General Hap Arnold to get in touch with Lindbergh. They corresponded regularly, and when Lindbergh returned to the States, he gave Arnold a very detailed picture of the Luftwaffe equipment and their defects. Arnold considered these a fresh justification for going ahead with the first of the B-17 production model.[6]

The Roman Warrior

In May, President Roosevelt, who had an uncanny ability to pick the right man, announced his choice to replace General Malin Craig as United States Army Chief of Staff, who was retiring on August 31, 1939. The selection of George Catlett Marshall was no surprise to the military, although the public hardly knew him. Marshall was jumped over the heads of twenty major and fourteen brigadier generals who were senior in rank. When Marshall took over, he was highly critical of the nation's readiness to fight any kind of war. He complained about the very low appropriations for defense since the end of the First World War. But he also deplored the lack of coordination of the different branches of service.[7]

Marshall, the shy, quiet, soft-spoken, austere, courteous ramrod soldier, was fifty-nine years old when appointed. He was tall, had a long face, and looked like a Roman warrior. His low, staccato voice had intensity. His credentials were impeccable; he was all military, strict, fair, demanding, and a good organizer.

He was not a brilliant student at VMI, but he loved history and understood political alliances and negotiations. It helped him to become captain of his cadet corps. He believed in discipline, self-denial and rectitude. Some said he was glamorous, but he was known more for his lack of vanity, his courteousness, and his strict obedience to superiors. He had what one writer called a "measured calm." It was often misunderstood as coldness.

The Chief of Staff was in charge of all land forces and the Army Air Corps. His first priority was the defense of the United States, the Panama Canal, and the Caribbean area. But under the Monroe Doctrine his jurisdiction extended to the entire Western Hemisphere. Marshall had extensive training as a chief of staff. He served in this capacity under Pershing and also with the First Army in France. When he left his staff duties in 1924, he was assigned to the Fifteenth Infantry in Tientsin, China, where he spent three years.

Marshall was sworn in on September 1, the day Germany invaded Poland. He commanded 227,000 persons (with equipment for only 75,000), some old Garand and Springfield rifles, twenty-year-old machine guns, and a handful of French 75 guns that were brought to the United States after World War I. To say that we were militarily unprepared was a joke. Dean Acheson quipped that "God looks after children, drunkards and the United States."[8]

Marshall, who was a native of Uniontown, Pennsylvania, and who was related to Chief Justice John Marshall, did not come from a military family, although his father did serve in the Union Army in the Civil War. George followed his older brother to Virginia Military Institute, after he was unsuccessful in obtaining an appointment to West Point.

After graduation, Marshall was assigned to the Philippines, where he first exhibited his great genius for organization. As a lieutenant, he drafted a very complicated field order for the defense of the Islands, for which he was labeled a soldier to watch. His peacetime orders took him to China; to Fort Benning, Georgia; to the Illinois National Guard; and finally to Washington, D.C. to work as a deputy to General Craig.

In one of his domestic assignments, Colonel Marshall commanded twenty-seven CCC camps. The idea of rehabilitating young unemployed boys excited him greatly. His interest was so intense that he tried to have his name placed as Director of the Corps. This effort failed. Nevertheless, it was said that Marshall "ate, breathed and digested CCC problems." He awoke very early each day and made his rounds of the camps. There was woe to those officers who were not "up and at them" when Marshall arrived for an inspection. As enrollments mounted, there were not enough regular Army soldiers to man the camps, which necessitated calling up reserves, many of whom were unemployed also.

Although the United States was not prepared to fight a world war in 1939, Marshall believed that we were a first-class military power, because we had an abundance of raw materials, a powerful economy, and the advantage of being separated by two oceans. He was aware of the growing range of modern bombers, and he came to support allocations for them. He made geography a key factor in setting military goals, which were extremely modest. He asked for only 350,000 new troops.[9]

Marshall set out to create balanced forces of Army, Navy, and Air Force. He got rid of the deadwood that had accumulated in the twenty-five years of peace and promoted young, bright men to positions of power and responsibility. He remembered that Roosevelt had picked him over several more-senior officers. He chose his assistants on purely military grounds—he cared not for the political ramifications of his choices.

He was known for his ability to spot men of great potential. He promoted younger men by abolishing the seniority system. In December 1939 he summoned Dwight D. Eisenhower to be his aide. Ike had spent the prior fourteen years in the Philippines, and he was capable of laying out the defense of the Islands and the Pacific area. It was the beginning of Eisenhower's rise to Supreme Commander. Marshall also chose General George Patton as a coming leader.

Air Power—The Redoubtable Weapon

By the fall of 1918, General Billy Mitchell was able to amass 1,500 aircraft along the St. Mihiel front. It was the first use of a sizeable force of aircraft in American history. It won him a commendation from General Pershing and convinced him that air power was the ultimate weapon.

When Mitchell was assigned to serve under an infantry general, he realized that there would be no dollars available "for the purchase of a new aircraft." He began stumping the country for funds for a separate air force. This idea was attacked by Assistant Secretary of the Navy Franklin Roosevelt, who favored putting funds into a stronger navy. Following the Army reorganization of 1920, the Air Service was placed under the Army and limited to only 1,516 officers and 2,821 aircraft.[10]

Frustrated, Mitchell declared that bombers could search out ships far at sea and sink them easily with a few well-placed bombs. The Navy sneered at this challenge, and offered to provide a few old ships for a test. Some naval officers offered to stand on the decks while Mitchell's bombers were dropping their bomb loads.

The tests began on June 20, 1921, when some Navy bombers sank a German submarine. Next came the big target, the battleship *Iowa*. On June 29, a dirigible started a sea search to locate the target for the bombers, which they promptly sank. But the real test of air power came against the *Ostfriesland*, a German battleship with double skins and supposedly unsinkable. Using Martin MB 2 bombers, the best of their day, Mitchell's flyers first wounded the big ship with 1,500-pound bombs and then sent her to the bottom with two thousand pounders. The Navy was stunned at Mitchell's complete victory. But it turned out to be hollow, because Navy brass took the sinkings to mean that the Navy should have its own air arm. Billy Mitchell got support from Italian General Guilio Douhet, who was the leading European exponent of using airplanes for offensive purposes. His book, *The Command of the Air*, was first published in

1921. In it, he compared an airplane to a large gun that fires from a vertical rather than a horizontal position and whose range was the plane's flying time.

When Mitchell criticized our national defense, President Coolidge ordered that he stand trial in a court-martial. Mitchell was found guilty of all charges and was ordered to forfeit all pay and allowances for a period of five years. Despite this setback, there were compelling reasons to create an Army Air Corps. General H. H. (Hap) Arnold was given the job in 1938, in the middle of the jurisdictional battle between Secretary of War Harry Woodring and his assistant Louis Johnson. While all the squabbling was going on, Arnold was "taboo" at the White House. He felt that he had "lost the President's confidence." But Arnold did have two friends in the White House: Chief of Staff George Marshall and Secretary Harry Hopkins.[11]

What changed matters was the Flying Fortress. On April 29, 1938, the new Boeing Y1B-17A went up for a test flight. It was powered by new Wright cyclone engines, with 4,000 horsepower—one fourth more than the prototype. High above ground, the pilot found himself in a violent thunderstorm, which tossed him and the crew around. The plane stopped and plunged into a spin, turning slowly as it fell. As they came into clear air, they were all amazed. The wings were still on! In bringing the plane out of its dive, they increased the forces that battered the Fortress. The recording instruments aboard the Y1B-17 showed that the stresses imposed during the dive had exceeded just about every maximum load for which it was designed. Under such stresses, the airplane should have burst its seams, but all they found were some loose rivets.

Three months after making its good-will tour of 1938, the 2nd Bombardment Group of the Air Corps was given a chance to demonstrate what it could do for coastal defense. It learned that the Italian liner *Rex* was seven hundred miles out to sea and headed for New York City. The Air Corps decided to find this dot in the ocean. It selected its best men for the search in three Flying Fortresses, with Lieutenant Curtis LeMay as chief navigator. The passengers on the ship were amazed to see the three large silver birds making a "bomb run" directly over the luxury liner. The crews estimate that they were 725 miles east of New York, which meant that they had traveled 1,500 miles for the round-trip journey. They had used a square search technique and had flown much of the time in cloud cover.[12]

While the crews celebrated, the reaction from Washington stunned them; they returned to find a severe reprimand and an order banning similar future flights. They learned later that the ban was initiated by Navy brass, who were guarding their control over the seas. General Hap Arnold accepted the new order, which confined the Air Corps to flights of less than "one hundred miles out from the shoreline."

In 1938, the Secretary of War settled the issue; after the additional Fortresses that were on order were built, no additional orders would be forthcoming. But Arnold was insistent. One of the reasons the United States needed a bomber that could fly at twenty thousand feet was the very noticeable improvement in antiaircraft guns.

The average improvement range is more startling. During World War I, planes could navigate a circle which would pass through Brussels and Paris, but a Flying Fortress stationed in England could bomb in a circle that reached to Kiev in Russia, Libya in Africa and even Iceland on the Arctic Circle. This was a combat radius of over two-thousand miles (a total journey of four thousand miles).[13]

In spite of its great achievement, no more Fortresses were built in 1938, but 1939 proved to be an excellent year for advocates of heavy bombing. The new plant in Seattle began delivering the advanced Y1B-17A, and the Air Corps quickly let it make its mark. It had a new load capacity of 11,023 pounds over a distance of 621 miles at an average speed of 259.39 miles per hour. Under combat conditions, it could carry a bomb load of 2,400 pounds, with a range of 1,500 miles.

When war began in Europe, the United States declared its neutrality; its stated policy was to keep the totalitarian powers out of the Western Hemisphere—a policy that was wholly consistent with the Monroe Doctrine. At the same time, the President took steps to expand the Air Corps. In his Presidential Message of January 12, 1939, he spoke of airplanes of "increased range, increased speed, increased capacity." He called the existing Air Corps "utterly inadequate." Within three months, Congress had authorized the procurement of 3,251 aircraft, and it approved raising the Air Corps total to 5,500 planes, 3,203 officers, and 45,000 enlisted men.[14]

This was bad news for the Boeing Company. It sent its representative, James Murray, to Washington to inform the War Department that its original price of $205,000 per airplane was predicated on a high volume of orders. Because these were not forthcoming, Boeing wanted to raise the price. The Air Corps staggered Murray by insisting that the price was too high. Murray told General George Brett, the Air Corps negotiator, that at that price Boeing would lose money for each plane sold, because of innovations in design. The atmosphere was tense. Finally, Murray asked Brett if he could go to see General Arnold, to which Brett replied, "You can see Jesus Christ for all I care."

When the stalemate continued, Boeing made its decision. The company was fed up; it would abandon production of the Flying Fortress. For the first nine months of 1939, the company had lost $2.6 million. The decision to emphasize heavy bombers had put the company at the point of bankruptcy. When Boeing played hard nose, the Air Corps gave in. It accepted several changes that made it possible for Boeing to survive at a price of $202,500 per bomber. It is no exaggeration to say that those negotiations altered the course of history. If they had failed and if Boeing had halted production of the Fortress, it would have deprived the United States of its best aerial weapon of World War II.

The United States was the only industrial country that developed its air power in the private sector, although the government offered help for the nascent industry through air-mail contracts and navigational aids. The process is evident in the history of commercial aviation. Donald Douglas, the head of Douglas Aircraft Company, designed a new kind of airplane, with honey-combed wings and an aluminum skin. Charles Lindbergh was asked to comment and he approved, but with one proviso: that the aircraft be able to take off with a full load on one engine. The DC-1 passed all its tests in 1934, as did the DC-2, and on December 17, 1935, the new twenty-one passenger DC-3 was introduced. It was purchased by almost all the American airlines, and in 1938, the U.S. Army became interested in the plane for transport service. The military interest stemmed from the large role the DC-3 played in the Spanish Civil War. Glines and Moseley called it "The Plane That Saved the Airlines," but its importance to the military far outweighed this. The military version, the C-47, was to air transport what the Flying Fortress was to strategic bombing, and both planes started as commercial designs.[15]

THE ILLUSION OF NEUTRALITY

After years of debate, the question of neutrality reached a climax as Germany and Italy began their policies of conquest. Roosevelt, who created the most powerful coalition in American political history, saw his support crumble when it came to foreign affairs. The politicians read the American fear correctly. Senators Burton K. Wheeler (Montana), Robert A. Taft (Ohio), Gerald P. Nye (North Dakota), Hiram W. Johnson (California), and Robert M. LaFollette (Wisconsin) led the isolationist, "America First" movement. They quoted Washington's Farewell Address and the Monroe Doctrine on the dangers of foreign tyrants and the need to avoid repeating the horrors of the First World War.

Arthur Vandenberg, sometimes called the "Big Michigander because of his portly demeanor," a Senator since 1928, battled Roosevelt over the kind of neutrality the United States should accept. With a run for the Presidency in mind, he went straight to the heart of every American mother by promising that he would oppose every vote that "would send your sons to war."[16]

The series of laws passed in 1935, 1936, 1937, and 1939 maintained the neutrality of the United States in European and Asian wars. The Act of 1935 authorized the President to embargo "the sale of guns, munitions, and war materials to belligerents upon his finding that a state of war existed." The 1936 Act added loans to the forbidden list. The 1937 Amendments to the Neutrality Act (sometimes called the Cash-and-Carry Amendments) were signed just as the old law was expiring. Divine tells us that it was a race against time. On April 30, a copy of the new legislation was flown from Washington to the Gulf of Mexico, where the President was on a fishing vacation. The document was then transferred to a Navy seaplane, which landed next to the presidential yacht. On the morning of May 1, Roosevelt signed the bill.[17]

The law specified four major restrictions. Whenever the President declared that a state of war or a civil war existed, which was a threat to the peace of the United States, automatic limitations went into effect: there would be an embargo on arms, ammunition, and war supplies; a ban on long-term loans; a prohibition on travel on ships of the belligerent nations; and a ban on arming American merchant ships trading with these belligerents.

Polls indicated that the American public favored mandatory legislation. Roosevelt, fearing further losses of support for his domestic agenda, preferred to allow Secretary Hull to carry the issue for him. The Neutrality Acts of 1935 and 1937 tied him in knots. He had no power to use against dictators. When Congress convened on January 4, 1939, the President delivered an animated address. He measured his words carefully, marking out the menacing aspects of events overseas, relating them to the neutrality issue. Roosevelt, who thought that war was inevitable, sent Hull before the Senate Foreign Relations Committee to request that it pass legislation to repeal the Neutrality Act. But the Committee, led by isolationist senators rejected Roosevelt's warning. "There will be no war this year," said Senator Borah.

Alluding to the Japanese situation, FDR urged that we avoid any action that might encourage or assist an aggressor. He stressed that our neutrality laws might actually give aid to an aggressor, and he suggested that we use all methods "short of war" to discourage aggression. The President refused to state a precise position on neutrality until Hitler made his next move: on March 15, 1939, the German army attacked Czecho-slovakia, negating the pledge Hitler had made at Munich. Now the American people wanted action. The Republicans quickly established a "National Committee to Keep America Out of Foreign Wars."[18]

In April 1939 Gallup reported the results of his poll on the Neutrality Acts. He found that 57 percent favored amending the Acts to allow the United States to sell war supplies to France and England and that 65 percent believed Germany should be boycotted. Over half of the respondents believed that there would be a European war in 1939, and that the U.S. would be drawn into the conflict.[19]

Roosevelt had to contend with the isolationist and the interventionist factions. His hands were tied by Congress and a doubting public. At one point he said, "You know I'm a juggler." On a very hot day in July he called several key senators to the White House. Republicans Charles McNary of Oregon and New Englander Warren Austin were joined by Alben Barkley of Kentucky, the Democratic Majority Leader, Independent William E. Borah, of Idaho, and Key Pittman of Nevada. Pittman, the southerner who had migrated to the West, represented the mining interests who would gain from a war.

Roosevelt, who was in his wheelchair, flanked by Cordell Hull and Vice President John Nance Garner, got to the business of the meeting. The State Department had informed FDR of the grimness of the situation: that the Nazis had over two million men in uniform and other countries were put on a war footing (civilians were practicing air-raid drills and soldiers were marching to their frontiers). Roosevelt told those present that the neutrality laws allowed him no freedom to deal with the deepening crisis, and he asked them to support repeal or modification of the Acts. He emphasized that the export embargo made it impossible for France and Britain to buy munitions from the United States.

But Borah, the very opinionated senator from the American West, was not about to grant Roosevelt's wish. The senator did not trust Roosevelt, who he thought was meddling in "power politics." Borah believed that our participation in World War I was a mistake, and he swore that American boys would never fight another European war. The arms embargoes were designed to prevent any future President from involving the United States in any foreign alliances. Davis maintains that this was the "most disappointing aspect of FDR's second term."[20] For him, Roosevelt's foreign policy was too cautious and allowed Europe to drift towards war. Davis implies that Roosevelt's policy was secret and devious, causing a credibility gap and lost opportunities to avoid war.

When World War II began, however, the President was obliged to respond. On September 5 he issued a proclamation of neutrality that embargoed all arms to belligerents and imposed restrictions on travel by American citizens. Then he began his campaign to revise the Neutrality Act by calling a special session of Congress.

On September 21, he addressed the Congress. The House chamber was packed; the galleries were filled, and there were representives from several nations, but none from Germany, Japan, or Italy. This time the President did not offer his usual wide grin. Divine assessed the situation: "It was a brilliant political speech. With unerring skill, Roosevelt had laid the case for repeal of the embargo on the altar of international law. Always stressing his desire to return to traditional American practice, he made the embargo appear as a dangerous and unwise experiment. He hammered away at the need to protect the United States from involvement in war."[21] After the speech, the President's support rose to 62 percent (from 50), and, of more importance, every region was in favor of repeal. The Congress listened. The Senate debated for 117 hours, 19 minutes, as sixty-eight senators spoke an estimated one million words.[22]

Saying that he would not play Mr. Hitler's game, Majority Leader Sam Rayburn of Texas endorsed revision of the neutrality law. On November 2, the House voted to repeal the embargo, 243-181; on the following day, the conference committee agreed on the final version of the legislation. They reported out the bill, and it passed by 55 to 20 in the Senate and 243 to 172 in the House. The effect of the law was to allow exporters to ship war supplies to all belligerents. When the law passed, the President was already working to establish naval patrols to ban ships from belligerent countries from American waters. At the same time, he was seeking bases for the protection of the hemisphere. He leased aircraft hangars in Bermuda and was looking for bases in the Caribbean.[23]

The fear of war in the United States swelled the ranks of isolationists. Public opinion swung heavily against American involvement. We were not so eager to save the world again for democracy. Americans were still bitter over the anti-American feelings that pervaded Europe in the 1920s. Robert Lockhart, a Scottish-American who toured the United States in early 1939 on a lecture tour, said this about America's attitude concerning European problems: "We Americans went into the last war to save democracy. We pulled you out of a hole and we received very grudging thanks. At Versailles and after Versailles you trampled on democratic ideals. Now, largely through your own fault, you are in trouble again and you want our help. Well, we've learnt our lesson."[24]

Public opinion polls changed with the winds of war. The Gallup poll of April 1939 reported that 65 percent favored boycotting Germany, and 57 percent wanted the neutrality act amended to allow the United States to sell war supplies to England and France, but a poll taken just after war was declared in Europe showed that over 90 percent of Americans favored staying out or having nothing to do with the war. Women were overwhelmingly against.

The America First Committee

Lindbergh provided the basis for the creation of the America First Committee, the work of a Yale Law School student. R. Douglas Stuart, Jr., the son of a Quaker Oats executive, enlisted the support of some powerful industrialists to make their isolationist pitch. Robert A. Wood of Sears Roebuck gave them prominence, as did Colonel Robert McCormick, publisher of the *Chicago Tribune*. The political right joined in, especially Congressman Hamilton Fish and Senator Burton Wheeler. The Committee was a mixture of pacifists and isolationists.

They agreed that Roosevelt was determined to bring the United States into the war on the English side. Lindbergh, the midwesterner, accused the liberal eastern press of supporting Franklin Roosevelt's policies of planning a war Americans did not want. Lindbergh's supporters included Irish-Americans, who prayed for British defeats in world affairs, because of her disgraceful treatment of Ireland; all those common Americans, who did not read the *New York Times* but who hated war; and the plain folks, who read no newspaper but who had some vague notion that people in the "monied East" would gain financially from war.

On September 15, 1939 Lindbergh and the America First movement scheduled a huge rally in Manhattan to assuage the fears of that large body of Americans who did not trust the newspapers, radio stations, or the newsreels. Before air time, Colonel Truman Smith, a presidential aide, delivered a message from Roosevelt, which expressed his concern over the tone of the proposed speech and which promised him a new cabinet post as Secretary of Air if he would not deliver the address. It was a great opportunity for Lindbergh to mold the United States Air Corps in his image, but he declined the offer. He refused to acquiesce, which infuriated Roosevelt. Freidel tells us that the President exploded, "If I should die tomorrow, I want you to know this, I am absolutely convinced that Lindbergh is a Nazi." On another occasion, the President called him a "Sunshine Patriot."[25]

Lindbergh's speech was a sensation. It negated many of the arguments that the President used in announcing the war. Millions of Americans agreed with Lindbergh, which angered and frustrated FDR. Lindbergh thought that a German victory was possible; Roosevelt knew that a German victory was unthinkable and unacceptable, because it would legitimize the Nazi philosophy and would allow the German notions about world conquest to remain unchallenged.

There was a more ominous aspect to Lindbergh's isolationist position. Besides wanting to stop Roosevelt, he harbored racist notions about the rest of the world. He wrote of the fear of the yellow, brown, and black races, and he called the large Jewish ownership of Hollywood a grave danger to democracy. Behind this debate, there lurked an untalked-of subject: Lindbergh's love of Germans. He didn't believe that the French and English had the mettle to stand up to the superior Germans. For this, his critics called him "Herr Lindbergh." Lindbergh's position was also bereft of morality. He was unconcerned about the movement of totalitarianism across Europe. His answer was that the United States was given a special destiny (presumably by the Creator).

Lindbergh supported Roosevelt's general recommendations concerning air power, but he did not favor early mass production in the absence of war. He preferred the production of fewer high-quality airplanes. This did not please Roosevelt who believed that the United States must produce enough airplanes for Europe as a deterrent to Hitler.

MYSTERY AIRPLANES

The President was certain that the United States could become a leading aircraft producer, and he was in the market for buyers. He was happy for the order the United States received from the French for one thousand of our newest fighter, the P-36. But the American aircraft industry could not fill so large an order, so, it was scaled down to one hundred planes.

The inability of American producers to meet the larger French order (they simply didn't have the mass production tools) upset FDR. He called in General "Hap" Arnold and told him that he wanted a greatly expanded air force, which pleased the General immensely. But Arnold informed him that airplanes, by themselves, were insufficient. There would be a need for navigational aids, new landing fields, more pilot training, and an expanded mechanics corps. Roosevelt suggested a long-term plan for building twenty planes per year for defense of the hemisphere (and to frighten off Adolf Hitler), but his immediate concern continued to be sending aid to France and Great Britain.

The isolationists on Capitol Hill were confirmed in their suspicions of the President when, in January 1939, they learned in an unusual way of his secret dealings with the French on arms purchases. The story, as it came out, showed that one of our newest bombers had crashed in a parking lot near the Los Angeles Municipal Airport. The test pilot, John Cable, was killed when his parachute failed to open. He had taken the twin-engine plane up to altitude and put the plane through power dives when it went into a spin and crashed. The mystery unfolded when a passenger survived the crash. He was identified as "Smithin," but the *New York Times* reported that his real name was Paul Chemidlin—a French test pilot. The plane that crashed in Los Angeles was the top secret Douglas A-20 bomber.

When the French first asked to see the plane, General Arnold refused. Frustrated, they went directly to Secretary of the Treasury Morgenthau who said that FDR approved. But in fact Morganthau had approved the request. When Morgenthau was questioned about it by the Senate, he said Arnold had approved the flight. FDR, knowing nothing about the episode, lambasted Arnold for telling the truth. The political Roosevelt would have handled it differently. He acknowledged that Chemidlin was here to look into the purchase of an experimental airplane. The Administration acted against the advice of Secretary of War Woodring and General Arnold. But the chief disclosure in the incident was the devious nature of Roosevelt's actions and explanations. Besides lying about the Frenchman's name, FDR said, at first, that the plane that crashed was a private aircraft, when, in fact, the military red, white, and blue markings were clearly visible.

French Premier Daladier was anxious to take up Roosevelt's offer. He sent economist-financier Jean Monnet to talk to Roosevelt. Their meeting was secret and bizarre. The President said that they could go around the Neutrality Act by building assembly plants on the Canadian side of Niagara Falls, where American companies could send parts for assembly. He even believed that enrollees in the National Youth Administration could be trained as airplane mechanics.[26]

EXTREMISTS ON THE LEFT AND RIGHT

The 180-Degree Turn

Franklin Roosevelt, the first Democratic President since Woodrow Wilson, ignoring much advice, recognized the government of Stalinist Russia. In 1933, FDR appointed William C. Bullitt as the first Ambassador to Russia. At that time, the United States had a Russian Section as part of the American Legation at Riga, Latvia. It was nothing but a research group that received Russian periodicals and wrote economic reports on conditions in the Soviet Union. George Kennan, who was one of the researchers at Riga and who was a leading hard-liner against recognition of Russia, was very fearful for the safety of the many Americans who had fled to Russia in the Depression seeking a better life.[27]

When Hitler seized power in Germany, many anti-Fascists in the United States joined the Communist Party USA. They were sympathizers of the Popular Front, and many joined the International Brigade in Spain. The Stalin-Hitler Pact of August 1939 had a devastating effect on them. Yet, they kept the communist faith. The Pact was chaotic for those who espoused leftist and rightist doctrines. The Russians had just ended a massive purge of "Fascists, counter-revolutionaries, spies and wreckers" that began in 1937. It resulted in the liquidation of party leaders, military advisers, and intellectuals. The NKVD, the Commissar of Internal Affairs, using stool pigeons, fabricated cases against innocent adults and children.

College students engaged in rhapsodic lamentations for a romantic time that never was. They could only pay tribute to their lost cause in the Spanish revolution and to bemoan the linking of despots. The CIO and Maritime Unions, heavily laced with communists, had no truck with college kids, but they could bemoan their lost causes.

The Nazi-Soviet Pact fractured the American Communist Party. The first effect was to deplete membership, but it also led to deep, internal conflicts in strategy. On the day after the German invasion of Poland and less than two weeks after the signing of the Pact, Whittaker Chambers, now a disillusioned party member, told Assistant Secretary of State Adolf Berle that two brothers, Donald and Alger Hiss—both State Department employees—were communists. Chambers provided Berle with a long list of persons who were party members or communist sympathizers.

In 1939 it was difficult for radicals to swallow what the Soviet Union had agreed to. By signing the Pact with Germany, it had revoked its support of the League of Nations, which called for sanctions against aggressor nations. The words of American Communist Dorothy Healey are particularly apt. She grew up as a "red-diaper baby," because her mother, Barbara Rosenblum, was a charter member of the party. In her growing-up years, Dorothy knew that she wanted to be a communist. And so at age fourteen, she joined the Young Communist League.[28] Her book, a narration with the subtitle, *A Life in the American Communist Party*, is an uncommon autobiography. Although quite young, she became an excellent negotiator for the exploited farm workers. But her personal life was in shambles. She had two failed marriages and several abortions. Even with the birth of her son, Richard, she never lost her zeal for her mission.

Healey became an apologist for the Soviets. She maintained that they were justified in signing the Pact with the Nazis. She has regrets, but she failed to deal adequately with the shock of American Communist Party members, who had to make 180-degree turns in policy, particularly concerning embracing a Nazi government that had been denounced by the communists as autocratic and despotic earlier. When Earl Browder, the leader of the party, was asked if he thought the Germans and Russians could ever reach an agreement, he answered, "I could easier imagine myself being elected President of the U.S. Chamber of Commerce."[29]

Hope Hale Davis's memoir of her life as a communist is another evocation of the idealism, romance and leftist buoyancy that was shattered by the "shock, incredulity. . . angry hopelessness" at the signing of the nonaggression Pact by Stalin and Hitler.[30] Davis recounts the history of the intellectual Utopians who joined the party in the expectation that there would be a "Great Day Coming." Her story is of the Washington, D.C. contingent who labored in the communist vineyard from 1933 until 1939, when the great day of disillusionment arrived.

She moved from Greenwich Village to Washington in the spring of 1933, where she worked in magazine publishing, and where she associated with a young Bohemian crowd that included Claud Cockburn, the British radical. Their connection produced what she called their "Revolutionary Baby"—Claudia. Because Davis was a person of means and was the product of a bourgeois family, she persuaded Claud to produce a marriage certificate as well.

Davis's first task for the party was to find a job in the new Roosevelt Administration, where many other leftists had flocked. They had doubts about his commitment to reform, but he was the only game in town. Davis followed the communist line of burrowing from within the Consumers Counsel, but her mind was taken off radicalism when she met Hermann Brunck, a young German economist. They fell in love, she disposed of Cockburn, and Davis and Brunck married and joined the Communist Party. This memoir confirms what many others have told: that life in the Communist Party was a heavy mixture of radical ideas and policies and sex.

The Davis memoir is important also because it says something about the activities of communists in the nation's capital. She writes of Gardner Jackson and Alger Hiss, but her narrative is more about her marriage than about American Communism. In fact, Davis details Hermann's mental collapse from overwork. He was unable to balance the demands of the party with those of his job and his love life. He was overcome by doubts and paranoia, and he was convinced that Hitler was tailing him. When he was incarcerated in a mental institution, he was treated by noted psychiatrist Frieda Fromm-Reichmann, who Davis claims manipulated him. Brunck committed suicide.

Peggy Dennis, a young Californian, joined the Communist Party USA in 1925. She married Eugene Dennis, who in 1946 became the Secretary General of the American Communist party. Initially, they were very active in Comintern affairs in the Far East, but in the mid-1930s, they returned to the United States. When they learned of the Hitler-Stalin Pact in their New York apartment, she exclaimed, "Say it isn't true!" Her husband calmed her saying that "the Soviet Union has outwitted the bourgeois democracies in their attempts to get Germany and the Soviet Union to fight each other while they stand by, then pick up the pieces."[31]

THE PARTNERSHIP THAT SAVED THE WEST

On September 11, 1939, President Franklin Roosevelt began a series of letters to Winston Churchill that Joseph P. Lash called "the Partnership That Saved the West." It was a remarkable episode, because it involved correspondence between a head of state and another person who was not in charge of the government or its foreign affairs. However, Churchill, as First Lord of the Admiralty, had obtained permission from the Prime Minister to correspond with FDR. Genealogists inform us that Roosevelt and Churchill were eighth cousins, both men tracing their family trees to John Cooke, who came on the *Mayflower*. One of Churchill's daughters was related to Sara Delano, Franklin's mother.

In making his first contact with Churchill, Roosevelt stressed that he was glad that Churchill was back at Admiralty and that they had a certain kinship because they had the same job in World War I. Roosevelt had served as Assistant Secretary of the Navy. The Roosevelt correspondence had the effect of propping up Churchill and may have aided him in becoming Prime Minister. Certainly, they were war hawks, unlike Chamberlain,

When Hitler swallowed up Austria, Joseph P. Kennedy recommended appeasement. His position infuriated FDR, who bypassed his Ambassador in favor of writing to Churchill, who was fiercely against Chamberlain's appeasement of Hitler. Churchill had failed in his effort to alert the British to the dangers of Nazism.[32]

Franklin's first letter emphasized German strength in its lightning-war tactic in Poland. Roosevelt wrote: "What I want you and the Prime Minister to know is that I shall at all times welcome it, if you would keep me in touch personally with anything you want me to know about. You can always send sealed letters through your pouch or my pouch."[33] On that same day, Ambassador Kennedy had sent a cable to the State Department urging the President to work up a new plan for peace. It was a call for appeasement, Munich style.

The long friendship between Roosevelt and Churchill that commenced with these letters was curious, because they stood on opposite ends of the political spectrum, and because in the United States, Churchill was viewed as a defeated statesman—a political also-ran. He alone had stood up in the Parliament and called the Munich accord a total defeat, just as in 1931, he had bemoaned the British course of disarmament. And as a conservative, his views were more compatible with those of Herbert Hoover than the preachings of FDR on New Deal matters, which Churchill believed involved too much experimentation. Their correspondence was a marriage of the head of American liberalism and the most right-wing advocate of British conservatism. But Roosevelt liked what he heard from this man, who Clive James said "sounded like he looked—like a bulldog."

Joseph Kennedy was certain that after Hitler cleaned up Europe he would be ready for peace with France and England. Sir Samuel Hoare, Lord of the Privy

Seal, agreed with Kennedy. Churchill, who had no love for Ambassador Kennedy, suggested that the Poles stand fast and "that they give up nothing." He had allies in Roosevelt and Hull, who were more interested in putting down the forces of appeasement. Hull's answer to Kennedy stated that the United States government would not support any policy that would "make possible a survival of a regime of force and of aggression."[34]

After Munich and before the beginning of World War II, Churchill told his friend Bernard Baruch that war was coming and that the United States would be in it, and he added, "I believe America is unprepared."[35] Roosevelt listened. He allowed several secret meetings between American and British naval chiefs concerning the command of forces in the Atlantic should war come. When King George VI visited Roosevelt in June 1939, they talked about how the United States could relieve the British of the need to patrol the South Atlantic. From these discussions, Roosevelt conceived of a unique plan to establish a "neutrality zone" in the entire Western Hemisphere (comprising an area from three-hundred to one-thousand miles) inside which the ships of all warring nations would be excluded.

The plan seemed to have no supporters; there was no precedent in law. The British called it a "chastity belt," and the Germans labeled it "a closed zone," but it was clear that the plan would restrict the ability of Nazi U-boats from prowling in Atlantic waters. To give the idea more respectability, Assistant Secretary of State for Latin American Affairs Sumner Welles told the delegates at the Inter-American Conference in Panama City on September 23, 1939, that the twenty one American republics were entitled to be free from hostile acts from belligerents. Roosevelt believed ernestly that the Neutrality Zone would "keep the war out of the Americas."

THAT WOEFUL SEPTEMBER SONG

While Hitler was attacking Poland, the klezmer bands played on. These klezmorim (musicians in Yiddish) were members of folk bands in Eastern Europe. They numbered about five thousand, and they were particularly adept at playing happy tunes at weddings and mournful, wailing ones at funerals. Their songs penetrated the foul air of concentration camps and dismal conditions of the pogroms.

They began in the streets, because Jews did not allow musical instruments in the synagogues. The klezmorim were not respected (they were low on the Jewish occupational scale), because they spoke Yiddish and were Ashkenazic, rather than Sephardic who spoke Hebrew. On September 1, while the klezmer bands played, the Germans concocted an "incident" on the Polish border. They dressed twelve German criminals, who had all received death sentences, in Polish uniforms, gave them poisonous injections, which killed them instantly. They put bullets in their bodies, then they released the phony story that these men had tried to take the radio station at Gleiwitz. It was the start of World War II.[36]

In the early morning, William Bullitt, the American Ambassador to France, called President Roosevelt from Paris telling him that the German Army had invaded Poland. Ambassador Joseph Kennedy in London said he was sure the British would soon declare war. Americans were not as surprised as they had been in 1914. Many were expecting it.

On September 3, 1939, President Roosevelt played up to our ambivalence. In his radio address, he stated categorically that we would stay out of the war, but he added, "I cannot ask that every American remain neutral in thought as well."[37] Most Americans were unmoved. There were those who asked why they should die to save a degenerate Britain or the vulgar French, who sneered at American culture, or lack of it, who sat drinking wine safely behind their Maginot line. The ones who laughed least in the United States were the eighteen to twenty-four-year-old males who would have to save the world again for democracy.

NOTES

1. "Roosevelt Asks for 10-Year Peace," *New York Times*, April 16, 1939, p. 1.
2. Ketchum, *The Borrowed Years*, p. 173.
3. Brinkley, *Washington Goes to War*, p. 26.
4. Perrett, *Days of Sadness; Years of Triumph*, p. 36.
5. "Hounds in Cry," *Timecapsule/1939*, p. 31.
6. *Time*, September 25, 1939.
7. *Time* did a cover story on Marshall in its July 29, 1940, issue.
8. Manchester, *The Glory and the Dream*, p. 202.
9. "Program for U.S in War Provides for 500,000 Men," *New York Times*, May 14, 1939, p. 1.
10. Mason, *The United States Air Force*, p. 83.
11. Arnold, *Global Mission*, p. 186.
12. Caidin, *Flying Forts*, p. 98.
13. *Background of War*, p. 227.
14. Craven and Cate, *The Army Air Forces in World War II*, p. 104.
15. The C-47, "The Peerless Airplane," served in three wars—World War II, Korea and Vietnam, and many are still flying.
16. It is an irony of history that isolationist Senator Vandenberg become such a strong advocate of a bipartisan foreign policy that in 1945 he was named a U.S. delegate to the San Francisco conference that led to the establishment of the United Nations.
17. Divine, *The Illusion of Neutrality*, p. 193.
18. Divine, *The Illusion of Neutrality*, p. 255.
19. *New York Times*, January 5, 1939, p. 1.
20. Davis, *F.D.R. Into the Storm*, 1993.
21. Divine, *The Illusion of Neutrality*, p. 296.
22. *New York Times*, October 29, 1939.
23. *Washington Post*, November 4, 1939, p. 1.
24. Sherwood, *Roosevelt and Hopkins*, p. 131.

25. Freidel, *Franklin D. Roosevelt*, p. 323.

26. Freidel, *Franklin D. Roosevelt*, p. 309.

27. Kennan, *Memoirs*, p. 55.

28. Healey and Isserman, *Dorothy Healey Remembers*.

29. Ketchum, *The Borrowed Years*, p. 187.

30. Davis, *Great Day Coming* (1994).

31. Quoted in Leonhard, *Betrayal*, p. 160.

32. Churchill, *The Gathering Storm*, p. 453.

33. Quoted in Gunther, *Roosevelt*, p. 15.

34. Lash, *Roosevelt and Churchill*, p. 23.

35. Lash, *Roosevelt and Churchill*, p. 29.

36. Tim Page, "Klezmer: Revival of the Traditionalists," *Washington Post*, June 9, 1996.

37. Langsam, *The World Since 1914*, p. 816.

Bibliography

Adair, Robert K. *The Physics of Baseball,* 2nd ed. New York: Harper: Perennial, 1994.

Allen, Frederick. *Since Yesterday*. New York: Harper and Bros., 1940.

———. *The Big Change*. New York: Harper, 1952.

Anderson, Sherwood. *Puzzled America*. New York: Appel, 1970.

Arnold, H. H. *Global Mission*. New York: Harper, 1949.

Arrow, Jan. *Dorothea Lange*. London: Macdonald, 1985.

The Artist in America. New York: W.W. Norton, 1967.

Asinof, Eliot. *1919: America's Loss of Innocence*. New York: Donald I. Fine, 1990.

Aster, Sidney. *1939: The Making of the Second World War.* New York: Simon and Schuster, 1974.

Background of War. Editors of *Fortune*. New York: Alfred A. Knopf, 1937.

Bailey, Anthony. *America Lost & Found*. New York: Random House, 1980.

Ball, Adrian. *The Last Day of the Old World*. London: F. Mueller, 1963.

Basinger, Jeanine. *A Woman's View.* New York: Alfred A. Knopf, 1993.

Baynes, N. H., ed. *The Speeches of Adolf Hitler,* Vol. I. London: Gordon Press, 1942.

Beard, Annie E.S. *Our Foreign Citizens*. New York: Thomas Crowell, 1968.

Beard, Charles A., and Mary R. Beard. *The Basic History of the United States*. New York: Hawthorne Library, 1944.

———. *America in Mid Passage*. New York: Macmillan, 1939.

Bennett, Edward M. *Franklin D. Roosevelt and the Search for Identity*. Wilmington, DE: Scholarly Resources, 1985.

Benny, Jack, and Joan Benny. *Sunday Nights at Seven*. New York: Warner, 1990.

Bergreen, Laurence. *As Thousands Cheer*. New York: Viking, 1990.

———. *Capone*. New York: Simon and Schuster, 1994.

Bernstein, Michael A. *The Great Depression*. New York: Cambridge University Press, 1987.

Bethge, Eberhard. *Dietrich Bonhoeffer*. New York: Harper, 1970.

Blakey, George T. *Hard Times and New Deal in Kentucky, 1929-1939*. Lexington: University of Kentucky Press, 1986.

Bloch, Michael. *Ribbentrop*. New York: Crown, 1992.

Bolino, August C. *A Century of Human Capital by Education and Training.* Washington: Kensington Historical Press, 1989.

———. *The Ellis Island Source Book.* Washington: Kensington Historical Press, 1990.

Bolitho, William. *Italy Under Mussolini.* New York: Macmillan, 1926.

Boston American, March 15, 1939 and March 31, 1939.

Brassai (no other names). *Picasso and Company.* New York: Doubleday, 1966.

Bridges, Antony. *Scapa Ferry.* London: Arrow Books, 1978.

Brinkley, Alan. *The End of Reform.* New York: Alfred A. Knopf, 1995.

———. *Voices of Protest.* New York: Vintage Books, 1983.

Brinkley, David. *Washington Goes to War.* New York: Alfred A. Knopf, 1988.

Brooks, John. *The Great Leap.* New York: Harper, 1966.

Browder, Earl. *Fighting for Peace.* New York, 1939.

Brown, Anthony Cave, and Charles B. MacDonald. *The Secret History of the Atomic Bomb.* New York: Delta, 1977.

Brown, James Seay. *Up Before Daylight.* Tuscaloosa: University of Alabama Press, 1982.

Bullock, Alan. *Hitler and Stalin.* New York: Alfred A. Knopf, 1992.

Busch, Harold. *U-Boats at War.* New York: Ballantine, 1955.

Buttitta, Tony and Barry Witham. *Uncle Sam Presents: A Memoir of the Federal Theatre, 1935-1939.* Philadelphia: University of Pennsylvania, 1982.

Caidin, Martin. *Flying Forts.* New York: Ballantine, 1968.

Calvocoressi, Peter, Guy Wint, and John Pritchard. *Total War.* New York: Pantheon, 1989.

Campbell, John W., ed. *Astounding Science Fiction.* Carbondale: Southern Illinois University Press, 1981.

Canady, John. *Metropolitan Seminars in Art.* New York: Metropolitan Museum of Art, 1958.

Cantor, Louis. *A Prologue to the Protest Movement.* Durham, NC: Duke University Press, 1969.

Capra, Frank. *The Name Above the Title.* New York: Macmillan, 1971.

Caro, Robert A. *The Power Broker: Robert Moses and the Fall of New York.* New York: Vintage, 1974.

Cash, W. J. *Of the Great Blight.* New York: Doubleday, 1939.

———. *The Mind of the South.* New York: Doubleday, 1954.

Caudill, Harry. *Night Comes to the Cumberlands.* Boston: Little, Brown, 1963.

Ceplair, Larry. *Under the Shadow of War.* New York: Columbia University Press, 1987.

Chadwick, Whitney. *Myth in Surrealist Painting, 1929-1939.* Ann Arbor: University of Michigan Press, 1980.

Chronicle of the Cinema. London: Dorling Kindersley, 1995.

Churchill, Winston. *Step by Step, 1936-1939.* London: Butterworth, 1940.

———. *The Gathering Storm.* Boston: Houghton Mifflin, 1948.

Cinel, Dino. *From Italy to San Francisco.* Palo Alto, CA: Stanford University Press, 1984.

Clark, Sidney. *All the Best in Mexico.* New York: Dodd, Mead, 1970.

Clark, Thomas D. *The Emerging South.* New York: Oxford University Press, 1961.

Clarke, Donald. *Wishing on the Moon.* New York: Viking, 1994.

Cochran, Thomas C. *The American Business System.* New York: Harper, 1957.

Colberg, Marshall. *Human Capital in Southern Development, 1939-1963.* Chapel Hill, NC: University of North Carolina Press, 1964.

Collier, James. *Benny Goodman and the Swing Era*. New York: Oxford University Press, 1989.

Collier, Peter, and David Horowitz. *The Kennedys*. New York: Pan Books, 1985.

Collins, Alan C. *The Story of American Pictures*. New York: Doubleday, 1953.

Collodi, C. [Carlo Lorenzini]. *The Adventures of Pinocchio*. New York: Blue Ribbon, 1927.

Conrad, David Eugene. *The Forgotten Farmers*. Urbana: University of Illinois Press, 1965.

Craven, Frank, and James Lea Cate. *The Army Air Forces in World War II*. Chicago: University of Chicago Press, 1948.

Craven, Thomas. *Thomas Hart Benton*. New York: Associated American Artists, 1939.

Cray, Ed. *General of the Army*. New York: W.W. Norton, 1990.

Curran, Edward L. *Franco: Who Is He? What Does He Fight For?* Brooklyn, NY: International Catholic Truth Society, 1937.

Current Biography. Bronx, NY: H.W. Wilson, 1940.

Cutler, John Henry. *Honey Fitz*. Indianapolis, IN: Bobbs-Merrill, 1962.

Davis, Francis. *The History of the Blues*. New York: Hyperion, 1995.

Davis, Hope Hale. *Great Day Coming*. South Royalton: Steerfort Press, 1994.

Davis, Kenneth S. *FDR: Into the Storm, 1937-1940*. Vol. IV. New York: Random House, 1993.

DeHart-Mathews, Jane. *The Federal Theatre*. Princeton, NJ: Princeton University Press, 1967.

Diggins, John P. *Mussolini and Fascism*. Princeton, NJ: Princeton University Press, 1972.

Divine, Robert A. *The Illusion of Neutrality*. Chicago: University of Chicago Press, 1962.

Dixon, Daniel. *Dorothea Lange: A Visual Life*. Washington: Smithsonian Press, 1994.

Dolan, Edward F., Jr. *Hollywood Goes to War*. New York: Gallery Books, 1985.

Dolgoff, Sam. *The Anarchist Collectives*. St. Paul, MN: Black Rose Books, 1974.

Dooley, Roger. *From Scarface to Scarlett*. New York: Harcourt Brace, 1981.

Dorothea Lange. London: Macdonald, 1985.

Douglas, Roy, ed. *1939: A Retrospect Forty Years After*. Hamden, CT: Archon, 1983.

Douglas, William O. *The Court Years, 1939-1975*. New York: Random House, 1980.

Drury, Allen. *Toward What Bright Glory*. New York: William Morrow, 1990.

Duncan, Joseph W., and William C. Shelton, "Revolution in United States Government Statistics, 1926-1976." U.S. Department of Commerce, October, 1978.

DuPont. Wilmington, DE: E. I. DuPont, 1952.

Dupuy, K. Ernest, and Trevor N. Dupuy. *The Encyclopedia of Military History*. New York: Harper and Row, 1970.

Ellis, Edward Robb. *A Nation in Torment*. New York: Coward-McCann, 1970.

Engle, Eloise, and Lauri Paananen. *The Winter War*. New York: Charles Scribner's Sons, 1973.

Esquire's Great Men and Moments in Sports. New York: Harper, 1962.

The Fabulous Century. New York: Time-Life, 1969.

"FDR and His Library," *Smithsonian*. December 1989.

Fehrenbach, T. R. *FDR's Undeclared War, 1939-1941*. New York: David McKay Co., 1967.

Fifty Years of Popular Mechanics. New York: Simon and Schuster, 1950.

Firestone, Ross. *Swing, Swing, Swing*. New York: W. W. Norton, 1993.

Flanagan, Hallie. *Arena: The History of the Federal Theatre*. New York: Duell, Sloan and Pearce, 1940.

Flannery, Tom. *1939: The Year in Movies*. Jefferson, NC: McFarland, 1990.

Fleischhauer, Carl, and Beverly W. Brannan. *Documenting America, 1935-1943*. Los Angeles: University of California Press, 1988.

Frankfurter, Felix. *Of Law and Men*. Hamden, CT: Archon Books, 1956.

Freidel, Frantz. *Franklin D. Roosevelt: A Rendezvous With Destiny*. Boston: Little, Brown, 1990.

Fromm, Erich. *Escape From Freedom*. New York: Rinehart, 1941.

Fuller, J.F.C. *The Conduct of War, 1789-1961*. New Brunswick, NJ: Rutgers University Press, 1961.

Fussell, Paul, ed. *The Norton Book of Modern War*. New York: W. W. Norton, 1990.

Gabler Neal. *An Empire of Their Own*. New York: Crown, 1988.

Gay, Ruth. *The Jews of Germany*. New Haven, CT: Yale University Press, 1992.

Gentry, Curt. *J. Edgar Hoover*. New York: W.W. Norton, 1988.

Gelernter, David. *1939: The Lost World of the Fair*. New York: Free Press, 1995.

Gilbert, Martin. *The Second World War*. New York: Holt, 1989.

Gill, Glenda E. *White Grease Paint on Black Performers*. New York: Peter Lang, 1988.

Glines, Carroll V., and Wendell F. Moseley. *The DC-3*. New York: Lippincott, 1966.

Goebbels, Joseph. *The Goebbels Diaries, 1939-1941*. Translated and edited by Fred Taylor. New York: Penguin Books, 1984.

Goodman, Benny. *The Kingdom of Swing*. Vol. III, 1937-1938. New York: Stackpole Sons, 1939.

Goodwin, Doris Kearns. *No Ordinary Time*. New York: Simon and Schuster, 1994.

Gosch, Martin, and Richard Hammer. *The Last Testament of Lucky Luciano*. Boston: Little, Brown, 1975.

Green, Stanley. *Ring Bells! Sing Songs!* New York: Galahad, 1971.

Gunther, John. *Inside U.S.A.* New York: Harper, 1947.

———. *Roosevelt in Retrospect*. New York: Harper, 1950.

Guttmann, Allen. *The Wound in the Heart*. Glencoe, IL: Free Press, 1962.

Haase, John E. *Beyond Category: The Life and Genius of Duke Ellington*. New York: Simon and Schuster, 1993.

Haines, C. Groves, and Ross J. F. Hoffman. *The Origins and Background of the Second World War*. New York: Oxford University Presss, 1943.

Hanighen, Frank C., and Felix Morley. *A Year of Human Events*. Washington, D.C.: Human Events, 1945.

Hardman, J. B. S. *Rendezvous With Destiny*. New York: Dryden, 1944.

Hayes, Carlton J. H., Marshall Whithead Baldwin, and Charles Woolsey Cole. *History of Western Civilization Since 1500*. New York: Macmillan, 1967.

Haynes, William. *American Chemical Industry*. New York: Van Nostrand, 1954.

Healey, Dorothy, and Maurice Isserman. *Dorothy Healey Remembers*. New York: Oxford University Press, 1990.

Heiferman, Ronald. *World War II*. Secaucus, NJ: Derbibooks, 1973.

Heilbron, J. L. *Lawrence and his Laboratory*. Berkeley: University of California, 1989.

Hemingway, Ernest. *For Whom the Bell Tolls*. New York: Scribner, 1940.

Henderson, Neville. *Failure of a Mission*. New York: G. P. Putnam's, 1940.

Hill, Frank E. *The School in the Camps*. New York: American Association for Adult Education, 1935.

Hitler, Adolf. *Mein Kampf*. New York: Reynal and Hitchcock, 1940.

Holiday, Billie. *Lady Sings the Blues*. New York: Doubleday, 1956.

Hollander, Zander. *Great American Athletes of the 20th Century*. New York: Random House, 1966.

Hooper, Arthur Sanderson. *The Soviet-Finnish Campaign*. London: A. S. Hooper, 1940.

Hudson, Winthrop S. *Religion in America*. New York: Scribner, 1973.

Huffington, Ariana S. *Picasso*. New York: Simon and Schuster, 1988.

Hughes, Terry, and John Costello. *The Battle of the Atlantic*. New York: Dial Press, 1977.

Humphrey, Hubert H. *The Political Philosophy of the New Deal*. Baton Rouge: Louisiana State University Press, 1970.

Hutchison, William R., ed. *Between the Times*. New York: Cambridge University Press, 1990.

Jacobs, Travis Beal. *America and the Winter War, 1939-1940*. New York: Garland Publishing, 1981.

Jakobson, Max. *The Diplomacy of Winter War*. Cambridge, MA: Harvard University Press, 1961.

Kaempffert, Waldemar. *Science Today and Tomorrow*. New York: Viking Press, 1945.

Kauffman, Andrew J., and William L. Putnam. *K2: The 1939 Tragedy*. Diadem Books, 1992.

Kee, Robert. *1939: In the Shadow of War*. Boston: Little, Brown, 1984.

Keeler, Robert F. *Newsday: A Candid History of the Respectable Tabloid*. New York: Arbor House/Morrow, 1990.

Kennan, George F. *Memoirs*. Boston: Atlantic, Little, Brown, 1967.

———. *Russia and the West Under Lenin and Stalin*. Boston: Little, Brown, 1960.

Kennedy, John F. *Why England Slept*. New York: Funk, 1961.

Kennedy, Joseph P. *I'm For Roosevelt*. New York: Reynal & Hitchcock, 1936.

Kennedy, Rose Fitzgerald. *Times to Remember*. New York: Doubleday, 1974.

Ketchum, Richard M. *The Borrowed Years, 1939-1941*. New York: Random House, 1989.

Keynes, John Maynard. *The General Theory of Employment, Interest and Money*. New York: Harcourt, Brace, 1936.

Kimball, Warren F. *The Most Unsordid Act, Lend Lease, 1939-1941*. Baltimore: Johns Hopkins University Press, 1969.

Kingsley, April. *The Turning Point*. New York: Simon and Schuster, 1992.

Klehr, Harvey, John Earl Haynes and Fridrikh I. Firsov. *The Secret World of American Communism*. New Haven, CT: Yale University Press, 1995.

Knox, MacGregor. *Mussolini Unleashed, 1939-1941*. Cambridge: Cambridge University Press, 1982.

Kobal, John. *Gods & Goddesses of the Movies*. New York: Crescent, 1973.

Kobler, John. *Capone*. New York: G. P. Putnam's, 1971.

Koestler, Arthur. *Arrow in the Blue*. New York: Macmillan, 1952.

———. *Darkness at Noon*. New York; Macmillan, 1941.

Kornbluh, Joyce L. *A New Deal for Worker's Education*. Urbana: University of Illinois, 1987.

Krock, Arthur. *Memoirs*. New York: Funk and Wagnalls, 1968.

La Guardia, Fiorello H. *The Making of an Insurgent*. Philadelphia: Lippincott, 1948.

Lally, Francis J. *The Catholic Church in a Changing America*. Boston: Little, Brown, 1962.

Lally, Kathleen A. "A History of the Federal Dance Theatre of the Works Progress Administration, 1935-1939." Unpublished Doctoral Dissertation, Texas Western University, 1978.

Lange, Dorothea, and Paul S. Taylor. *An American Exodus*. New York: Reynal and Hitchcock, 1939.

Langsam, Walter Consuelo. *The World Since 1914*. New York: Macmillan, 1950.

Lanouette, William, and Bela Szilard. *Genius in the Shadows*. New York: C. Scribner's Sons, 1992.

Lash, Joseph P. *Eleanor and Franklin*. New York: W.W. Norton, 1971.

———. *Roosevelt and Churchill*. New York: W. W. Norton, 1976.

[Law, Bernard]. *The Memoirs of Field-Marshall Montgomery*. Cleveland: World Publishing , 1958.

Lekachman, Robert. *The Age of Keynes*. New York: Random House, 1966.

Leonhard, Wolfgang. *Betrayal*. New York: St. Martin's Press, 1989.

Leuchtenberg, William E. *Franklin D. Roosevelt and the New Deal*. New York: Harper and Row, 1963.

———. *The FDR Years*. New York: Columbia University Press, 1995.

Levine, Suzanne Braun, and Susan Dworkin. *She's Nobody's Baby*. New York: Simon and Schuster, 1983.

Lewis, Tom. *Empire of the Air*. New York: HarperCollins, 1992.

Lifton, Robert Jay. *The Nazi Doctors*. New York: Basic Books, 1986.

Lindbergh, Anne Morrow. *War Within and Without*. New York: Harcourt, Brace, Jovanovich, 1980.

Lindsay, Michael. *The Unknown War*. London: Beergstrom and Boyle, 1975.

Linn, Ed. *Hitter*. New York: Harcourt Brace, 1993.

Lounsbury, Myron O. *The Origins of American Film Criticism, 1909-1966*. New York: Arno, 1966.

Lucas, Laddie. *Wings of War, 1939-1945*. New York: Macmillan, 1983.

The Luftwaffe. Alexandria, VA: Time-Life Books, 1982.

Lukas, Richard C. *The Forgotten Holocaust*. Lexington: University of Kentucky, 1986.

Lyons, Eugene. *David Sarnoff*. New York: Harper and Row, 1966.

Maas, Peter. *The Valachi Papers*. New York: Putnam, 1968.

MacDonald A. *The United States, Britain and Appeasement, 1936-1939*. New York: St. Martin's Press, 1981.

MacDonald, Charles B., and Anthony C. Brown. *On a Field of Red*. New York: Putnam, 1981.

Malcolm X. *Autobiography*. New York: Grove Press, 1965.

Malone, Dumas, and Basil Rauch. *War and Troubled Peace*. New York: Appleton-Century-Crofts, 1960.

Maloney, T. J., ed. *U. S. Camera, 1940*. New York: Random House, 1939.

Manchester, William. *The Glory and the Dream*. Boston: Little, Brown, 1974.

———. *The Last Lion*. Boston: Little, Brown, 1988.

Mangione, Jerre. *The Dream and the Deal*. Boston: Little, Brown, 1972.

Manvell, Roger. *Film*. Gretna, LA: Pelican Books, 1944.

Marrus, Michael R. *The Holocaust in History*. New York: New American Library, 1987.

Marshall, Ray. *The Negro Worker*. New York: Random House, 1967.

Mason, Herbert Malloy, Jr. *The United States Air Force*. New York: Mason Charter, 1976.

Massock, Richard G. *Italy From Within*. New York: Macmillan, 1943.

Mast, Gerald, and Bruce F. Kawin. *A Short History of the Movies*. Needham, MA: Allyn and Bacon, 1995.

Meikle, Jeffrey L. *Twentieth Century Limited: Industrial Design in America, 1925-1939*. Philadelphia: Temple University Press, 1979

McBride, Joseph. *The Catastrophe of Success*. New York: Simon and Schuster, 1992.

McCausland, Elizabeth. "100 Years of American Standards of Photography," *U. S. Camera, 1940*. New York: Random House, 1939.

McCombs, Don, and Fred L. Worth. *World War II Super Facts*. New York: Warner Books, 1983.

McDonald, William F. *Federal Relief Administration and the Arts*. Columbus: Ohio State University, 1969.

McGilligan, Patrick. *George Cukor*. New York: St. Martin's Press, 1992.

McWilliams, Carey. *Factories in the Field*. Boston: Little, Brown, 1939.

Medvedev, Roy A. *Let History Judge*. New York: Alfred A. Knopf, 1972.

Merkin, Richard. *Leagues Apart*. New York: William Morrow, 1995.

Messick, Hank. *John Edgar Hoover*. New York: David McKay, 1972.

Metropolitan Museum of Art. *Life in America*. New York: Scribner, 1939.

Meyerson, H., and E. Y. Harburg. *Who Put the Rainbow in the Wizard of Oz?* Ann Arbor: University of Michigan Press, 1993.

Millbank Memorial Fund. *New Light on Old Health Problems*. New York: 1939.

Mitchell, Otis C. *Nazism and the Common Man*. Lanham, MD: University Press of America, 1981.

Moellering, Ralph Luther. *Modern War and the American Churches*. New York: American Press, 1956.

Mollenhoff, Clark R. *Atanasoff: Forgotten Father of the Computer*. Ames: Iowa State University Press, 1988.

Molotov, Vyacheslav M. *The Third Five-Year Plan for the National-Economic Development of the USSR*. Moscow: Foreign Language Publications, 1939.

Morgan, Ted. *On Becoming American*. Boston: Houghton Mifflin, 1978.

Morison, Samuel Eliot. *The Oxford History of the American People*. New York: Oxford University Press, 1965.

Morley, James William ed. *The Fateful Choice: Japan's Advance into Southeast Asia, 1939-1941*. New York: Columbia University Press, 1980.

Mumford, Lewis. *Faith For Living*. New York: Harcourt, Brace, 1940.

Murray, Williamson. *The Change in European Balance of Power, 1938-1939*. Princeton, NJ: Princeton University Press, 1984.

Nasaw, David. *Going Out: The Rise and Fall of Public Amusements*. New York: Basic Books, 1993.

Newman, Roger K. *Hugo Black*. New York: Pantheon, 1994.

The New York Times Index: A Book of Record. New York: New York Times Co., 1940.

The New York Times Obituaries Index. New York: New York Times Co., 1970.

Nicholson, Harold G. *Marginal Comment*. January 6-August 4, 1939. London: Constable, 1939

Paananen, Eloise. *The Winter War, 1939-1940*. New York: Scribner's, 1973.

Pagano, Grace. *Contemporary American Painting*. New York: Duell, Sloan and Pearce, 1945.

Parkes, James W. *The Emergence of the Jewish Problem, 1878-1939*. Westport, CT: Greenwood Press, 1970.

Payne, Robert. *The Life and Death of Adolf Hitler*. New York: Praeger, 1973.

Perrett, Geoffrey. *Days of Sadness; Years of Triumph*. New York: Coward, McCann and Geoghehan, 1973.

Phillips, Cabell B. H. *From the Crash to the Blitz, 1929-1939*. New York: Macmillan, 1969.

Phillips, H. B. *Felix Frankfurter Reminisces*. New York: Reynal, 1960.

Pope, Edwin. *Ted Williams*. New York: Manor Books, 1972.

Popper, David H. *America Charts Her Course*. New York: Foreign Policy Association, November 1939.

Porter, David L. *The Seventy-Sixth Congress and World War II*. New York: Columbia University Press, 1979.

Powers, Richard G. *Secrecy and Power*. New York: Free Press, 1987.

Preston, Paul. *Franco*. New York: Basic Books, 1994.

———. *Revolution and War in Spain*. New York: Methuen, 1984.

Radzinsky, Edvard. *Stalin*. New York: Doubleday, 1996.

Rauch, Basil, ed. *Franklin D. Roosevelt, Selected Speeches*. New York: Rinehart, 1957.

Rauschning, Hermann. *Hitler Speaks*. Zurich: Europa Verlag, 1940. RCA Institute. Technical Paper, 1919-1939, 1940.

Reynolds, Clark G. *America at War*. New York: Gallery, 1990.

Ribowsky, Mark. *The Power and the Darkness*. New York: Simon and Schuster, 1996.

Rice, Grantland. *The Tumult and the Shouting*. New York: A. S. Barnes, 1954.

Robinson, Ray. *Iron Horse: Lou Gehrig in His Time*. New York: W.W. Norton, 1990.

Roosevelt, Eleanor. *My Day*. New York: Pharos, 1989.

Rosenburg, John M. *The Story of Baseball*. New York: Random House, 1964.

Rosenman, Samuel. *Working with Roosevelt*. Vol. I. New York: Harper, 1952.

———, ed. *The Public Papers and Addresses of Franklin D. Roosevelt*. 13 vols. New York: Random House, 1938-1950.

Ross, Barbara. *J. E. Spingarn and the Rise of the NAACP*. New York: Atheneum, 1972.

Rosten, Calvin. *Hollywood*. New York: Harcourt Brace, 1941.

Rupp, Leila J. *Mobilizing Women for War*. Princeton, NJ: Princeton University Press, 1978.

Russell, Francis. *The Secret War*. Alexandria, VA: Time-Life, 1981.

Schechtman, Joseph. *The United States and the Jewish State Movement*. New York: Herzl Press, 1966.

Schisgall, Oscar. *Eyes on Tomorrow*. New York: Doubleday, 1981.

Schlesinger, Arthur Meier. *Political and Social Growth of the American People, 1865-1940*. New York: Macmillan, 1941.

Schoenberg, Robert. *Mr. Capone*. New York: William Morrow, 1992.

Schuller, Gunther. *The Swing Era*. New York: Oxford University Press, 1989.

Schwartz, Rudolph. "Non-Military Education in the United States Army and Air Force, 1900-1960," Unpublished Doctoral Dissertation, New York University, 1963.

Schwarz, Jordan A. *The New Dealers*. New York: Alfred A. Knopf, 1992.

Secrest, Meryle. *Frank Lloyd Wright*. New York: Alfred A. Knopf, 1992.

Seidel, Michael. *Ted Williams*. Chicago: Contemporary Books, 1991.

Seldes, George. *One Thousand Americans*. New York: Boni and Gaer, 1947.

Settel, Irving, and William Laas. *A Pictorial History of Television*. 2nd ed. New York: Grosset and Dunlop, 1983.

Seydewitz, Max. *Civil Life in Wartime Germany*. New York: Viking, 1945.

Sforza, Count Carlo. *Contemporary Italy*. New York: E. P. Dutton, 1944.

Shaw, Artie. *The Trouble with Cinderella*. Santa Barbara, CA: Fithian Press, 1992.

Sherwood, Robert. *Roosevelt and Hopkins*. Vol. I. New York: Harper, 1948.
———. *The White House Papers of Harry L. Hopkins*. Vol I. London: Eyre and Spottiswoode, 1948.
Shindler, Colin. *Hollywood Goes to War*. London: Routledge and K. Paul, 1979.
Shirer, William L. *Berlin Diary*. New York: Alfred A. Knopf, 1941.
———. *Midcentury Journey*. New York: Farrar, Straus and Young, 1952.
———. *The Rise and Fall of the Third Reich*. New York: Simon and Schuster, 1960.
Snow, Thad. *From Missouri*. Boston: Houghton Mifflin, 1954.
Snyder, Louis L. *The War: A Concise History, 1939-1945*. Raleigh, NC: Bell, 1960.
Sobel, Robert. *RCA*. New York: Stein and Day, 1986.
Solzhenitsyn, Aleksandr I. *The Gulag Archipelago*. New York: Harper and Row, 1974.
Speizman, Milton D. *Urban America in the Twentieth Century*. New York: Thomas Y. Crowell, 1968.
Sulzberger, Cyrus Leo. *World War II*. New York: McGraw-Hill, 1970.
Summers, Anthony. *Official and Confidential*. New York: Putnam, 1993.
Susman, Warren. *Culture as History: The Transformation of American Society in the Twentieth Century*. New York: Pantheon, 1984.
Sweet, William Warren. *The Story of Religion in America*. New York: Harper and Row, 1950.
Tanner, Vaino. *Winter War*. Palo Alto, CA: Stanford University Press, 1957.
Taubman, Howard. *The Maestro*. New York: Simon and Schuster, 1951.
Terkel, Studs. *"The Good War"*. New York: Pantheon, 1984.
These Are Our Lives. Chapel Hill: University of North Carolina Press, 1939.
Thomas, Brinley. *Migration and Economic Growth*. Cambridge: Cambridge University Press, 1954.
Thomas, Gordon, and Max Morgan-Witts. *Voyage of the Damned*. New York: Stein and Day, 1974.
Thomas, Hugh. *The Spanish Civil War*. New York: Harper and Row, 1977.
Time Capsule/1939, New York: Time-Life, 1968.
Todd, Charles L. "Okies Search for a Lost Frontier." *New York Times*, August 27, 1939.
Tolischus, Otto D. *Through Japanese Eyes*. New York: Reynal and Hitchcock, 1945.
Tucker, Mark, ed. *The Duke Ellington Reader*. New York: Oxford University Press, 1993.
Turner, William W. *Hoover's FBI*. Los Angeles: Sherbourne Press, 1970.
U.S. Department of Agriculture. "Food and Life." *Yearbook of Agriculture*. 1939. U.S. Government Printing Office, 76th Congress, House Document Number 28.
U. S. National Resources Committee. *Progress Report*, 1939.
Villacorta, Aurora. *Ballroom Dancing*. Danville, IL: Interstate, 1974.
Watkins, T. H. *The Great Depression*. Boston: Little, Brown, 1993.
———. *Righteous Pilgrim: The Life and Times of Harold Ickes*. New York: Henry Holt, 1990.
Watt, Donald Cameron. *How War Came: The Immediate Origins of the Second World War, 1938-1939*. New York: Pantheon, 1989.
Wecter, Dixon. *The Age of the Great Depression, 1939-1941*. New York: Macmillan, 1948.
Weinberg, Gerhard. *A World at Arms*. Cambridge: Cambridge University Press, 1994.
———. *The Foreign Policy of Hitler's Germany*. Chicago: University of Chicago Press, 1980.
Wertheim, Arthur F. *Radio Comedy*. New York: Oxford University Press, 1979.

Wexler, Jerry, and David Ritz. *Rhythm and the Blues*. New York: Alfred A. Knopf, 1993.

Whitcomb, Ian. *Tin Pan Alley*. New York: Paddington Press, 1975.

White, E. B. *One Man's Meat*. New York: Harper, 1944.

Whyte, William Foote. *Street Corner Society*. Chicago: Univerisity of Chicago Press, 1943.

Wilder, Alec. *American Popular Songs*. New York: Oxford University Press, 1972.

Williams, Robert C., and Philip L. Cantelon. *The American Atom*. Philadelphia: University of Pennsylvania Press, 1984.

Williams, Ted. *My Turn at Bat*. New York: Pocket Books, 1970.

Wiltz, John E. *From Isolation to War, 1931-1941*. New York: Thomas Y. Crowell, 1968.

Wittke, Carl. *We Who Built America*. Cleveland, OH: Case Western Reserve, 1967.

The World's Greatest Airport: La Guardia. New York: Air Cargo News, 1979.

Wright, Frank Lloyd. *An Organic Architecture*. Boston: MIT Press, 1939.

Wyden, Peter. *The Passionate War: A Narrative History of the Spanish Civil War, 1936-1939*. New York: Simon and Schuster, 1983.

Index

About the Author

AUGUST C. BOLINO is Professor Emeritus in the Department of Economics and Business at The Catholic University of America and Vice President for Research of the Ellis Island Restoration Commission. He is the author of numerous books, including *The Ellis Island Source Book* (1990), *A Century of Human Capital by Education and Training* (1989), and *The Watchmakers of Massachusetts* (1987).